the Psychiatric Disorders of Childhood

the Psychiatric Disorders of Childhood

Charles R. Shaw, M.D.
Staff Psychiatrist
and Director of Research
Hawthorn Center, Northville, Michigan

Appleton-Century-Crofts
Division of Meredith Publishing Company
New York

Copyright © 1966 by

MEREDITH PUBLISHING COMPANY

PRINTED IN THE UNITED STATES OF AMERICA
M–80206

PREFACE

Every book must have a point of view. This book could be said to represent a fusion of two: the scientific and the compassionate.

From the scientific poi of view, man is a creature in evolution, an organism singularly adaptabl n almost any environment. His success in evolution lies in his wide div y and in his capacity to produce a great variety of individuals from \ struggle for survival. But eve heterogeneity, so necessary to a expense of producing a certain isms; these are the weak, and the

Man, then, is a creature hav motivation, in response to stress, i upon to perform. And some indivic or excessive stress, break down. In one way or another, they become malfunctional. The ways in which this occurs are legion, and their list constitutes the catalogue of human pathology. In most cultures of man, the maladaptive are not destroyed; they are protected and cared for and, if possible, made better. Their care is the charge of medicine; if the symptoms are largely emotional or behavioral, it is the concern of psychiatry.

In fulfilling its charge, psychiatry must be aware of the important advances in knowledge taking place both within and without its immediate field. Major developments in genetics, biochemistry, neurophysiology, experimental psychology, and in many other fields are contributing to our understanding of human behavior, and they must be incorporated into a psychiatry which presumes to the status of a dynamic and scientific discipline.

Fused with this scientific point of view is one which the author chooses to call the compassionate. It sees man as a creature who thinks, feels, believes, wants, remembers, struggles, and loves. It sees him as a fascinating, terrible, and lonely being, desperate, gregarious, passionate, and cruel. It sees him as a being who feels pity, which Thomas Wolfe called "more than any other, a learned emotion"; who laughs, and who has a sense of humor, which George Meredith considered "the ultimate civilizer."

The compassionate view finds psychiatry to be a challenge, a joy, and a grave responsibility. And perhaps the gravest responsibility is to the children, who carry the future. To the child psychiatrist come the troubled children—angry, afraid, miserable, unhappy, defiant. They are brought to us, usually against their will, and we try to help, even when they don't want our help, hoping to alleviate some of their misery, to direct them to more productive ways, ways less troublesome to themselves and others.

This point of view knows that psychiatry is not really very scientific, that it is still largely a personal encounter, an experience into which the psychiatrist as well as the patient brings his personality and his feelings. In the psychiatric session there must be spontaneity, warmth, and the capacity for a mature feeling of love. These things are not learned from books or laboratories, or even from teachers. They develop out of the psychiatrist's own childhood.

It is hoped that this book will impart something of the feeling between a psychiatrist and a child. Children are wonderfully spontaneous, and almost anything can happen in a child psychiatrist's office. These happenings sometimes fracture professional dignity; but the loss is small and is replaced by something infinitely more valuable, the capacity to help a troubled child.

Together, the scientific and compassionate points of view can form an amalgam that incorporates the best of knowledge and experience, and can make psychiatry a discipline better able to treat the mentally ill. If this book can provide the reader with some understanding of how this amalgam may be achieved, it will have succeeded in its purpose.

Some teachers inspire; others impart knowledge. Ralph Rabinovitch and Sara Dubo, my teachers in child psychiatry, together combine the best of both worlds. My first debt in the conception of this book is to them.

Then there is always to be acknowledged one's gratitude to one's wife —for sympathy, understanding, keeping the house clean, that sort of thing. My own wife, Margery, a physician and scientist, first earned her acknowledgment by suggesting that I write the book. Then she typed most of the first draft, skillfully edited every page, and finally did most of the indexing. Meanwhile our cleaning lady took care of the house.

My colleague Alexander Lucas contributed immeasurably in getting the book from its middle stages to completion. He reviewed and edited the entire work, added large sections, and wrote the chapter on pharmacologic treatment.

I am also much indebted to Ruth Schelkun, University of Michigan, who not only edited the entire manuscript but also suggested and helped write several additional sections. Peter Klaver, University of Michigan, also edited the final manuscript.

Many others contributed in various ways: Ila Emmons typed the beginning, at that crucial stage when something needs to be put down on paper; my colleagues Morris Weiss, Harold Lockett, Martin Fliegel, James Sonnega, Beverly Sutton, Kiyoko Ching, and Gerald Fuller read certain chapters and made valuable suggestions.

However much help he receives, the author is, of course, finally responsible for all that is in his book. That there are defects is admitted, but I shall not point them out; that is the prerogative of the critic.

CHARLES R. SHAW

CONTENTS

CONTENTS

xi

the Psychiatric Disorders of Childhood

SECTION ONE

BEHAVIORAL INDIVIDUALITY: THE GENESIS OF MENTAL ILLNESS

The term *mental illness* suggests an entity, and implies a clear-cut distinction between the states of mental health and disease. Actually, there is a continuum of emotional adjustment. People vary widely in all aspects of behavior,* and in some, their deviations from the norm are so extreme as to be considered mental illness.

What makes people different? What determines that some persons are intelligent while others are dull, some are alert and interested, others indifferent, some relatively happy and untroubled, others in continuous anger, turmoil, and discontent? The causes of behavioral variation and mental disorders are problems of enormous complexity. Their investigation presents many facets and many points of view. Much of the subject is controversial, with strong opinions held which are too often based on insufficient evidence or outright prejudice.

The one point on which there is now general agreement is that mental illnesses *do* have a cause, or causes. The demonstration of this profound truth was perhaps Freud's greatest contribution. Most of these causes, however, must remain incompletely understood until subjected to prolonged and careful research.

Nevertheless, at least in mentally ill children, some of the factors that led to the disturbance can usually be determined. The child, unlike the adult, is still living in the environment which nurtured him. Much of this

_____
* The term *behavior* is used in its broad sense, and includes not simply observable response, but all central nervous system function.

1

can be directly observed, by talking with his parents, assessing the emotional tone of his family, meeting the other persons who are significant in his life: his teachers, friends and family. Additionally, much can often be learned from his parents of what he was like in early infancy: his temperament, his plasticity, the repertory of behavior with which he came into the world. Thus, to a significant degree, both the congenital and experiential factors that have contributed to the child's personality can be assessed.

In this section on the genesis of mental illness, specific causes of the individual psychiatric disorders are not considered—these appear in the chapters on the various disorders. Rather, the general question of behavioral differences is here explored. While man's concern is primarily with man, much of his knowledge of behavioral variation is derived from experimental studies of animals, and certain of these studies are cited here without apology.

Table 1 outlines the various factors which have a determining influence on human personality and, concomitantly, on mental illness. While these are noted as separate functions, they are inextricably interrelated, and operate continuously throughout life.

TABLE 1

A. Hereditary Factors
   1. Genetic Determinants of Behavior
   2. Instinct
   3. Constitutional Predisposition to Mental Disease
B. Environmental Factors
   1. Learning
   2. Interpersonal Experience
   3. Culture
   4. Organic Damage of the Brain

Some cases of mental illness are determined by a single and obvious cause. For instance, a child may have brain damage because he experienced a period of apnea immediately after birth. Or he may be neurotic because his mother was mentally ill and was never able to provide for his wants and needs in a consistent and empathic way. Most psychiatric disorders, however, are caused by multiple factors. A child with the "constitutional predisposition" to be hypersensitive and anxious, if raised by a mother who is tense, narcissistic, and rejecting, may develop a severe anxiety neurosis. If the same child were raised by a mother who is warm, mature, and loving, and who can understand and adequately satisfy his needs, he will be more likely to grow up to become a normal, well-adjusted, even though sensitive and somewhat tense individual.

Although some disorders have a single and specific cause, additional factors always operate to determine the personality and emotional adjustment of the individual. The brain-damaged child mentioned above will adjust better in one environment than another; on the other hand, some children make a reasonably good adjustment in the most deprived and primitive homes because they seem to have a constitutional strength and resiliency to withstand these vicissitudes.

This section considers, in the order presented in Table 1, the factors that determine behavioral individuality. Chapter 1 deals with heredity, Chapter 2 with environment. The last topic listed in Table 1, organic brain damage, appears separately in Chapter 8.

1

THE CONTRIBUTIONS OF HEREDITY

The fact of genetic variation is documented throughout the biological world. Every species of organism, plant and animal, demonstrates great heterogeneity. This is the basis of evolution, the chief factor which determines that some individuals will succeed better than others in what Darwin so vividly termed "the struggle for existence." Man is perhaps the most protean of all living creatures. Indeed, it is his wide range of variability which has made him virtually infinitely adaptable within his earthly environment.

GENETIC DETERMINANTS OF BEHAVIOR

Many people tend to think in terms of physical traits when they consider the hereditary variables which effect an organism's survival and evolution; they think of such things as physical strength, protective coloration, and resistance to disease. But evolutionists have long been aware that behavioral factors are equally important in determining the survival of a species. These factors include such functions as reproductive behavior (strength of sex drive, ability to attract a mate, copulatory success), food-getting behavior (hunting, hoarding), escape behavior, adaptability (learning), and social behavior. All these categories have been operative in the evolution of the human species.

The fascinating problem of behavioral genetics as it applies to evolution is not within the scope of this book, and the interested reader is referred to the excellent compilation by Roe and Simpson. The point here is that, for any understanding of human behavior, it must be appreciated that the behavioral traits and capacities of man have been acquired through the long and arduous process of natural selection. Many of these are simple, primitive behaviors, such as food-gathering, a diurnal sleep-wake pattern, and copulation. Others are "higher level," such as man's great learning capacity, and his ego identity (awareness of self as separate from

5

the environment). But all of these capacities and behaviors have a genetic base, and they all vary from one person to the next.

Man's knowledge of behavioral genetics in man is extremely limited. Research in this field is difficult, and many of the difficulties appear virtually insurmountable. There are three major stumbling blocks. One is that man cannot be used in present-day culture as an experimental animal; thus, selective breeding, an essential technique of the behavior geneticist, cannot be employed. A second difficulty resides in the long life span of the human organism; genetic analyses often require data on several generations, and any scientist is understandably reluctant to undertake an experiment, the results of which can be obtained only long after his own death. A third difficulty is that any study of behavior must consider not only hereditary but also environmental factors, and many of these are at present indefinable or unmeasurable. All behavior is affected by learning, and only by knowing what the subject's experience has been throughout his life can conclusions be made about the genetic influences on his behavior.

The science of genetics has made tremendous strides during the past decade in working out some of the fundamental problems of gene action and the physical-chemical structure of the chromosome. The essential structure of the chromosome has been determined to be a long double strand of deoxyribonucleic acid (DNA) arranged in helical coils and surrounded by a protein coat. Genes are functional segments of the chromosome. The particular effect exerted by a gene is determined partly by the sequence of the four different nucleotides which make up the nucleic acid, and partly by the total genetic make-up of the organism. The coded information contained in the nucleotide sequences is imparted to the organism by directing the synthesis of enzymes which are involved in the cell's growth or metabolism. Thus, genes act by directing the production of a single protein or, more accurately, the amino acid sequence within a particular polypeptide.

Despite the great advances in biochemical genetics, the important question of the hereditary determination of normal variations in behavior and in central nervous system physiology are as yet virtually unexplored. It is expected that much research in this direction will be forthcoming, and psychiatry and psychology will follow this work with great interest. Some interesting findings in this area have resulted from the metabolic study of animals which are inherently prone to epileptiform seizures. Ginsburg has shown that this behavioral trait, along with other associated ones, results from a defect in any one of several enzymes involved in the intermediary metabolism of nerve cells. Other examples of single-gene effects on brain function are the well-known clinical examples of metabolic blocks with

associated mental deficiency such as galactosemia, phenylpyruvic oligophrenia, and Wilson's disease. While these provide the important information that a defect in a single gene can produce major disruption of brain
function, and, additionally, that the integrity of many genes is necessary for
normal functioning, they tell little about normal differences between individuals.

POLYGENIC INHERITANCE

"Normal" differences between human beings which are caused by a
single gene are relatively rare. An example is the ability to taste the chemical substance phenylthiocarbamide (PTC). Some people find this substance completely tasteless, others experience a bitter taste when a drop of
PTC solution is placed on their tongues. This difference is determined by a
single gene. Other examples of monogenically-determined normal variations in humans occur in the various blood types (ABO, Rh, and so on), in
certain specialized serum proteins called haptoglobins and transferrins
(Smithies & Connell), and in an ester-splitting enzyme found in the red
blood cells (Shaw and others).

Most of the hereditary differences among human beings, however, are
affected by several pairs of genes which produce complex interacting effects
through their control of growth and metabolism. This hereditary influence
on a particular trait by more than one pair of genes is termed *polygenic*
inheritance. Familiar examples of polygenically-inherited traits are body
stature and skin color. Another instance is intelligence, although this is a
more complex, less definable trait, and is actually a combination of many
functions, some of which are themselves probably polygenically determined.

SELECTIVE BREEDING

A nice example of polygenic inheritance is seen in Tryon's classic
study of maze-learning in the rat. This experiment is worth considering in
some detail, as it illustrates one of the two major techniques of the behavior geneticist, selective breeding.

Tryon investigated the question of whether maze-learning ability in
rats is genetically determined. His method was to selectively breed animals
for high and low performance in a maze. He first tested a large number of
rats (142) in the maze, then selected those that performed at the low end
of the scale and bred them with each other; he also inbred those from the
high end of the scale. He then tested the offspring from each group, again

selected those that performed best and those that performed worst and interbred them, and continued this process through more than twenty generations.

The results of Tryon's study are represented in Figure 1. The graphs shown are those of the original group of animals and the offspring in the first, second, sixth, seventh, and eighth generations. Scores of the offspring from the poor performers (maze-dull) are indicated by the dotted line, those of the maze-bright by the solid line. Note that there was no apparent difference between the two groups of first-generation offspring, but that in the second generation a definite separation of the two groups began to appear. The separation gradually increased through the next several generations; at the sixth, there was still some overlap; by the seventh, separation was almost complete; and by the eighth, there was virtually no overlapping of the two groups. Beyond the eighth generation, further separation did not occur.

Tryon's results demonstrate that maze-learning ability, under the particular circumstances of his experiments, is inherited, and further, that it is affected by several genes. There has been extensive re-evaluation of Tryon's work, and much additional study of his two strains of animals. These two strains have been maintained and are still available today. The studies were originally intended to investigate the problem of inheritance of intelligence, but there is some question as to whether Tryon was actually measuring intelligence. The two strains of rats may have been exhibiting differences in fear of the apparatus, or differences in motivation (Searle). Whatever was measured, the fact remains that the experiment demonstrates a polygenically-determined behavioral trait.

Selective breeding for specific behavioral traits has actually been carried out by animal breeders for many centuries. Darwin noted (*The Origin of Species*) that, ever since the domestication of animals began, men have known something of the principles of selective breeding and have mated those animals which have desirable traits, both physical and behavioral. Many of these traits survive in the strain long after the purpose for which they were originally developed no longer exists. Scott cites the interesting example of the spaniel, which was developed in seventeenth-century England. It was used for hunting birds, and would approach the covey, then crouch low to the ground so that the hunters could draw a net over the spaniel and drop it onto the birds. This trait of crouching when given a sharp command is today still seen in many cocker spaniels.

Selective breeding, although an ancient technique, has unfortunately not provided nearly as much information as it might have, since, until recently, it was not employed as an experimental method for the elucidation of the genetics of behavior. The records of animal breeders are notori-

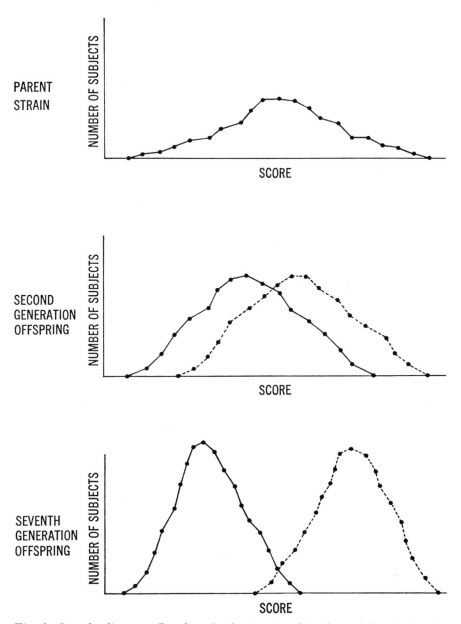

Fig. 1. Sample diagram: Results of selective breeding for a behavioral trait which is polygenically inherited. (Adapted from Tryon.)

ously incomplete, and it is common practice for them to omit observations of "undesirable traits" in a strain, as this may reduce the monetary value of their product. Moreover, they obviously do not breed for both low and high levels of performance, but simply eliminate the poor performers in each generation.

STRAIN DIFFERENCES

A second technique of the behavior geneticist is to study differences between existing strains of animals. From such studies the kinds of behavioral differences that may be inherited can be learned. Additionally, by crossbreeding strains of animals which have marked differences, much is to be learned about the modes of inheritance of the trait. Perhaps the most extensive systematic studies of strain differences in animal behavior have been carried out by a group of workers at the Roscoe B. Jackson Memorial Laboratory, Bar Harbor, Maine, under the direction of John Paul Scott and John L. Fuller. These workers have continued investigations for some twenty years, chiefly on strains of dogs, rats, and mice. Comparing five different strains of dogs (beagle, cocker spaniel, Shetland sheep dog, wire-haired terrier, and African basenji) they find marked differences in such traits as spatial orientation, motor activity, impulsiveness, docility, and responsiveness to a human trainer. Terriers generally perform best on tests which require confidence in strange situations. Basenjis are best in tasks requiring "independent action and visual observation of relations." Cockers excel in obedience training and leash control. These examples are but a sample of the many different kinds of tests and the many differences demonstrated among these five strains. Fuller and Thompson conclude that "perhaps the most important aspect of this research lies in its illustration of the great complexity of so-called intelligent behavior, and the necessity of isolating rational units before proceeding to genetic analysis."

INHERITANCE OF BEHAVIOR IN HUMANS

If analysis of hereditary differences in animal behavior is so complex, how much more complex must it be in man. Much of today's theory about human behavior is inferred from animal studies, and such inference has many pitfalls. However, more conclusive data on humans can be obtained through the following techniques: (1) Longitudinal study, beginning with the newborn infant; and (2) the twin study method, which utilizes the principle that identical twins have identical genetic make-up. Some examples of the kinds of information obtained by these two methods will now be considered.

LONGITUDINAL STUDIES

Every mother knows that no two babies are alike. Marked differences are apparent from the day of birth, often even *in utero*. A mother may report that her infant sleeps most of the time or that he sleeps very little, that he "fusses" if not fed immediately upon waking or that he never seems to get upset over anything, that he likes to be held or that he squirms and kicks all the time he is held, that he is very energetic or very quiet, that he suckles strongly or weakly, and so on.

These inborn differences in behavior are important determinants of personality. Not only do they determine the behavior of the individual, but also the ways in which others react to that individual. Motor activity of newborn infants was measured by Fries and Woolf and, according to the amount of activity displayed, the infants were divided into five groups, which the authors termed *congenital activity types*. They studied infants for periods of several months to several years, noting particularly the responses of mothers to infants of different types. There were marked variations in the relationships that developed between these different infants and their mothers, relationships depending both on the motor activity of the child and on the personality of the mother. For instance, one infant who was quiet, rarely cried, and slept most of the time "was welcomed by her parents, since she did not disturb their work." Another mother preferred a more active, aggressive infant, "finding narcissistic gratification from the child's motor achievement such as walking and climbing." These infants related with their environments and learned to test reality in quite different ways. The less active child "absorbed experience by predominantly visual, auditory and olfactory introjection rather than by active muscular experimentation." The more active child related with his environment by physical contact and exploration. When parents were well adjusted, children in both the active and the quiet groups tended to modify their behavior toward the median, while if the parents were ambivalent or poorly adjusted, the children tended to deviate toward the extremes.

This pioneering study of Fries and Woolf is important because it represents an attempt in the human field to demonstrate the ongoing relationships between hereditary and environmental factors. It antedated by several years the suggestion of Karon and Saunders that we "cease asking what percentage of the variance is due to this or that, and ask instead, what is the nature of the hereditary and environmental mechanisms which underlie this or that phenomenon." Fries and Woolf were careful to point out that the congenital activity type may not be determined exclusively by heredity, as other factors such as prenatal nutrition and birth trauma may influence early motor activity. However, there seems little doubt that such activity is largely hereditary.

The above study measured only one variable in early behavior. A more extensive investigation of early human differences is that of Chess and others. In a study which is still in progress, these workers have observed infants at regular periods beginning at age 2 months, and have followed some into adolescence. From direct observation and from standardized interviews with parents, the children were measured on a three-point scale in each of the following categories:

1. Activity—Passivity
2. Regularity—Irregularity
3. Intense Reaction—Mild Reaction
4. Approacher—Withdrawer
5. Adaptive—Non-Adaptive
6. High Threshold—Low Threshold
7. Positive Mood—Negative Mood
8. Selective—Non-Selective
9. Distractible—Non-Distractible

Chess and her co-workers found that early patterns did not necessarily persist in a static way, but that they were altered by the growing child's experiences. However, they found, as did Fries and Woolf, that the primary reaction patterns determined in great degree how a particular child reacted to a particular experience. The authors observe:

> We do not believe that there is any one-to-one correlation between the primary reaction pattern and the specific character of the personality structure that develops in each child. . . . Personality structure appears to emerge out of the interplay and interaction of the various forces involved in psychological development. . . . Psychological organization may be the resultant of a highly complex set of interactions in which primary reactivity functions as a significant variable.

Chess points out that, in the practice of child psychiatry, the concept of primary reaction patterns obviates the assumption that all behavioral phenomena necessarily have a psychodynamic basis. For example, extreme negativism in a child, while sometimes an expression of underlying hostility or anxiety, may also occur as an expression of the child's primary reactivity.

Such studies represent important beginnings in understanding human behavior. Several large-scale longitudinal programs are in progress, and as more data are gathered, and new techniques for handling masses of interrelated data are applied, important developments in this vital area of human research can be expected.

STUDIES OF TWINS

Human twins have always excited much interest and curiosity. Somehow there is a fascination in seeing a person existing in duplicate, and the similarities between twins are so well known that they would hardly seem to deserve discussion in a textbook. But twins provide research material par excellence for the human geneticist, whose investigations have been as much concerned with the differences as with the similarities in twins. How much are twins really alike, and how greatly can they differ? There is no simple answer to this question; the answer depends largely on what factors are measured. It is worth considering the question in some detail; the findings provide much insight into the problem of how much of human behavior is "immutably" determined by inheritance.

One approach has been to compare identical with fraternal twins. The hypothesis here is that, since both kinds of twins have been reared together and have had essentially identical environments, any differences which are greater between the fraternal than the identical twins are presumably due to heredity. Kallman and Slater have employed this method with much success in studies of schizophrenia, and their findings will be cited in the chapter on that disease (Chapter 6). Some workers question the validity of the identical twin-fraternal twin comparison method; they point out that, since fraternal twins are different from the time of birth, their environments are not identical, because people react toward them in different ways. However, early differences are seen also in identical twins, and many observers feel that they induce just as different responses from their environment as do the fraternals. Burlingham has described a pair of identical twins in which the "dominant" behavior of one twin over the other shifted suddenly when the originally dominant twin developed an acute but transitory medical illness. This shift was apparently permanent. The report is of interest, not only because it demonstrates an aspect of the interrelationships between genetic and environmental influences, but also because it points up the vicissitudes and unpredictable influences to which the developing personality is subjected.

Newman compared 50 pairs of identical with 50 pairs of fraternal twins; then, by statistical methods, he calculated how much the variability of certain traits was due to heredity and how much was due to environmental effects. He concluded that physical traits such as height, weight, number of finger ridges, and so on, were almost entirely hereditarily determined, general intelligence was about 75 per cent determined by heredity, while motor activity and "emotional balance" were about equally affected by environment and heredity.

Newman's twin studies have been criticized as being superficial, and lacking in psychological sophistication. Certainly one might wish that his case material had been examined in somewhat greater depth and with the application of more definitive psychological methods. Nevertheless, for its time (1940), it represents a remarkable and valuable compilation of data. Especially illuminating are the case studies of 20 pairs of identical twins who had been reared apart. Both the similarities and the differences between some of these twins are striking. Unfortunately, it is not always clear why certain of the twins are more alike or more different than others, so that the vital question of how much influence experience has on heredity is by no means definitively answered.

The accounts of these 20 pairs of twins who were reunited after many years of separation would each make a wonderful "human interest" newspaper story. Most of the twins had not even known of their opposite twin's existence, as they had been adopted in infancy. There is the story of Edwin and Fred, neither of whom knew that he had a twin brother, and who at the age of 22 were brought together by chance. The similarities between these two separately-reared twins were remarkable. They had been adopted in infancy by two families who lived in the same town in New England. They were both reared as only children in families of about the same social status. They went to the same school for a short time and had often noticed how much alike they were but never suspected that they were twin brothers. When the boys were eight years old their two families moved to different Midwestern cities about 1,000 miles apart. They lived strangely parallel lives, received about the same amount of education, were both interested in electricity, and both became expert repairmen in different branches of the same telephone company. They were married in the same year to young women of about the same age and type. Each had a baby son and each owned a fox-terrier dog named Trixie! Newman reports:

When we examined these twins we found them to be as nearly similar physically as almost any pair of twins brought up together. They were strikingly similar in mental ability and in personality. Edwin scored a shade higher on mental tests and was a little more flexible, a little more emotional, a little more talkative, and a little more easily aroused, but they were no more different in these or in other respects than the average pair of one-egg twins reared together. From this case one might be led to infer that the identical heredity and closely similar environments had interacted to produce almost identical results.

Contrast the case of the above twins, who had been reared in different but similar environments, with the twins Mabel and Mary, whose environments were quite dissimilar. Mary was reared in a city, and completed high school, while Mabel completed only the 8th grade in a small country school near her farm home. Their ways of life were very different. Mary had been motivated to study music and became a music teacher, while Mabel had done hard physical work on the farm. When tested on the Stanford-Binet, at the age of 29, Mary achieved an I.Q. of 106, Mabel 89—a difference of 17 points. Newman states:

Mabel, the farm woman, was slow and phlegmatic; Mary was far more excitable and responsive, almost neurotic. On the other hand Mabel was more aggressive and was evidently the leader and manager. She had fewer fears and was less readily shocked by unpleasant words and ideas. She walked about with a firm, almost masculine stride, in contrast with Mary's lady-like step and manner. The two women seemed totally unlike in overt behavior and gave the impression of having very different personalities.

This is truly a remarkable case of major personality differences in identical twins. One would wish that a psychiatric evaluation of the families of these two twins could have been performed, to provide information on the influences that made them so different.

Gesell introduced the co-twin control method. This technique evaluates the effects of environmental differences by experimentally providing a specific training or teaching experience to one twin, while the other twin, the control, does not receive such an experience. Gesell and Thompson utilized this method in an extensive study of a pair of twins, T and C, who were followed from birth to adolescence.

The co-twin control method should, in principle, provide much valid information on the effects of different experiences on identical twins. Unfortunately, this method has not been used extensively, and, where it has been employed, the environmental differences to which the twins were exposed have generally been minimal. Obviously the extent to which environment can be manipulated in a human experiment is limited; nevertheless, techniques could be developed which would control such important factors as emotional tone of the environment, techniques of handling and of enforcing discipline, and relationship with a passive-type versus an aggressive-type mother figure; these would be expected to provide more vital information than training in motor skills such as stair-climbing.

Gesell and Thompson concluded that the major differences between twins T and C were differences which were essentially present in very early infancy. T was always the more active, aggressive, and energetic of the two. The authors ask, "What is the source of this difference? It probably is not motive in the ordinary sense, a desire to excel, or a reaction to inferiority, for it was displayed by T in early infancy. It persists to this day in acts of motor execution, whether of legs, feet, hands, fingers, or eyes. T is more highly geared. She was more lively as a neonate. She probably was more lively as a fetus." It is illuminating to see how early differences manifested themselves in later personality differences. T was always more independent, more aggressive, and less in need of help. C was more passive, and sought more relationship. She wanted and received more love; in growing up she was more sociable.

C's amiability attracted a greater portion of the affection which the mother gave to both twins. Thus once more, endowment proves its priority over environment. The greater maternal affection enjoyed by C did not initiate a greater degree of sociality in C. Indeed, this was evident through-out infancy. C had a tithe more of the quality or state of being lovable, and this deflected the environment. It was not the environment, per se, which created the quality or the state.

Gesell appears prejudiced on the side of heredity. While his studies are important, and his voluminous compilation of longitudinal data is a valuable contribution to the literature of psychology, some of the interpretations must be tempered. He perhaps goes a bit far in saying that, "In last analysis, the organism plays the primary role in determining environment."

SUMMARY

The major techniques used for determination of hereditary influences on behavior have now been considered. These include, in animals, selective breeding and comparison of pure strains; in the human, longitudinal studies beginning in infancy, and studies of twins. In the above discussion of each of these methods, examples have been given in order to clarify the kinds of information that can be obtained with each method.

For a better perspective and a more complete view of the contributions of heredity to behavioral and personality differences, the following table has been compiled. This is a list of the various functions and behavioral processes which have been shown through one method or another to be determined in whole or in part by heredity. The list is by no means exhaustive. Much of it represents findings from animal research, and there is no claim that all of it applies to the human animal. There has been no attempt to include all the references to the original studies on which the list is based. However, most of the items have been presented with full references in Fuller and Thompson's *Behavior Genetics*. This book is highly recommended to the interested reader. It is a readable, scholarly, and concise account of this fascinating and rapidly developing field, and it has filled a large gap in the literature of behavior.

TABLE 2

BEHAVIORAL FUNCTIONS AFFECTED BY HEREDITY

A. Motor Activities

1. Running Time
2. Exploratory Behavior
3. Congenital Activity Type
4. Sand Digging (field mouse)

B. Sensory and Perceptual Processes

1. Temperature Preference
2. Taste Threshold
3. Visual and Olfactory Acuity
4. Other Visual Functions: Flicker fusion
   Müller-Lyell illusion (ability to block out
   extraneous stimuli)
   Spatial Orientation
5. Auditory Functions
   Acuity
   Pitch Discrimination
   Musical Memory
6. Sensory Preference (food, odors, etc.)
7. Habitat Preference
8. Craving for Alcohol

C. Response Processes

1. Autonomic Balance
2. Motor Skill
3. Ingestive Behavior
4. Hoarding
5. EEG Pattern
6. Handedness (laterality)
7. Sexual Behavior (drive, courtship, mating activities, mate preferences)
8. Parental Behavior (broodiness, care-taking, grooming of young,
   nursing)
9. Muscle Tone

D. Intellectual Capacities

1. General Intelligence
2. Special Abilities (verbal, mathematical, etc.)

E. Emotional Functions

1. Aggressiveness
2. Fearfulness
3. Dominance (pecking order)
4. "Neuroticism"

F. Response to Drugs

(Wide range of behavioral and physiological responses)

All these functions and many others operate within a wide range of variability, and, interacting with the individual's infinitely variable and distinctive environment, result in the personality that is unique for every individual.

INSTINCT

What is instinct? To some, the word conjures up the wonderful phenomena of nature such as the annual return of the swallows to Capistrano or the weird mating dance of the sandhill crane. In psychiatry, instinct is generally equated with "drive," and the major drives are thought of as hunger, sex, and aggression. There is probably no more controversial subject in the whole of psychiatric literature than that concerned with the problem of instinct.

Less confusion exists about instinct in the field of animal behavior. This is partly because the workers in this field, animal ethologists, can carry out more definitive experiments than could be done with the human animal. Also, the animal ethologists are more "research oriented" and have approached the problem in a more systematic way.

INSTINCT IN ANIMALS

When a mother thrush perches on the edge of her nest holding a morsel of food, her babies all turn toward her with mouths gaping. She thrusts the morsel deep into the nearest throat, then flies quickly off for more. A delightful picture of maternal devotion and filial trust. However, if a human finger is held near the nest, the baby thrushes will turn toward *it* with gaping mouths; and if a small block of wood with a red hole in the end is placed in the nest, the mother will thrust the morsel of food into the block of wood.

Tinbergen defines an instinct as "A hierarchically organized nervous mechanism which is susceptible to certain priming, releasing, and directing impulses of internal as well as of external origin, and which responds to these impulses by coordinated movements that contribute to the maintenance of the individual and the species." The concept of a hierarchy of nervous mechanisms is an important part of this definition. It means that there are levels of nervous-system organization, beginning with the individual motor unit and proceeding upward through coordinated movements of whole extremities, the entire body, and finally including the organization of the highest centers of the nervous system. In certain instinctual responses, only the lower levels in the hierarchy are involved, as in ordinary locomotion. In others, the whole organization of the nervous system up to the very highest centers is functioning, as when a young man at a party is seeking an introduction to a young lady.

An instinct is a response to a specific stimulus or group of stimuli. The instinct is not itself the stimulus, a point often confused in psychiatric literature. A part of the instinctual response may be a subjective feeling, such as the feelings associated with hunger and the sexual response. However, the conscious affective experience is only a part of the instinct, major portion of the central response pattern occurring at unconscious levels.

The example of the thrushes cited above is a simple, direct type of instinctual reaction. The gaping response is elicited by a specific stimulus, and the response is a specific, stereotyped motor reaction. Ethologists employ the term *innate releasing mechanism* (IRM) to designate the specific stimulus which produces an instinctual response. In the case of the young thrushes, the IRM has been found to be an object which is moving, which is at least 3 millimeters in diameter, and which is presented above the level of the young birds' eyes.

The innate releasing mechanisms for many different instinctual responses of animals have been worked out in detail. These have encompassed all of the sense modalities: temperature, vision, hearing, touch, taste, and others. Certain of the visual stimuli involve rather complex Gestalt patterns. For example, a simple silhouette bird model when moved across a young bird's visual field will induce escape behavior if the wings of the model are located near the front, but not if the wings are near the tail; the value of this response is that a bird with wings near the front most resembles a bird of prey (Tinbergen).

"Supernormal" IRM's have been described (Tinbergen) in which the experimental stimulus is more effective than a naturally occurring one. The ringed plover will sit on a white egg that has been painted with large black dots in preference to its own egg which is light brown with dark brown spots. An amusing example of a supernormal IRM is seen in a bird called the oystercatcher, which, when given a choice, will always sit on the larger of two eggs. In Tinbergen's book there is a picture of an oystercatcher attempting to incubate a herring gull's egg, which is so large that the bird can barely straddle it.

Certain highly complex patterns of instinctual behavior have been shown to consist of a series of simple reactions to different stimuli. Tinbergen calls such behavior "chain reactions," and has worked out in detail the chain-reaction mating behavior of the stickleback fish. Using dummy fish, he showed that each act in this complex pattern of behavior depends on an appropriate stimulus; each resultant act in turn induces the next response.

*The male's first reaction, the zig-zag dance, is dependent on a visual
stimulus, the swollen abdomen of the female. The female then reacts to
the zig-zag dance of the male by swimming toward him. This movement
induces the male to turn around and swim to the nest. This, in turn, en-
tices the female to follow him, thereby stimulating the male to point its
head into the entrance of the nest. This behavior now releases the female's
next reaction: she enters the nest. This releases a quivering reaction in the
male which induces spawning (egg laying). The presence of fresh eggs in
the nest makes the male fertilize them.*

An instinctual response thus depends on a specific stimulus to initiate
it. But it is modified by other factors. It is modified by learning, and also
by "internal factors," such as hormonal balance, and level of satiation. Examples of hormonal effects on instinctual behavior are so well known as
not to require presentation here.

There next follows a brief consideration of some of the animal experiments which demonstrate effects of learning on instinct.

INTERRELATIONSHIPS BETWEEN LEARNING AND INSTINCT

Some kinds of fish care for their young, herding them together in a
school, shepherding them out of danger, and the like, much as a hen cares
for her brood of chicks. This appears to be purely instinctual parental behavior. But if a young pair of cichlid fish during their first breeding season
are given eggs of another species in exchange for their own, they will accept
them and raise the young. From then on they will never again raise young
of their own species; they will kill their own young as soon as they hatch.
Here then is an example of a complex behavior system, the care and feeding of young, which can be markedly altered by early learning (Tinbergen).

A more familiar instance of the effects of early learning on an instinctual response is the so-called imprinting, or following, response in birds.
The German ethologist, Konrad Lorenz, in *King Solomon's Ring*, has described his early studies of imprinting in ducklings. Noting that ducklings
would follow a foster mother of another duck species, he concluded that
the essential stimulus was the quacking sound. To test his theory, Lorenz
decided to become a mother duck. He describes the following experience
with a new-hatched brood of Mallard ducks:

*I took the babies, as soon as they were dry, under my personal care,
and quacked for them the mother's call note in my best Mallardese. For
hours on end I kept it up, for half the day. The quacking was successful.
The little ducks lifted their gaze confidently towards me, obviously had no*

fear of me this time, and as, still quacking, I drew slowly away from them they also set themselves obediently in motion and scuttled after me in a tightly huddled group, just as ducklings follow their mother.

Lorenz discovered a complication to this procedure, however. He noted that the mother figure must be a relatively small, moving object, so that as long as he remained bent over, the ducklings followed him, but as soon as he stood upright they no longer did so; the stimulus of a tall upright figure is not a sufficient IRM. He noted that when he would stand up, "they gave up, peered searchingly on all sides, and then began that penetrating piping of abandoned ducklings that we are accustomed simply to call crying. So I was forced to move along, squatting low." Lorenz found that, once having adopted his children, he could not give them up, nor would they give him up. It became a common sight to the neighbors around Lorenz' Danube farm to see him and his brood waddling about the farmyard. He concludes that "The ducklings were most demanding and tiring charges, for, imagine a two-hour walk with such children, all the time squatting low and quacking without interruption!"

Laboratory study of the following-response in ducks and other birds (Hess) has demonstrated that: 1. The mother object must be a relatively small, moving figure. 2. The stimulus must be presented at a fairly specific period of time following hatching, usually between the twelfth and the twenty-fourth hour of life. The quacking sound, or any other sound, does not appear to be essential. At a somewhat later time, generally about the forty-eighth hour after birth, presentation of the stimulus, if it has not been presented previously, will produce an opposite effect; that is, the duckling avoids, and appears to fear the mother figure.

Is the above behavior instinctual or learned? Obviously, it is both. It requires the functioning of specific inborn neural or behavioral patterns, and for its completion it requires a specific learning experience which must occur at a critical time in the organism's life. Probably all instinctual behavior is affected by learning. Even the simplest reflex reactions in the intact organism probably vary according to differences in higher-level functioning of the organism.

HUMAN INSTINCT

It is not universally accepted that true instinctual behavior occurs in the human. The dissidents point out that even the more primitive inborn behavior responses such as sucking require a certain amount of learning, and that the newborn infant does not suck as well as he does after one or two days' experience. The controversy is largely a semantic one. It is patently absurd to deny that there are inborn, complex behavioral responses to specific stimuli. The fact that these are affected and altered by learning does not negate their occurrence. The crucial question is not what to call these behaviors but what the behaviors are, how much they vary between individuals, and in what ways they determine subsequent behavior.

Bowlby, in a formulation of the factors which effect the infant's tie to its mother, has described five types of instinctual response in the human infant. He concedes that there may be others. They are: sucking, crying, smiling, clinging, and following. Bowlby concludes that these instinctual responses are largely determined by inborn neural patterns and that they have developed phylogenetically and are important in assuring the survival of the race. He notes that the strength of these responses varies greatly among infants, and that the responses are markedly affected by experience.

Bowlby points out further that the instinctual responses do not function continuously throughout life, but operate at specific periods of development, appearing and then later dropping out. However, they may reappear during times of stress and regression. The crying response, the infant's distress call, so essential an operation in the early years, has little function in the older child and adult, and is for the most part controlled and suppressed by higher centers. But at times, even in the mature adult, it may break out of control.

Much of the controversy about human instincts concerns the question of whether an instinct is a stimulus or a response. Some psychiatrists feel that the confusion arises from the translation of the German word *Trieb*, as used by Freud. Some translate this as meaning "instinct," while others feel that it should be called "drive." A resolution of this semantic conflict will by no means clear up the problem. As noted above, some feel that there is no true inborn behavior response, that everything is learned; other workers, notably Jung and his followers, believe that there are highly-organized inborn neural patterns, including the highest levels of abstract thought, so that they hypothesize the occurrence of inborn religious feelings and complex social and ethical responses.

Freud himself held that specific symbolic thoughts, such as fear of certain objects, are inherited, and that they assist in the survival of a race. He observed (Freud 1956a):

When we speak of our archaic heritage we are generally thinking only of the id and we apparently assume that no ego is yet in existence at the beginning of life. But we must not overlook the fact that id and ego are originally one, and it does not imply a mystical overvaluation of heredity if we think it credible that, even before the ego exists, its subsequent lines of development, tendencies and reactions are already determined. The psychological peculiarities of families, races and nations, even in their attitude towards analysis, admit of no other explanation. Indeed, analytic experience convinces us that particular psychical contents, such as symbolism, have no other source than hereditary transmission.

Nor is this an expression of Freud's earlier writings which he later found cause to alter. It appeared in 1937 in what was perhaps his last major piece of writing.

Freud's "biological orientation" and his intense interest in "constitutional" factors in the determination of personality and mental disorder have largely been deplored and de-emphasized by most of his followers. For example, Hartmann notes: "Freud argues that the intensity of the fear of castration experienced by the male child in our civilization is unaccountable if we consider it as a reaction to the actual threats to which the boy is being exposed in the phallic phase; only the memory of the race will explain it." Hartmann argues that a boy in our civilization may not be exposed to actual, but only to symbolic castration threats, and that these account for what psychoanalysts consider the universality of castration anxiety. Hartmann concludes that "The recourse to the past of the race transmitted by the inheritance of acquired characteristics, inspiring as it is in Freud's presentation, does not find sufficient empirical support in our present knowledge of heredity."

Actually, advances in knowledge of heredity since Freud's time, important as they have been, neither add to nor detract from this concept of Freud's. Moreover, recent advances in animal ethology and in evolution theory would suggest that such a concept is entirely feasible. It is known that birds have an inborn fear response to complex visual Gestalt stimuli (Tinbergen). It is not inconceivable therefore that the human animal may likewise inherit certain fear responses. Such reactions undergo much modification and elaboration in the human, so that later representations of a fear response bear little resemblance to the original. Nevertheless, the original response must assert itself at some time in the early life of the organism.

Experimental study of the fear response in primates discloses that young chimpanzees experience a "primal" fear toward objects which are similar to but not identical with familiar objects. Thus, at 4 months, the chimpanzee is intensely frightened by humans other than its handlers, or by another chimpanzee which has been anesthetized, yet he is not frightened by objects which are completely unfamiliar.

Psychoanalysis presently considers that there are at least two major instincts, or drives: the hunger drive and the sex drive. The aggressive drive is also regarded by many analysts as one of the instincts, but, as will be discussed in Chapter 2, this would no longer appear tenable. The death instinct, or Thanatos, has now been generally rejected in psychoanalytic literature, and this has been a major area of disagreement between Freud and modern psychoanalysts. Freud apparently clung firmly to this notion of a death instinct, even though during his later years it met with much outspoken disagreement. Some of his last writings are concerned with what he considered evidence in support of the theory: the return of all living material to the inanimate state. He thus saw the death wish as a kind of universal drive toward the return to the inanimate. It is this sort of thinking in Freud's "biological orientation" that his detractors have most violently objected to, and not without justification.

Ernest Jones discussed Freud's unwillingness to incorporate pertinent knowledge of animal behavior into analytic theory, and also his insistence that man has but two instinctual drives. In a remarkably candid revelation, Jones remarks:

There would appear to be two reasons for this rather curious omission on his (Freud's) part. One was his almost obsessional determination to confine himself to two sets of instincts only. These sets several times differed in kind, but they were invariably two in number. Then again Freud seems to have followed his ancestral traditions in feeling aloof from the animal world. . . . Freud seems never to have paid much attention to the zoological aspects of natural history, confining his observations to the botanical ones.

The application of other principles, more reliable than numerology and a sense of aloofness from the animal world, confirm that man is driven by a number of instinctual behaviors. These vary widely in strength and duration. Many of them are much altered by learning—they are suppressed, redirected, symbolically represented. In a sense, man is less firmly "instinct-bound" than other animals. But he is by no means entirely free.

CONSTITUTIONAL PREDISPOSITION

By the term *constitutional predisposition,* which he used interchangeably with *hereditary predisposition,* Freud apparently meant all those factors in biological and psychological functioning which are hereditarily determined. He saw the constitutional factors as operating in continuous relationship with the organism's ongoing experience, the resultant interaction producing the individual's personality and his mental health or illness. Usually, the term *predisposition* was employed to mean a tendency toward developing mental illness. Freud once wrote(1956b):

In the pathogenesis of the major neuroses heredity plays the part of a condition, potent in all cases and even indispensable in the majority of them. It cannot do without the assistance of the specific causes; but the importance of hereditary predisposition is demonstrated by the fact that the same specific causes operating on a sound person would produce no manifest pathological effect, while its presence in a predisposed person will precipitate a neurosis, the development of which will be in intensity and extent proportional to the degree of hereditary predisposition.

Freud in his writings on constitution never got beyond the level of generalities, chiefly, perhaps, because there was not much data available in his time. He would no doubt have been interested in, and perhaps would have incorporated into his writings, much of the information which has appeared recently from the fields of animal behavior, genetics, and neurophysiology. On the other hand, there is strong evidence that he either ignored or was unaware of the major facts of modern genetics even though these had been available during the last 25 years of his life. For example, Freud apparently believed as late as 1937 that some learned or acquired traits could be passed on to one's offspring by heredity (1956a).

The concept of constitutional predisposition, largely rejected in psychiatric writings for several decades, is again coming into prominence. This movement has been effected from several directions. One has been the pioneering work of Anna Freud and other child analysts who have employed research methods of longitudinal observation beginning in infancy. These studies have helped to clarify knowledge of the inborn differences between infants. Modern psychoanalytic thinking on ego psychology has incorporated the concept of constitutional variation, and has investigated the role of the autonomous functions of the ego in the determination of personality and neurosis. These developments are exemplified in the writings of Hartmann, Kris, and Lowenstein.

Other work which has contributed to the clarification and acceptance of the notion of constitutional predisposition are the studies cited earlier on variations in animal behavior. Additionally contributory has been research and clinical practice in child psychiatry, which has taken cognizance of the many kinds of variations in the child's capacity in such areas as intellectual functioning, conceptual thinking, perceptual functioning, frustration tolerance, and delay of gratification. In daily practice, we psychiatrists are continuously aware that the differences between children are in part differences which were present from birth. It is impossible to practice child psychiatry without this concept. An understanding of the child and of his difficulties requires that the origins be understood, that something should be known of what the child was like when he first came into the world, how he expressed his needs, how he reacted to satisfaction and frustration. Also, the time and the manner in which his responses first became "difficult," when he first began to overreact, to become nonadaptive, should be determined. This must be perceived as an ongoing operation, an interrelation between the child and his environment; the kinds of experience must be assessed which the environment presented—the mother and her personality, her needs, her feelings, the father, the siblings—both in terms of what they are and of what they meant and presently mean to the child.

In a sense, the practice of child psychiatry is continuous, longitudinal research into the genesis of personality and mental illness. Clinical psychiatry is supplying many answers. Much knowledge of the causes and treatment of childhood disturbances has accumulated as child psychiatry has grown over the past three decades. But there is a great deal yet to learn; there are still far more questions than answers. Good research and good clinical practice can continue to improve man's understanding. This requires an avoidance of prejudice, an effort to encompass or at least to be aware of the multiplicity of aspects of each problem. Investigators from many disciplines appear to be increasingly aware that all disciplines and all approaches must contribute. Typical of this growing awareness is a statement made by Kris in 1950, in which he discussed the necessity for both longitudinal observation and reconstruction through historical material obtained from the patient, in order to understand the genesis of a disorder. Kris concudes:

It seems that in each of the areas further research is required; and in each the test of the advanced hypothesis could best be reached by a convergence of two sets of data, those gained in analysis and those which, assembled over many years, may have been tested by predicting short-term steps. Moreover, once we have decided on such coordination of data we shall sooner or later have to include the problem of hereditary factors in our investigation.

REFERENCES

Bowlby, J. The Nature of the Child's Tie to His Mother, Int. J. Psychoanal., 39: 350, 1958.

Burlingham, D. The Relation of Twins to Each Other, Psychoanalytic Study of the Child, New York, International Universities Press, 1948, Vol. 3/4.

Chess, S., Thomas, A., Birch, H., and Hertzig, M. Implications of a Longitudinal Study of Child Development for Child Psychiatry, Am. J. Psychiatry, 117: 434, 1960.

Freud, S. Analysis Terminable and Interminable, Collected Papers, London, Hogarth Press, 1956a, Vol. 5.

Freud, S. Heredity and the Etiology of the Neuroses, Collected Papers, London, Hogarth Press, 1956b, Vol. 1.

Fries, M. and Woolf, P. Some Hypotheses on the Role of the Congenital Activity Type in Personality Development, Psychoanalytic Study of the Child, New York, International Universities Press, 1954, Vol. 8.

Fuller, J. L., and Thompson, W. R. Behavior Genetics, New York, John Wiley & Sons, 1960.

Gesell, A., and Thompson, H. Twins T and C from Infancy to Adolescence; a Biogenetic Study of Individual Differences by the Method of Co-twin Control, Genet. Psychol. Monog., 24: 3, 1941.

Ginsburg, B. Genetics as a Tool in the Study of Behavior, Perspect. Biol. & Med., 1: 397, 1958.

Hartmann, H., and Kris, E. Genetic Approach in Psychoanalysis, Psychoanalytic Study of the Child, New York, International Universities Press, 1945, Vol. 1.

———— Kris, E., and Loewenstein, R. M. Comments on the Formation of Psychic Structure, Psychoanalytic Study of the Child, New York, International Universities Press, 1946, Vol. 2.

Hess, E. Imprinting, Science, 130: 133, 1959.

Jones, E. The Life and Work of Sigmund Freud, New York, Basic Books, 1957, Vol. 3.

Karon, B. P., and Saunders, D. R. Some Implications of the Eysenck-Prell Study of "The Inheritance of Neuroticism": a Critique, J. Ment. Sci., 104: 350, 1958.

Kris, E. Development and Problems in Child Psychology, Psychoanalytic Study of the Child, New York, International Universities Press, 1950, Vol. 5.

Lorenz, K. King Solomon's Ring, New York, Thomas Y. Crowell Co., 1952.

Newman, H. A. Multiple Human Births, New York, Doubleday, Doran & Co., 1940.

Roe, A., and Simpson, G. G. Behavior and Evolution, New Haven, Yale University Press, 1958.

Rutter, M., Birch, H. G., Thomas, A., and Chess, S. Temperamental Characteristics in Infancy and the Later Development of Behavioral Disorders, Brit. J. Psychiatry, 110: 651, 1964.

Scott, J. P. Animal Behavior, Chicago, University of Chicago Press, 1958.

Searle, L. V. The Organization of Hereditary Maze-brightness and Maze-dullness, Genet. Psychol. Monogr., 39: 279, 1949.

Shaw, C. R., Syner, F. N., and Tashian, R. E. New Genetically Determined Molecular Form of Erythrocyte Esterase in Man, Science, 138: 31, 1962.

Smithies, O., and Connell, G. E. Biochemical Aspects of the Inherited Variations in Human Serum: Haptoglobins and Transferrins, in Biochemistry of Human Genetics, ed. Wolstenholme and O'Connor, London, J. & A. Churchill, Ltd., 1959.

Stern, C. Human Genetics, San Francisco, W. H. Freeman Co., 1960.

Tinbergen, N. The Study of Instinct, New York, Oxford University Press, 1951.

Tryon, R. C. Individual Differences, in Comparative Psychology, F. A. Moss, ed., New York, Prentice-Hall, 1942.

2

THE EFFECTS OF EXPERIENCE

This chapter will consider the impact of environment upon the developing child, and the ways in which experience effects differences in individuals. Because personality is never static, and because the needs of a child at each period of his development vary with his past experience and with his genetic make-up, there can be no simple formula to determine specific effects of a particular experience at a particular age. Thus, although generalizations are admittedly risky and always incomplete, a few will here be attempted.

The first generalization is that every child needs to be loved, and that without love he will grow up seriously distorted and disturbed. This love has nothing to do with the satisfaction of the child's physiological needs such as feeding and cleansing. It is a need in itself, as great as the need for food, and, as Spitz has shown, without the love object an infant may die.

A second generalization is that rarely if ever is emotional disorder caused by a single episode or brief period of trauma. Rather it is determined by the total milieu, the total emotional tone of the child's environment, and by the repeated experiences to which he is subjected during prolonged periods, usually during his entire early life. There are, as in all generalizations, exceptions. Severely traumatic episodes, such as in the case of a 7-year-old boy who accidentally killed his young brother with a revolver, have sometimes induced a major emotional reaction in a child who would otherwise probably have remained normally adjusted.

A single episode such as a parent's death has permanent effect, but here the experience is not an isolated event but a deprivation that extends over years. There is also the possibility that single episodes in very early infancy may have lasting effects, episodes which, for example, determine a particular way of reacting to frustration, so that the child, frustrated at every turn, quits trying and withdraws, and thus sets a habit pattern which becomes fixed. This is, in essence, one-trial conditioning, which thereafter reinforces itself. The extent to which this occurs is not known, and represents a major area for research. For the most part, however, the generalization holds that emotional disorder does not result from a single experience.

This chapter on experience consists of three sections: Learning; Interpersonal experience; Cultural factors.

As in Chapter 1, the general rather than the specific will be discussed. It is not intended to explain a particular episode or illness, but rather to impart some understanding of the multiplicity of ways in which an individual's world determines his personality.

LEARNING

Learning is usually defined as a change produced in subsequent behavior as a result of experience. Psychiatry is much concerned with learning: all mental disorder is, to some degree, a learned phenomenon. Thus, any knowledge which improves understanding of the learning process should increase understanding of mental illness.

Learning theory is that branch of formal psychology concerned with the process of learning. It has a long, generally dignified, and at times controversial history (Hilgard). It has produced some famous names in psychology. However, learning theory has thus far contributed disappointingly little to psychiatry. For one thing, it has largely ignored the fundamentally important problem of individual variation. The classical approach to the study of learning has generally involved "overcoming" individual variation by using a large number of subjects, so that the variations average out. For example, in studying visual discrimination in the rat, a large number of animals would be taught to jump toward a particular geometric figure for a food reward. It might be shown that the group of rats would learn, in an average of 50 trials, to discriminate between a square and a circle while requiring 100 trials to discriminate between a square and a triangle. But such a study ignores what might well be more interesting and significant questions, such as why some of the rats jump quickly while others sniff at the apparatus, peer about the room, or cower trembling at the edge of the jumping stand.

At the theoretical level, one important contribution of learning theory to psychiatry has been the demonstration that permanent behavior disorders, or "experimental neuroses," can be produced in animals by conditioning methods. This was an incidental finding, and occurred in many animals being studied in conditioning procedures which forced them into states of conflict from which there was no escape. Liddell has pointed out that although Pavlov in his later years studied the experimental production of emotional disorders, he apparently never fully appreciated the severity of disorder, the "total emotional bankruptcy," that he produced in his experimental animals.

The studies on experimental neurosis, important as they are, could be much more meaningful to psychiatry if they were carried out and reported with more attention to the problem of individual variation. It is apparent from the reports that animals vary greatly in their susceptibility to "neurosis." However, it is usually not made clear whether all animals can be "broken." Nor has there been much attempt to determine in advance which individual animals are more likely to become disturbed. Another fascinating area for exploration would be to investigate the factors which determine in what way the animal reacts to the intolerable situation. Masserman commented in 1943 that his cats reacted in different ways to the conflict-producing situation, some cowering in the corner of the cage, others spitting or attacking angrily. Such studies should provide important clues to the problem of symptom choice and to effective methods of dealing with frustration in the human child.

CONDITIONING

Another contribution of learning theory, the importance of which is perhaps too little appreciated, is the demonstration that conditioned responses do occur. This means that a reaction can occur in response to a stimulus other than the one which originally produced it. The implications of this finding for human functioning are enormous. It has done much to take the magic out of man's thinking, and to make logical, or at least theoretically logical, much in human behavior and human thinking that would otherwise seem inexplicable. It helps to explain phobias, compulsions, love and hate, all those vicissitudes and peculiarities of human behavior which occur because they "mean," or symbolize, something else, and because they were associated in early life with some particular meaningful experience. Actually, less may be known about all these things than is generally thought, since the phenomenon of conditioning itself is by no means well understood, and the fundamental problem of learning, namely, the neurophysiological basis of the memory trace, remains an enigma.

The phenomenon of conditioning has been given further meaning by the elucidation of the principles of *generalization* and *discrimination*. *Generalization* states that the conditioned response may be elicited by stimuli which are similar to, but not identical with, the original conditioning stimulus. This exigency was necessary in evolution, as it avoided the requirement that a situation be exactly reproduced in order for the organism to have learned anything, a proviso obviously not possible. *Discrimination*, of course, limits generalization, so that the organism does not respond to every stimulus which has any slight resemblance to the original condition-ing stimulus. Thus, experimentally, the animal may discriminate between a metronome clicking at 60 times per minute and one clicking at 100 times per minute. In nature, differentiation permits the infant to distinguish the voice of his mother from that of strangers, and other such knowledge which is fundamental to all appraisal of the environment and growth of the personality.

Of major significance was the demonstration that some conditioned responses are elicited more readily than others, and that some responses cannot be conditioned at all. This finding gives further meaning to the concept of instinct. It suggests that there is a continuum of learning, ex-tending from those responses which occur without previous learning (in-stinctual responses), through responses which are readily learned after one or two trials, to others which are learned with greater difficulty, and finally to those which can never be learned. These levels of learning are presuma-bly functions of the organism's neurophysiology.

The demonstration of variations in ease of conditioning quickly led to a realization that learning was not merely a matter of contiguity, that is, a simple function of the temporal proximity of the unconditioned and con-ditioned stimuli. This in turn led to elaborations of learning theory, and to the investigation of such concepts as motivation, strength of drive, rein-forcement by reward vs. reinforcement by punishment, the principle of drive reduction, and "mental set." All these are fundamental, and are in-cluded in any major theory of learning. The "schools" of learning theory differ chiefly in their emphasis on one or another aspect of learning.

THE NEUROPHYSIOLOGICAL BASE

Olds demonstrated that when an electrode is implanted in a certain area of an animal's midbrain and attached to an apparatus by means of which the animal can press a lever and apply an electric shock to its own brain, the animal will press the lever repeatedly for as long as it is permit-ted to do so. Under certain conditions a hungry animal will prefer this electrical stimulation to eating, and in some cases it will endure pain in order to reach the lever and give itself the shock. The areas of the brain in which this self-stimulation is produced have been called "reward" centers, although Olds prefers the term "positive reinforcement area." Whatever term is used, the demonstration that such an area exists is of profound sig-nificance to learning theory and to any theory of behavior. There is a won-derful specificity about it; it takes out of the realm of the vague and of the abstract such phenomena as pleasure, reward, and satisfaction. Such things become simply those phenomena which produce or obtain electrophysiological discharge into the reward centers. This definition, however, will obviously not satisfy the philosopher.

To complement the discovery of the areas of positive reinforcement, Olds additionally found areas of negative reinforcement. When the electrode is implanted in these areas (which are of smaller extent than the positive reinforcement areas) the animal will carefully avoid the shocking lever after having experienced it once or twice. At first thought this might not appear unusual; it seems normal not to want to give one's self a shock. However, it must be remembered that the brain is generally insensitive to direct stimulation; it has no sensory endings, and can be cut, torn, or burned without any feeling. Thus, the demonstration of the primary avoidance was a significant achievement.

Olds' findings are too recent to have as yet been incorporated into any major theories of learning and behavior. However, this is currently being done, and it represents an important step in the growing relationship between neurophysiology and psychology.

LEARNING THEORY AND PSYCHIATRY

In psychiatry, both in theory and in practice, principles of learning theory are applied all the time, but without thinking in such terms. In therapy, the patient's responses are continually being reinforced, positively or negatively, by the psychiatrist's approval or disapproval. The aim is to "condition" certain reactions and to "extinguish" others. The therapist determines what things seem to motivate the patient best. The patient is then helped to achieve drive reductions in ways which are socially acceptable and least conflict-producing. An understanding of the principles of learning theory can clarify everyone's thinking about "higher" learning such as object relationship, identification, and transference.

But the limitations of learning theory must be known and appreciated. Any theory developed from a study of animal behavior cannot be allsufficient for the human. The difference between the human and lower animals is more than a quantitative one. There is the matter of the phenomenal memory of man, which insists on bringing long-ago happenings into the present situation. Man is not "stimulus-bound" as are other animals. Then there is the phenomenon of language, which enormously complicates the picture; man can learn a thing without experiencing it, simply by being told about it by another person. Grey Walter once remarked:

No other animal is equipped for being sapiens. It is in fact a difference of equipment and not of opportunity. In terms of behavior, the gist of it is that, when we come across something new, we do not necessarily respond

to it at once in a particular manner. We think it over. We can imagine one
of a number of possible responses, and imagine it so clearly that we can see
whether it would be, if we made it, a mistake, without having to commit
ourselves to action. We can make our errors in a thought and reject them
in another thought, leaving no trace of error in us.

And Hebb more recently protested:

Surely it is time for the work of the conditioned response diagram
makers to abandon the assumption that the conditioned response is the
simple prototype of learning and that it depends only on the establishment
of a one or two step pathway from a sensory to a motor structure. Because
a simple task could, theoretically, be handled by a simple mechanism does
not mean in fact that the brain handles it that way. Other mechanisms
may insist on getting into the act and turn simple tasks into complex ones.

There is evidence of increasing application of learning theory in psychotherapy. Wolpe applied the term "reciprocal inhibition" to a technique
which is based on causing the neurotic patient to re-experience a stimulus
or a situation which formerly produced unadaptive behavior. By succes-
sively increasing the stimulus in a reassuring, non-anxietous situation, the
learned anxiety gradually becomes unlearned. Rachman and Costello, in
England, have applied principles of learning theory to the treatment of
children's phobias. They state that "the essence of Behavior Therapy is
clearly deducible from theory. If neurotic behavior is acquired (learned), it
should be amenable to 'un-learning' in a manner similar to that whereby
non-neurotic behavior is extinguished."
Russian psychiatry has, of course, been profoundly influenced by
learning theory (Winn) and, as communication between American psychiatrists and their Russian colleagues improves, it may be anticipated that
the best of their principles will be incorporated. The apparent conflict between learning theory and psychoanalytic theory must eventually be resolved, and these two disciplines will undoubtedly be shown to complement and explicate one another.
It is likely that "practical" application of academic psychology may
first occur on a wide scale in child rather than adult psychiatry because of
child psychiatry's emphasis on the total milieu of the developing child, on
methods involving major changes in environment, and on techniques of re-
training and education.

INTERPERSONAL EXPERIENCE

The child learns from interaction with his physical and human environment. As he explores the objects and the space about him, he devel-

ops a concept of reality, and a concept of himself as an object distinct from his environment. This learning requires an intact and developing nervous system. It cannot proceed normally in the presence of those biological defects called brain damage and schizophrenia. The ways in which learning is disrupted by these disorders will be described in chapters later.

The physical environment is relatively constant. The infant's crib always presents to him hard wooden sides and a soft floor. A ball is always a small round object. There may be occasional surprises, as when the ball rolls out of reach, or bounces up and hits him in the nose, or the side of the crib may suddenly drop. But these variations can be predicted and learned.

In addition to living in the physical environment, the child lives in a human environment. This is highly variable, changeable, often unpredictable, and its variations can have profound effect upon the child's developing personality.

THE NEEDS OF CHILDREN

To understand how interpersonal experience can adversely affect emotional adjustment, there must first be some consideration of what the human environment must supply if the child is to develop normally.

Erik Erikson has most concisely and beautifully expressed the needs of the organism, in his chapter on "The Eight Stages of Man"; this chapter has become one of the classics of psychiatric literature. Following is a summary, in outline form, of Erikson's eight stages, with notation as to the approximate age at which each occurs, the basic functions and concepts which should develop at that stage, and the major defects which occur if these functions do not develop normally.

1. *Early Infancy.* The time for development of a basic sense of trust. The needs are for warmth, comfort, and food. If these needs are met by a sensitive, empathic mother or mother figure in response to the infant's discomforts and hungers, the child soon learns to integrate the vague feelings of discomfort, to learn what hunger means, and how to signal for its satiation. "In his gradually increasing waking hours he finds that more and more adventures of the senses arouse a feeling of familiarity, of having coincided with a feeling of inner goodness." He learns gradually the permanence of objects in his world, that things which are out of his sight are not gone forever. His "first social achievement is his willingness to let the mother out of sight without undue anxiety or rage, because she has become an inner certainty as well as an outer predictability."

Thus a basic pattern of trust in his environment is early established in the child. Without it, without consistent and sensitive care, a basic mistrust develops, and this may be enduring. For adequate maternal care there are no written rules; it cannot be learned from a book. Erikson emphasizes this: "The amount of trust derived from earliest infantile experience does not seem to depend on absolute quantities of food or demonstrations of love, but rather on the quality of their maternal relationship. Mothers create a sense of trust in their children by that kind of administration which in its quality combines sensitive care of the baby's individual needs and a firm sense of trustworthiness within the trusted framework of their culture's life style."

Having achieved a basic sense of trust, the developing infant is able to tolerate the frustrations which are inevitable, the postponement of satiation, the pain of teething and of sickness, the sharing of the mother's love with siblings and father. With a sense of trust, a sense that things are all right, a certainty that comfort will come soon, there are few frustrations which the growing child cannot somehow endure. "Parents must not only have certain ways of guiding by prohibition and permission; they must also be able to represent to the child a deep, an almost somatic conviction that there is a meaning to what they are doing. Children become neurotic not from frustrations, but from the lack or loss of societal meaning in these frustrations."

2. *First to Third Years.*   The development of autonomy. With the development of skeletal and sphincter musculature, the growing infant begins to have some control over himself and his environment. He has the capacity for choice between two basic social modalities: holding on and letting go. The uses of this control may be hostile or benign, depending on the growing personality and its essential peace or anger, and depending on the degrees of frustration or assistance which the child encounters.

In this period the child needs to explore and experiment with his new-found powers and with his environment. There is danger in this, "for if denied the gradual and well-guided experience of the autonomy of free choice (or if, indeed, weakened by an initial loss of trust) the child will turn against himself all his urge to discriminate and to manipulate. He will over-manipulate himself, he will develop a precocious conscience. Instead of taking possession of things in order to test them by purposeful repetition, he will become obsessed by his own repetitiveness."

At this age the child needs wise and understanding external control; he must be allowed to experiment and manipulate, but not too much. He must be frustrated at times, but the frustration need not and should not be damaging. Parents must be firm but loving. It is at this time that shame first appears. This is the feeling of being exposed and disapproved of, and it is the precursor of guilt. Guilt is "a sense of badness to be had all by one's self when nobody watches and everything is quiet—except the voice of the superego." These feelings, shame and guilt, are the incorporation into the growing personality of environmental disapproval. It is a normal process; everyone has got to accomplish it. But it may be too intense, or overwhelming, so that the world always remains an alien and a hostile place.

3. *Third to Sixth Years.* The age of initiative. This is the age when jealousies are formed and resolved; it is the time for incorporation of taboos and cultural restrictions, the time of overpowering love and disappointment in love. "Infantile sexuality and incest taboo, castration complex and super-ego all unite here to bring about that specifically human crisis during which the child must turn from an exclusive, pregenital attachment to his parents to the slow process of becoming a parent, a carrier of tradition."

The child now begins to have a sense of past and future, to perceive that tomorrow he will want what he wants today, but may not be able to have it. At this age begins pleasure in attack and conquest. Differentiation of the sexes appears: the male the aggressor, the intruder; the female the attracter, the receiver. These attitudes may be partly instinctual; they are certainly much learned, from parents, peers, and adults. In this time, as in the previous, there is need for guidance, and firm but gentle control. The mother who must withhold part of her love must also continue to give part of it. She cannot be too protecting or too rejecting. The father must not be too stern, or too approving.

The child at this age is learning the first steps toward parenthood; the balance of love and hate. "The problem, again, is one of mutual regulation. Where a child, now so ready to overmanipulate himself, can gradually develop a sense of paternal responsibility, where he can gain some insight into the institutions, functions, and roles which will permit his responsible participation, he will find pleasurable accomplishment in wielding tools and weapons, in manipulating meaningful toys—and in caring for younger children."

Because he perceives himself as responsible, as the agent of consequences, earlier shame now turns into guilt. The sense of his new-found powers may induce inordinate self-blame for difficulties, as well as inducing pride in accomplishments. At this time he may take the blame for everything, no matter how illogical.

4. *Years 7 to 12.* The age of industry. At this age the child begins to get out into the world and to accomplish things. His universe is no longer the home but the community. "He has experienced a sense of finality regarding the fact that there is no workable future within the womb of his family, and thus becomes ready to apply himself to given skills and tasks." In civilized cultures, the child goes to school, he learns organized modes of

play and work, he becomes a member of a peer group, and he seeks recognition in the group. He enjoys the rewards of diligence.

"His danger at this age lies in a sense of inadequacy and inferiority." If his skills are insufficient, or if his early experiences have left him without a firm sense of trust, autonomy, and initiative, he is unable to enter the society of peers with confidence and motivation.

5. *Adolescence.* The age of identity. This is the advent of sexual maturity and the end of childhood. At this age all the accruing earlier skills and confidences form into a personality that seeks its new role at the beginning of adulthood. This is the time of seeking a mate, and of embarking on a career. The sense of future is more organized, and conscious, and expressed in the question: "What am I and what will I become?"

The danger of this stage is role diffusion. Where this is based on a strong previous doubt as to one's sexual identity, delinquent and outright psychotic incidents are not uncommon. If diagnosed and treated correctly, these incidents do not have the same fatal significance which they have at other ages. It is primarily the inability to settle on an occupational identity which disturbs young people. To keep themselves together they temporarily over-identify, to the point of apparent complete loss of identity, with the heroes of cliques and crowds. This initiates the stage of "falling in love," which is by no means entirely, or even primarily, a sexual matter— except where the mores demand it.

6. *Young Adulthood.* The age of intimacy. This is the time of finding a mate, and the end of seeking a mate. It is also the beginning of productive work and of establishing one's self in the community of adults.

In the "self-abandon of intimacy with a sexual partner" there must be sufficient assurance of self and purpose to prevent loss of identity, with its accompanying anxiety and fear of intimacy. This is the time of the understanding of human dignity, and of a knowledge that dignity resides in man, not in spite of but because of his capacity for sexual intimacy.

Erikson observes that psychoanalysis has at times overemphasized, or seemed to overemphasize, heterosexual orgasm as the key to mental health. Actually, much more important is a strong sense of identity, sufficient drive, and the capacity to sublimate the drive when necessary. "A human being should be potentially able to accomplish mutuality of genital orgasm, but he should also be so constituted as to bear frustration in the matter without undue regression wherever considerations of reality and loyalty call for it." In any marriage there is conflict, resentment, even hate; marriage imposes restrictions, takes away freedoms, reawakens old jealousies and fears that have been dormant since childhood. But sexual intimacy, the mutual sharing of this high experience "in some way breaks the point off

the hostilities and potential rages caused by the oppositeness of male and
female, of fact and fancy, of love and hate."

7. *Adulthood.* The age of parenthood. This is the time of what
Erikson has called "generativity," which is primarily "the interest in establishing and guiding the next generation." At this time the adult who has
matured well can raise his children without overreacting, without obsessive
need for love, for anger, for punishment. Having sufficient self-strength, he
can give of himself to his children, and can sympathize genuinely with
their feelings. This is the time when mental health or mental disorder is
transmitted to the next generation.

8. *Maturity.* This is the time after the children leave home. It is
often the time of emptiness and despair; it is also the time of greatest productivity in the sense that it is the age of most of the world's great leaders.
Erikson calls it the period of ego integrity. "Only he who in some way has
taken care of things and people and has adapted himself to the triumphs
and disappointments adherent to being, by necessity, the originator of
others and the generator of things and ideas—only he may gradually grow
the fruit of these seven stages."

These are the years of greatest perspective. They may also be the years
of narrowing perspective, of fear of approaching death, and of constriction
of interests. They may be a happy time or a sad time. This seems to depend almost entirely on what happened in childhood.

CHILD-REARING PRACTICES

Beyond these generalizations about what the developing child needs
from his environment, it is difficult to be specific, and to develop child-
rearing principles which are clearly superior. There are two main reasons
for this: 1) As stated in Chapter 1 children vary greatly in all aspects of
behavior, and what works well for one child may fail completely with another. 2) There is simply not enough long-term information available on
results of specific rearing practices with specific types of children.

It is known, for example, that all infants must be fed. But it is not
known with certainty that one particular method of feeding, or schedule,
or way of holding the baby, and the like, is preferable to another. A study
by Levy in 1928 suggested that infants needed a certain amount of "oral
gratification" by being allowed to suckle, and that if this was not sufficiently attained, serious disturbances could occur. But a later and better-
controlled study by Davis and others, indicated that no apparent distress
resulted from reduced sucking activity.

Distress, discomfort, and misery can be produced in any child by
withholding ordinary gratifications or by frustrating his endeavors. But this

does not mean that such an experience is "bad" for the child. As Chess has pointed out, some conflict and frustration is necessary for the child's maturation. "Human growth is stimulated by conflict. A child would have little incentive to learn to speak if his inability to express a wish did not interfere with its being granted." But it is to be noted that while one child will respond to frustration by trying harder, another will turn away in quick defeat.

PSYCHOANALYTIC CONCEPT OF INADEQUATE NEED FULFILLMENT

The reader will have recognized that Erikson's stages of man coincide with the psychosexual levels of development as described in psychoanalytic theory. The following table, adapted from Erikson, relates his eight stages of man to the psychosexual periods of development of classical analytic psychology. Erikson's stages are here designated by terms which indicate the major accomplishment of that period, followed by the major defect if development does not occur normally through the period.

TABLE 1

PSYCHOSEXUAL STAGES OF MAN

	Age	Psychosexual Stage	Major Achievement	Major Defect
1.	0–1	Oral	Trust	Mistrust
2.	1–3	Anal	Autonomy	Shame, doubt
3.	3–6	Oedipal	Initiative	Guilt
4.	7–11	Latency	Industry	Inferiority
5.	12–18	Adolescence	Identity	Role diffusion
6.	19–25	Young adulthood	Intimacy	Isolation
7.	25–45	Adulthood	Generativity	Stagnation
8.	45+	Maturity	Integrity	Disgust, despair

From Erikson. *Childhood and Society.* W. W. Norton & Co.

Psychoanalytic psychology conceives that the developing child, as he passes through the successive stages of psychosexual development, consecutively invests the majority of his libido, or sexual pleasure, in certain organ systems.

In the oral stage, the infant's pleasure is concerned mainly with sucking, biting and swallowing. At the anal stage, pleasure is in bowel functions, in controlling and letting go his excreta, in playing with feces. In the phallic stage, also called the Oedipal stage, there is great interest in genital pleasures, and presumably sexual interest in the parent of the opposite sex.

Next is the latency period, an unfortunate term since it suggests that nothing really important is happening and that the child is simply waiting for puberty to begin. The later stages of adolescence, young adulthood, adulthood, and maturity are, of course, standard terms and not a contribution of psychoanalysis.

The psychosexual fixation theory of neurosis states that at any time in development the child may experience undue difficulty in the satisfaction of his needs of the particular period, and may then fail to give up the needs of that particular period and to pass on to the next. Thus he becomes "fixated" at that particular level, and this determines in large measure both his personality and the symptoms of the neurosis which develops from the conflict.

Fenichel has listed the kinds of experience that favor the development of such fixations:

1. Excessive satisfaction at a particular psychosexual stage, with the result that that stage is later renounced reluctantly or incompletely.

2. Excessive frustration at a particular stage, so that the child refuses to advance, "demanding the withheld satisfactions."

3. A combination of excessive satisfaction followed by excessive frustration, so that the person is unable to bear the later frustration.

4. Particularly abrupt changes in either satisfaction or frustration.

5. Most frequent of all causes of fixation: satisfaction of the psychosexual instinct "which simultaneously gave reassurance in the face of some anxiety or which aided in repressing some other feared impulse."

The fixation theory of neurosis is an ingenious one, and it undoubtedly serves to explain certain of the symptoms in some disturbed children. However, it usually represents an oversimplification; most disorders do not fit so neatly into a formula. The child and his parents rarely select a particular period of development in which to invest all the difficulties, while providing normal gratifications and restrictions during the other periods. Usually, a child who is overindulged at one time will be over indulged at other times, a child who is unwanted and rejected the first year will be unwanted and rejected his second, third, fourth, and later years.

Another complication regarding the fixation theory is the fact that there is considerable overlapping of the psychosexual periods. The child does not suddenly give up his oral pleasures and take up anal ones; instead, there is a gradual shifting of interests from one zone to the next, and there is also much shifting back and forth from one area of interest to another.

Nevertheless, despite these complications, fixations do occur. Children with oral fixations, for example, are by no means uncommon in the psychiatric clinic. These children appear with symptoms such as obesity, vomiting, and anorexia nervosa. Difficulties relating to the other stages are also seen: true Oedipal neuroses, for example, though not common, are occasionally seen. However, the vast majority of the emotional disorders of childhood which primarily have been environmentally produced display symptoms related to all the developmental periods.

EGO, ID, AND SUPEREGO

Ego, which is the Latin word meaning "I" or "myself," is a group or constellation of functions of the central nervous system. As understanding of personality development has increased, and because *id* and *superego* are rather clearly defined, ego has come to include all psychological functions not covered by the terms *id* and *superego.* This probably encompasses much more than Freud originally had in mind. The following table, adapted from Bellak, presents in outline form the functions which are now considered to constitute the ego.

TABLE 2

EGO FUNCTIONS

1. Relation to Reality
   A. Adaptation to reality
      a. Differentiation of figure and ground
      b. Role-playing
      c. Spontaneity and creativeness; regression in the service of the ego
   B. Reality-testing
      a. Accuracy of perception
      b. Soundness of judgment
      c. Orientation in time, place, person
   C. Sense of reality
      a. Good "self-boundaries"
      b. Unobtrusiveness of ordinary functioning
2. Regulation and Control of Drives
   a. Ability to engage in detour behavior
   b. Frustration tolerance (neutralization of drive energy)
   c. Anxiety tolerance
   d. Integrated motility
   e. Ambiguity tolerance
   f. Sublimation
3. Object Relations
   a. Capacity to form satisfactory object relations
   b. Object constancy

4. Thought Processes
   a. Selective scanning
   b. Ability to avoid contamination by inappropriate material or drives
   c. Good memory
   d. Sustained ability to concentrate
   e. Abstracting ability
5. Defensive Functions
   a. Repression (as a barrier against external and internal stimuli)
   b. Sublimation, reaction-formation
   c. Projection
   d. Denial, withdrawal, and other defenses
6. Autonomous Functions
   a. Perception
   b. Intention
   c. Intelligence
   d. Thinking
   e. Language
   f. Productivity
   g. Motor development
7. Synthetic Function
   a. To unite, organize, bind and create the ego's ability to form Gestalten
   b. Neutralization
   c. Sublimation
   d. Somatic "homeostasis"

Alexander in 1948 had suggested a somewhat different categorization of the ego functions than appears in the above table. He divided ego into synthetic, adaptive, and cognitive functions. In addition, he listed the functions of perception, integration, and executive action, all of which he considered as primarily concerned with sensory-motor operations.

The ego resides in the central nervous system. This fundamental but often-ignored fact was refreshingly reiterated by the distinguished neuro-anatomist, James Papez, who localized many of the ego functions in the thalamus. In specific thalamic nuclei, Papez notes, "the self as an individual is represented." These nuclei have extensive connections with frontal cortex, and the two systems deal with conscious ego functions, such as self-consciousness, self-vigilance, self-realization, self-direction, creative capacity, personal hygiene, and enterprise. In these and other nuclei of the thalamus, Papez adds, are the ego functions of "original thinking, imagination, language elaboration, general awareness of pain, suffering, anxiety, embarrassment, . . . an appreciation of body schema and of stereognosis."

It is apparent that the various functions of the ego are so interrelated that it is artificial to consider them as separate functions. Thus far, for example, reality-testing is partly achieved through motor activity in exploring the environment, together with perception and memory, all of which are integrated through higher cognitive functions. Even the development of motor behavior is a learning process, involving a kind of motor memory.

Because the concept of ego was devised by a physician whose observations were mainly of pathology, the ego was first conceived as being concerned largely with conflict and defenses against anxiety. Now the notion of "conflict-free" ego functions (Hartmann) has been reached and it has become a case of the tail wagging the dog, because by far the major and most used ego functions are conflict-free. Analytic psychology has come by a circuitous route to these understandings, which academic psychology approached more directly, but in so doing it has contributed a considerable amount of dynamic meaning to all of psychology.

Just as it is artificial to separate and compartmentalize the ego, so it is also of doubtful validity to divide the "mind" into three separate parts: id, ego, and superego. Certainly the earlier concept of these three components has undergone modification. Alexander noted that the superego was at first considered to be a function which was acquired early, remained unconscious, functioned automatically, and was not easily changed by later influences. He stated: "I question whether today such a rigid structural distinction is possible. In the normal individual most of the early regulations are slowly modified by later influences."

Alexander further observed that the notion of the id, as originally defined, is problematical. "Strictly speaking, a completely unorganized, inherited mass of instinctual urges is not found even at birth." As already indicated, the belief that there are only two or three basic drives (hunger, sex, and aggression) has undergone or is undergoing much modification, so that there are really many kinds of responses which are partly instinctual. Further, to separate what is inborn from what is learned in the developing organism becomes more and more unfeasible.

The vivid, graphic representation of the struggles between id and superego, with the ego interposed between them, first weak and ineffectual, gradually growing in strength until able to take charge and direct most actions in the battle—such a picture, wonderfully lucid though it may be, is vastly oversimplified. Taken literally, it presents a point of view and a presumed knowledge which are quite spurious, and may close avenues of learning which ought to be kept open.

THE CRITICAL PERIOD

At what age does an experience exert its maximum effect on the developing personality? To this fundamental question there is no simple answer. Knowledge of the subject comes from many sources—from animal ethology, from learning theory, from longitudinal observation of children, and from clinical experience.

Hess, discussing "imprinting" in animals, supplies three basic principles about the effects of early experience:

1. Early habits are very persistent and may prevent the formation of new ones.

2. Early perceptions deeply affect all future learning.

3. Early social contacts determine the character of adult social behavior. Hess thus emphasizes the importance of early learning, and has shown in his own experiments that baby birds such as ducklings must be exposed to the mother sometime within the first 24 to 36 hours in order to develop the "following" response, that is, the social attachment to its mother. Other studies of imprinting, such as that of Moltz and Rosenblum indicate that the critical period extends well beyond the limit set by Hess; however, all agree that early learning is crucial.

On the other hand, there appears to be a time very early in the newborn when learning occurs very little or not at all. Fuller and Scott found that conditioning in dogs cannot occur before the age of about 2 weeks, and Scott (personal communication) has expressed doubt that any experience other than one producing physical damage can have a permanent effect in a puppy younger than 2 weeks. Experience with human infants likewise suggests that very early experience is of relatively little importance in determining personality development. This is the so-called "period of undifferentiated id," when the infant's perceptions are a diffuse mass of incoming stimuli, when he cannot distinguish between himself and his environment, when he cannot differentiate between living and nonliving objects, and when he has not yet learned that his own behavior may be used to signal for attention and for the relief of discomforts.

Scott uses the term *critical period* to mean specifically the period for what he calls "primary socialization." He observes that all social animals exhibit a process of socialization which can be divided into two parts. Primary socialization, which usually takes place relatively early in life, determines the group of animals to which an individual will become attached. Secondary socialization to other animals and groups may take place later in life, as in the formation of sex relationships. The results of primary socialization usually influence the kind of secondary socialization which may take place. Scott further notes that in some species primary socialization must occur within a few hours after birth, as in the case of ducklings, while in others it may take place over a period of years. The critical period, and also the strength of social attachments, is greatly affected by heredity, and varies within species.

Primary socialization is thus a learned phenomenon which occurs at a particular time in the developing organism. It seems to be a kind of permanent conditioned response; the evidence from both clinical and experimental work demonstrates that, once learned, it is rarely unlearned, and if the critical period is passed without its having been learned, it will probably never be learned. This phenomenon of failure of primary socialization in children is considered at length in the chapter on Psychopathy (Chapter 11).

In addition to the primary social response, or the so-called "following" response, there is in most animals a time of primary fear or avoidance. Usually this period occurs shortly after the period of primary socialization, and in the higher animals seems to involve a primary attachment to one love object to the exclusion or fear of others. The fear reaction of baby chimpanzees to unfamiliar objects has already been cited; it appears about the 4th month. In human infants this occurs around the 9th month. In ducklings the avoidance response occurs during the second day of life. If the duckling is not exposed to a mother figure (such as a moving duck model) during the time when the "following" response would be elicited, and is then presented with the mother figure soon thereafter, it will avoid the moving duck, fleeing from it in alarm as it approaches. This avoidance response often persists throughout the animal's life, and he remains a solitary, unattached duck (Waller, P., and Waller, M., personal communication).

In the human animal, the fear response to strangers eventually subsides and the attachment to the mother object becomes generalized toward other humans. However, this primal fear reaction is never altogether lost; it persists in the unconscious, and may appear later as a fear of strange places, of the dark, of crowds, etc. There is in all humans some residual fear of the unfamiliar; there is in all the need for a continuous input of familiar stimuli, and even the most stable and mature adult will feel uneasiness or panic in strange situations such as being alone at night in a woods, or deep under water in a diving suit, or suspended in an experimental sensory-deprivation tank.

Why are the effects of these early experiences permanently retained? What is the basis for the critical period? Neurophysiology and experimental psychology can answer these fundamental questions at least partially. First of all, it has been shown in puppies that primary socialization cannot occur before the animal is able to receive adequate stimuli from the environment; that is, the visual and auditory apparatuses must be functioning. Further, such socialization cannot occur before learning can take place, as evidenced by the capacity to perform conditioned responses. Additionally, certain changes in the EEG must have occurred, which are in the nature of more adult-like patterns. At this time the animal is able to perceive the environment, and is further able to differentiate objects in the environment and to associate specific objects, such as the mother or the human handler, with the gratification of needs and the alleviation of discomforts. The permanence, then, of this association, and this continued seeking of further contact with the "love" object, is perhaps explained by the phenomenon which experimental psychology calls "reinforcement." This principle states in part, that a response which has resulted in gratification of a need or reduction of a drive will tend to be repeated when the situation is repeated. It is a kind of habit formation. Thus, the young animal learns, as soon as it is capable of learning, that the mother or mother figure is associated with pleasant experiences, and a pattern of thinking develops which is self-perseverating. Its effects are permanent. The child is committed forever after to being a social animal. This early love, if sufficiently gratified and allowed to express itself, will be the foundation on which the child's whole personality, character, and later loves will grow. It will be the means by which he learns self-control and discipline in his formative years, for it is through love and the fear of loss of love that children are controlled and patterned, and through these that they make their identifications. Insufficiently or inconsistently gratified or rejected, this primary love will be the basis for later conflict, disappointment, chronic anger, self-rejection, and all the many forms of maladjustment and unhappiness that the human animal has devised.

Are there critical periods in the life of the growing child other than the periods of primary socialization and of primary avoidance? And, of even more practical pertinence to child psychiatry, how late in life can experiences have permanently damaging effects? Some theories hold that only very early experience is of critical importance, that it sets the patterns for all later attitudes and responses, and that later experiences produce little significant change in the individual. Most workers take a more moderate view, conceding that early experience is a major determinant of later responses, but that throughout childhood and adolescence the individual is further affected by his experiences. Obviously there is much variation, and at all ages some children are better able than others to withstand adversity. In some, traumatic experiences even beyond childhood and into old age may produce emotional breakdown. It is well known that men who have shown no previous evidence of psychiatric disorder may break down in military combat, although there is a somewhat higher incidence of previous neurotic symptoms in those who break down under combat than in those who do not (Rose). And the "brain-washing" techniques used on prisoners of the Communists have demonstrated that any man, no matter what his strength and courage, can be permanently "broken" (Meerloo).

Thus, in a sense, the notion of a critical period is a relative one, in that there is no period of his life in which the individual is, psychiatrically, free from danger. Nevertheless, the first year of life is by far the most critical, and if the infant achieves in this time a basic sense of trust toward the world, his chances for psychiatric survival are reasonably good. Susceptibility to environmental vicissitudes diminishes steadily thereafter, except for a transient increase during adolescence.

CULTURAL FACTORS

In the Brooks range of Alaska, north of the Arctic circle, lives a small tribe of nomadic Eskimos who subsist by following and hunting the caribou herds. The leader of the tribe, an old man named Noah, once traded one of his sons to another man in the tribe in return for a sled dog. There was no evidence that this was considered in any way unusual. Such a happening in Western culture would represent a most extreme form of parental rejection.

This story has been selected to illustrate that the most important aspects of child-rearing practices are not so much in the particular techniques, the mechanics, but rather in the parental and cultural attitudes, that is, in the whole emotional tone of the child's environment. This point has been made by many psychiatrists and anthropologists. For example, much importance was once attached to the institution of swaddling among certain cultures, but it is now conceded that most of the effects attributed to this practice are better explained by general parental attitudes and feelings toward the infant (Benedict).

The ways in which a culture affects personality development and the occurrence of mental disorder depends largely on the age at which the most important learning occurs. There is no general agreement on this subject. Some schools of psychology hold that the experiences of an infant's first year are the major determinants of personality, while others maintain that the Oedipal period and the years through adolescence contribute most to the shaping of the personality and the development of many of the major psychiatric disorders. This question has already been touched upon, and is mentioned here again as it involves influences of the culture.

Cultural influences during the first year or two of a child's life are imparted chiefly through the child-care practices of his family, especially the mother. All aspects of child care can be influenced or determined by the culture, including not only the mechanical aspects such as feeding schedules, toilet training, and so on, but also the amount of attention and affection which the parent bestows on the infant, the kinds of punishment employed, and the like. Linton cites the example of the Marquesan women who rarely nursed their babies because the chief function of women in this society was a sexual one, designed to attract and satisfy as many husbands as possible. Shapely breasts were an important part of the woman's armamentarium. Linton describes the feeding practice of the Marquesans as follows: "It consisted in laying the child on its back on a flat stone, taking a handful of the mixture (breadfruit and coconut milk) and letting it trickle down on the child's mouth. The child would sputter and gasp and swallow as much of the mixture as it could. The mother then wiped off the child's face with the edge of her hand, took another handful and poured it on. One can easily imagine the feeling of these children toward their parents! This method of feeding was certainly not conducive toward developing a lot of affection and warmth, particularly toward the mothers." This practice is apparently not "harmful" to the Marquesan children, perhaps because of the fact that the feeding practice fits in with other customs and value systems of their culture. A child fed in such a way in our Western society, then expected later to function according to value systems requiring close maternal care and affection, considerable restriction of sexual expression, and so on, would undoubtedly find himself a misfit. Linton has emphasized the above point, that it is not so much the cultural practices and attitudes, but deviations from these attitudes within the culture, which lead to difficulty for the individual.

Every society has had its misfits, and each has devised various ways of dealing with them. This in itself often determines the severity of a mental disorder. Sexual deviants such as homosexuals, and transvestites, are generally poorly tolerated and are often isolated from society in various ways. However, certain cultures have been able to accept them and to incorporate them into the routine of life. In Madagascar (Linton), males who have exhibited feminine traits from birth often are raised as females, dress as females and pursue feminine occupations. The writer once observed an Eskimo woman, living in a village on the Bering Sea, who was obviously a hallucinating schizophrenic. She would emerge daily from her little shanty during the summer time, stand for hours on the beach gazing at the sea, or stoop and scrabble among the rocks and shells, talking or singing to herself. The children exhibited a neutral attitude toward her, neither avoiding nor approaching her unduly. She was tolerated by the village, her simple wants were met by her family, and she created no apparent tension or disturbance. It is doubtful whether such treatment could be accorded her in Western society. Her presence in the family would at least be a severe embarrassment and she would be strongly resented and rejected.

CHANGING CULTURES

In a stable society, as compared with a changing one, the stresses and demands placed upon the individual are relatively few. Roles are clearly defined, the growing child learns what is expected of him at each particular level of development, and, when he is old enough to conceptualize adequately, he knows what to expect of the future. True, each of the developmental steps requires some degree of readjustment, such as weaning, the Oedipal period, and the onset of sexual maturity.

On the other hand, when the culture is in a state of evolution, the conflicts mount tremendously. Kardiner has described the dissolution of the Comanche Indian culture when this warlike tribe was restricted to a reservation. The whole training and experience of every member of the tribe, both male and female, had always been toward the direct expression of aggression. The activities and value systems of the entire tribe were geared to the maintenance of the war party. When this function no longer existed, there was simply nothing for the Comanche to do. Listlessness, apathy, and depression set in, many of the Comanches committed suicide, disease increased, reproductive activity diminished, and the tribe deteriorated.

In present-day society there are many occasions to observe all about and even within one's own home the effects of a changing culture. Where a role is not clearly defined, the children are puzzled and uncertain. Even the deeper and supposedly eternal values, such as paternal love, are being subordinated to the culturally determined pressures toward social status and material gain (Josselyn).

CULTURE AND HEREDITY

The effects of culture are often confused with characteristics that are genetically determined. For example, the warlike traits of the Comanche are attributed to his early training. It is likely, however, that the trait is in part inherited; or more accurately, that the capacity for learning the trait is inherited. A fundamental principle of genetics and evolution is that in any population those traits are selected which have survival value within that population. In general, selection for a trait is primarily effected through increased relative fertility (number of surviving offspring). Thus, one may speculate that those Comanche braves who were more successful in war were also more successful in procreation.

The important question of the interrelationships between learned and inherited traits was discussed in Chapter 1. It is mentioned here again, to emphasize that all the differences between various cultures cannot be considered as determined exclusively by learning.

CULTURE AND PSYCHOANALYTIC THEORY

Much objection has been expressed against certain of the tenets of psychoanalytic psychology on the grounds that Freud and some of his followers did not take sufficient cognizance of cultural factors. It has often been pointed out that Freud lived in a highly patriarchal society, where the father was the epitome of the Prussian type, stern, aloof, and lacking in feelings of tenderness and affection. Likewise, Freud lived in a Victorian culture, where even the mention of sex was taboo and where the only portions of her anatomy that a woman exposed were her face and hands. Such a culture was bound to engender a strong Oedipal conflict, with the great contrast between the gentle, passive mother and the forbidding, unapproachable father. It was also ideally suited for the suppression of the sex drive and the development of strong conflict over sexual matters.

It is true that psychoanalysts have often made the mistake of overgeneralizing, even to the point of believing that the Oedipal conflict and castration anxiety are the sole determinant of neurosis. In a sense, however, it is perhaps fortunate that Freud lived in the age and the culture in which he did; perhaps no culture could have been better suited for the demonstration of those disorders which led him to his most fundamental discoveries. And, while many of the details and later developments of psychoanalysis can no longer be considered valid, these most basic principles, including the theory of unconscious mechanisms and of the continuity between early experience and adult personality, remain as major and permanent contributions. Freud never thought of psychoanalytic theory as finally conclusive or static; the best proof of this is his own continued efforts to develop and improve upon it throughout his life.

Erikson has contrasted Freud's culture with the present one as follows: "The patient of today suffers most under the problem of what he should believe in and who he should be or become; the patient of early psychoanalysis suffered most under inhibitions which prevented him from being what and who he thought he knew he was." Essentially, this suggests that the major problems for the individual of today are problems of identity in a changing world. Erikson concludes that "The study of identity, then, becomes as strategic in our time as the study of sexuality was in Freud's time." He notes, however, that the subjects are relative, and that the patients of both periods had problems of sexuality as well as of identity, with one or the other preponderant. "Different periods thus permit us to see in temporary exaggeration different aspects of an essentially inseparable whole."

POSITIVE ASPECTS OF CULTURE

Psychiatry is inclined to view the individual's culture as a set of rules and restrictions with which he is in constant conflict and under the stress of which his ego sometimes breaks. This view is perhaps engendered by psychiatry's distorted perspective; we psychiatrists see only the ones who break down. Actually, all the cultures of man, from the earliest and most primitive to the highest and most recent, must have to some extent fostered the development of the best attributes and the highest attainments of which their members were capable. Some cultures succeeded better than others, some flourished long and well, while others were short-lived. But even the worst of them certainly had their positive aspects. Each culture succeeded in giving most of its members a sense of identity, some degree of security, freedom from fear and conflict, and also provided an atmosphere in which the members could carry out their activities and achieve some rewards. Erikson has emphasized this aspect of a culture: "To understand either childhood or society, we must expand our scope to include the study of the way in which societies lighten the inescapable conflicts of childhood with a promise of some security, identity and integrity. In thus reinforcing the values of the ego, societies create the only condition under which human growth is possible."

Man is, by inheritance, a social animal. Without his society he is nothing. The tragedy is in those individuals who are not permitted, or who are not able, to adapt to their society.

CULTURE AS A DETERMINANT OF MENTAL DISORDER

As in all aspects of the causes of psychiatric disease, there is a great deal that is not known about cultural determinants. Both psychotic and neurotic disorders occur in every culture thus far studied, which might lead one to conclude that the culture has little or no etiological influence. However, frequency of these disorders probably varies considerably, and certainly the form which the disorder takes, its content, varies markedly.

Comparative data on the incidence of mental disturbances among the various societies is difficult to obtain and even more difficult to evaluate. Much of the data on primitive cultures comes from the observations of non-psychiatrists, and the diagnosis is often questionable. Even data determined by trained psychiatrists comparing the incidence of psychosis among modern civilized nations indicates some degree of disagreement. Criteria for diagnosis are by no means uniform throughout the world or even, sometimes, within a definite locality. Nevertheless, cases are described from every culture which would certainly be diagnosed as schizophrenia. The content, as noted above, is determined by the person's environment and past experience; a schizophrenic in fifteenth-century France would not have delusions of persecution by radio waves. But the basic process, the dereistic thinking, the dysidentity, appears to be present in all cultures.

In modern America, the incidence of psychosis has been found to vary with social class. Hollingshead and Redlich noted that in the city of New Haven, Connecticut, the frequency of schizophrenia increased greatly as one descended the social scale. In the fifth or lowest social class the incidence was twelve times as high as in the highest class. This finding has not been satisfactorily explained. An obvious partial explanation is that families in which psychosis occurs tend to gravitate to the lower social classes. A further cause may be that marriage and reproduction of psychotics is more accepted in the lower social classes. Both of these explanations, of course, would argue against the environment within the class as a determinant of schizophrenia.

The above explanations seem less adequate in the face of the later demonstration by Dunham that, while incidence of schizophrenia was greatest in the lower economic areas of Chicago, manic-depressive psychosis was most frequent in higher economic areas.

The relation of neurosis to culture is perhaps an even more complex problem than that of psychosis. Data on incidence in various cultures is

unreliable, partly because diagnostic criteria vary tremendously. Nevertheless, there are several studies which illustrate the great influence which culture can exert on neurotic disorders. Linton has described the various
forms which the hysterias take within different societies, and has noted
that hysterias flourish in some cultures while being virtually absent in
others. Within the present century in America, the incidence of hysteria
has diminished considerably. Linton observes that "One form of hysteria
which has definitely vanished within my own life time is that of the fainting lady. Nowadays fainting has simply gone out. I want to stress, however,
that there is no question that these Victorian faints were genuine." Linton
also pointed out the high degree of suggestibility, including autosuggestibil-
ity, of the hysterical person. He noted that the cases of *grand hysterie*
which Charcot described simply do not appear in present-day clinics. What
Charcot apparently did was to take hysterics who had certain tendencies
and "build them up" into true cases of *grand hysterie*. Then, when they
grew sufficiently violent and had extreme physical reactions, they were rewarded by being pointed out as a wonderful case and were displayed to all
the students.

The secondary-gain aspect of hysterical behavior has often been
emphasized. It is seen today in the histrionic acting out of adolescent girls,
and these patients can create such disturbance and frantic agitation within
the family, the school, or the hospital ward that those in attendance are
willing to give in to almost any demand, in order to quiet them. The secondary gain of conversion hysteria is usually apparent, and the increased
incidence of these disorders among combat soldiers is well documented.
While many such cases were earlier regarded suspiciously as "malingering,"
there is little doubt that many of them were quite real and that the mechanisms involved were largely unconscious. It is interesting, however, that
these almost invariably occurred among enlisted men, rarely among officers.
Within the members of the officer culture, even the unconscious was unable to accept this form of reaction to conflict.

The absolute frequency of neurotic disorders undoubtedly varies from
culture to culture, but the degree to which cultural factors determine this
cannot be known with any degree of accuracy. The point is that in psychiatry there must be an awareness of cultural differences, and an endeavor to
understand how these differences interact with the multiplicity of other
factors that determine the personality of the individual. Subcultures within
present-day Western society sometimes present as much variation as cultures of primitive areas of the world, and there is a great deal of difference
in the psychodynamics, say, of stealing, in a child who comes from a run-
down farm home in Arkansas and one who lives in a tri-level house in
Westchester County.

THE ENVIRONMENT AND ITS VICISSITUDES

To what extent, then, does environment determine mental illness? This varies tremendously, in fact all the way from 0 to 100 per cent. Some children are born disturbed, and no matter what kinds of handling and experience they receive, they will remain mentally ill. On the other hand, there are many children born with all the capacities to grow up normal and healthy, whose life experiences are so damaging that they become emotional cripples. The majority of disturbed children fall somewhere between these extremes, and the relative effects of inborn and experiential factors varies with the diagnosis. The accompanying scale illustrates the relationship by placing the various diagnostic categories on a a scale ranging from 100 per cent biologically determined to 100 per cent experientially determined.

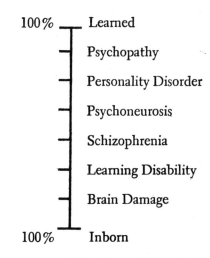

```
100% ——  Learned

       -  Psychopathy

       -  Personality Disorder

       -  Psychoneurosis

       -  Schizophrenia

       -  Learning Disability

       -  Brain Damage

100%  ——  Inborn
```

There is, of course, considerable variation in the above scheme. It should be noted that brain damage is not placed at the extreme bottom of the scale. The disturbance seen in children diagnosed as brain-damaged is always affected by the child's experience. With proper handling and attention to his special needs, the brain-damaged child can make a relatively good adjustment, while if mishandled and not properly understood, his disturbance may become extreme. Just as the disturbance in brain damage is not all "biological," neither is that of personality disorder and psychopathy 100 per cent experientially determined. It is well known that many children "survive" almost unbelievable degrees of emotional neglect and deprivation. This is often seen in the siblings of children with personality disorders, children who come from severely deprived, punitive, and disorganized homes; and while these "normal" siblings could usually not be said to represent the ideal of American youth, nevertheless they often show a surprising degree of ego strength and good capacity for relationship. One can only conclude that such children came into the world better equipped than their less fortunate siblings.

It is generally supposed that most emotionally disturbed children come from disturbed homes. This is, however, by no means true. It depends both on the severity and the kind of disorder. In an unselected sample of 50 children referred to the Hawthorn Center outpatient clinic, near Detroit, Michigan, approximately half of them had one or both parents who were considered to be either neurotic or psychotic. This means also that half of the children had parents who were reasonably well adjusted. (Actually, the sample was not entirely unselected, as only those children were included in the study whose parents were both living and were both willing to come to the clinic for evaluation. Thus, those cases were not included who came from broken homes or one of whose parents was unwilling or unable to come in. Nevertheless, the fact remains that a substantial number of the children had normal parents.) On the other hand, the writer's study (unpublished) of 100 mentally disturbed children in a state hospital disclosed that all but three came from seriously disturbed homes. These children were on the whole more disturbed than those in the outpatient group. Approximately 30 per cent were schizophrenic and most of the remainder had severe personality disorders with histories of chronic maladjustment and antisocial behavior. This finding of 97 per cent disturbed homes is striking evidence of the fact that disturbance begets disturbance, whether it be through heredity, or environment, or both.

Thus, life experience determines not only the severity of maladjustment but the kind of maladjustment. There is a great deal of difference in the disorder of a child who has been overprotected and of one who has been neglected, although both may be of equal severity. The chronically neglected child learned early to trust no one; it is virtually impossible to hurt him, his defenses are firm. The overprotected child has inadequate defenses; he is dependent, without self-reliance, and easily hurt.

What kinds of experience may be harmful to a child? It is impossible to catalogue them. They run the gamut of human misery. As a generalization, too much or too little of anything is harmful, and children are seen whose disorder is caused by too much or too little love, too much or too little attention, too much or too little control—the list is endless. But there is a thread running through all of it, common to all of the environmental misfortune and mistreatment, and that is a lack of love. Not the narcissistic, overindulgent and inconsistent love of an immature mother, but the empathic, sensitive and sustained love of warm, mature and well-motivated mothers, fathers, teachers, older siblings, and others who are authority figures in the child's world. Louise Despert, in her book on children of divorce, has entitled the last chapter "Love is Enough." Surely this is true, and where there is love there will be an emotional tone and a continuous experience that will support and sustain the child through fears and conflicts, that will compensate for all the inevitable mistakes and blunders, and that will assure his developing early a sense of trust, confidence, self-reliance, and warmth toward other humans. Without love, he is lost. Love, then, is the great need, the only need. "That—and no more, and it is everything."

Unfortunately, there are a few children for whom love is *not* enough. These are the ones who are born with special deficiencies and handicaps and who require special kinds of upbringing and training. For these, the ordinary care of loving and well-meaning parents is not sufficient. These children constitute an important segment of the children who need psychiatric help.

Child psychiatry, then, is concerned mainly with two kinds of children: those who have had insufficient love, and those for whom love is not enough.

In these first two chapters the problem of individual differences, and the biological and environmental influences which make every human being different from every other human being have been considered. It was noted that the uniqueness of an individual may be sufficiently extreme so that he is considered abnormal, and that such extremes may be determined by heredity or by environment or by both.

The next three chapters are concerned with "practical" matters. They consider the problem of the troubled child: how he manifests his disturbance, how he gets to the psychiatrist, and how the psychiatrist determines what is wrong with him.

REFERENCES

Alexander, F. Fundamentals of Psychoanalysis, New York, W. W. Norton & Co., 1948.

Beach, F. A. Current Concepts of Play in Animals, Am. Naturalist, 79: 523, 1945.

Bellak, L. Schizophrenia, New York, Logos Press, 1958, p. 7.

Benedict, R. M. Child Rearing in Certain European Countries, Am. J. Orthopsychiatry, 19: 342, 1949.

Chess, S. An Introduction to Child Psychiatry, New York, Grune & Stratton, 1959.

Davis, H. V., Sears, R., Miller, H. C., and Brodbeck, A. J. Effects of Cup, Bottle, and Breast Feeding on Oral Activities of Newborn Infants, Pediatrics, 2: 549, 1948.

Despert, J. L. Children of Divorce, Garden City, N.Y., Doubleday and Co., 1953.

Dunham, H. W. Sociological Theory and Mental Disorder, Detroit, Wayne State University Press, 1959.

Erikson, E. Childhood and Society, New York, W. W. Norton & Co., 1950.

Fenichel, O. The Psychoanalytic Theory of Neurosis, New York, W. W. Norton & Co., 1945.

Fuller, J., and Scott, J. P. Genetic Factors Affecting Intelligence, Eugenics Quarterly, 1: 28, 1954.

Hartmann, H. Ego Psychology and the Problem of Adaptation, New York, International Universities Press, 1958.

Hebb, D. O. Alice in Wonderland, or Psychology among the Biological Sciences, in Biological and Biochemical Bases of Behavior, ed. Harlow and Woolsey, Madison, University of Wisconsin Press, 1958.

Hess, E. Imprinting, Science, 130: 133, 1959.

Hilgard, E. R. Theories of Learning, New York, Appleton-Century-Crofts, 1957.

Hollingshead, A. B., and Redlich, F. C. Social Stratification and Schizophrenia, Am. Sociological Review, 19: 302, 1954.

Josselyn, I. Cultural Forces, Motherliness, and Fatherliness, Am. J. Orthopsychiatry, 26: 264, 1956.

Kardiner, A. The Psychological Frontiers of Society, New York, Columbia University Press, 1945.

Levy, D. M. Finger-sucking and Accessory Movements in Early Infancy: Etiologic Study, Am. J. Psychiatry, 7: 881, 1928.

Liddell, H. Emotional Hazards in Animals and Man, Springfield, Ill., Charles C Thomas, 1956.

Linton, R. Culture and Mental Disorders, Springfield, Ill., Charles C Thomas, 1956.

Masserman, J. Behavior and Neurosis, Chicago, University of Chicago Press, 1957.

Meerloo, J. A. M. The Rape of the Mind, New York, World Publishing Co., 1956.

Moltz, H., and Rosenblum, L. A. Imprinting and Associative Learning: The Stability of the Following Response in Peking Ducks, J. Comp. Physiol. Psychol., 51: 580, 1958.

Munroe, R. L. Schools of Psychoanalytic Thought, New York, Dryden Press, 1945.

Olds, J. Adaptive Functions of Paleocortical and Related Structures, in Biological and Biochemical Bases of Behavior, ed. Harlow and Woolsey, Madison, University of Wisconsin Press, 1958.

———— and Milner, P. Positive Reinforcement Produced by Electrical Stimulation of Septal Area and Other Regions of Rat Brain, J. Comp. Physiol. Psychol., 47: 419, 1954.

Papez, J. Neuroanatomy, in American Handbook of Psychiatry, ed. S. Arieti, New York, Basic Books, 1959.

Pavlov, I. P. Experimental Psychology, New York, Philosophical Library, 1957.

Rachman, S., and Costello, C. G. The Aetiology and Treatment of Children's Phobias: a Review, Am. J. Psychiatry, 118: 97, 161.
Rose, A. M. Factors in Mental Breakdown in Combat, in Mental Health and Mental Disorder, ed. A. M. Rose, New York, W. W. Norton & Co., 1955.
Scott, J. P. Animal Behavior, Chicago, University of Chicago Press, 1958.
Spitz, R. Hospitalism, Psychoanalytic Study of the Child, New York, International Universities Press, 1946, Vol. 2.
Walter, W. G. The Living Brain, New York, W. W. Norton & Co., 1953.
Winn, R. B. (translator and editor), Psychotherapy in the Soviet Union, New York, Philosophical Library, 1961.
Wolpe, J. Psychotherapy by Reciprocal Inhibition, Palo Alto, Stanford University Press, 1958.
———— The Systematic Desensitization Treatment of Neuroses, J. Nerv. Ment. Dis., 132: 189, 1961.

CHAP.] EFFECTS OF STIMULI, ETC.

SECTION TWO

THE CHILD COMES
TO THE PSYCHIATRIST

3

THE SIGNS OF TROUBLE

When a child breaks his leg, he is taken to the doctor, the condition is diagnosed, and he is treated appropriately. Here, the indications for medical attention are obvious, and there is general unanimity as to the procedure. In the case of emotional illness, the situation is often much less clear-cut. The disorder is usually chronic and fluctuant, its manifestations are not inevitably regarded as pathological, and there is rarely unanimity among the various interested persons that psychiatric help is indicated.

What are the symptoms which cause a child to be taken to the psychiatrist? Mainly, they are disorders of behavior, rather than disorders of feeling. The child rarely complains of the symptom. He does not often say, as does an adult, "I've been feeling so depressed lately," or "I have this awful pain in my chest and can't seem to get my breath." Rather, he expresses in his behavior that something is wrong.

Much of the behavior of disturbed children differs only in degree from that of normal children. The child may get angry and cry, he may fight with other children, he may sit in his room and sulk, he may defy his mother's authority. Normal children do all of these things. The disturbed child does them more often, or more readily, or with greater intensity. The parent of a disturbed child, usually the father, will sometimes say to the psychiatrist, "There's nothing wrong with that, all kids do that." And usually he is right. Macfarlane and others determined the occurrence of behavior problems in 252 normal children who were followed from infancy to adolescence. They found a considerable incidence of disturbance, much of which if severe or protracted, would be an indication for psychiatric referral. Table 1 indicates the percentage of normal children who at some time exhibited the indicated behavior problems.

Lapouse and Monk (1959, 1964), who studied a randomly selected non-psychiatric sample of 482 children ranging in age from 6 to 12, found a surprisingly high percentage of behavior which is commonly thought of as pathological. For example, 43 per cent of the children were reported as

TABLE 1

SYMPTOMS PRESENT IN 252 NORMAL CHILDREN

Behavior	Incidence (Percentage)	
	Boys	Girls
Disturbing dreams	20	26
Poor appetite	13	15
Excessive modesty	14	17
Nail-biting	17	23
Speech problems	12	9
Lying	24	18
Stealing	6	3
Destructiveness	13	6
Overdependence	13	16
Oversensitiveness	37	44
Shyness	11	24
Mood swings	22	22
Temper tantrums	50	37
Jealousy	34	29
Excessive reserve	30	41

From Macfarlane et al. A Develpmental Study of the Behavioral Problems of Normal Children between Twenty-one Months and Fourteen Years. University of California Press.

having 7 or more fears and worries out of a list of 30 about which the mothers were questioned. Deviant behavior was reported most in the younger children and in boys. This would lend support to the thesis that many of the symptoms are transient and improve with increasing age. Table 2 shows the reported incidence of a number of behavioral symptoms reported by Lapouse and Monk (1959), in close agreement with Mafarlane's findings.

On the other hand, certain symptoms are more than merely exaggerations of normal behavior; they are qualitatively different and intrinsically pathological. Much of the behavior of the schizophrenic child is in this category: the autism, in which the child is totally involved in his own world, uncommunicative, unresponsive, seemingly unaware of the things and the people about him; the disordered speech, echolalic, neologistic, meaningless to the listener. There is a qualitative difference in the behavior of the empty, affectionless child: a bland unconcern for the feelings of others, a total narcissism, a complete lack of response to social and moral controls in a way that is puzzling and baffling to all those with whom he comes into contact. There is the "catastrophic" reaction described by Goldstein in brain injury, and also seen in schizophrenia and in neurosis, in which the patient exhibits complete ego rupture, an experience outside the comprehension of the normal person; the patient is overwhelmed, unable to function in an organized way, intensely agitated, and without any direction or object to his emotion.

TABLE 2

SYMPTOMS PRESENT IN 482 NORMAL CHILDREN

Behavior	Incidence (Percentage)
Fears and worries, 7 or more present	43
Wetting bed within the past year	17
Nightmares	28
Temper loss	
Once a month or more	80
Twice a week or more	48
Once a day or more	11
Stuttering	4
Unusual movements, twitching, or jerking (tics)	12
Biting nails	27
Grinding teeth	14
Sucking thumb or fingers	10

From Lapouse and Monk. Am. J. Orthopsychiat., 29: 803, 1959.

THE MAJOR SYMPTOMS

In psychiatry, as in all of medicine, a symptom is the effect of disorder. It is also an integral part of the disorder. But a particular symptom may occur in more than one disorder. Just as fever or anemia are present in many different diseases, so such symptoms as compulsiveness, withdrawal, apprehension, and rage outbursts occur in more than one kind of emotional disturbance. All of these symptoms, for example, have been found to be present in children with psychoneurosis, brain damage, and schizophrenia.

Psychiatric illness, like any illness, is more than a complex of symptoms. While certain of these illnesses may be diagnosed on the basis of the major symptoms alone, a real understanding of the disorder requires a deeper penetration into the background of the child, a knowledge of his environment, and especially some awareness of his inner thoughts and feelings. As Kanner has expressed it, the symptom is a signal. The psychiatrist must concern himself not with turning off the signal, but with trying to find out what information it is seeking to convey.

To delineate the most common symptoms presented by emotionally disturbed children, the records of 500 consecutive patients seen in the outpatient clinic of Hawthorn Center were reviewed. The reasons for referral were tabulated and are listed in Table 3. The ten most common symptoms which led to psychiatric referral, in order of frequency, were:

Poor academic achievement
Behavior problem (acting-out behavior)
Reading problem
Aggressiveness
Hyperactivity
Stealing
Oppositional behavior
Poor peer relationships
Temper tantrums
Anxiety

Located near a large metropolitan area, and serving the entire state of Michigan, the Center sees a representative sampling of severely disturbed and moderately disturbed children and adolescents. Of the 500 children 380 (76 per cent) were boys and 120 (24 per cent) girls. This represents a ratio of 3:1. The age range was from 2 to 18 with a mean age of 10.4 for boys and a mean age of 10.6 for girls. Figure 1 illustrates the age distributions. The distribution curve shows two peaks, occurring at ages 8 and 13 for boys, and smaller peaks at ages 7–8 and 12 for girls. With boys there was a sharp decline of referrals after age 14, but with girls there was a relatively level incidence of referral throughout pre-adolescence and adolescence through age 16, which is the arbitrary upper age limit for referral to Hawthorn Center. Since there is a waiting list of approximately six months from the time of referral until the child can be seen, and since a period of time usually elapses before a referral is initiated, the actual period of greatest disturbance probably occurs a year earlier than represented in Figure 1.

The total number of children listed is considerably more than 500 because frequently more than one reason was given when, for example, a child was referred because of poor academic achievement, enuresis, and aggressiveness. By far the largest number of children (44 per cent) had poor academic achievement as one of the reasons for referral, or as the sole reason. An additional 10 per cent had a reading problem. This is in part a reflection of the fact that approximately half of the children were referred through their schools. But even the children referred by other agencies showed a high incidence of school problems. The entire list is reproduced here to stress the vast variety and ubiquity of the symptoms. In many cases the parent's wording is retained to convey more vividly the nature of the symptom. Of interest is the infrequency with which some of the "classical" symptoms such as compulsions and phobias are represented.

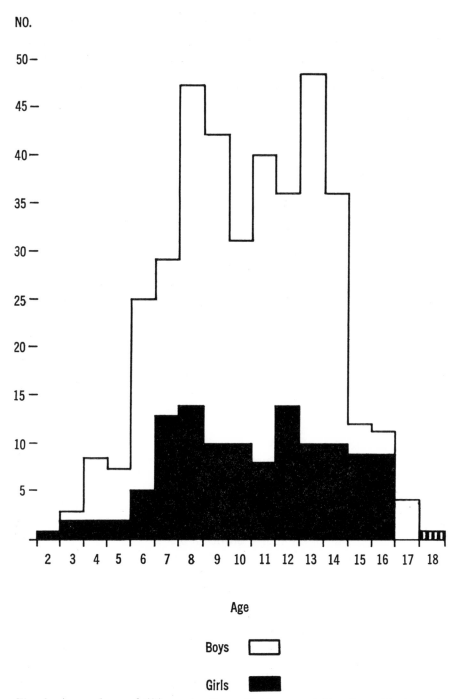

Fig. 1. Age and sex of 500 consecutive patients seen at Hawthorn Center out-patient clinic.

Naturally, many disturbed children have fears, but, as Lapouse has shown, so do normal children, and apparently fears rarely become the major reason for psychiatric referral.

The list cannot be used to estimate the incidence of symptoms in disturbed children. Only the major presenting symptoms were given for each child. Many more than 2 per cent were, for example, enuretic—but in only 2 per cent was this the reason for referral.

UNHAPPINESS

In psychiatric circles unhappiness is not accorded the status of a genuine symptom. Yet, in the larger sense, it is the symptom, the *sine qua non*; it is the very reason for psychiatry's being.

The symptom of unhappiness is implied or subsumed within a large constellation of symptoms including: anxiety, depression, apathy, withdrawal, anger, fear, panic, and jealousy. Unhappiness is all of these, and yet it is none of them. It is the absence of happiness. It is the absence of joy, of pleasure, of delight, of all those feelings that are pleasant, satisfying, and interesting, and that cause a person to feel positively toward other people and toward life.

Somehow, unhappiness in a child seems more tragic than unhappiness in an adult. Happiness and fun are associated with childhood—it is one of the natural rights. Also, unhappiness in a child appears more intense; children show their feelings, their emotions are "near the surface." When a child is happy, he laughs and shouts; his whole body and all of his movements express his happiness. When he is sad, he is sad all over.

The goal of psychiatry is not to remove illness. It is to restore happiness. Nor is such a view an oversentimentalization. It represents the orientation of many psychiatrists who feel that there has been in the past too much emphasis on pathology, on the negative aspects of the child's adjustment, on the major motivating forces being fear of loss of love, castration anxiety, and jealousy of the father. Suttie emphasized the positive aspect of development when he said "the child wakes up to life with the germ of parenthood, with the impulse to give and to respond already in it. This primal love, while it subserves self-preservation by maintaining a nurtural relationship to the mother, is something more than the sum total of organic needs and gratifications."

Bender has emphasized the positive, in a paper listing the instinctive needs and drives of children: "The child has an inherent capacity or drive for normality. He has an inborn capacity to relate to the mother or parent figure, and by identification to experience the emotional things of life which make us all human beings, capable of loving and being loved."

TABLE 3

TABLE 3

REASONS FOR REFERRAL IN 500 CONSECUTIVE PATIENTS SEEN
AT HAWTHORN CENTER OUTPATIENT CLINIC

Reason for Referral	Number	Percentage
Poor academic achievement	216	44
Behavior problem (acting-out behavior)	67	13
Reading problem	49	10
Aggressiveness	43	8
Hyperactivity	42	8
Stealing	30	6
Oppositional behavior	29	6
Poor peer relationships	28	6
Temper tantrums	26	5
Anxiety	26	5
Disruptiveness	25	5
Placement problem	24	5
Withdrawn	24	5
Speech problem	22	4
Immaturity	21	4
Uncontrollable	18	4
Depression	16	3
School exclusion	16	3
Poor motivation	16	3
Belligerence	15	3
Hostility	14	3
School refusal	14	3
Mental retardation	13	3
Impulsiveness	13	3
Bizarre behavior	12	2
Enuresis	12	2
Sexual acting out	11	2
Delinquency	10	2
Daydreaming	10	2
Fearfulness	9	2
Truancy	9	2
Short attention span	8	2
Mutism	8	2
Slow development	7	
School planning	6	
Manipulative	6	
Drivenness	5	
Obesity	5	
Destructiveness	5	
Tics	5	
Low self-confidence	5	
Masturbation	5	
Somatic complaints	5	

TABLE 3 (continued)

Reason for Referral	Number	Percentage
Encopresis	5	
Lying	4	
Distractibility	4	
Poor co-ordination	4	
Delayed speech development	4	
Fire-setting	4	
Provocativeness	4	
Delinquent identification	4	
Suicidal attempt	4	
Convulsive disorder	4	
Evaluation for adoptability	4	
Autism	3	
Suicidal preoccupation	3	
Moodiness	3	
Asthma	3	
Blindness	3	
Homosexuality	3	
Apathy	3	
Runaway	3	
Hypersensitivity	3	
Inadequate adjustment to physical problem	2	
Vandalism	2	
Drooling	2	
Disorganized behavior	2	
Passivity	2	
Bulemia	2	
"Projection"	2	
Drinking	2	
School dropout	2	
Excessive fantasy life	2	
Irritability	2	
Inattentiveness	2	
Demandingness	2	
Unpatterned behavior	2	
Sibling rivalry	2	
Evaluation of relationship capacity	2	
Parents unable to accept child's limitations	2	
Cries frequently	2	
Vomiting	1	
Episodes of sighing and gasping	1	
Unpredictability	1	
Effeminacy	1	
Whining	1	
Poor adult relationships	1	
Echolalia	1	
Perseverativeness	1	
Uninhibited	1	
Sloppy	1	

TABLE 3 (continued)

Reason for Referral	Number	Percentage
Narcissistic	1	
"Emotionally disturbed"	1	
"Emotional"	1	
Projection of mother's problems	1	
Denial of physical illness	1	
Jealousy	1	
Falsifying report card	1	
Compulsions	1	
Rocking	1	
Regression	1	
Muscular dystrophy	1	
Sullenness	1	
Planning for illegitimate pregnancy	1	
Celiac syndrome	1	
Poor attitude	1	
Thumbsucking	1	
Loss of appetite	1	
Erratic behavior	1	
Malicious behavior	1	
Nightmares	1	
Low self-percept	1	
Molested by older boy	1	
Accidental shooting of playmate	1	
"Doesn't like school"	1	
Poor frustration tolerance	1	
Worrying	1	
Constricted	1	
Preoccupied	1	
Over-submissive	1	
"Writing threat notes to self"	1	
Incest	1	
Threatening sister with knife	1	
Aggressive fantasies	1	
Sadistic behavior	1	
Fetishism	1	
Excitable	1	
Over-critical	1	
Over-competitive	1	
Attention-seeking	1	
Phobia (of crowds)	1	
"Lack of superego"	1	
"Sexual difficulties"	1	
Mannerisms	1	
Question of brain damage	1	
Congenital malformation of orbit	1	
Labile	1	
"Increasingly emotional behavior"	1	
Bickering	1	

Bowlby emphasized the positive when he described the smiling and "following" responses as primary instincts which determine the child's tie to its mother.

By helping the child to develop positive relationships, chiefly through the psychiatrist's own relationsip with the child, he is helped not only to give up his symptoms but to attain those feelings of happiness and wellbeing that are every person's right.

REFERENCES

Bender, L. The Genesis of Hostility in Children, Am. J. Psychiatry, 105: 241, 1948.

Bowlby, J. The Nature of the Child's Tie to His Mother, Int. J. Psychoanal., 39: 1, 1958.

Goldstein, K. The Brain-Injured Child, in Pediatric Problems in Clinical Practise, ed. Michal-Smith, New York, Grune & Stratton, 1954.

Kanner, L. Child Psychiatry, 3rd ed., Springfield, Ill., Charles C Thomas, 1957.

Lapouse, R., and Monk, M. A. Fears and Worries in a Representative Sample of Children, Am. J. Orthopsychiatry, 29: 803, 1959.

——— and Monk, M. A. Behavior Deviations in a Representative Sample of Children, Am. J. Orthopsychiatry, 34: 436, 1964.

Macfarlane, J. W., Allen, L., and Honzik, M. P. A Developmental Study of the Behavior Problems of Normal Children Between Twenty-one Months and Fourteen Years, Berkeley, University of California Press, 1954.

Suttie, I. The Origins of Love and Hate, New York, The Julian Press, 1950.

4

THE SOURCES OF REFERRAL

The procedures for bringing together psychiatrist and child function with widely varying efficiency. In most situations it is a rather hit-or-miss operation, although in some communities and school systems there are now excellent facilities for obtaining psychiatric referral of troubled children.

How is the decision arrived at that a child should be taken to a psychiatrist? Usually some crisis occurs, or a series of crises. The child's temper outbursts may become more frequent and intense until finally there is a scene in the family. Or, a serious episode may occur, as in the case of a boy who suddenly ran out into the street, firing his rifle through the walls of the neighbors' houses. Or perhaps there is no critical event. The mother may simply find the father in a relaxed and receptive mood one evening, and talk with him about their child's troubles. Often the fact of a child's moving to a new neighborhood, transferring to a new school, or entering another class in school is the determining factor in his being referred to a psychiatrist. His new teacher, more alert to the signs of emotional disturbance, telephones the parents or talks with them at the regular parent-teacher conference. A visit to relatives or friends who have not seen the child for some time may cause them to comment on how much he has changed.

Parents are understandably reluctant to accept the idea that their child is emotionally disturbed, and may continue to deny it long after his disorder has become obvious to everybody else. This denial by the parents may be mostly unconscious; they are convinced that the child is "all right," that he is just being mischievous, or that he is "going through a phase." Mental illness in the family is always a threatening experience, and when it involves one's own child, the threat is even greater. It implies that one has failed as a parent. Every parent has some feeling of responsibility for his own child, no matter how rejecting and unloving that parent may be.

A parent's reactions to having a mentally ill child can take a variety of forms. There may be anger and resentment, coupled with an unconscious or even conscious wish to be rid of the child. There is usually guilt in parents, and it is often more intense in the parent who has been a poor parent. Such guilt may be totally narcissistic, it may be tinged with self-pity rather than pity or love for the child. Or the guilt may reflect the anguish felt at having failed a much-loved child or one who has been tenderly cared for. Or the child may have been too much cared for, too much overprotected, and this may be the basis of the problem.

When parents cannot see that their child is in trouble, they must somehow be convinced—their denial has got to be penetrated. This is a problem for the teacher, the social worker, a friend, or the family doctor. It is often a difficult task, and occasionally it cannot be accomplished at all. There are many approaches, many techniques. The teacher may have to "work with" the family for months. Sometimes it requires only a single interview. Often a threat is useful; this may at first glance seem unkind or even brutal, but if it has the effect of getting help for the child, it is justified. If a father is told directly that his child will probably "end up in prison," this has much more meaning to him than the information that his child is "in need of professional assistance."

REFERRAL SOURCES

Who refers children to the psychiatrist, and for what reasons? These vary, depending on the community, its culture, its facilities, and its level of psychiatric sophistication. The sources of referral will generally be different in New York City from those in a rural community in Michigan. And in a community where psychiatric treatment is readily available and widely accepted, less severe cases will be referred than in more primitive areas where psychiatry has less acceptance and where only the most severe and obvious disturbances are reluctantly turned over to the physician.

Table 1 has been compiled to indicate the sources from which a child psychiatry clinic may receive its cases. It lists the referral sources of all children seen in the outpatient clinic at Hawthorn Center during a one-year period, with an indication of the percentage of cases from each source. The Center is located in the country, near Detroit. Thus the data should be fairly representative of clinics serving a metropolitan-suburban area.

SCHOOL REFERRALS

The fact that the schools refer the largest number of cases is partly a reflection of the fact that many Michigan school systems have a "visiting-teacher" service which is concerned with seeking out and assisting children who are in difficulty. Such a service has become an important part of preventive psychiatry, as it assures that more of the quiet, withdrawn, and depressed children receive attention. The natural course of events has hitherto always been that the acting-out child, the trouble-maker, gets the special attention, while the harried teacher, grateful for any respite, leaves "the quiet one" alone.

TABLE 1

SOURCES OF REFERRAL TO HAWTHORN CENTER

		Percentage
1.	Schools	47
2.	Physicians	20
3.	Social Agencies	13
4.	Courts	6
5.	Guidance Clinics	5
6.	Parents	3
7.	Others	6

Academic difficulties and emotional difficulties are inextricably interrelated, and when both occur, cause and effect are not always obvious. While it has long been accepted that learning problems occur secondarily to emotional difficulties, it is now known that the reverse also occurs. Both situations require that the school and the psychiatrist work in close cooperation, as the therapeutic approach to many of these problems is through special-education methods.

PHYSICIAN REFERRALS

Cases sent by other physicians may constitute the chief referral source for psychiatrists in private practice, while psychiatric clinics receive a smaller percentage of their referrals from physicians. The public clinics are more utilized by other public agencies such as the schools and courts, as there is closer communication between the workers of these organizations; also, most of the children coming to the attention of these agencies are financially unable to afford private psychiatric care.

From physicians come many of the pediatric problems which have attendant emotional difficulties. This includes the large group of psychosomatic problems such as ulcerative colitis, asthma, anorexia nervosa, and so on. It also includes children with acute or chronic medical illnesses who are overreacting emotionally to their disease. In this handling of these children the psychiatrist can be of real help to the pediatrician. This, of course, requires that there be good communication and close co-operation between the two specialties. The psychosomatic disorders and the reactions of children to medical illnesses will be dealt with at greater length in Chapter 14.

REFERRALS FROM SOCIAL AGENCIES

The agencies which refer children to the psychiatrist are mainly those concerned with the care and placement of orphaned and neglected children. These agencies provide an almost endless source of problem children, and they generally seek psychiatric help for only the most serious problems. In some cases, the needs are obvious; usually institutional placement is indicated, and the social worker seeks the help of the psychiatrist largely to enlist his added influence in effecting such placement. This is a valid referral, and the psychiatrist does what he can.

In many cases, however, the needs are not so obvious. These children present a variety of disorders—the results of neglect are not uniform. As always, recommendations are based on diagnosis, plus a realistic appraisal of available facilities. Most social agencies carry a large caseload, the staff is overworked, the problems and demands which they face are immense, and most of the measures which they employ are based on practical necessity. The social worker who takes half a day to bring a child to the clinic has wasted her time if, at the end of the session, she receives merely the information that the child "is neurotic, has low self-esteem, and needs consistent ego support." She wants to know what to do for the child, and how soon, and where, and for how long.

Sometimes, of course, no one can give her the answers—not even the omniscient psychiatrist.

COURT CASES

The courts principally refer to the psychiatrist two types of cases: (1) The child who has been charged with committing an act of delinquency, and (2) the neglected child, whose parents have been legally charged with neglect.

Only a small portion of children brought before the court are referred to the psychiatrist. This varies, depending upon the attitudes toward psychiatry of the judge and the court worker, the state of the county budget, the community feeling about "juvenile delinquency," and the availability of psychiatric services.

Some of the larger courts maintain their own full-time or part-time staff of psychiatrists or clinical psychologists. When this is so, children brought to the court are "screened" by these professional workers, and those considered to need further psychiatric evaluation are selected. The court psychiatrist may refer certain cases further, if he believes an additional opinion is desirable.

Courts refer children to psychiatrists because they want to know what to do for them. The problem is invariably a practical one, such as whether to keep the child in a detention home, whether, following divorce, to have him live with his mother or his father, or whether to obtain psychiatric treatment. Some kind of disposition is always needed, and the court wants the psychiatrist's help in making the best disposition. The judge is usually not interested in a detailed report of the psychodynamics of the case. He finds little value in the information that "this child is acting out his displaced hostility which stems from an inordinate attachment to the over-protective and over-indulgent mother and an inability to resolve the intensified Oedipal conflict." Much more meaningful to the court would be a statement like this: "This boy's aggressive behavior will undoubtedly continue if he remains in his present environment, and it is recommended that he be placed in a semi-closed institution such as ——, where he can receive the controls and patterning which he needs."

GUIDANCE CLINIC REFERRALS

The frequency or referrals to and from guidance clinics will depend upon the situation in the particular community. The guidance clinic may itself be the only clinic in a particular area that can provide child psychiatric evaluations. In the case of Hawthorn Center, referrals are received from guidance clinics for several reasons. Children referred from these clinics have usually had a fairly complete work-up, and may be referred when there are specific diagnostic questions, or for further evaluation of cases who have failed to respond to outpatient treatment in the clinics. Frequently referrals are made for inpatient or day-care treatment.

REFERRALS DIRECTLY FROM PARENTS

Many psychiatrists and clinics prefer not to have patients referred directly by the parents. As in the other medical specialties, the usual rules of professional ethics apply. Requiring that another physician or agency refer the patient has the advantage that information about the child is obtained in addition to that supplied by the parents. Generally, referrals from professional caseworkers are more informative than those from private physicians; the case reports supplied by the former are generally detailed and carefully prepared, while the physician may send no more than a hastily scrawled note requesting: "Please examine Johnny Jones regarding misbe-havior in school." A detailed case report not only saves the examining psy-chiatrist much time, but makes the evaluation more complete and accurate; it may even make the difference between a correct and an incor-rect diagnosis. Information which has come to the caseworker or to the family physician as a result of their long contact with the family cannot always be obtained from parents in a single psychiatric interview. If the fa-ther beats the child daily with a buggy-whip, or if the mother has frequent male visitors while the father is away at work, such vital information may never get to the psychiatrist except from some outside source.

Most calls from parents are not true emergencies, but it must be rec-ognized that, to the parent, the matter is at least urgent. The problem may be a long-standing one which has finally been "brought to a head," either by some incident a little worse than the others or simply by the parents' having talked about the problem that day and having decided to "get something done about it." These calls must of course be handled with sympathy and understanding, and an appointment arranged as soon as is feasible. On the other hand, there are real emergencies. When a father phones and says, with desperation in his voice, "My boy just tried to stab me with a hunting knife," one obviously doesn't say "I'm sorry, but you'll have to have your family doctor send a referral," or "We can give you an appointment three weeks from next Tuesday." Such calls are by no means uncommon in a clinic for disturbed children, and it is significant and grati-fying that psychiatric facilities are being turned to increasingly for prob-lems involving children, where formerly the only recourse was to call the police. This is not to suggest that the psychiatrist should replace the police-man, and the majority of cases of juvenile delinquency remain in the prov-ince of the law enforcement agencies rather than the psychiatric clinics. Nevertheless, spending a night in jail can be a terrifying and traumatic ex-perience for an emotionally disturbed child, and can shatter the little that remains of his self-esteem and his capacity for defense.

These are the various ways children get to the psychiatrist. It was noted at the beginning of the chapter that the system of referral is not al-ways efficient. Many children who need help badly are never referred. The other side of the problem, referral of children who don't need it, has not yet reached serious proportions.

Improving the referral system is a multifaceted problem, and requires the cooperative effort of a number of agencies. The child psychiatrist can help, but he is usually too busy seeing patients.

When the patient arrives, the psychiatrist first seeks to determine what is wrong with him. This is the subject of the next chapter.

5

THE DIAGNOSTIC PROCESS

Early in a physician's training, in his pathology course, he is taught the catalogue of diseases. He learns that there is a more or less finite number of disorders, that each involves certain of the organ systems, and that each has a specific cause. If the cause is unknown, the disease is called "idiopathic," a somewhat plaintive term suggesting that there must be a cause but it has not been discovered.

Following the course in pathology, the medical student enters his clinical years. Here he is taught diagnosis, or how to recognize in a patient the disease which he learned about in pathology. Next he learns therapeutics, meaning what to do to alleviate or cure the disease. There is a nice logic and orderliness about such an approach to human misery. It works out reasonably well, and the patient usually gets better. Some doctors call this approach "recipe medicine." The term carries overtones of contempt.

Medicine is, of course, not so cut-and-dried as the young medical student might at first be led to expect. Many cases cannot be treated by recipe, and many diseases do not present a textbook picture. Every physician eventually learns this—some better than others. To some it is a source of annoyance and bafflement. To others it is a challenge, an invitation to discover why patients differ so greatly, why they respond in such various ways to the same therapies.

In psychiatry, too, the first thing the psychiatrist does is to diagnose the case. Diagnosis is, to paraphrase Lowrey, the process of finding out what is the matter. Then, having determined what is the matter, the next step is to apply the appropriate label. This label can communicate to one's colleagues a general notion of the patient's disorder, its probable causes, the behavior he presents, the kinds of treatment most likely to be effective, and the eventual outcome. All of this can frequently be imparted in one or two words, a not unremarkable achievement. And for many cases the system works reasonably well.

However, in psychiatry the diagnostic approach is less satisfactory than in the other medical specialties. Why?

1. There is a continuum extending from excellent emotional adjustment to severe mental illness, with all gradations between. In psychiatry, it is not a simple matter of black or white, of sickness or health. Many individuals are only moderately healthy, or somewhat disturbed. Also, the severity of disturbance fluctuates in many patients, sometimes over a considerable range from relatively good functioning to seriously disabling illness. Thus, diagnosis must often be qualified, according to the patient's behavior and reactions in various situations and at various times. A simple one- or two-word label is here not sufficient.

2. Treatment of a psychiatric disorder is determined not only by the diagnosis, but also by the patient's life situation. The requirements of a neurotic child living in an intact home are quite different from those of a neurotic child living with a psychotic parent or one living in an institution for homeless children. Or the requirements of children with different disorders may be essentially similar. For example, schizophrenic and brain-damaged children often need similar kinds of treatment including a routinized, non-stimulating environment, much individual attention, and firm but sympathetic control. On the other hand, they may have markedly different requirements. Thus, for example, the brain-damaged child often needs special education which would be of little or no value to the schizophrenic.

3. Treatment in psychiatry involves to a considerable extent the personality of the individual therapist. Psychotherapy is always a personal process, and a therapeutic approach to a particular disorder which works well for one therapist may not work at all for another. John Whitehorn studied the relationship between the personality of the psychiatrist and his success in treatment of various disorders. He found that most therapists are more successful with one type of disorder than with another.

4. Criteria for diagnoses in psychiatry are not universally established. There is disagreement among psychiatrists over what constitutes a particular disease entity. Different psychiatrists emphasize one or another aspect of the disorder, and make their diagnosis on the basis of the presence or absence of that particular dysfunction. For example, schizophrenia is variously considered to be an affective disorder, a thinking disorder, a disorder of central integration, or a developmental lag. It is perhaps all of these and more. Some feel that schizophrenia is a single entity; others, that it is a group of related disorders. There is similar confusion, although perhaps not so great, over diagnosis of some of the other mental disorders.

This confusion is compounded by the fact that each psychiatrist or local group of psychiatrists tends to develop his or their own diagnostic cri-

teria which work well for them. The writer finds that, through long association, he can communicate readily with close colleagues, so that when he
speaks of a child as being schizophrenic, or as having primary reading
disability, his colleagues will have a fairly clear notion of what that child's
problem is. However, with psychiatrists from other areas, communication
is often more difficult, and requires that the diagnosis be presented in several sentences or paragraphs rather than in one or two words.

These, then, are the major reasons why recipe medicine does not work
well in psychiatry. One cannot simply make the diagnosis, look up in a
book the appropriate treatment, and prescribe. However, this is by no
means to suggest that diagnosis is not important in psychiatry. Indeed, it is
perhaps more important than in most medical diseases. In no other branch
of medicine is the patient so likely to be damaged by incorrect therapy. In
some circles there has been an unfortunate trend toward treatment without diagnosis. It is not uncommon to see children who had been in "therapy" for months or years, where the psychodynamics, the family interrelationships, and the child's feelings had all been exhaustively explored, but
the therapist obviously had no notion of what the basic difficulty was. In
this context, Lowrey remarked, "There is danger of jumping headlong into
therapy, and of recent years I have been puzzled by what seems to be a
tendency to treat first, and then inquire afterward what was the matter."

Errors in diagnosis are usually in the direction of underestimating or
ignoring the biological aspects of the disorder, and overemphasizing the experiential. Much harm can come from such errors. Because of them, there
are undoubtedly countless thousands of parents who are guilt-ridden, convinced of their failure as parents, when in fact they have given their children thoroughly adequate care. To treat a child as neurotic when he is
brain-damaged is not only poor psychiatry, it is often cruelty, both to the
child and to his parents. The parents must know the nature of the problem, they must know when it was caused by something beyond their control for which they are not responsible, and they must understand the
special needs of such a child.

THE DIAGNOSTIC WORK-UP

The beginner in child psychiatry, when first confronted with an emotionally disturbed child, is sometimes inclined to run and hide. These
children can be very upsetting; they often have no regard for the proprie-
ties; they may kick, scream, bite, grab things out of one's pockets or off the
desk; they may sit sullenly and refuse to look at the examiner. But, one
soon learns to deal with the "difficult" children, and most children do not
present such difficulties. The majority of those seen for psychiatric evalua-

tion are quite tractable, they sit more or less quietly in the waiting room, they come to the office when invited, and they answer questions when asked.

The diagnostic work-up varies widely among different psychiatrists and clinics, but whatever the procedure, there must be some flexibility. It is not feasible to attempt to fit each case into a fixed routine. Some children should have several psychological tests, others do not need any. Some can be adequately diagnosed in a five-minute interview, others must be seen several times or even admitted to the inpatient unit for a month's study. On the other hand, the efficient operation of an office or clinic necessitates scheduling of patients, with some notion of the time and personnel that will be required for each case. For most diagnostic work-ups half a day is sufficient. In this time the parents can be interviewed, the social and personal history obtained, psychological tests administered, and the child seen in psychiatric interview. The social history may be taken either by the psychiatrist or the social worker. Many psychiatrists prefer to take it themselves, especially if the referring agent has already submitted some social history. A history taken by the psychiatrist is usually not as complete or as well organized as one by a social worker, but by taking it himself, the psychiatrist has more contact with the parents, discussing with them such matters as family relationships, the other children, the neighborhood, and so on. This gives the psychiatrist a better "feel" for the patient's environment than he would get from a written report.

In any case, the psychiatrist must always interview the parent or parents, at least briefly. This is assuming, of course, that the parent accompanies the child. Some children either have no parents, or their parents are so disinterested that they do not come to the clinic, allowing the child to be brought by the "worker." Because of this, some clinics have a policy of not seeing children or not taking them into treatment unless the parents can also be involved. Such a policy is indefensible. The child whose parents are not interested needs as much help as the child whose parents are, and often a good deal more. Most of these children can be helped, some by being placed away from home, some by other treatment even though they continue to live in their disordered environments.

In medicine, it is taught that a careful history is of the essence, as the diagnosis is most often made from the history. In child psychiatry, the opposite holds. The clinical examination is everything. This does not mean that a history is superfluous: it is helpful to know, for example, that the child was a foundling, or that he witnessed his mother shooting his father, or that at the age of 7 he stole a car and wrecked it in a chase with the police. It is sometimes helpful in differential diagnosis to know details of the child's behavior in early infancy, such as whether he relaxed easily in his mother's arms or constantly kicked, squirmed, and did not want to be held; or whether he began to walk and to talk at unusually late ages. But the majority of children can be diagnosed from the initial psychiatric interview, and without benefit of history. The chief purpose of a complete history is to assist in planning the treatment program or whatever disposition needs to be worked out; for this, one needs to know the life situation.

THE DIAGNOSTIC DIMENSIONS

Diagnosis is fundamentally a process of measurement. What are assessed are the presence, or absence, and sometimes the quantity, of certain functions. In medical illness these include such things as pain, nausea, weakness, blood pressure, and serum bilirubin. The internist has a more-or-less-standardized checklist of dimensions which he uses. Diagnosis is not merely the filling out of a checklist; however, an orderly procedure is the backbone of most good diagnoses.

In the psychiatric interview it is useful, especially for the inexperienced, to have an organized list of diagnostic measurements. These may be in the form of an actual written checklist which may be glanced at either during the interview or before and after. Such a checklist is not used in the way a pilot prepares his airplane for takeoff, by starting with item one and proceeding in order. Rather, it serves as a reminder to attend, at some time during the interview, to each of the functions listed.

Following is a list of important capacities or functions to be evaluated in the diagnostic session. Each psychiatrist will have his own modifications and variations, and this list does not lay claim to representing the only pertinent functions. However, if all those listed here are measured with some accuracy, an accurate diagnosis can probably be reached. This list has been adapted from an outpatient record employed at Hawthorn Center:

1. Relationship capacity
2. Affect—especially anxiety, depression, and anger
3. Intellectual capacity and intellectual functioning
4. Neurological integration (motor, perceptual, conceptual)
5. Reality-testing
6. Motivation
7. Acculturation

It can be seen that the above list consists mainly of certain of the "ego functions." For those who employ this frame of reference, it may be useful to measure all of the ego functions, as well as those of the id and superego. A table of the ego functions appears in Chapter 2.

How does the psychiatrist proceed in obtaining the diagnostic measurements? First, and perhaps most important, he attempts to get a feeling of how the child *relates* with him. His response to overtures is noted, whether he is warm or aloof, interested or disinterested, trusting or suspicious, outgoing or guarded. The ability to judge the quality of the child's relationship is perhaps the most important single attribute of a good psychiatrist. It can be learned, but it is not learned easily. It is a capacity which is contained within the psychiatrist's own personality; it is in part empathy, and a feeling of warmth toward, and interest in, the child. In order to measure the child's capacity to relate, the psychiatrist must be able himself to relate with him. There is no way to simulate such a feeling; it must be genuine.

The child's *intellectual level* is important, and can be evaluated in several ways. His use of, and understanding of, language give a clue to his intelligence. His level of conceptual thinking can be judged. Sometimes this must be specifically tested, by asking such questions as how long did it take him to drive to the clinic. Often the child is asked to read a paragraph or two from a standard reading test, to judge his reading-grade level. The diagnosis of reading disability has often been missed for the simple reason that it was not looked for. To evaluate a child's intelligence, one must know approximately what level of functioning is normal for each age. This requires experience, but it can be more quickly learned by specific study and application. It is an important part of training in child psychiatry, and is, unfortunately, too often overlooked. Psychological tests are often done in the initial evaluation, and usually provide the most accurate measure of intellectual functioning. However, they cannot always be employed, and the psychiatrist must train himself to evaluate these functions clinically. A favorite exercise among child psychiatrists is to estimate what the child's test scores will be.

Affects, especially anxiety, are evaluated in the diagnostic interview. How is anxiety in a child recognized? Sometimes it cannot be. Reactions to anxiety vary greatly, and some children appear to react not at all. In evaluating a child, the psychiatrist depends largely on observation of his behavior; he will not often verbalize, even on direct questioning, that he feels nervous, or tense. Some children are so guarded, so mistrustful, that they cover up evidences of anxiety, and appear bored, or scornful, or sullen, or "tough." Sometimes these poses are quite patent, sometimes they are not. When a child does not "give out" in the interview, when he is guarded and unresponsive, and because it is important to know how he feels, an attempt may be made to stimulate a reaction. This can take the form of direct threats, or some comment about the gravity of the problem. If one says, for example, "You know, John, your mother is completely broken up over all this," or "How do you think your father feels, knowing his son may be arrested?" Such an approach will often mobilize a child who has been sitting sullenly through such platitudes as "You know, John, I want to help you."

In the initial interview one assays *motor functioning*, especially tension, clumsiness, tremor, and facial expression. These help to evaluate neurological integration as well as level of anxiety. *Motivation* is important and one tries to ascertain the amount of interest which the child shows in his situation. One looks for guilt and hostility. These are judged usually by projective or indirect methods rather than by direct questioning. The child's response to controls has to be evaluated, sometimes by applying direct controls. Here the level of firmness and authoritarianism which is required must be carefully judged; sometimes a mild word of command or reprimand is sufficient, sometimes real anger and a stern voice are needed.

Acculturation, a term borrowed from anthropology, refers to the manner in which the child has assimilated the customs, beliefs, and values of his culture. This cultural indoctrination occurs both consciously and unconsciously through the influence of the parents and other important adults such as teachers. A child is thought of as being normally acculturated if he successfully emulates the ideals of his elders. The evaluation of the effectiveness with which a patient has accomplished this task requires that the psychiatrist have a working familiarity with the subcultures from which his clinic population is drawn. In many clinics that serve a large metropolitan area this will encompass a broad range of socioeconomic and ethnic groups, from upper to lower class. Symptoms must be evaluated in the light of their cultural conformity. Behavior which may be quite acceptable in a primitive unpatterned family situation could represent serious pathology in an upper middle-class family.

For a discussion of the evaluation of *reality-testing* the reader is referred to Chapter 6.

THE "TONE" OF THE INTERVIEW

The initial interview in psychiatry is sometimes maintained at a "neutral" tone. This will vary with the individual psychiatrist, with his particular orientation, experience, and personality. However, interviews with children are usually not neutral. They are most effective and most productive if emotion is felt, expressed, and stimulated. If the child is apprehensive, he must be reassured. If he is sullen, he may be reprimanded. Always some contact must be made, some genuine feeling stimulated for initiating a working relationship. The child may leave the interview hating the psychiatrist—but this is better than indifference.

Humor is used a great deal in child psychiatry. Many psychiatrists depend much on the humorous approach for establishing a good relationship. Some are intuitively more adept than others at the use of humor; however, it is a technique which can be to some extent learned. In the initial interview, the humorous approach is reassuring and also flattering to the child. It indicates to him that the interviewer is genuinely enjoying his company. It is, of course, implicit that the examiner actually be able to enjoy the humor at the child's level, or to enjoy the child's enjoyment. The writer once observed that "Humor is the projective technique *par excellence* in the psychiatric interview with children. It can always be used, and something can almost always be learned from its use." Children of all intellectual levels can enjoy humor, and the level of humor to which the child responds is one of the best indices of his intelligence and his capacity for abstraction. A 6-year-old boy, I.Q. 70, will laugh gleefully if the therapist makes some ridiculous remark such as, looking at the boy's bright red shirt, "Why Stanley, what a lovely green shirt!" Jerry, a bright, ten-year-old neurotic boy will "get" most adult-type jokes, and will feign boredom or contempt if the joke is too patent or "juvenile."

Important clues to diagnosis may be obtained from the child's response to an initially humorous approach. The depressed or the schizophrenic child seldom responds to humor; and there is a difference in their unresponsiveness. The depressed child will only hang his head a little lower, or he may make a fleeting attempt to smile, but give it up as a bad job. The schizophrenic usually does not understand the joke, he looks puzzled, or confused; this is a signal to drop the humor immediately, as the child is already having enough difficulty with reality-testing. The uncontrolled, acting-out child may see the humor as a signal that "anything goes," and he may quickly get out of hand. The brain-damaged child may perseverate in the humor, laughing and repeating the same joke *ad nauseam*. But whatever the child's response, a joke here and there is not amiss in the psychiatrist's office; it clears the atmosphere, and it usually sets a tone that leads readily to better understanding and relationship between psychiatrist and child.

The tone of the interview is not invariably light and humorous. A satisfactory diagnostic interview may be an orderly, sober, dignified process; the child may not enjoy such an interview as much as one kept at a light tone, but, after all, he does not come to the psychiatrist to be entertained. Yet, no child can tolerate a situation which is too stiff, too formal. This may be taken as an inviolable rule. There must be a little opportunity for relaxation, for warmth, and for fun. If a therapist is unable to relax his dignity, then probably he should not attempt to treat children. This is a reality which must be recognized; not every physician can become a successful child psychiatrist. No particular disgrace need be implied in such an admission; neither would all medical school graduates make good surgeons, or good astronauts.

RULES FOR THE DIAGNOSTIC INTERVIEW

It was mentioned above, somewhat facetiously, that there are few good rules governing the diagnostic interview, and that even these seldom work. The point to be kept in mind is that the interview is largely a personal matter, and the way it is carried out depends upon the personality of the examiner, the ways in which he relates best with children, and the techniques which have, in his experience, worked best. The writer has tended to emphasize here his own particular techniques and methods, suggesting the type of interview which is generally relaxed, unstructured, with considerable verbal give and take, bantering, use of jokes, of humor, and with the opportunity for emotional display both by therapist and by patient. Such an approach to an emotionally disturbed child works well for some examiners. This is not to say that it is the *only* good approach. Other therapists get equally good results with entirely different methods. Some would be uncomfortable and unsuccessful with the techniques just mentioned, and accordingly they use techniques which they themselves prefer and which they have developed and found successful.

Following are a few other lesser rules, all of which could be arrived at by the application of good judgment and common sense. They are listed here as a guide to the inexperienced. They are not inflexible, and may undergo considerable modification as the therapist, with experience, develops his own individual methods.

1. Don't whisper or talk about the patient when you don't want him to hear what is being said. This rule is so obvious as to appear ridiculous, yet it is broken much too often and by persons who should know better. If there are comments or instructions which one wishes to make to the parents or to the accompanying social worker, then it is important enough to take sufficient time to conduct the persons into the office while having the child remain in the waiting room. If the child tries to come along and "get in on" the conversation, he should be firmly told to stay out, that the conversation is not for him to hear. Children understand and usually accept that they cannot be allowed to hear certain things, and this is far better than to attempt to deceive them by whispering behind their backs and by having them overhear things which may be quite harmful.

2. Don't wear a white physician's coat. The emotional impact of the dreaded white coat can be a powerful one. In some cases it can interfere irrevocably with the opportunity of developing a good relationship with

the child. There is no particular need or advantage for the child psychiatrist to wear a white coat and, even if the rules of the institution require this uniform, it can be left off in the privacy of one's office.

3. Always greet the child in the waiting room at the beginning of the session and again as he leaves. This is part of the overall principle of making the child feel as if he is the chief object of interest and not merely an unwanted onlooker.

4. Don't try to deceive the child about the reasons why he is seeing the psychiatrist or about the fact that he is seeing a psychiatrist. Parents often ask in advance what they should tell the child about the reasons for his coming. Usually a direct and honest answer is preferable to any attempts to deceive. The child is directly told that he is coming to the doctor because of the particular difficulty that he has, whether it be an acting-out problem, a school academic problem, or whatever. Most children are perfectly aware that they are having trouble. In the initial interview one may ask the child outright if he knows why he has been brought to the psychiatrist. The answer is often revealing, and the subsequent discussion can be an important part of the diagnostic procedure.

MEDICAL EVALUATION

It is always safe to recommend that the diagnostic evaluation of an emotionally disturbed child include a complete medical examination. Actually, however, this is not often indicated. Most of these children are quite obviously healthy physically, and no more in need of a medical evaluation than any other healthy child. This is a matter of judgment by the person or persons responsible, and the psychiatrist will presumably have a voice in the matter.

Neither are special medical investigations often indicated. A neurological examination is of little or no help in the diagnosis of most of the psychiatric problems of children, including brain damage and aphasia. Nor is electroencephalography, the clinical value of which continues to be mainly in the verification of brain tumors and the epilepsies.

STANDARDIZATION IN DIAGNOSIS

Child psychiatry historically developed as an offshoot of adult psychiatry. This created a variety of distortions and misconceptions which are gradually being eliminated as experience with children demonstrates that emotional disturbances in the early years are not merely immature versions of adult disorders. One of the greatest areas of confusion has been in diagnosis. Soddy observes that, "Exact diagnosis depends upon an accepted pathology, which is lacking in child psychiatry. . . . It does not help to assign names to the phenomena described, as if they were diagnostic entities. Terms borrowed from adult psychiatry, like anxiety, neurosis, hysteria, obsessions, and compulsions reveal nothing useful about when and how the condition arose, nor do they enable a prognosis to be made."

One of the most vexing aspects of diagnosis in disturbed children is the child's propensity for change. Children seem to have no respect for the rules of psychodynamic formulation. It can be most annoying to get a child nicely evaluated and classified, only to have him come up with a new symptom-complex so that one finds that he has to be picked out of one pigeon-hole and put into another. Ackerman, commenting on the difficulties of devising a satisfactory diagnostic scheme, observes:

The common symptom pictures of children do not display anything like the stability and consistency of adults. In children, the manifestations of pathology show sensitive changes with a shift in time, social setting, and total life situation. A set of symptoms which dominates the clinical picture at one age may be replaced by a new set at a later age. . . . The younger the child and the less formed its personality, the more difficult it is to discriminate between normal reaction to stress and pathological anxiety responses.

Reading the literature, one might conclude that every author has his own system of diagnostic terms and criteria. Fish, for example, in 1960 employed only three major categories: schizophrenia, organic brain disease, and behavior disorder. The latter apparently included all those problems caused primarily by the child's experience, thus obviating the differentiation between neurosis, personality disorder and psychopathy. Such a system has some merit, in that it avoids the inevitable bickering about questionable cases, but it is so nonspecific as to impart little meaning. In 1965 Fish developed a more elaborate categorization which appears to have a greater prognostic significance (Fish and Shapiro).

An example of a diagnostic scheme transposed from adult psychiatry, and representing the exclusively "psychogenic" school, is the one proposed by Pearson in 1949. He classifies disturbed children under the following nine headings:
1. Direct Reactions to Environmental Errors
2. Acute and Chronic Anxiety States
3. Anxiety Hysteria
4. Conversion Hysteria
5. Organ Neuroses
6. Compulsion Neuroses
7. Perversions

8. Psychoses

9. Character Neuroses

Whatever merit this system may have is obscured by the fact that it would probably apply to no more than half of the children referred to the psychiatrist.

Chess, proposing a diagnostic scheme admittedly her own, succeeds in encompassing most of the published evidence for the various pathologic entities. Here is the grouping she suggests:

1. Normal

2. Organic brain disturbance

3. Reactive behavior disorders

4. Neurotic behavior disorders

5. Neurotic character disorders

6. Neurosis

7. Schizophrenia and psychosis

8. Psychopathy

9. Mental retardation

The above system corresponds closely with the one employed in this book. It is also in agreement, in most areas, with the scheme recommended by Ackerman, which has been, with certain modifications, suggested by the American Psychiatric Association (APA). The APA classification of childhood disorders has not found wide acceptance among child psychiatrists. Its use has been limited mainly to record-filing applications, rather than for communication among psychiatrists. Its adoption perhaps represented a premature effort to impose the views of a limited number on the entire profession. The Group for the Advancement of Psychiatry (GAP) is currently attempting to work out a diagnostic classification for childhood disorders. A preliminary report (*Diagnostic Classification in Child Psychiatry*) of their recommendations suggests that there is still much work to be done before a satisfactory system is evolved.

In the present volume, the writer has sought to employ those diagnostic terms and criteria which appear to have widest current acceptance in the United States. The matter of diagnosis is not an altogether arbitrary one, and the accumulating clinical and research evidence confirms that a certain clustering of disorders exists among the population of emotionally disturbed children. One may apply whatever criteria he wishes in separating these clusters. Soddy, for example, uses age of onset as the major criterion for classification. The most usual criterion, and that which is employed here, is etiology. Thus, the major diagnostic entities have different causes as their chief measures of distinction. It is almost certainly on this base that the diagnostic system will continue to evolve.

ACCURACY OF DIAGNOSIS

It has become almost a truism in medical circles that diagnosis in psychiatry is haphazard and inaccurate, and that no two psychiatrists agree on what is wrong with a patient. Certainly there is no dearth of individual cases in which diagnostic opinions have differed widely. Yet what is the over-all picture? How bad is the situation? Or, to put it in the positive, what are the validity and reliability indices in psychiatric diagnosis?

There have been several reported studies of reliability in the diagnosis of psychiatric disorders in adults, and these were recently reviewed by Kreitman. Reliability measures the amount of agreement between two or more independent observers. Kreitman found wide variations in the reliabilities reported, depending in part on the methods of assessment, and in part on the diseases studied. There was generally better reliability in the diagnosis of the psychoses than of the neuroses and personality disorders, ranging from around 90 per cent to 30 per cent.

The reported studies are usually interpreted as supporting the view that reliability of psychiatric diagnosis is horribly poor, but Kreitman has pointed out that most of the studies, by the nature of their design, lead to unfairly low results. One reason is that the degree of discrepancy is usually ignored. Thus, if two observers disagree only slightly in their evaluation, one for example, making the diagnosis of mild chronic schizophrenia and the other, schizoid personality disorder, this would be reported as a disagreement as wide as if the two diagnoses were, say, paranoid schizophrenia and fetishism.

The problem of reliability is largely a matter of training in diagnosis, and, through better methods of communication and standardization, it is hoped that this can be improved.

Validity of diagnosis is another matter altogether. This is the true measure of accuracy. A valid diagnosis is one which can be proved to be correct. The problem of "objective" confirmation is, in many cases, insurmountable. Moreover, reliability does not prove validity. A dozen psychiatrists may agree that a patient has an Oedipal neurosis, but they may all be wrong.

Improving the validity of psychiatric diagnosis is a long and painstaking process, and it can develop only as psychiatry itself develops, through careful clinical practice and research.

In child psychiatry, there has thus far been little systematic attempt to evaluate the diagnostic process and to standardize nomenclature and criteria. The reliability of diagnosis among child psychiatrists is probably lower than in the adult field.

The specific emotional disorders of children are considered in the next section. Each is treated in a separate chapter, as follows:

1. Childhood schizophrenia
2. Psychoneurosis
3. Brain damage
4. Specific learning disabilities
5. Personality disorder
6. Psychopathy
7. Mental retardation
8. Psychosomatic disorders

Most disturbed children will fit into one of the above categories, some more certainly than others. Some represent a combination of two or more of the disorders. The writer has seen one child who clearly possessed no less than four and probably five of these eight, in addition to being congenitally blind. A few children defy all attempts at classification, but the number of these can be significantly reduced by thorough diagnostic study.

REFERENCES

Ackerman, N. W. Psychiatric Disorders in Children—Diagnosis and Etiology in Our Time, in Current Problems in Psychiatric Diagnosis, eds. Hoch and Zubin, New York, Grune & Stratton, 1953.

Chess, S. An Introduction to Child Psychiatry, New York, Grune & Stratton, 1959.

Diagnostic Classification in Child Psychiatry. Ed. Jenkins and Cole, Psychiatric Research Report #18, Washington, D.C., The American Psychiatric Association, 1964.

Fish, B. Drug Therapy in Child Psychiatry: Psychological Aspects, Comprehensive Psychiatry, 1: 55, 1960.

———— and Shapiro, T. A Typology of Children's Psychiatric Disorders I. Its Application to a Controlled Evaluation of Treatment, J. Amer. Acad. Child Psychiat., 4: 32, 1965.

Kreitman, N. The Reliability of Psychiatric Diagnosis, J. Ment. Sci., 107: 876, 1961.

Lowrey, L. G. Symposium: Training in the Field of Orthopsychiatry, Amer. J. Orthopsychiatry, 20: 674, 1950.

Pearson, G. H. J. Emotional Disorders of Childhood, New York, W. W. Norton, 1949.

Shaw, C. R. The Use of Humor in Child Psychiatry, Amer. J. Psychotherapy, 15: 368, 1961.

Soddy, K. Clinical Child Psychiatry, London, Bailliere, Tindall & Cox, Ltd., 1960.

Whitehorn, J. C. and Betz, B. J. A Study of Psychotherapeutic Relationships between Physicians and Schizophrenic Patients, Amer. J. Psychiatry, 111:321, 1954.

SECTION THREE

SPECIFIC DISORDERS

6

CHILDHOOD SCHIZOPHRENIA

REPORT OF A CASE

Francis R. is a 14-year-old boy who has shown bizarre behavior since infancy. For the past five years he has lived on the children's ward of a state hospital; it is likely that he will be institutionalized for the rest of his life.

Francis is the third of four children in an average, middle-class, suburban family. His father works in the office of a large manufacturing company, and his salary is adequate for the family's standard of living. Mr. R. is a college graduate, in good health, mature, stable, and interested in his family. Mrs. R. is a housewife, a high school graduate, of above-average intelligence, also in good health and reasonably well-adjusted. She has occasional tension headaches in the afternoons, and attributes these to situational problems in the home when the children are unusually noisy or demanding. The other three children are all healthy. They are of about average intelligence except for the older sister who is an honor student; none of the three has presented any serious behavior problem; they have many friends and pursue normal interests and activities.

Francis' paternal uncle has paranoid schizophrenia. This was first diagnosed when he was in college at the age of 21. He has been in and out of state hospitals several times. Francis has seen this uncle briefly on several occasions but has never had any prolonged contact with him.

Mrs. R.'s pregnancy with Francis was normal, as were her other three pregnancies. She was 24 when Francis was born. Delivery was without any unusual event; the baby breathed immediately, appeared healthy, and suckled well. He was nursed for about two weeks, at which time the mother "lost her milk" and he was placed on a bottle. He continued to eat and gain well and appeared normal in every respect throughout the first year. He was described as "a good baby," was not unusually demanding, slept well, and began to babble at about seven months. Before he was a year old he could say "Mama," "Dada," and "Hi." He smiled and laughed readily, and enjoyed being thrown into the air by his father. His motor co-ordination was not good; the parents felt that he was clumsier as an infant than were their other children.

Then, at the age of 14 months, Francis began to have panic attacks. The first of these occurred when he was taken onto a bus; as the bus door closed he began to scream uncontrollably. Soon he was afraid of going into stores, or sometimes even of going out of his house. He continued to be very frightened of buses; the parents gave up altogether trying to take him anywhere on a bus, and sometimes it was even necessary when they were driving in a car to turn down a side street whenever a bus appeared in the distance. Loud noises also frightened him terribly.

From the age of 1 to 3 Francis was content most of the time to sit alone and rock and play with a few familiar toys. He would sit in the sand-pile for hours on end, shoveling sand and throwing it from one spot to an-other. The only time he would show anger was when someone took his toys from him; except for this emotion, he evidenced little affect and never seemed concerned about other people. He showed little interest even in his parents; he did not appear to recognize them as familiar objects, and stran-gers could take care of him as well as his parents could.

From about the age of 1 to 5 Francis never spoke any meaningful words. The few words which he had exhibited earlier disappeared, and his speech during this time consisted of unintelligible sounds or meaningless words, repetitious or rhyming sounds like "too choo choo too," hisses, squeals, and loud screams. Between 5 and 6 he began to try to imitate words which his mother would say to him or to make rhyming words to her words. He began to use an occasional meaningful phrase, such as "don't know" or "mother won't." At this time other speech developed, which appeared to be without meaning and which he would recite in repeti-tious fashion, often interspersed with a tuneless humming. This speech was apparently not intended for communication, but was a kind of autistic play with vocal sounds. Francis' speech has not developed beyond this level. He is now able to express a few things in recognizable language, such as saying "No, no," when told to eat a certain food which he does not want. Otherwise, his speech is infrequent, usually autistic, and of an echolalic and repetitious nature.

At 4½, Francis began to be interested in drawing, and in cutting out pictures with scissors. He developed food fads, and for periods of time would eat only one food such as oranges, bananas, or milk. Later he began to be interested in preparing his own food, and some of his concoctions were unique: for example, he liked to put chocolate syrup on his mashed potatoes.

Until about the age of 6 Francis had to be supervised most of the time. He had no social judgment, he might wander away from the house and into other houses, and would wander into stores if taken downtown and stand posturing and gesturing peculiarly in front of the display counters. The parents noted that he did not seem to differentiate between people and inanimate things, and would attempt to talk and gesture to non-living objects. Also, when addressed by a person, he would obviously hear the person, would sometimes obey if given a command, but otherwise "didn't seem to know you were there"; there was no evidence of recognition, no indication of any feeling toward other persons. He would usually not look at the person when spoken to, almost as if he were receiving the sounds from an indefined direction and from far away. He always seemed to be alone, living within himself and with his own thoughts, and he did not like to have them intruded upon.

After about 6, Francis began to require less external control; he could remain unsupervised and would usually keep out of trouble. However, he could not go to school because he was totally uninterested in the school activities and was distracting to the other students.

Francis was first seen for psychiatric evaluation at the age of 4½. The diagnostic impression was childhood schizophrenia. The parents were given a great deal of assistance in his management and a realistic appraisal of the prognosis. Francis continued to live at home until the age of 9, at which time the management problems had become greater. This was due to the fact that he was bigger, and was considered potentially dangerous because of his lack of social judgment and of feeling for other people. It was feared that he might, if frustrated or enraged, seriously injure or even kill another person without any feelings of concern. He was therefore admitted to Hawthorn Center for a period of intensive study, then was transferred to the children's ward of a state mental hospital, where he has remained.

Psychological tests given at intervals from ages four and one half to nine showed progressive deterioration of Francis' intelligence. On the first test, his I.Q. was estimated at 105. By the age of 6 this had dropped to 75, and at 9 years it was down to 54. Performance on most of the subtests was always extremely uneven, marked by occasional insights and successes much above the boy's general level of achievement. Testing was difficult due to lack of attention and poor communication, and Francis was completely unmotivated toward most of the problems. Yet he would sometimes perform with amazing rapidity, especially in making drawings. The psychologist observed that "the quality of Francis' drawings, especially the rapidity with which they are produced and their lack of any definite quality, suggests a very active fantasy life. They also suggest very inadequate conceptualization of mother and family. Francis seems to identify himself with a house."

The report on Francis' tests at age 9 concludes: "It appears that this boy's ego development has been arrested within the age limits of four to seven years. The basic intellectual functions are non-operative or extremely immature. Motility and speech are very disturbed. Identification is confused. Diagnostic impression: Severely impaired intellectual function related to childhood schizophrenia. Prognosis: poor."

The prognosis is indeed poor. At our present level of knowledge about this disease, it is hopeless.

Francis is a classical case of childhood schizophrenia. The onset, course, and prognosis are typical.

What manner of disorder is it, this most fascinating and most severe of all the mental illnesses of children? What causes it? Can anything be done to prevent it? Can anything be done to cure it? The answers to these and other important questions concerning childhood schizophrenia are not marked by unanimity. However, as experience and research findings have accumulated in the past two decades, some light is appearing. There is at least fairly general recognition that the disorder occurs, that it is an entity, or perhaps a group of entities; and criteria for its diagnosis have become reasonably clarified. Concerning its etiology and its relationship to adult schizophrenia, there is less conclusive information and, consequently, less agreement.

The literature is confused by the variety of names which have been applied to this disease. Accounts of psychosis of children, which appeared in the medical literature as early as 1763, were designated by such terms as "insanity" or "maniacal conditions," and were obviously a heterogeneous group of diseases often confused with mental retardation. In 1896, Kraepelin coined the term *dementia praecox*, which suggested both the progressive deterioration and the early onset, usually in adolescence. During the first decade of this century Sante de Sanctis described a group of children as "dementia praecocissima" which was regarded as a form of dementia praecox in younger children. It was later found that this syndrome also represented a heterogeneous group of disorders. At the same time Heller described "dementia infantilis," now known as Heller's Disease, which resembled schizophrenia symptomatically. It has since been demonstrated by brain biopsy and autopsy that this disorder is a progressive degenerative disease of the central nervous system.

Bleuler, in 1911, introduced the word *schizophrenia*, which he preferred because it suggested the splitting of the mental processes, without implying the hopeless prognosis of "dementia."

Potter, in 1933, was apparently the first to apply the term *schizophrenia* to children. He accurately described the symptoms and obviously recognized the disorder as a distinct clinical entity.

Another term still used in the literature is "early infantile autism," described by Kanner (1944) as a specific syndrome beginning as early as the first year of life. It is now generally considered synonymous with childhood schizophrenia of very early onset. The term *autism* is also widely used, but lacks specificity since it is actually a symptom seen not only in schizophrenia but also in other disorders. Beata Rank and her co-workers apply an even less specific designation, "the atypical child," which they unfortunately use to cover a heterogeneous group of disorders, including childhood schizophrenia.

As diagnostic criteria became clarified, reports of rather large series of cases began to appear in the literature, and the controversy soon developed over terminology and over whether the disorder should be considered a type of schizophrenia. While the term *childhood schizophrenia* is now the most widely accepted, this is by no means an indication that all who use the term agree that it is simply adult schizophrenia of an earlier onset. It will be worthwhile to examine the studies which clarify the relationship between adult and childhood schizophrenia.

The three major lines of evidence are:

1. Long-term follow-up studies of schizophrenic children
2. Comparison of the psychopathology in children and adults
3. Family studies

The largest series of long-term follow-up cases is that of Bender (1953, 1955), who found that between 85 and 90 per cent of 143 childhood schizophrenics became adult schizophrenics. The diagnosis was confirmed in most cases by independent examiners.

The writer is personally familiar with a small group of patients (16) who were definitely diagnosed childhood schizophrenics and who have now reached young adulthood. All of these are still clearly schizophrenic, their most marked feature being an autistic quality, an absence of true communication and relationship with others. Some of them retain characteristic mannerisms of speech and behavior which typify them as "grown-up childhood schizophrenics." Thus, they are in some ways different from the usual kinds of schizophrenia which begin in adolescence or later.

Follow-up studies are not sufficiently inclusive to resolve the question as to whether childhood and adult schizophrenias are the same process. The fact that there are certain differences between adults who became schizophrenic in adulthood and those who became schizophrenic in childhood does not prove either one view or the other. One would expect some differences between the personality of an individual who had been severely psychotic since childhood and one who had been relatively intact in his early years.

Further evidence linking the childhood and adult forms of schizophrenia is the similarity in the basic psychopathology between the two. Rabinovitch describes the "core disturbance" of childhood schizophrenia as an inability to "experience a clear-cut percept and to appreciate with clarity the reality of identities, boundaries and limits." Freeman and others consider the basic disturbance in adult schizophrenia as "a defect of ego-feeling, or the inability to differentiate self from environment"; and Federn likewise describes the fundamental psychopathology of adult schizophrenia as an ego defect, with loss of ego boundaries and a failure to differentiate between self and the external world.

The evidence from family studies will be discussed below under Etiology, and shows that there is a significantly higher incidence of schizophrenia in the adult relatives of schizophrenic children.

Summarizing the available evidence, Shaw and others (1959), conclude:

It is not yet finally certain whether childhood schizophrenia is a special type of schizophrenia or whether it represents merely an early or severe form of simple adult schizophrenia. Resolution of this issue must await further studies along the lines of familial patterns, physical and chemical evaluations, and continued longitudinal clinical and sociological studies. Nevertheless, as more and more information is being accumulated, it appears likely that the basic disorder is the same whether it occurs in children or adults.

INCIDENCE

Accurate data on the frequency of childhood schizophrenia in the general population is not available, since no published study has specifically sought to determine the incidence. Such a study would probably meet with insurmountable difficulties, as there is no general agreement regarding diagnostic criteria among the various clinics and agencies which might report their cases. For example, many of these children are in schools for the mentally retarded, because many actually function at a retarded level. Kanner (1957) has observed that, in addition to the problems posed by uncertainties in diagnostic criteria, many instances have been implied in the literature by hindsight, hinting that some schizophrenic symptoms of adults had made their first appearance before puberty. Illness whose onset occurred in middle or even late adolescence has often been reported as childhood schizophrenia, although it is generally agreed that the onset of the disorder occurs before the age of 11.

Childhood schizophrenia is fortunately rather rare, although perhaps not so rare as was formerly supposed. In the Hawthorn Center outpatient clinic, approximately 4 per cent of the children seen for diagnostic evaluation are schizophrenic. This figure is probably higher than that of many clinics, as a generally higher proportion of severely disturbed children is referred there. Bender (1947) has reported on the incidence at Bellevue Hospital over a period of 18 years. Of a total of 6,500 disturbed children, almost 10 per cent were schizophrenic; their age ranged from 2 to 13 years; and their sex ratio was about 2.6:1, as between boys and girls. In a state hospital in Michigan, the writer personally studied 100 consecutive cases of children committed to the hospital. Of these, 24 were diagnosed as having childhood schizophrenia (unpublished data).

Thus, schizophrenia would seem to be rather common within the group of most severely disturbed children. However, its incidence is certainly far lower in children than in adults, whose number includes the "grown-up childhood schizophrenics," as well as those whose disorder developed at adolescence or later.

ETIOLOGY

The cause of childhood schizophrenia, like that of its adult counterpart, is not known. Much has been written on the subject and much investigation has been carried out; there are many opinions, and some of them are rather firm. Nevertheless, when everything that is known is put together, it still adds up to an enigma. So little is known about the cause or causes of the disorder that there is still a major controversy over whether it is determined by biological factors or by early experience. When Hendrickson reviewed the literature on the etiology, he noted the existence of two major "schools": the predominantly biological theory emphasized by such workers as Bender, Rabinovitch, and Erikson, and the largely experiential viewpoint emphasized by Kanner, Despert, Putnam, Rank, and others.

According to Mahler, there are at least two different types of childhood schizophrenia, which she considers as distinct disorders: "autistic" and "symbiotic" child psychoses. Although emphasizing the importance of constitutional predisposition in both types, she implies that this hereditary influence contributes more heavily in the autistic type (which may appear as early as the first year of life). She believes that the symbiotic type (which usually appears at about the third or fourth year, when the normal symbiotic attachment between mother and child would ordinarily begin to be severed) results mainly from the close and constant overprotection of the child's mother. It should be noted, however, that the majority of children experiencing either overprotection or the traumatic incidents mentioned do not become psychotic; they either adjust normally or develop the maladjustments of neurosis or personality disorder.

Other workers have supported Mahler's view that there are at least two types of childhood schizophrenia, although it is not always clear whether the classifications are in agreement: Eisenberg (1956) supports the separation of early infantile autism from other cases of childhood schizophrenia; Goldfarb (1961) divides his cases into "organic" and "non-organic" subgroups. Clarification of this basic issue must await further study.

The central problem in making an accurate etiological formulation is the difficulty in sorting out the causes-effect relationships. Those who espouse the "psychogenetic" position point to the abnormal attitudes and feelings of the mother toward the schizophrenic child. Szurek notes that: "We have observed mothers speak about their own child who is present, as if he were absent or as if he could not understand. We have also observed many parents who during visits on the ward, show much more interest in other children than in their own child, who then often also shows little or no interest in his own parents." But which is cause and which is effect? Erikson considers that the basic defect is more likely to be in the child than in its parent. He questions the role of maternal rejection or special circumstances, noting that these children may very early or subtly fail to return the mother's glance, smile, and touch, showing an initial reserve which makes the mother, in turn, unwittingly withdraw.

Reports on psychopathology in the families of schizophrenic children vary widely. Kaufman and others studied the parents of 80 schizophrenic children and classified them according to four major types of maladjustment. Their report suggests that all the parents were, in one way or another, mentally abnormal, as none is included in a normal category. Eisenberg and Kanner, observing "the emotional frigidity in the typical autistic family" suggests "a dynamic experiential in the genesis of the disorder in the child." But they admit that some 10 per cent of the parents do not fit the stereotype (refrigerator parents) and that those who do have raised other normal, or in any event, non-psychotic children. Moreover, they add that similarly frigid parents are seen who do not give rise to autistic progeny.

Other workers, however, find a much higher incidence than 10 per cent of parents who do not fit the stereotype, and who could in fact be considered normal and well-adjusted individuals. Several writers (Peck and others; Bender and Grugett) have noted the great variety of personalities among the parents of schizophrenic children. Bender and Grugett compared the "emotional climate" of the families of 30 schizophrenic children with those of 30 disturbed non-schizophrenics. Each family was evaluated independently and, by over-all judgment, designated as providing better-than-average, average, or poor emotional climate. The two groups of children are compared in Table 1. It can be seen that the family environments of the schizophrenic children were, in general, superior to those of the children with other disturbances.

TABLE 1

Family Climate	Schizophrenic	Non-schizophrenic
Poor	8	23
Average	14	7
Above Average	8	0

Experience with a considerable number of normal families of childhood schizophrenics has convinced many workers, including this writer, that at least a large proportion of these children are born with the disorder. Talking with the mothers, the fathers, and the normal siblings, it is clear that the environments of many such children has been reasonably normal and healthful, and could in no conceivable way have produced such severe maladjustment. It is further apparent that these children from very early times failed to respond to the mother in a normal way—that they indeed, to quote Erikson, "fail to return the mother's glance, smile and touch." Such a reaction is puzzling and disturbing to the mother, who often becomes discouraged and distressed over trying to reach the child. Certainly the relationship is abnormal—but such a child would never relate normally with any mother.

On the other hand, there is a large group of childhood schizophrenics who do have psychotic parents, and whose life experience from earliest times has unquestionably been severely disorganized. Bender (in her 1953 study and later with Grugett) reports that approximately 40 per cent of childhood schizophrenics have at least one schizophrenic parent; and Shaw, in an unpublished study of 50 schizophrenic children, has concurred, in finding that 42 per cent had at least one schizophrenic parent. (Yet over 30 per cent of these children had families in which both parents were considered entirely normal.) Meyers and Goldfarb found, in a study of 28 schizophrenic children, that 30 per cent had at least one schizophrenic parent.

Kallman considers childhood schizophrenia, like adult schizophrenia, to be genetically determined. His studies of adult schizophrenic twins are well known. In brief, he has found in adult schizophrenia that the concordance (percentage of affected co-twins) is 80 per cent in identical twins and only 14 per cent in fraternal twins. These findings have led most persons to believe that adult schizophrenia has a strong genetic component

(Kallman, 1952). In a study of "preadolescent" schizophrenia, Kallman and Roth examined 17 pairs of identical and 35 pairs of fraternal twins, in which at least one member was schizophrenic. The concordance rate was 88 per cent in the identical twins, as compared with 22 per cent in the fraternal twins, figures which agree closely with Kallman's previous findings in adult schizophrenics. Twin studies are always more convincing, however, if one can observe twin pairs who have been reared separately, but cases of schizophrenic twin children who have been reared separately are of course rare. Kallman (1952) has reported findings on only one pair of identical and four pairs of fraternal schizophrenic twins who were reared separately. All four of the fraternal twin pairs reared separately were discordant as to childhood schizophrenia; that is, only one of each member of the pair had childhood schizophrenia. In the case of the identical twins reared separately, one twin became schizophrenic in childhood while the other developed schizophrenia after adolescence, at the age of 18 years.

The evidence, therefore, is strong that childhood schizophrenia is, at least in part, hereditarily determined. The mode of inheritance is not known, and there is as yet insufficient data for accurate genetic analysis. Because there is no apparent clear-cut pattern of inheritance, it seems doubtful that the disorder is caused by a single dominant gene or a single pair of recessive genes; it is more likely that a polygenic system is involved. Those who support the "environmental" view of etiology point out, with some justification, that the presence of schizophrenia in other members of the family is no evidence for genetic transmission, as the disorder may have been environmentally imparted through the child's experience of having lived with a schizophrenic parent. However, as will be discussed below, it would seem unlikely that the basic psychopathology of childhood schizophrenia can be a learned phenomenon.

When one has come to some understanding of the meaning of body image, and has witnessed its distortion in a schizophrenic child, one's conception about the etiology of this disorder is somewhat clarified. For it is difficult to conceive that such a disorder, such a total absence of the integrative function of the nervous system, could be a learned defect. Most of these children have had the usual opportunities to perceive and explore their environment, to see and hear and touch, to feel hunger and its satiation, to know anger and frustration, to be comforted. Furthermore, it is known from the study of other kinds of disturbed children that early neglect, deprivation, and rejection lead to other kinds of disorders—to neurosis, psychopathy, and personality disorder; such early experiences do not produce the complete disruption of ego functioning which is designated *childhood schizophrenia*. Such a dysfunction must almost certainly be a disorder contained within the physiology of the central nervous system, a defect of integration, an inability to call out from stored information the necessary associations and patterns by which the individual can "test" reality and think logically.

Thus, this writer aligns himself with those who believe that childhood schizophrenia is primarily a "biological" disorder. It is probably genetically determined, although evidence for its inheritance is far from complete. This is perhaps one of the most fascinating areas of child psychiatry, and one in which research can be most rewarding. For the study of this disease pertains not only to the one child or less per thousand who has childhood schizophrenia, but also to adult schizophrenia, that most severe of the major mental diseases of adults, which fills more hospital beds than any other single disease.

PSYCHOPATHOLOGY

Although various workers emphasize this or that aspect of the total psychopathologic picture, most agree that the schizophrenic child presents a major disruption in ego functioning, with autistic, isolating behavior and an inability to differentiate between reality and non-reality.

Rabinovitch has noted that schizophrenic children, like schizophrenic adults, may present a multiplicity of symptoms which vary with age of onset, developmental level, the nature of the defense mechanisms, and the child's early experience. Rabinovitch further states, however, that a core disturbance, which he has termed "dysidentity," is common to all cases regardless of behavior. This is the child's inability to experience a clear-cut percept and to appreciate with clarity the reality of identities, boundaries, and limits. Experiencing subjectively no sharply defined limit to his boundaries, it is as though the child merges diffusely with the objects in his environment. This formulation finds wide agreement and perhaps expresses most succinctly the consensus as to the basic psychopathology of this disease.

Elizabeth Norman has described with clarity and insight the distortions in thinking which schizophrenic children evidence. She notes that they are often intensely attentive to particular aspects or details of objects, such as the color of a toy or the small parts of a doll, exploring the object over and over again. She notes, however, the strong impression that something important is left out: What appears to be missing is the function and the use of the object and all that is related affectively to it. The child seems unable to integrate all the aspects of the object into a whole which has particular uses and functions. According to Norman the behavior of these children toward objects suggests a failure of generalization with great stress on particulars—a concrete rather than conceptual way of thinking even at this perceptual level. They seem to put their objects together, detail by detail and property by property. She points out that, for normal functioning, one glance at a desk, for example, can show us a hard solid thing which obviously has a back and underneath surface, no matter at what exact distance it is seen, or at what angle. For the schizophrenic child this experience does not occur adequately. The child often seems to fail to achieve objects as such, and is left with a color or a shape or a number of details poorly organized as a whole.

Piaget has described how the normal child begins, in the first year of life, to develop a concept of the world about him through the integration of his remembered experiences with objects and with people. It is this integrative capacity which appears to be missing or defective in the schizophrenic child. He can perceive, he can remember, but he cannot integrate his perceptions and his memories into an organized, persisting, and reality-sustaining environment.

Thus, the schizophrenic child is constantly perplexed, and totally without stability. Often he cannot even differentiate between the animate and the inanimate worlds. Norman has described how one little girl tried to dismember the examiner just as she did her doll, making no distinction between the live person and the toy. Schizophrenic children will often attempt to move other persons around physically just as they do toys, use another's hands as tools to grasp objects, walk over people, or jump onto them as though they were a part of the room or the furniture.

In a like manner, the schizophrenic child may not differentiate his own body from other objects in the environment. He may be observed playing with a part of his own body, such as a hand or a foot, just as if it were another toy. Norman described such behavior in one little girl who kept pulling her hand in and out of her sleeve with rapt attention; "When one hand became the object of visual attention, she treated it as part of the external visual world."

These children may evidence their confusion between self and others by sometimes regarding their own speech as coming from someone else. One boy, speaking of his toy, said, "It's a big soldier." Then he immediately followed this with, "I heard someone say it's a big soldier." Use of incorrect pronouns is common among schizophrenic children, evidencing further their confusion of identity. A schizophrenic child may often refer to himself as "he" or "you." Also, he may frequently speak of himself by using his own first name: "Carl wants to see it."

The concepts of body image and ego boundaries are difficult to grasp. The normal individual takes for granted his own ego identity, and the notion that some persons have difficulty differentiating themselves from their environment is a strange and perhaps incomprehensible idea. Yet, reflection will disclose that a certain amount of integrated information must have been utilized at some time in man's development in order for them to know such things as whether a stimulus comes from inside or outside of their bodies, or approximately how far they must be from an object in order to reach out and touch it. The psychoanalyst, Paul Schilder, has probably contributed most to the understanding of the processes by which the body image is formulated, and it was his wife, Lauretta Bender, who early (1947) pointed out that this function is impaired in childhood schizophrenia.

The experiences and sensations which go into the formation of body image would include the earliest experiences of the child, perhaps even those occurring before birth. These include the kinesthetic and visceral sensations which constantly impinge upon the central nervous system, the surface sensations such as touch and pain, and the special sensations (chiefly sight, hearing, and smell) which scan the surrounding environment and which function in teaching the child about distance and space. The affective states, too, contribute to body image: neurotic excitement, fear and anger, satiety and hunger, comfort, discomfort, and the feelings of tension and relaxation. All of these experiences are incorporated somehow into a child's brain, are stored, form patterns and associations, acquire meanings, and are utilized to give the child, and later the adult, an organized and meaningful picture of a world which has some stability, some continuity; a world in which the individual is himself a discrete part, and a part which he knows, with which he is familiar, and which he can differentiate with certainty from the surrounding environment.

Such a world is missing for the schizophrenic child. For him there is little certainty, much confusion; he literally does not know who he is, and the anxiety and anguish within him is often total and overwhelming. The misery of these children is enormous, the disintegration and disorganization of their functioning being at times complete. Nothing can reach them, nothing can comfort them, and to be faced with such a child in the midst of one of his panic attacks or rage outbursts is a helpless and frustrating experience.

SYMPTOMS

It may be helpful here to consider briefly the behavior of some typical childhood schizophrenics:

Billy, age ten, appears to believe that he is an automobile tire, periodically lies on the floor in a deflated and motionless heap until someone "pumps him up." Gary, age nine, identifies with a steam radiator, hisses all day and stares for hours at "other" radiators or at the pipes that supply them. Alfred, now adolescent, continues (as he has done since early child-hood) to converse, in a language meaningless to others, with the storage cabinets standing in the hospital corridors. Margaret, age 11, never speaks at all, but cowers silently in a corner of the room or the playground, whimpering when another child comes too near her. Robert, when left alone, repeats "doughnuts, doughnuts" endlessly—showing no interest at all in actual doughnuts when these are given to him. Jack, obsessed with the idea of infancy and the feelings of a baby, goes about for days saying "prickly heat, prickly heat" and writing these words on the walls and furniture.

Eisenberg (1957) considers that there are two cardinal symptoms pathognomonic of childhood schizophrenia. These are: 1) extreme self-isolation present in the early years of life, and 2) obsessive insistence on the preservation of sameness. Not all authors would agree that these two symptoms are restricted to childhood schizophrenia; however, when occurring in combination with other evidence of illogical or dereistic think-ing, these symptoms are strongly suggestive of childhood schizophrenia. The autistic behavior (self-isolation) and the constant attempts to preserve sameness in the environment should probably be regarded as restitutive at-tempts, which are reactions to the basic psychopathology.

The major manifestations of childhood schizophrenia may be classi-fied under four headings, the first three occurring with varying severity in all cases and the fourth being seen infrequently. The disorders occur in (1) speech and language, (2) relationship, (3) emotion, (4) physiological function.

1. *Disorders of speech and language* include the severest form of lan-guage disorder, mutism, which is common in schizophrenic children. In many, there is a history of some speech having been present in the earlier years, but disappearing as the child's illness became more severe. Many of these cases probably never resume speech, although sufficient long-term data has not yet been compiled for a conclusive statement. Other children who are not totally mute fail to use language for communication. Such children have a private language consisting of generally unintelligible vocal-izations. They may repeat words which are spoken to them, in an echolalic manner and without any real communication. Mutism may be transient, but when speech returns it is seldom normal.

There is much language distortion, with primitive forms—such as shortened sentences and the use of single words or the minimum number of words needed to impart meaning, much like the language of a baby who is just learning to speak. The speech may have other uses than communica-tion: There is much word play, with repetitious or sing-song verbalization of a word or a phrase. Obsessive preoccupation with a particular object may thus be verbally expressed, and the child may continue for many months with this preoccupation.

The language disorder of schizophrenic children is the verbal reflection of their total disorder in thinking, of their inability to organize and to integrate information into patterns of logical thought. Normal language is a highly abstract function, a conventional system in which particular sounds have particular meanings. Words represent objects, things, functions, ideas; and all these complex associations between the sounds and their meanings must be learned. This level of abstraction is too much for the ordinary schizophrenic, who does well to learn the simplest, most concrete meanings of words, such as the names of colors and of familiar objects. On the other hand, some schizophrenic children exhibit amazing capacities for abstraction in certain areas: one schizophrenic child who is now a young adult is a brilliant mathematician, a recognized authority in his particular subspecialty; yet he has no notion of how long an hour is.

Just as schizophrenic children cannot use language adequately, neither can they use speech correctly for communication. Speech and language are distinct processes, speech being the sounds which are produced, language being the communication system, the content. We human beings communicate not only in words themselves; by such subtleties as inflection, pitch, and tone of voice, we impart particular meanings and emotions. Normal children learn all the complex, subtle variations in the use of speech through imitation. The schizophrenic child fails to learn these speech functions, and his failure imparts a peculiarity to his speech that is puzzling and at times bizarre. Goldfarb and others, studying the speech patterns of schizophrenic children, found that most or all of them showed deviations in the quality, volume, pitch, duration, rhythm, intonation, articulation, and use of appropriate facial and body reinforcements. In effect, then, schizophrenic children were unable to convey mood or emotion by the sounds of their voices. Goldfarb's study questions the widely held view that schizophrenic children lack mood and emotion; it is more likely that the observers are reporting the absence of communication signals that are normally expected—the very ones which carry meanings for normals.

Perhaps the most striking feature of the speech of many schizophrenic children is the high pitch, with a rising inflection at the end of each statement or sentence, making everything sound like a question. For example, the child may say "Turn off the light" with a rising inflection, which gives the utterance a questioning, uncertain quality: "Turn off the light?"

2. *Disorders of relationship* are always found. One of the most obvious and constant features of childhood schizophrenia is the lack of attach-

ment to other people. Mothers may complain that the child "looks at me as if I'm not there," or that he "talks right through me." These mothers, who are puzzled and distressed, may develop an inordinate amount of guilt and search desperately in themselves for the defect which has made their children so unresponsive. Many of these mothers are patient and devoted, and literally contribute most of their waking hours to the needs of their schizophrenic children.

The inability to relate does not mean that the child does not form any attachment to another person. He may in fact form a very close attachment to his mother, or to a therapist, or to any person who has become familiar and who has been able to provide some constancy in his environment. But this is not a normal interpersonal relationship; rather it is an intense narcissistic attachment which has a characteristic distant, vacuous quality.

3. *Disorders of emotion* may cause violent behavioral outbursts; anything can set these outbreaks off. Schizophrenic children seem always on the edge of panic or of all-consuming rage, and their emotions appear constantly ready to overwhelm them. Their wish for "sameness" in the environment, if frustrated, can set them weeping, shouting, kicking, and striking out, so that they completely "fall apart." Nothing can be done to help them, and each outbreak has to run its course, its course frequently being quite prolonged. Kanner (1944) has observed that changes of routine, of furniture arrangement, of a pattern, of the order in which everyday acts are carried out can drive them to despair. Obviously, their children's outbursts can also drive the parents to despair.

The outbreaks of rage of schizophrenic children are qualitatively different from those seen in undisciplined and neurotic children, the distinctive quality being a lack of integration and direction. Since the outbursts are similar to the rages seen in impulsive, brain-damaged children, they have sometimes caused the examining physician to suspect temporal-lobe seizures. The anxiety attacks, too, differ from those of the neurotic children, in that the attacks are more all-pervasive. A "flattened" affect has been said to be one of the common features of schizophrenia, but in many schizophrenic children the affect is anything but flattened, the affective response being heightened into tantrum. However, as these children grow older, their personalities may become flattened, perhaps as a defensive mechanism, a careful avoidance of involvement with or affective response toward anything. Some of these persons, however, who walk a narrow path between overwhelming anxiety and total withdrawal, manage surprisingly well.

4. *Disorders in physiological function* include, mainly, abnormal patterns of motility and of vasovegetative functions. Many child schizophren-

ics exhibit a characteristic motor pattern which is graceful and dainty, almost birdlike in character, so that they seem to be flitting rather than walking. Their touch is light and delicate, and when one holds such children on his lap there is a fragile and evanescent feeling about them. They conform easily to the configuration of the person who holds them, feeling almost as if they would melt into the holder's body or evaporate into the air. This is especially true of the very young schizophrenic children, those five years of age or younger. Bender (1947) has described the motility in childhood schizophrenia as follows:

"One can obtain complete motor compliance from the child by contact through the palmar surfaces and induce *cerea flexibilitas*, or push the child about at will. The child's motor compliance suggests a strong need or impulse to be completely dependent upon the body of another person which can be used to control his own disorganizing impulses and undetermined ego boundaries." The younger schizophrenic child may become largely preoccupied with motor play which is composed of what Bender describes as "many inter-revolving systems of reflex activity." Efforts to get the child to conform to a pattern of life about him by acquired habit patterns may give the impression of awkwardness and dissociative behavior, but when left to his own devices, he carries on endless rhythmic and graceful dancing behavior with changing tempos. Bender further describes various impulsive activities of a darting nature, plus an uncertain control of the facial muscles, which leads to grimaces (often associated with oral mannerisms), and vocal sounds (which may be repetitiously employed in a kind of complex motor and vocal play). Such behavior has sometimes dubiously been interpreted as hallucinatory.

Rachman and Berger's recent controlled observations support the findings earlier described first by Bender (1953) and later by Goldfarb (1961) that both whirling behavior and deficient postural control are relatively common in schizophrenic children.

Disorders of autonomic functioning have often been described in the schizophrenic child. Actually they are not frequent, probably occurring in less than one-fourth of the cases. The child may appear excessively pale and may flush or perspire easily. He may have cold, almost cyanotic extremities, and his lips may appear blue, with a circumoral pallor, making him resemble a child who has been swimming in cold water. Bender (1947) has observed that such a child may react to a severe infection with little or no fever or may show excessive febrile response to slight illness. Other physiological dysfunctions include abnormalities in the usual rhythmic patterns of daily living, such as sleep and eating patterns. Schizophrenic children may sleep or wake at odd hours, their dietary habits and appetites show unusual fluctuations, and they often appear undernourished. Anorexia is not unusual; one severely schizophrenic boy in a state hospital periodically refuses to eat or drink altogether, and requires admission to the medical ward for gastric tube feeding.

PSYCHOLOGICAL TESTING

The psychologist who insists on a child's producing a valid, scoreable performance on tests may be baffled, because the schizophrenic child does not perform in a consistent way. In fact, inconsistency is perhaps the single most characteristic feature of psychological testing in childhood schizophrenia. On the Wechsler Intelligence Scale for Children (WISC), for example, the child may fail to answer several questions, then will off-handedly answer correctly one that is at a much more difficult level. On the object-assembly subtest (a kind of jigsaw puzzle) he may play aimlessly with the pieces, then suddenly, when the allotted time is almost up, or after having failed easier figures, he may quickly and dexterously fit the pieces together.

The Bender Gestalt drawings may be equally haphazard and diffuse. Often the figures overlap or merge into one another. Bender (1952) stresses the uncertainty of boundaries in the schizophrenic's drawings, and the tendency for figures to be repeated, enlarged, gone over several times, sometimes with elaborations and embellishments. She notes: "The total product makes a pattern itself with a great deal of fluidity based upon vertical movement."

Drawings of human figures often reveal a similar fluidity of movement, a graceful, airy, evanescent quality. Body boundaries are uncertain, revealing the child's own uncertainty. Often the productions are bizarre, but bizarreness is by no means limited to schizophrenic children.

Psychological testing seldom contributes more than a confirmation of the diagnostic impression, and in some cases even this is lacking. In the structured, circumscribed situation of psychological tests, many schizophrenic children are able to perform better than in a more free, spontaneous atmosphere. Nevertheless, testing of schizophrenic children should be attempted, as tests often provide a measure of the degree of disturbance.

DIFFERENTIAL DIAGNOSIS

In differentiating schizophrenia, one must consider the following: (1) Deafness; (2) Aphasia; (3) Mental retardation; (4) Brain damage; (5) Psychoneurosis; (6) Personality disorder with severe behavior disturbances.

1. *Deafness.* Many deaf or partially deaf children, because of their isolation, tend to become autistic. Some are mute, being unable to learn

language. Diagnosis of deafness in young children is sometimes difficult, especially if the diagnosis is not specifically considered. Even then, it may not be easy, although an experienced audiometrician can usually determine at least the relative degree of deafness. Clinically, one tries to determine whether the child can hear sounds, especially ones which should be familiar even to retarded children, such as his own name and "mother." Care must be taken that the child is not in a position to read lips, or even to see when the examiner is speaking, as some of these children are quite skilled at the use of non-auditory cues. Heffernan found that, of 50 children referred for suspected deafness, 15 were "pseudo-deaf" (that is, they appeared deaf but could actually hear), while another 5 could not be adequately assessed. Of these 20, 12 were thought to be autistic with evidence of brain damage, mental retardation, or probable schizophrenia. The probable schizophrenics showed characteristic behavior quite different from that of children with simple deafness. They were unresponsive to people, obsessively interested in inanimate objects, and would spend long periods stepping on pipes, spinning coins, stroking fur, rocking, rotating, or walking in tiny circles. The author notes of this group: "Their hearing behavior was characterized by inconsistency. Testing them was extremely difficult. They would sit in the testing room with the sound (audiometer) turned up to pain-level intensity without batting an eyelid. Half an hour later, sitting in the office, they would turn and look at the telephone when it rang." Thus, there are some schizophrenic children who are referred as being deaf, and vice-versa. The differentiation is usually obvious if one pays particular attention to it.

2. *Aphasia.* A child with severe aphasia, like the deaf child, is relatively isolated and may withdraw into an autistic pattern, especially when his difficulties have been compounded by severe early neglect or rejection. Such a child can be a diagnostic puzzle, because he relates poorly, is apathetic and unresponsive. He is sometimes mute or may have a private language which he uses in an autistic or repetitive way. On the other hand, a child who is actually schizophrenic may be diagnosed as aphasic. One such child, who had been seen in three language clinics because of mutism, had been so diagnosed. Attempts at speech therapy had been without effect. When seen by the psychiatrist, the diagnosis of schizophrenia was clear. The child's parents were extremely warm and intelligent, and, in such an environment, no degree of aphasia could have produced the severe disturbance and withdrawal which this child exhibited. Additionally, he had the characteristic motility patterns described earlier.

3. *Mental Retardation.* Some schizophrenic children, who function at an intellectually retarded level, are mistakenly diagnosed as retarded. Training schools for the mentally retarded usually contain a few cases of

childhood schizophrenia. Since such children perform unevenly on psychological tests, an accurate estimate of their intellectual capacity is impossible. Many of them score in the defective range, and for practical purposes they are mentally retarded. However, one usually finds evidence that they are capable of higher functioning: They may readily answer a difficult question after having missed several easier ones, or, after playing in a disorganized way with the blocks in the first three block designs, they may suddenly become interested in the fourth one and quickly reproduce it. Many schizophrenics, being concrete in their thinking, cannot grasp the concept on certain of the standard questions testing abstract thought, such as: "In what way are a peach and a pear alike?" Thus, in the area of abstract thinking, they are usually definitely retarded.

Just as schizophrenia is often mistaken for simple retardation, the reverse is also true, especially in families where the retarded children have received unsympathetic treatment and have become socially isolated. Such children may present an autistic picture difficult to distinguish from that of the schizophrenic: They sit quietly in a corner for hours, engaging in repetitive motor or verbal play; they exhibit silly laughter or uncontrollable weeping; their emotions may be incomprehensible. Such children sometimes require prolonged study before one can understand what processes are involved in their behavior. When a relationship has been established with such children, and when they have become motivated to learn and to perform, it becomes apparent that they do not have the extreme disorganization of schizophrenia.

4. *Brain Damage.* Like the others in this list, the brain-damaged child is more likely to simulate schizophrenia if he has experienced traumatic and neglectful early handling. He may exhibit emotional lability, diffuse or erratic responses, an inordinate need for consistency in the environment, and autism. However, most brain-damaged children should not be confused with schizophrenics. As will be seen in the chapter on Brain damage (Chapter 8), the clinical picture is usually of a quite different nature, with hyperresponsiveness to the environment rather than autism.

5. *Psychoneurosis.* Severely neurotic children may show behavior which in some ways resembles that of the schizophrenic child and, conversely, schizophrenic children may form neurotic symptoms and defenses restitutively. In a child who demonstrates the whole gamut of neurotic symptoms, with severe anxiety, obsessive-compulsive, phobic, and depressive symptoms, schizophrenia should be strongly suspected, but the diagnosis rests on the demonstration of the basic core disturbance. The differentiation between obsessive-compulsive versions and schizophrenia with obsessive-compulsive defenses may be difficult, and Despert has emphasized that this is done on the basis of the adequacy of reality-testing. The

neurotic child is aware that his compulsions are "foolish," despite his inability to control them.

An active fantasy life is seen in many normal and neurotic children and can include elaborate and organized systems, such as imaginary playmates. This is often considered a "break with reality," which it is not. The child knows that his fantasies are not real, but he may not readily admit this realization to an intruder. Schizophrenic children also fantasy, but they usually are less able to distinguish fabrication from reality. Their fantasies are often more freely verbalized than those of other children.

Common in childhood schizophrenia, mutism is sometimes seen in deaf, aphasic, and mentally retarded children, as well as in neurotics who refuse to talk (Miller). The latter form has been termed "elective" mutism (Pustrom and Speers).

Withdrawal is an ill-defined symptom which seems to mean avoidance of social communication. This is seen in varying severity in certain children of all diagnostic categories. More a personality trait than a symptom, it develops in response to many intense feelings—including resentment, hostility, feelings of rejection, depression, and low self-esteem. It is common in schizophrenia, but the majority of children presenting such behavior are not schizophrenic.

6. *Personality Disorder with Severe Behavior Disturbances.*   Bizarre, unusual, primitive, and regressed behavior may appear in severely neurotic, brain-damaged, or schizophrenic children, and particularly in children with severe personality disorders. They include such activities as mutilation of animals, food fads, and bizarre vocalization (such as shrieking, wild laughter), repetitive sounds (such as clucking, hissing, and snorting—which may be vocal tics). An example of extreme behavioral aberration is that of a 10-year-old boy who would kick younger children without provocation, laugh aloud in the classroom when nothing was apparently funny, and urinate in the corner of the classroom. Once, on the way to school he picked up a baby duckling which some children had found lying dead on the ground, chewed a hole in its abdomen, and ate some of the intestines. Obviously severely disturbed, this boy came from a primitive and rejecting home with a brutal, alcholoic father; he was depressed and without motivation or self-esteem, but was not schizophrenic. He verbalized his feelings toward his parents and about himself, recognized the abnormality of his behavior, and even had some insight into its meaning. His thinking was logical, and there was no uncertainty of identity.

In the preceding discussion of the disorders which may be confused with childhood schizophrenia, it should be noted that the experience of the children in most cases included abnormal early upbringing. That the schizophrenic child, on the other hand, may come from a normal family, can at times be a major point in the differential diagnosis. Differential diagnosis is not always easy, however, and cases are by no means rare in which competent psychiatrists and psychologists disagree over whether or not the child is schizophrenic. Nor is the question an academic one. Treatment and goals of therapy are quite different—for example, in aphasia and schizophrenia. Sometimes trials of therapy are useful, and may be combined with diagnostic evaluation. Here, the help of special-education teachers is invaluable.

TREATMENT

At present there is no therapy which will cure the disordered thinking, which is the basic dysfunction of childhood schizophrenia. Whatever the treatment, the schizophrenic child remains schizophrenic. However, this does not mean that nothing can be done, and in fact there is a great deal that can be done for him to relieve the symptoms and to effect some improvement in adjustment. Although the treatment goals are limited, therapy is well rewarded in most cases. Bender (1947) considers that treatment should be aimed at: (1) Relieving anxiety; (2) Strengthening the defenses; (3) Stimulating maturation. To effect these aims is a long-term process. The approaches are several, and depend on the family situation as well as on the child's own capacities and needs.

The first need is for an environment which is relatively constant and not overly demanding of the child. Sometimes this environment can be provided at home, sometimes not. Many cases require hospitalization or placement in a long-term group setting. Whatever the setting, those with whom the children have daily contact must try at all times to be patient, warm, supportive, and sensitive to the children's feelings. In such an atmosphere these children often improve remarkably: Their anxiety lessens, their panic ceases, and many are able to become involved in organized activities and educational programs.

Psychotherapy is usually helpful, and it is reassuring for the children to come to a familiar office, where they sit or play with the familiar therapist for two, three, or four scheduled hours each week. The psychotherapy should generally be of the type known as "supportive," and non-interpretive (interpretive therapy being definitely contraindicated). Psychotherapy consists mainly in re-educating and reassuring the patient about his identity and his relationships with his environment. Inquiry into his feelings about his disorder is helpful for planning of therapy, but not for interpretation to the patient.

Des Lauriers considers that the essential function of the therapist in treatment of childhood schizophrenia is to "lend" the child his own ego. The therapist becomes, in a sense, a part of the child's ego, and the part that is most consistent, dependable, and sustaining. He performs functions which the child is unable to perform, directing the child in the laborious process of learning how to live in a social world. The therapist must be available whenever he is needed, and this can be most wearing and demanding, but often he is the only person who can relieve the child's panic. The child knows that his therapist will try patiently to understand what is causing his anxiety, and thus the child will usually talk to the therapist, seeking to explain his feelings; whereas, with others when he becomes panicky, he only screams the louder.

One small boy, for example, was having frequent and uncontrollable panic attacks. After much careful questioning, the therapist learned that the cause of his anxiety was "the wheels." Further observation disclosed that, whenever the child saw a wheel spinning (such as a wagon wheel on a television show, or a wheel on a toy truck), he would gaze fascinated at it, as if mesmerized, closing out the surrounding world; then, in a sense of dissolution, he would panic. The therapist carefully explained to the boy that he must not look at the wheels, and gradually, the child became "trained" to avert his gaze whenever he saw a turning wheel.

Another boy, whose panics were caused by clothes being too tight around his wrists and neck, learned to avoid tight clothing. Another was upset by the loud voice of one of the counselors, a jovial, friendly man who happened to talk and laugh quite loudly. The child interpreted the loudness as aggression, and it was therefore carefully explained to him that, when the man was smiling, it meant that he was not angry. The boy learned to approach this man and ask, "You're smiling, aren't you?" whereupon the man would always smile broadly and reassure the boy.

The therapist's main function, then, may be to work with the specific uncertainties which these children have, such as feelings of dissolution, concern about the environment and about their own body images, and concern about other identities. This requires that they be told or reassured many times about such elementary things as their own names, who they are, where they are, whose office is next door, and what is down the hall. One small boy, who would often inquire plaintively "Subbasement?" (referring to a hallway in the building which was below the basement level), had to be certain that the subbasement was still there, and his question would require that somebody take him by the hand to lead him down to the subbasement. Here he would walk slowly along, with his hand lightly touching the wall; then, satisfied that the subbasement was indeed still there, he could be taken back to the ward. If his question were ignored, he would go into a panic.

Gradually, painstakingly, the child can be "habilitated" to live in the outside world. The process is not unlike teaching a mechanical boy how to be a real person, or, rather, how to pretend that he is a real person. He must be taught how to act appropriately, how to avoid saying silly things, how to know when people are joking and when they are serious. One little boy learned, after much instruction, that he must not talk about several different things at once, in the disorganized way that is so characteristic of these children. He learned well, and would, in the middle of a meaningless sentence, stop, put his hands over his mouth, and say, "Oh, I changed the subject."

Some schizophrenic children learn so well that they are able to go to school, to play with other children, and to perform so much like normal persons that only those close to them know that they live in a private world.

In some cases the treatment program should include work with the parents, many of whom feel inordinately guilty over their child's illness. Having no notion of its etiology, they feel responsible, and believe that they have failed as parents. Their feelings create complex tensions, resentments, and misunderstandings between themselves and the child, as well as in other aspects of their home life. The family can be helped if the therapist will devote some time and attention to exploring their feelings and to helping them understand and work out their attitudes in regard to the child's disorder. This is important whether the child remains at home or is institutionalized. The guilt may be even greater if the child has to be placed away from home, and the home atmosphere can be improved and made ready for his eventual return if the parents are given some help.

Peck and others have reported gratifying results from a program of group treatment for the parents of schizophrenic children. The authors note that the most common initial attitude among the parents is deep confusion. The parents are totally puzzled by their children and many have traveled from clinic to clinic or from doctor to doctor, often to receive uncertain or conflicting opinions which have added to their confusion. The parents were much disturbed by the frequent social pressures which they experienced outside the home, as for example, when taking their children into stores or out on the streets where their bizarre behavior provoked much attention and often considerable fear or resentment. These parents seem to have been helped a great deal by the group situation, in realizing that other people have to face the same problems, and on learning from others how best to handle these problems. The majority of these schizophrenic children have been helped, some to a remarkable degree, through their parents' increased insight and the diminution of tension in the home.

However, one cannot generalize about the approach to parents of schizophrenic children, because of the wide diversity among them. These families run the gamut from thoroughly intact to grossly psychotic. With the former, one can usually give a realistic appraisal, and expect them to work out successfully their guilt and misconceptions. With schizophrenic or "borderline" parents, the problem is complex; often, one parent is relatively intact, and must be enlightened to help guide and protect the more disturbed parent in their joint decisions regarding the child.

The attitude of therapeutic nihilism which existed during the first decade after childhood schizophrenia came to be clinically recognized has been replaced by much interest in trying various therapies, coupled with some optimism. Ekstein and others, in their extensive survey of the literature, found that in the decade from 1949 to 1958, reports concerned with therapy made up 40 per cent of all the literature on childhood schizophrenia, whereas in the previous decade the figure was only 4 per cent. The authors caution, however, that "The powerful optimism which pervades the literature concerning the treatment of a number of schizophrenic children is as yet not supported by evidence concerning the prognosis for the whole group."

Nor is it likely that any therapy will evoke a major success until the basic problem of etiology is clarified. For this reason, approaches directed toward evincing aberrations in metabolism or neurophysiologic function would seem to present the most hopeful avenues of research. The few attempts thus far made (Shaw and others, 1959, 1960; Syner and Shaw) on amino acid metabolism in schizophrenic children, while producing negative results, should by no means discourage further effort; instead, they represent a bare beginning, and the areas for further study are limitless.

PROGNOSIS

Follow-up studies of schizophrenic children (Bender 1953, Eisenberg 1956, 1957) show that approximately one third make some degree of adequate social adjustment, one third remain in the community but poorly adjusted, and one third are more or less permanently institutionalized.

The best single index of prognosis is the presence or absence of useful speech at age 5. Eisenberg (1956) has reported on a follow-up study of 63 cases of "infantile autism." Thirty-one of these cases, or approximately half, had had severe language disturbances ranging from total mutism to an absence of useful speech. Eisenberg found that all but one of these made an extremely poor adjustment in adolescence. Of the 32 children who had had some useful speech, half made a "fair or good" adjustment, while the other half did poorly.

Brown also found that mutism indicated an unfavorable outcome.

Other signs of poor prognosis in Brown's study were inability to use objects
or toys for their intended functions, repetitious motor play, and severe
autism. Good prognostic signs included interest in environment, good
speech and communication, and directed aggression. Of no apparent significance to outcome were: age when therapy was begun, duration of therapy, and experience of therapist. Whether or not therapy made any difference at all was not determined.

The ultimate outlook for the schizophrenic child is that he will remain schizophrenic: Such children will never know the joy, pleasure,
happiness and love that are the privilege of normal people, and they will
often feel a deeper pain and terror than most of us human beings ever experience. Yet, with the help, guidance, and understanding of those about
them, many of them can learn to tread a cautious path of relative tranquility, to avoid the edge of panic, and to occupy themselves in productive
work.

REFERENCES

Bender, L. Childhood Schizophrenia: Clinical Study of One Hundred Schizo-
phrenic Children, Am. J. Orthopsychiatry, 17: 40, 1947.
——— Child Psychiatric Techniques, Springfield, Ill., Charles C Thomas,
1952.
——— Childhood Schizophrenia, Psychiatric Quarterly, 27: 663, 1953.
——— Twenty Years of Clinical Research on Schizophrenic Children Under
Six Years of Age, in Emotional Problems of Early Childhood, ed. G. Caplan,
New York, Basic Books, 1955.
——— and Grugett, A. E. A Study of Certain Epidemiological Factors in a
Group of Children with Childhood Schizophrenia, Am. J. Orthopsychiatry,
26: 131, 1956.
Brown, J. Prognosis from Presenting Symptoms of Preschool Children with
Atypical Development, Am. J. Orthopsychiatry, 30: 382, 1960.
Des Lauriers, A. M. The Experience of Reality in Childhood Schizophrenia,
New York, International Universities Press, 1962.
Despert, J. L. Differential Diagnosis between Obsessive-Compulsive Neurosis
and Schizophrenia in Children, in Psychopathology of Childhood, ed., P. H.
Hoch and J. Zubin, New York, Grune & Stratton, 1955, p. 240.
Eisenberg, L. The Autistic Child in Adolescence, Am. J. Psychiatry, 112: 607,
1956.
——— The Course of Childhood Schizophrenia, A.M.A. Arch. Neurol.
Psychiat., 78: 69, 1957.
——— and Kanner, L. Early Infantile Autism, 1943 to 1955, Am. J. Ortho-
psychiatry, 26: 561, 1956.
Ekstein, R., Bryant, K. and Friedman, S. Childhood Schizophrenia and Allied
Conditions, in Schizophrenia, ed. L. Bellak, New York, Logos Press, 1958.
Erikson, E. Childhood and Society, New York, W. W. Norton Co., 1950.
Federn, P. Ego Psychology and the Psychoses, ed. E. Weiss, New York, Basic
Books, 1953.

Freeman, T. Cameron, J. L., and McGhee, A., Chronic Schizophrenia, London, Tavistock Publications, 1958.

Goldfarb, W. Childhood Schizophrenia, Cambridge, Harvard University Press, 1961.

———— Braunstein, P. and Lorge, I., A Study of Speech Patterns in a Group of Schizophrenic Children, Am. J. Orthopsychiatry, 26: 544, 1956.

Heffernan, A. A Psychiatric Study of Fifty Preschool Children Referred to Hospital for Suspected Deafness, in Caplan, G., Emotional Problems of Early Childhood, New York, Basic Books, 1955.

Hendrickson, W. J. Etiology in Childhood Schizophrenia—an Evaluation of Current Views, The Nervous Child, 10: 9, 1953.

Kallman, F. J. Genetic Aspects of Psychoses, in The Biology of Mental Health and Disease, New York, Paul B. Hoeber, 1952.

———— and Roth, B. Genetic Aspects of Preadolescent Schizophrenia, Am. J. Psychiatry, 112: 599, 1956.

Kanner, L. Early Infantile Autism, J. Pediat., 25: 211, 1944.

———— Child Psychiatry, Springfield, Ill., Charles C Thomas, 1957.

Kaufman, I., Frank, T., Heims, L., Herrick, J., Reiser, D. and Willer, L. Treatment Implications of a New Classification of Parents of Schizophrenic Children, Am. J. Psychiatry, 116: 920, 1960.

Mahler, M. S. On Child Psychosis and Schizophrenia—Autistic and Symbiotic Infantile Psychosis, Psychoanalytic Study of the Child, New York, International Universities Press, 1952, Vol. 7.

McMillan, M. B. Extrascientific Influences in the History of Childhood Psychopathology, Am. J. Psychiatry, 116: 1091, 1960.

Meyers, D. and Goldfarb, W. Psychiatric Appraisal of Parents and Siblings of Schizophrenic Children, Publication No. 21, Childhood Schizophrenia Project, New York, Henry Ittleson Center for Child Research, 1961.

Miller, B. M. Communication with a Non-verbal Child, Am. J. Psychol. 20: 1, 79, 1960.

Norman, E. Reality Relationships of Schizophrenic Children, Brit. J. Med. Psychology, 24: 126, 1954.

Peck, H. B., Rabinovitch, R. D. and Cramer, J. B. A Treatment Program for Parents of Schizophrenic Children, Am. J. Orthopsychiatry, 19: 592, 1949.

Piaget, J. The Construction of Reality in the Child, New York, Basic Books, 1954.

Potter, H. W. Schizophrenia in Children, Am. J. Psychiatry, 12: 1253, 1933.

Pustrom, E., and Speers, R. W. Elective Mutism in Children, J. Amer. Acad. Child Psychiatry, 3: 287, 1964.

Rabinovitch, R. D. An Evaluation of Present Trends in Psychotherapy with Children, J. Psychiatric Social Work, 24: 11, 1954.

Rachman, S., and Berger, M. Whirling and Postural Control in Schizophrenic Children, J. Child Psychol. Psychiat., 4: 137, 1963.

Rank, B. Intensive Study and Treatment of Preschool Children Who Show Marked Personality Deviations, or "Atypical Development," and Their Parents, in Emotional Problems of Early Childhood, ed. G. Caplan, New York, Basic Books, 1955.

Rank, B. and MacNaughton, D. A Clinical Contribution to Early Ego Development, Psychoanalytic Study of the Child, New York, International Universities Press, 1950, Vol. 5.

Schilder, P., Image and Appearance of the Human Body, London, Kegan Paul, Ltd., 1925.

Shaw, C. R., Lucas, J., and Rabinovitch, R. D. Metabolic Studies in Childhood Schizophrenia: Effects of Tryptophan Loading on Indole Excretion, Arch. Gen. Psychiatry, 1: 366, 1959.

—— and Sutton, H. E. Metabolic Studies in Childhood Schizophrenia: II. Amino Acid Excretion Patterns, Arch. Gen. Psychiatry, 3: 519, 1960.

Syner, F. N. and Shaw, C. R. Effect of Schizophrenic Serum on the In Vitro of Glutamine and Gamma-Amino-butyric Acid, Comprehensive Psychiatry, 3: 309, 1962.

Szurek, S. Psychotic Episodes and Psychotic Maldevelopment, Am. J. Psychiatry, 26: 535, 1956.

7

PSYCHONEUROSIS

REPORT OF A CASE

Billy S. was first brought to the psychiatrist by his mother at the age of 8 because of progressive anxiety, extreme fearfulness, night terrors, and phobias. He had been unable to attend school for the previous eight months because of these symptoms. At home he spent most of his time with his mother or playing and reading alone in his room, although occasionally he would play with his one good friend in their clubhouse in the back yard. He had many interests, and was seldom bored. He liked to make things with his hands, was inventive and imaginative, and most of the time appeared content. However, his panic attacks and apprehension would come on at least once every day. These seemed worse when they happened in the evening at about the time his father was due to come home, or later at bedtime. Sometimes he would lie awake in his room in utter terror, imagining that there were strange creatures in the closet, or that the shadows in the room were moving, and he would hold his breath for fear that he might be heard. Sometimes, after lying rigid for a long time, he would suddenly leap out of bed and rush into his parents' room.

Billy had other symptoms which annoyed the family and which interfered with their daily living. He was phobic about dirt, germs, and bugs. He would meticulously wash his hands before each meal or whenever he had touched anything which he considered dirty. He had many somatic complaints, and would often develop a headache, or a stomach-ache, or say that he was tired, or sometimes just that "I feel bad all over."

FAMILY HISTORY

Billy's parents were both older people. Mrs. S., by a previous marriage, had a son 16 years older than Billy. She was thin, bright, cheerful, and an outgoing person. She was also rather tense and emotional, given to occasional episodes of "nervous exhaustion," and suffered from severe bronchial asthma which incapacitated her much of the time each winter. Mr. S., by contrast, was a stoical, apathetic but quick-tempered man who worked as a laborer, had few interests, limited ambition, and whose life consisted of going daily to work, eating his meals, reading the evening newspaper, and sleeping. To Billy, his father was a stranger who, for most of his hours at home, sat silently in his chair, but who would suddenly and unaccountably burst into loud and terrifying anger. Billy lived in fear of his father, could only relax when he was out of the house, and would begin to get tense as the afternoon wore on and it became time for his father to return home.

Between Billy and his mother there was a close bond. She recognized that she was overprotective, and that the relationship was abnormally close, but, as she explained to the psychiatrist, "What else can a mother do when her child is so wretched and unhappy?" The overinvolvement between them was further enchanced by the mother's asthma. During her severest attacks both she and Billy were fearful that she might die. At these times he would remain by her for hours on end, or, if she were in the hospital, he would sit alone in her room at home in a kind of deathwatch. The onset of his severe symptoms and his refusal to attend school had occurred at the time of her worst asthma attack eight months prior to his psychiatric evaluation.

PERSONAL HISTORY

Billy's birth and early development were normal. However, in his first year of life he was far from healthy. He had severe colic which continued long past the usual three-month period. His mother said that he screamed almost constantly during his first year of life, seldom being able to sleep longer than two or three hours at a time.

It was apparent early that Billy was an unusually bright child. Language developed precociously; he soon became quite verbal and used words far beyond his years. He developed an excellent sense of humor, engendered by his mother's somewhat wry, understated humor. He was sensitive, empathic, an altogether charming and appealing little boy, well liked by adults, but never at home in the society of his peers. He would spend long hours in his room with a book; here he felt comfortable and safe, and would allow nobody to interfere. By the age of seven he had expressed the concept that you couldn't "trust" anybody; he had been disappointed and hurt so often, and the solution seemed to be to stay away from people.

In school, Billy did well, but not as well as he was capable of doing. The teachers noted that he was often preoccupied, and that he could not "apply himself," so that his work was often incomplete. He was frequently late to school, and also late getting home; he dawdled, and was painfully slow in nearly everything, to the exasperation of his teachers and parents.

PRESENT ILLNESS

Things became progressively worse: His schoolwork fell off badly, his panic attacks and social isolation increased. Matters came to a head with his mother's most severe asthma attack. This coincided with the time between semesters at school, and when school resumed Billy became upset, cried, and refused to leave home. His mother, by her own account, was "too sick to insist," so Billy stayed home, and thus the pattern was set. When his mother's health improved, in about a month, she tried to get him to return to school, but he only cried and begged to stay home. The family physician eventually referred him to the psychiatric clinic, and he was admitted to the inpatient unit at age 8 years, 3 months.

COURSE IN THE HOSPITAL

At first, as was expected, Billy was terribly homesick. However, almost immediately his night terrors disappeared. The first night, he went to bed readily in his new room and went immediately to sleep, sleeping the entire night. This improvement in the night terrors persisted throughout his hospitalization, with only an occasional mild relapse. He went to the inpatient school his first day, participated readily, and it was immediately apparent that he would be a superior student. He learned a great deal during the nine months of his hospitalization and easily caught up academically, so that he was able to resume his regular class when he returned home.

Socially, Billy also made impressive gains, although not so rapidly as in the academic sphere. He never became close friends with any of the other children, and while he participated in many of the games and other activities he continued to be a peripheral member of the group. He avoided rough play, such as wrestling and football, and rarely got into a fight. However, he learned vicariously to enjoy the roughness and the fighting of the other children. This was also true of the profanity, the foul language, and the displays of anger in which many of the children indulged. At such times, Billy could be seen quietly observing, often with a small grin. He never came to use profanity himself, but he expressed to his therapist that, while the language of the other children had at first shocked and upset him, he later came to "not mind it so much."

However, if Billy could not allow his language to become "dirty," the same could not be said of his person. His meticulousness and his compulsiveness soon disappeared. He began literally to wallow in dirt, with complete abandon and obvious enjoyment; he became for a time one of the filthiest children at the Center (no minor achievement). Later, in his personal cleanliness he swung back to a middle-of-the-road policy.

For the first half of his hospitalization, Billy's relationship with his therapist was friendly but distant. The therapy hours were spent almost entirely in conversation. Unlike most younger children, Billy preferred not to, as he himself put it, "waste the time playing," so that such things as games and drawing had little part in his therapy. From the beginning, Billy wanted to talk about his symptoms. He wanted desperately to understand them, and to learn how to make them "disappear." He wanted to go straight to the heart of the matter, and could not accept that it was helpful to talk to his therapist about such things as his friends back home, his daily activities, and his roommate in the cottage. He enjoyed these conversations, and his sense of humor was superb, but it was obvious that he was dissatisfied with the therapy, that he felt he was somehow being cheated, and that his therapist was "putting him off."

The major step in Billy's treatment occurred dramatically one morning in the sixth month of his hospitalization. He had been in bed with a severe cold for three days, was to return to school that morning, but after breakfast had been found sitting alone on his bed, crying. His therapist went to see him, and, when he asked what was wrong, Billy burst into tears, and said, "Everything has gone wrong." They talked for a while. Billy began to cheer up a bit, but when the therapist suggested that perhaps he should go down to school rather than sit around in the cottage, he again burst into tears saying, "That's what the trouble was before I came here. When my nerves were like this, I didn't feel like going to school but they made me go and then I would feel worse."

At this point it was felt that Billy wanted desperately to relate with the therapist, and that his reserve was gone. It was suggested that he might like to come down to the office, and he eagerly accepted. There, he poured out all of his feelings and thoughts which he had kept to himself for so long, and told in great detail the fears that he had felt, especially toward his father, fears that his father might kidnap him, that he might do terrible things to him. He had fantasies that the father was a member of a bandit gang, and that at times when they were out driving in the car, the father intended to deliver him to this gang. He felt that his mother wanted to protect him, but that she had to give in to the father's will. He resented her for this weakness, and felt that she had failed him.

He talked of other fears, and said that all his life he had seemed to be afraid of things. "As far back as I can remember, when I heard about witches and things, I would get scared. Sometimes walking along the street if I saw a woman walking toward me I would think she was a witch. Even when people were mad at somebody else and weren't mad at me, I'd get scared, and would feel like they would turn on me next." He said that his mother had told him about his having colic as an infant, and it seemed to him that he could even remember those very early times, that he could remember screaming and being afraid and that the earliest memories he had were of being afraid.

At length, he began to talk of his great need to tell somebody about all these fears, and of the awful feeling he had that he could never be close enough to anyone to confide in them, that nobody could really understand or accept his feelings, and that, if he told somebody, they would laugh at him, or at least would not be able to understand him, so that he would feel even worse, and would be more lonely. The word that he used often was "trust," and he said that he had never felt that he could "really trust anyone." Finally I asked him (here a secret is revealed: the writer is the therapist) if he trusted me, and he looked directly at me and said with real feeling, "Not completely." I asked if he was afraid of me and he said "Sometimes. I don't entirely trust you, and I think I should tell you about things but I couldn't." I pointed out that he was telling me about many things at this time, and he said, "Yes, and you're the only person I could tell these things to. I couldn't tell them to my mother or dad or any other doctor or any other counselors, or anybody." I then told him that the fact that he could now tell me these things was a very good sign. He looked thoughtful, then smiled and said, "Maybe I can get to trust you, then it will spread to other people and then I will get better."

This interview continued for over two hours. It had obviously been a major emotional experience for Billy, and he recognized this openly, and said that he wanted to go back to his room and think about all the things that had been said. As he left, he referred to his great misery at the beginning of the morning, and said "I was sitting there on my bed feeling terrible, then I saw the door open and I saw these trousers and jacket coming in and I thought 'Here is more trouble coming.' Then I looked up and saw that it was you, and it seemed like a miracle."

When Billy said that his feeling of trust would spread to other people and that he would get better he had previewed the eventual outcome of his illness. He did indeed get better. He returned home, and to school. There were some bad times, some recurrences of the old fears, but he mastered them. He continued as an outpatient, returning for weekly visits for about a year. Then his family moved out West, partly for the climatic benefits for the mother's asthma, partly to start a new life in another community. This has worked out well, and the annual letters from the mother disclose that Billy has continued to be a good student, is maturing normally, is well liked by his peers, and plans to go to medical school. This wish of his to become a doctor is the only apparent remaining link with his therapist. He does not write, and, according to his mother, he seldom mentions Hawthorn Center. All this is as it should be. This is one of the ironies of the practice of psychiatry: Those patients whom we help the most are those that most completely abandon us. A major aspect of their health is a capacity to dissociate themselves from the troubled and unhappy past. And good therapy consists not only in being able to give the patient good treatment when he needs it, but also in being able to let him go when he no longer needs it.

INTRODUCTION

Psychoneurosis is the most frequent of the emotional disorders of children. More has been written about it perhaps than all the others combined, and it has produced the greatest amount of disagreement and controversy. Everyone who has dealt with disturbed children has seen many neurotics, and many different disciplines have contributed their special philosophies to the large and growing body of knowledge pertinent to this disorder. The neurophysiologist, the experimental psychologist, the clinical psychologist, the learning theorist, the psychoanalyst, the cultural anthropologist, the sociologist, the animal ethologist, even such unlikely specialists as the economist and the electronics engineer—all these and many others have devised or expressed or expounded upon theories of childhood neurosis.

Not all of these points of view will be dealt with here. Some, for example, learning theory and animal ethology, have already been considered. Others, the writer is not qualified to deal with. The fact that there is such a large body of theories suggests that all these groups are still in the process of trying to understand this disorder, and that so far no theory or group of theories has been devised which is adequate.

There is no sharp line between adjustment and maladjustment. Most children go through periods of "normal" maladjustment. Gesell and his coworkers have emphasized the cyclical and recurrent patterns of difficult behavior in all children, and every parent is familiar with these. But most children adapt to the new problems and new modes of life, and the intense emotional reaction is transient. Davis pointed out that following any traumatic experience there is a tendency to be preoccupied with the experience, and that this is particularly true in children. Gradually, however, the vividness of the experience diminishes, the child's preoccupation with it declines, he no longer thinks, dreams, and fantasies so intensely about the experience; repression occurs, and the normal child returns to a less troubled way of life. But the neurotic child does not. He overreacts, he continues to be troubled and preoccupied, he anticipates further difficulties, and usually finds them. The trauma may be too often repeated, and this is sometimes etiological.

How long must the disorder persist, and how intense must it be, before the child is designated as being neurotic? This may be an arbitrary designation; it often depends on the parent's degree of concern about the child. Usually, however, the presence of emotional disorder is apparent to anyone who sees the child (except perhaps his parents).

Neurosis (or psychoneurosis) is treated here, in order to facilitate communication, as though it were an entity. However, it is not an entity. In a sense, it is not even a disease, or a group of diseases. It is almost a way of life. It takes many forms, it induces a multiplicity of symptoms. It may seemingly begin at any age, its duration ranges from a brief span to a lifetime. It baffles precise definition and concise description. Yet, through all its many forms and faces there runs a common thread: unhappiness. No neurotic child or neurotic adult escapes being miserable, being unhappy, being in anguish. And his anguish is far greater than man's normal share, greater than that amount which all of us humans must experience. The misery of the neurotic, if not always with him, is at least always lurking just around the corner.

No attempt at classification of the neuroses has ever been entirely satisfactory, and no attempt to classify them will be made here. There is no more justification for classifying the cases by symptom (the most usual approach) than by, say, age of onset, or predominant defense, or intellectual level. For example, the two most frequent symptoms in neurotic children are anxiety and academic failure. Yet to lump together all cases under either of these headings would be misleading, because the children presenting these symptoms include a heterogeneous group of disorders, both neurotic and non-neurotic. Again, a widely used method of classification is to differentiate between the neurotic children who "act out" and those who "internalize" their conflict. This, too, is unsatisfactory in a great number of cases, because many children present both kinds of behavior, either together or alternately.

Therefore, while some kind of diagnostic classification is employed by nearly everyone dealing with neurotic children, the fact is that at least a sentence or two rather than a word or two must usually be employed in describing the individual case at all adequately. Thus, the case of Billy might be variously diagnosed, depending on the particular bias or orientation of the classifier, as psychoneurotic reaction, obsessive-compulsive type; or, psychoneurotic reaction, phobic type; or psychoneurosis with anxiety and depression; or school phobia; and so on. More meaningful is the description: a neurotic boy of superior intelligence with anxiety, night terrors, depression, aggression inhibition, and school refusal.

ETIOLOGY

Earlier it was emphasized that personality develops under the influence of both hereditary and experiential factors, and that these various factors are interrelated in complex and constantly changing ways. This will be the major thesis in the consideration of the causes of neurosis which follows.

It is really known what causes a neurosis? The answer in many cases is a qualified "yes." Sometimes the cause seems grossly obvious, as in the case of an eight-year-old boy whose spiteful grandmother enlisted his aid in getting rid of his mother by having him put rat poison in her coffee. Yet, even in as transparent a case as this, there are many and complex factors other than the single overt episode, and a long history of distorted experiences and relationships must be evaluated, going back to the child's earliest days. Moreover, though it is often obvious why a child is disturbed, it is seldom apparent why his disturbance takes the particular form that it does. Symptom "choice" remains largely an enigma, and must take its place along with etiology of schizophrenia as one of the major research challenges confronting psychiatry today.

There follows an examination of some of the constitutional and experiential factors known or considered to be involved in the genesis of childhood neurosis.

HEREDITY

Hereditary, or constitutional, influences have received relatively minor attention up to now in the literature and research on neurosis. The preponderance of investigation has been directed to the child's environment, to the disturbing and distorting experiences which seemed to have major influence in producing his maladjustment. Many workers have acknowledged the importance of constitutional factors, but have for the most part done little investigation of them. The prevailing attitude was well expressed by Margaret Gerard (1957) who said, in discussing the etiology of neurosis in childhood: "Probably there is a constitutional variation in an individual's capacity for ego development. On the other hand, since so many other factors enter into these formulations, and since it is impossible to evaluate the constitutional elements involved, practical analysis in symptom formation will assume that variations in innate ego strength or instinct may be possible, if not probable, but are too problematic to discuss dynamically." This generally pessimistic attitude toward elucidation of the constitutional determinants is presently undergoing some revision, and a resurgence of interest in their study and clarification is now visible, both clinically and in the research setting.

How important, actually, is heredity, in the etiology of neurosis? Is any child born neurotic? This is not known with certainty. Some children seem to be born with almost no capacity to adapt, and would fall at the extreme end of Chess's scale of "adaptable-non-adaptable" and of "intense reactor-mild reactor." Such a child, although he has apparently received excellent care, motherly affection, normal family surroundings, and has normal siblings, is nevertheless neurotic, fearful, socially maladjusted, unhappy. It could almost be said that such a child was born neurotic. Yet one cannot state with certainty that, in another family, with a different kind of "normal" care, he would not have made a good adjustment. Fries and Woolf studied the interaction between infants of different levels of motor activity and different types of mothers. They found that a very active child was much enjoyed by some mothers, who delighted in his performances; on the other hand, some mothers resented the extra attention and care demanded by an active child, and much preferred a more quiet, passive one. These studies were not sufficiently extensive to learn which if any of the children later made a poor adjustment. However, they do indicate with rare clarity an aspect of early adjustment, involving the participation of both heredity and environment. They further show that children varying over a normal range of behavioral differences may, under certain conditions, make an easy adjustment and, under other conditions, a difficult adjustment.

There is little substantial evidence that "neuroticism" per se is inherited. Studies have demonstrated an abnormally high number of neurotic persons in certain families. However, such studies usually represent a biased point of view, and do not adequately take into account the learning factor. There are, no doubt, certain behavioral traits which are strongly affected by a single gene or by a small finite number of genes, and these may predispose the individual to becoming neurotic. These would include such traits as hyperexcitability, non-adaptiveness, and so on. But the inheritance of neurosis is a problem of the sort which geneticists term "messy": It is too complex, there are too many variables and too many indeterminables. The experiments cannot even be designed, let alone carried out. Yet, given time, some of them will surely be done, better measurements of behavior will be devised, and a painstaking amount of data will be accumulated.

Meanwhile, we must continue to see the patients.

ENVIRONMENT

The basic psychopathology in neurosis is psychological conflict. It follows that, in seeking the causes, one should look for the things in the child's environment that induce conflict. Central to the problem of etiology is the condition that the conflict situation be one from which *there is no escape*. Experimental work with animals as well as clinical experience amply confirm the necessity of this inescapability factor. The neurotic child is imprisoned in his family's psychopathology. He struggles to escape, but cannot; he is caught in a web of emotional distortions and overreactions, until he becomes a part of it, and it becomes a part of him.

If there be a single factor which can be pointed to as fundamental in the environmental etiology of neurosis, it must surely be the *emotional tone* of the child's family. For it is out of this emotional tone, out of all the complex feelings and distortions in the young child's family, that come the mishandling, the rejection, the hatred, the excesses of love, of attention, of protection, and disappointment. All of these deny the child the gratifications that he needs, and make it impossible for him to find comfort and emotional adjustment.

It is impossible to catalog in the space of a single chapter all the variety of entanglements, jealousies, interactions, fears and overreactions that may beset a family and that profoundly affect the child's emotional adjustment. Finch has approached the matter by describing various family "types," such as the tense family, the hostile family. This approach, while illustrative of some of the kinds of interpersonal difficulties, must necessarily be cursory and incomplete. There are too many variables, and it is seldom valid to fit a family into any one type. For example, consider the family of Billy, in the case presented at the beginning of this chapter. How would one classify his family? It is a family of older parents; it is, in a sense, a family with an only child, since the half-brother was so much older than Billy; it might be called a "tense" family, as the mother is certainly a tense woman, and there was much tension between the parents. It is a family with a bright child, a bright mother, and a dull father; a family with an overprotective mother and a jealous father; a family with a sensitive child and an unempathic father. How many variations are there? The number is virtually infinite.

In the families of most neurotic children, one can find psychopathology. But this is not invariable. Nor is it possible always to ascribe the child's disorder to the family psychopathology. What is necessary is to explore, to understand as fully as possible how the child and his environment interact.

ETIOLOGY OF SPECIFIC DISORDERS

So far in this chapter, general causes of neurotic disturbance in the child have been considered. But what about specific neurotic disturbances? Is it possible to point with certainty to particular kinds of experience which lead to neurotic depression, for example, or to conversion hysteria, or to aggressive acting out? Unfortunately, there are few situations where a clear-cut relationship of this kind has been found. Generalizations about the etiology of specific neuroses, so popular early in this century, have, upon further examination, been found largely inaccurate. For example, the notion that obsessive-compulsive neurosis resulted from difficulties in bowel training is without substance, for most neurotic children. In fact, a "pure" obsessive-compulsive neurosis is rare in children—these children have apparently not read the psychiatric textbooks; they insist on having extraneous symptoms which do not fit into any of the "typical" patterns.

Nevertheless, with some reservation, certain generalizations can be made about specific causes of some of the major neurotic patterns. They are here presented with the understanding that most are in need of more research before they can be considered verified. They are:

1. Counter-aggressive acting out is most often seen in children whose families display much aggression. Such children have actually been taught to fight, as this is the way emotions are handled within the family.

2. The aggression-inhibited child, highly repressed and constricted, most often comes from a rigid, overcontrolled family. Often the father sets the tone in such a family, and he may be moralistic, strict, sternly religious. Emotional display, including anger and affection, are not condoned. This leads, in the child, to anxiety, and sometimes to depression.

3. Refusal to attend school is seen in the passive, dependent child with an overprotective mother. School phobia, as it is sometimes called, is actually a fear of being away from the mother and of losing her love. Additionally, there is a component of immaturity, as the child has not been permitted or has not wished to become independent of his mother and to develop normal social relationships with his peers.

4. The hypochondriacal child, the neurotic child with somatic complaints, is also likely to have been overprotected. Often he or she has learned the somatic orientation directly from a sick or complaining parent. Thus, one eleven-year-old girl developed chest pains and fears of death following her father's death from a heart attack. She would lie on the couch

where he had lain, would complain intensely of the pain, and would refuse
to go upstairs to sleep for fear that she would never awaken. Often these
children complain of multiple somatic symptoms, such as stomach-ache,
backache, and headache. They may search from one area or organ to another to see which feels worst; later, one organ becomes favored over the
others, and there the symptom becomes fixed.

5. Delinquent or antisocial behavior is often induced by a parent who
unconsciously and vicariously enjoys and stimulates the child's delinquency. This phenomenon has been termed *superego lacuna* by Adelaide
Johnson, and she regards it as a major cause of delinquency in children.

6. A feminine, passive-dependent orientation frequently occurs in
boys who have no father, or whose father is himself a passive, ineffectual,
and unmasculine person. Such a boy has low self-esteem, is afraid of aggression, does not get along well with his peers and often prefers the company of younger children. He may become overtly homosexual.

As indicated, the above generalizations do not apply in all cases. There
are variations on each theme, and the ways in which a child reacts to and
adjusts to his particular conflicts and difficulties depends on many factors.
Reaction formations often develop, so that the passive, effeminate child becomes an aggressive bully. One boy who had always been a "sissy" found at
the age of 13 that he had grown bigger and stronger than his peers. He
began to beat them up, was admitted to a neighborhood gang, and within
a year had been arrested for being involved in over 40 breaking-and-
entering episodes. Or the child who is involved in many fights within the
family, where this behavior is routine, finds, when he goes off to school,
that such behavior is not acceptable. He may be beaten up a few times,
and forced to suppress his aggression. He thus becomes inhibited and anxious.

Each case is a unique one, each has its individual and peculiar facets,
and each must be studied individually. Making facile conclusions about the
cause of a child's disorder on the basis of a cursory knowledge of the presenting symptoms is to be avoided. Just as universal symbolism has gone
out of fashion, so also has universal etiology.

PSYCHOPATHOLOGY

To repeat, the fundamental psychopathology in childhood neurosis, as
in adult neurosis, is psychological conflict. Conflict to an abnormal degree
is present in every neurotic, and it is the basis for all of the various symptoms.

Not only does the neurotic have much conflict, but he also has a high
degree of emotional response to the conflict. Indeed, this is considered by

some to be the basic pathology. In other words, there is heightened response to the conflict, rather than the presence of an abnormal degree of conflict. Actually, the two are inseparably associated: the overreaction results in further conflict, which induces further anticipation of overreaction. Thus there is early established a highly charged cycle of conflict-hyper-reaction-conflict, which is almost self-perpetuating. The pathology of neurosis is, in a sense, a quantitative phenomenon. It is an exaggeration of normal functions. Everyone experiences psychological conflict, everyone reacts emotionally to it, but in the neurotic, both conflict and reaction are excessive.

What are the major areas of conflict in the neurotic child? There are many. It was at one time believed, and still is in certain of the psychoanalytic schools, that there was one basic conflict, and that all others were representative or symbolic of it. This was, of course, the Oedipal conflict, which is produced by the young boy's love for his mother and jealousy of his father, and vice-versa for the little girl. Oedipal conflict, with secondary castration fear, was considered to occur in every child. Those who resolved the conflict developed normally; those who did not resolve it adequately became neurotic. It is now known that there are many kinds of conflict in neurotic children, and that most of them are not basically Oedipal.

One feature is common to all neurotic conflict, and is, in fact, the basis for the conflict. This is the presence of object relationship. Relationship with other persons underlies all of the conflict which the neurotic child experiences. His feelings toward meaningful persons in his life conflict either with other relationships or with certain instinctual wishes.

The kinds of conflict which the child experiences vary with his age; those of the 1-year-old are quite different from those of the 8-year-old. To understand the major areas of conflict at each level of development, reference is again made to Erikson's eight stages of man, specifically to the first five stages, from infancy to adolescence. It will be recalled that Erikson designated each stage by noting the major struggle or conflict characteristic of that stage. These are:

1. Trust vs. basic mistrust—the "oral" period, first year.
2. Autonomy vs. shame and doubt—the "anal" period, second and third years.
3. Initiative vs. guilt—the Oedipal period, fourth to sixth years.
4. Industry vs. inferiority—the "latency" period, seventh to twelfth years.
5. Identity vs. role diffusion—adolescence.

The first period is full of discomforts, frustrations, pain, rage, and hunger. It may also be the time of greatest comfort, ease, peacefulness, and oblivion. Conflicts occur daily, many of them, and in this stage it is the child's mother who is most instrumental in resolving them. The sensitive and loving mother helps the child to learn that his environment and his own body can be trusted. Aggression, too, with anger, is experienced even at this early stage, as well as the beginnings of control over aggression, of gaining confidence that the aggression will not get out of hand and will not destroy or drive away the loved one. If these things are not learned, major and perhaps permanent conflicts are established.

In this first stage, perhaps more than in any of the later ones, the child's sense of identity develops, his awareness of who he is, his feeling of confidence that things will be all right rather than that they will be all wrong.

In the second stage, the child begins to have some control over his environment: he is able to manipulate. Here he needs, perhaps more than anything else, consistent external controls which will prevent him from taking charge too much. He needs to develop most at this period a realistic sense of autonomy, and an awareness that he can control himself and his environment in realistic ways and ways consistent with social needs; this involves also an awareness that he will not overcontrol, or get out of control. Erikson believes that at this stage a "sense of badness" may develop, and with it a feeling of shame, which is a sense of being exposed and being looked at by the world. This can be terribly frightening and overwhelming, and the child may never truly recover from it.

The conflicts of the third stage are social and sexual, and the two are interrelated. Sexual curiosity increases, and at the same time, social taboos are met with. Social relationships become more complex; the child is no longer a baby, there are far more things to know about, more nuances of behavior which are acceptable or unacceptable. Emotional attachments are stronger, and jealousies occur. All these are conflict-producing.

When the child leaves home and goes to school, along with his peers, he is for the first time truly on his own. Here he needs very badly not to feel inferior, and he needs to be able to do the things which other children can do. The child may leave home willingly, and with confidence; or he may leave reluctantly, longing, consciously or unconsciously, to remain home and to be protected. This is a crucial time. It is often the time at which emotional illness becomes manifest.

What the adolescent needs most is to be identified with the group. At the same time he needs a true sense of personal identity. The struggle is often between identification with family versus identification with the social group. The struggle is also between being a child and being an adult.

Thus, it can be seen that a child experiences many kinds of conflict in the course of his development. There are conflicts over self-identity, as he struggles to master himself and his environment. Early, he learns the simple, physiological achievements concerned with obtaining food and physical comfort. Later, as self-awareness grows, he learns to differentiate between himself and his environment; his feelings become more complex, he experiences love and a fear of loss of love. And he must somehow incorporate, integrate, and adapt to all these conflicting and seemingly irreconcilable wishes, needs, and frustrations: to be independent and dependent; to be like a baby and to be like an adult; to do many things which are pleasant but forbidden. Later come all the social conflicts, the sexual feelings, the aggressive feelings, love and hate, tenderness and harshness. All these conflicts occur many times and in many ways. At any age they may become overwhelming.

The child's reactions to his excessive conflict take a variety of forms. These may be fairly consistent and predictable—one child may invariably "blow up" with anger, another will run away from home, another will sit in his room and sulk. More commonly, a variety of reactions to conflict are shown by the child. These reactions are usually classified into two categories: symptoms, and adjustment mechanisms. Yet the two are not always separable—they merge, and they operate together. A symptom can also be a defense, and vice-versa. For example, depression is a symptom, yet it may have the effect of avoiding further conflict, and in his depression the child may regress, which is another defense mechanism.

Below, the more common defense, or adjustment, mechanisms of children will be discussed. These are included here, not because they are limited to neurosis, but because they are central to the psychopathology of neurosis. They operate also in all the other emotional disorders of childhood. They operate also in normal children.

THE ADJUSTMENT MECHANISMS

The term *defense mechanism*, like so many of the terms in the jargon of any discipline, is an unsatisfactory one. It imparts only the negative connotation of the mental mechanisms, when in fact their operation results not only in the avoidance of unpleasure but in the acquisition of pleasure. Olds' rats (Chapter 2) press the lever and give themselves an electrical stimulus into the "pleasure center" not to avoid pain or to reduce a drive; they apparently do it simply because they want to. It is a positive and desired experience. Just so does the child who fantasies that he is the pilot of a rocket ship enjoy his fantasy: it gives him true pleasure; it is fun. Admittedly, the child's fantasy is a much more complex phenomenon than the electric shock to the rat's brain; it has many meanings, conscious and unconscious, it includes many mechanisms, including denial, projection, and identification with the aggressor. But the fantasy is a positive experience, and provides pleasure as well as serving to avoid unpleasure.

It might be supposed that the mental mechanisms are peculiarly human functions. The animal ethologists would not agree. The frontis-piece of Tinbergen's book on animal instinct is a picture of a fish employ-ing the mechanism of displacement. The fish, a stickleback, thwarted in its efforts to drive another fish out of its territory (the other fish is actually its own reflection in a mirror) is reacting to the conflict and presumably re-ducing tension by frantically digging a nest for which it has no use what-ever. This is not unlike the adolescent boy who, after an argument with his girl, leaps into his hotrod and hurtles down the highway at 80 miles an hour.

Anna Freud (1946a) has attempted a chronological classification of the defense mechanisms, thus recognizing that some develop earlier than others. She concludes that such a classification is tenuous because of indi-vidual variability. Nevertheless, she notes that while projection, introjec-tion, regression, reversal, and turning against the self appear early, usually repression and sublimation develop rather late. Fenichel likewise desig-nates certain of the defense mechanisms as occurring earlier than others. He considers the earliest or most "archaic" to be denial, projection, and introjection, while some which vary in age of onset are isolation, undoing, regression, and reaction formation.

Psychiatric work with children confirms that certain of the adjustment mechanisms occur in young children while others arise only in late child-hood or adolescence. Some of the mechanisms are ill-defined, and there is much overlapping among them. One cannot often say with certainty that at a particular moment in a particular situation the child is employing, say, projection or denial—he may be doing both, and other things as well. When a child gets angry at his playmate, and stamps his foot, several mech-anisms are involved. There is a direct expression of motor tension; there is displacement of anger; there is probably some introjection, with identifica-tion with the aggressor; there may be a turning against the self; there may be regression. Fenichel has noted the great complexity involved in every psychological experience, and the difficulty of attempting to describe and classify the mental mechanisms. He observes:

Actually, defensive conflicts are more complicated than description in-dicates. An isolated conflict between one particular drive and one particu-lar opposing anxiety rarely occurs. More frequently there are complex and powerful interactions between the drives and many anxieties. Certain expe-riences may invoke the return of what has been warded off in the defense, which may in turn necessitate defenses against the defenses. There are re-

action formations against reaction formations. Conditions favorable to and opposed to the objectionable impulses arise, so that many contradictory layers develop.

The major adjustment mechanisms used by children are listed, somewhat arbitrarily as follows: denial, projection, identification, displacement, constriction, fantasy, regression, somatization.

Aggression might also be considered as a "defense" mechanism; it is one of the most usual ways for a child to deal with his conflicts. *Repression* must also be considered among the common defenses of childhood. Repression has a unique position, and is usually considered to precede the occurrence of the other defense mechanisms. The tension which results from repression of the wish or drive then induces other defense mechanisms. In children, where most of the ego functions are still in the process of development, and where the superego is still rudimentary, repression is inconstant; much more of the forbidding comes not from within but from the child's environment, from the reprimands of his parents, from coercion by his peers. Thus, in these earlier years, repression does not necessarily precede each of the other mechanisms. For example, a 3-year-old boy reacts to his jealousy of his new baby brother with aggression or regression. In his case, little is repressed. But the 6-year-old must not express himself so directly, and other mechanisms, such as fantasy and displacement, will come into play.

Denial is one of the most primitive of the defenses, yet it persists throughout life. A 15-year-old girl, desperately unhappy over her father's frequent alchoholic bouts and his deteriorating health, denies that she is concerned about him, and when asked by the therapist how her father is doing, blithely replies, "Oh, he's fine." The human being's capacity to delude himself in the face of reality is sometimes astonishing. Extreme denial may be perceived by the unwary psychiatrist as "poor reality testing" and can lead to an erroneous diagnosis of schizophrenia. Yet, denial is for the most part a normal mode of adjustment. In milder degrees it shades gradually into forgetting, which is the fate of most experiences. They sink into unconsciousness, and if a bit of active denial submerges them more rapidly, the harm is usually minimal. On the other hand, denial can be a treacherous and undependable defense. When it fails, it can fail suddenly and completely, leaving the individual defenseless and exposed. The use of denial normally diminishes during the middle years of childhood; the demands of reality make it largely untenable.

Projection and *displacement* are a step beyond denial in maturity. They find an object to accept the guilt or the anger. Projection, though primitive, persists into adulthood, and much of it is seen in the parents of child patients. These are the parents who blame the school, or "that terrible boy down the street," or their own mates—anybody but themselves and the child. Displacement is the precursor of *sublimation*, which is largely a happy and acceptable device. The growing child gives up kicking the wall, and plays cops-and-robbers, or, later, argues politics.

Identification is a major and normal process in personality development. It is the beginning of the child's own adult identity. It generally attains importance around the fifth year, when the child is proceeding from the home world to the peer world. He (or she) takes with him, hopefully, a positive image of the parent of the same sex. "Good" identification can be most comforting and reassuring to the child; it relieves him of so much responsibility, helps so much in decisions, gives him a sense that things are all right. At this age, children, especially boys, defend their parents fiercely against their playmates, and need desperately to be proud of them. Early identification has lasting effect. In adolescence, there is a transient rejection of the idea of parental omniscience and authority as the child struggles for his own adult identity. Later, the more mature young adult accepts the parents again, but in a less dependent way.

The beginnings of true identification are also considered, in psychoanalytic theory, to be the beginnings of superego formation. The customs and taboos of the culture are incorporated or introjected, along with other aspects of the identified-with parent. Superego development is later modified by association with peer groups and other authorities. It is largely completed by early adolescence, but is considered to undergo some modifications up to the beginning of adulthood.

A special form of identification has been described: identification with the aggressor. This device permits vicarious expression of aggressive feelings, and may function throughout life. It explains the success of professional football as a spectator sport, and of the Western and crime-detective shows on television. It is largely a harmless, not seriously pathological operation in a society where aggression is strongly forbidden; but it can be serious, and is an important determinant of social delinquency in an adolescent who identifies with a delinquent parent or peer.

Identification is sometimes a powerful factor in psychotherapy, and the chief function of the therapist may be to provide an adequate ego ideal. It is also a vital function of teachers, often much more important than their academic teaching; it is the major reason why teachers should be mature and insightful persons, and why they can never be replaced by audio-visual aids (Rasey).

Constriction is the overcontrol or reduction of emotional response. It is an important function in the adjustment of every child. It comes from learning that some responses cause trouble or produce displeasure, so that such responses are no longer made. In psychopathology, constriction means that too much response has been omitted from the child's behavior, and in extreme forms he responds to virtually nothing. The constricted child may be chronically fearful or he may be relatively bland. Constriction is to be differentiated from undermotivation, which occurs chiefly in the child who has never been stimulated and who never developed much interest in anything.

Fantasy is probably a uniquely human endeavor. It means just thinking about things. It is thus a passive pursuit, but its content can be wonderfully aggressive. The earliest fantasies are probably those of the baby thinking about his mother's breast. Adolescents fantasy about breasts, too. In between, there is piloting a rocket plane or batting-in the winning run in the World Series. Billy S., the boy in the case history with which this chapter began, was an expert fantasizer, and for a long time the only way he could express aggression was in recounting his fantasies to the therapist. Telling of an old lady down the street whom he feared and despised, he said, "I'll take this airplane and fly over her house and push this big barrel of bricks out and they'll go right through her roof; then I'll drop a note saying, 'Please pardon the interruption.'" He would fantasy elaborate devices to trap people who came too near his clubhouse: machines operated by electric eyes which would drop a loop of wire around the prowler's neck, or a huge grappling hook which would reach out and drag the victim into the clubhouse. These could hardly be called "healthy" fantasies, but there is no doubt that they had an important function in helping with Billy's needs for counter aggression.

Fantasies can assume most bizarre forms, and are often not unlike dreams in their distortions, reversals, and condensations. They may thus in large part involve primary-process thinking. This is characteristic of the disordered thought processes of the schizophrenic, and has sometimes led to the mistaken diagnosis of schizophrenia in a child who verbalizes his fantasies. The distinction is important. Children usually know and admit when they are fantasying. But sometimes the fantasies are too important, and the child will insist they are true—this is still not schizophrenia.

Regression ordinarily means going back. In psychiatry, it means a return to an earlier, more primitive level of behavior. Everyone regresses at times, and there is in all human beings, more or less consciously, the wish to return to the old, simple ways, to the time when there was less responsibility, when wishes could be directly gratified, when one did not have to put off satisfaction, when one was taken care of, and everything felt safe and secure. Regression occurs when the stresses of life are too much. The child cries, and rushes into his mother's arms. The man turns to his wife for comfort and support. The capacity to regress can be a fortunate thing, and a good marriage rests in part on the recognition of this need between mates. But, like all the adjustment mechanisms, regression can occur in pathological degree, in the child and in the adult. The child is a crybaby or overdependent, unable to grow up into the company of his peers. This may be engendered by the overprotective mother whose need to keep her child as a baby outweighs her desire to have him mature. Later, reaction formation against the strong dependency wishes may develop; the adult then becomes unable to accept his own wishes to be cared for and loved. Often such persons find they can regress by drinking alcohol, and many alcoholics are those with strong passive-dependency wishes which they can indulge only when intoxicated.

Somatization is discussed in Chapter 14, under the heading of Psychosomatic Disorders.

These, then, are some of the usual ways that the child "deals with" emotional conflict. They are more or less successful in enabling him to achieve comfort, pleasure, relaxation, and happiness. They are mainly unconscious operations, although some of their effects come into consciousness. The child does not deliberate and make a decision as to which mechanism to use, and the reasons for the selection of a particular one are often obscure. However, once begun, the mechanism tends to be self-perseverating. Learning theory uses the term self-reinforcing, which psychoanalysis calls "repetition-compulsion." Somehow, the particular response has become associated with pleasure, or relief of tension, and is repeated when the situation recurs. It may not be the best possible solution, but the individual cannot risk giving it up in order to try others. In pyschotherapy, the therapist is advised against "tearing down" the patient's defenses unless better ones can be provided. Thus expressed, the operation sounds a bit like demolishing an old building, brick by brick, in order to replace it with a new one; the operation is actually not quite so direct, and the therapist has less control over his patient's ego than a bricklayer has over his bricks. Nevertheless, the comparison is valid.

The mental mechanisms are discussed in this chapter because their malfunctioning is crucial in neurosis, but, as already noted, they operate also in the other disorders. They must be evaluated in every disturbed child, whatever his diagnosis, and a part of treatment must always be concerned with bolstering his defenses and helping organize his adjustment mechanisms. The schizophrenic child, for example, uses much withdrawal and constriction; the brain-damaged child much aggression, projection, and denial. Regression is common in all the disorders, and it is important to know when to allow the child to regress, to infantilize and support him, and when to insist that he try again to draw on his own strength and to take a step upward in maturation.

In addition to acting out his anxiety, or employing any of the various adjustment mechanisms, there is yet another alternative: The child may simply tolerate the anxiety. This is one of the capacities of a mature ego— anxiety tolerance. The child experiences the anxiety, finds it unpleasant, but manages to endure it and to keep functioning. Some children, and some adults, lack this capacity. It appears to be largely inborn, but it is modified by experience. It is almost completely absent in the schizophrenic and the brain-damaged child; it is diminished in the neurotic child. The child whose anxiety-tolerance is low needs to develop strong defenses; he is likely to have a "rigid" or "brittle" personality. His control is precarious, and under stress, his defenses are likely to fail. Lippman, who emphasized the importance of anxiety tolerance and its increase under therapy, concludes: "For most of the neurotic children, therapy was not directed toward solving the underlying unconscious causes of the neurotic symptoms. Instead, the aim was to make it possible for the child to tolerate emotional stress and live more comfortably, even under difficult conditions."

SYMPTOMS

Masserman observed that when cats were made experimentally "neurotic" they usually reacted to the insoluble conflict in one of two ways: some would snarl, spit angrily, and attack anyone who came near the cage; others would cower in the back corner, trembling and immobilized. These two reaction patterns typify the two major symptom groups in the neurotic child: fight or withdraw; act out or suppress; turn anxiety outward or inward. Most of the symptoms of neurosis can be classified under one of these two headings. Funkenstein has related these differences in behavior, which he calls "anger-out" and "anger-in," to physiological changes resembling reaction to excessive norepinephrine and epinephrine respectively. Masserman could not explain why some cats reacted one way while others reacted another way. Nor can psychiatrists explain this in children. It is probably largely constitutional; Chess and others found that some infants were congenitally "approachers," while others were "withdrawers." Yet the possibility exists that response patterns are not inborn but are learned very early. It may then be largely a matter of chance that an initial reaction occurs in a particular way, becomes fixed, and is perseverated.

The two types of reaction are not mutually exclusive; some children express both. Some even vacillate from one to the other; an 11-year-old tiqueur would swing pendulum-like in periods of about one week, at one time having his tics and high tension, at the other time being constantly embroiled in fights, but without tics.

In adult psychiatry, neuroses are classified according to the major type of symptom, and this has resulted in the expectation that neurosis commonly occurs as one of the classical forms, such as obsessive-compulsive type, phobia, and conversion hysteria. Attempts to apply the adult classification of neuroses to children have met with frustration, as few neurotic children present the necessary symptoms. It would seem more satisfactory simply to designate the case as psychoneurosis, followed by a list of major symptoms, as was suggested in the case of Billy, above.

What are the major symptoms of childhood neurosis? To give the reader some perspective as to the frequency with which the various symptoms occur, the following list has been compiled. Records of 50 consecutive cases (38 males and 12 females) which had been diagnosed as neurotic were drawn from the outpatient files at Hawthorn Center, and the major presenting symptoms were noted. These symptoms are listed below in relative order of frequency, and the number of times each occurred is indicated. Since most children had more than one presenting symptom, the total number in the list is considerably more than 50.

Academic Failure	23	Sexual Delinquency	2
Anxiety	18	Lethargy	2
Oppositional Behavior	11	Sadistic Behavior	2
Social Isolation	11	Fire-setting	2
Temper Outbursts	6	Tics	2
Depression	6	Nightmares	2
Aggressive Behavior	5	School Truancy	1
Apathy	5	Stuttering	1
Somatic Symptoms	4	Suicidal Preoccupation	1
Enuresis	4	Obesity	1
Stealing	3	Histrionic Behavior	1
Aggression Inhibition	3	Encopresis	1
School Refusal	3	Conversion Symptoms	1
Vandalism	3	Compulsiveness	1
Excessive Masturbation	3	Phobias	1

This list does not represent the total number of symptoms present in these 50 cases. For example, considerably more than 18 of the 50 had overt anxiety; however, anxiety had not been recorded as one of the symptoms for which the child was brought to the clinic, although it was often elicited in the history and examination.

There is one symptom present in all neurosis: anxiety. Anxiety is central to neurosis, and is the accompaniment of conflict. Without anxiety there is no neurosis. There are, however, many levels and many kinds of anxiety, and its presence is not always readily apparent. Moreover, it may occur early in the disorder and then diminish, as adaptation occurs. The

problems and conflicts remain, but they arouse less anxiety; they have become "ego-syntonic." By the time the child is brought to the psychiatrist,
he may appear indifferent to his troubles. This is seen much in the acting-
out children, the ones who steal, and fight, and truant from school. Yet, if
the child is neurotic, his indifference is superficial, his denial patent, and
his emotional control precarious. Anxiety can easily be found beneath the
surface.

All of us have experienced anxiety many times; it is an old familiar
friend. To speak of anxiety as a friend is not romantic, or fatuous; it
is scientifically accurate. Anxiety and pain are the protectors of men's
lives, the guardians of our survival. Without them all men would long
since have been dead or confined to an institution. The warning of these
two signals teaches man what to approach and what to avoid. These two
functions have been built into the human animal through the long,
arduous process of adaptation and selection. The fittest, those who have
survived, contain the capacity for these responses, anxiety and pain, in neither too great nor too small a degree. It was perhaps with this aspect in
mind that Alexander designated anxiety as one of the defenses.

On the other hand, anxiety can become an enemy. Experienced too
often, or too intensely, it can destroy one's happiness and render one unable to function as a normal social being. Anxiety is always unpleasant, and
an experience to be avoided.

Masserman's classical studies with cats have demonstrated the extreme
agitation of the animal in a state of conflict. Masserman induced the conflict by setting a situation in which the animal experienced simultaneously
both approach responses and avoidance responses. One technique was to
teach the animal to open a box and receive food when a bell was sounded.
Then, just as the cat was opening the food box, he was given a short blast
of air directly into his ear, an experience which a cat seems to find singularly unpleasant. After several such experiences the animal became completely "neurotic." He would crouch shivering, and, when the signal for
food was sounded, would make frantic attempts to escape.

In the psychiatric evaluation of a child, an attempt is always made to
evaluate the amount of anxiety. But, because it is a subjective experience, it
is difficult to determine how much anxiety another person is feeling. The
psychiatrist tries to estimate it by observing the child's behavior; but the
ways in which people or children react to anxiety vary tremendously.

There are autonomic dysfunctions associated with anxiety, such as
flushing or pallor of the skin, excessive sweating of the palms, dryness of
the mucus membranes, and increased heart rate. Objective measurement
of these autonomic phenomena is often employed to estimate anxiety in experimental procedures and in the "lie-detector test." Galvanic skin resist-

ance is an indicator of the amount of moisture in the skin, and is considered one of the most sensitive objective tests of anxiety. But these tests are only relative; they cannot determine absolute amounts of anxiety or even compare the level of anxiety of two different individuals; they can only determine when the anxiety in a particular individual increases or decreases.

The problem of anxiety is a difficult and complex one. There is much disagreement about it and much that is still little understood. In practice it is seldom seen in pure form; it is associated with other symptoms, other emotions. Sometimes it is confused with other emotions. It is akin to fear and to anger. Different kinds of anxiety have been described, and there is no doubt that the anxiety of the neurotic is of a different quality than that of the schizophrenic or of the brain-injured child. These will be dealt with further in the chapters on the specific disorders.

The fact that *academic failure* heads the list of symptoms is no doubt partly a reflection of the fact that the schools are the chief referral source to Hawthorn Center. Yet, among any group of neurotic children, academic troubles will be a major problem. It should be noted here that these cases do not include the cases of primary learning and language disability, which are discussed in a separate chapter (Chapter 9), and in which academic difficulty occurs in even greater frequency. The reasons for the academic difficulty of neurotic children are several. Many are too preoccupied and too anxious to apply themselves to school work, and the teacher may say of such a child, "He just sits and stares out of the window," or "He just can't seem to apply himself." Other children, the ones who act out their feelings, are constantly in trouble in the classroom, frequently being sent home or to the principal's office. Many of them are the "class clowns," whose behavior usually represents an attempt at restitution, a status-seeking device; they talk out in class, are adept at "needling" the teacher, at exploiting the comic relief, and they practically always find a ready audience. Some children fail because they are too inhibited, afraid to participate, and when the teacher tries to involve them, they become even more anxious; they may shake visibly, or cry. The teacher is often too busy with other difficult children, and is content to leave them alone. Some fail out of a need to fail. These are the children with low self-esteem and the conviction that they are no good. They demonstrate it over and over again and seem to take a masochistic pleasure in failure. Some fail as an act of retribution or aggression against their parents. It becomes a kind of oppositional behavior, and a blow against the parents' authority. School achievement and school failure have many meanings, and a hasty conclusion as to the reason for a child's failure is to be avoided. Academic failure is a serious symptom; its consequences are invariably unfortunate, and, once begun, it tends to be self-perpetuating. Its presence is a strong indication for immediate and positive measures.

Oppositional behavior is a frequent cause for referral of a child to the psychiatrist. It takes many forms. In the school, the child may simply refuse to work, or he may defy all authority, getting out of his seat whenever he wishes, leaving the classroom, talking aloud, until his behavior disrupts all order and drives the teacher to distraction. In the home, the mother may be unable to cope with the child as he refuses to obey her slightest command. Oppositional behavior may take subtler forms, and this is perhaps more frequent among girls. The child may be painfully slow in following an order, may become an expert at changing the subject, at evading an issue. She becomes a "manipulator," an evader, an arguer, setting any number of traps for the unsuspecting parent, playing one member of the family against another until all lines of authority and control in the household are reduced to shambles. In the younger child, extreme forms of negativism occur as refusal to take food, to move his bowels, to go to the toilet, even refusal to talk.

Oppositional and *aggressive behavior* often occur in the same patient. Both represent in part an expression of hostility, and the negative child, if pressed, may react with rage and aggression. Oppositional behavior in the very young child need not have a hostile aspect, but as others in his environment, especially the mother, begin to oppose his negative behavior, hostility becomes directed toward them.

Oppositional behavior in a child provokes negative emotional responses in the person against whom it is directed. Anger, frustration, resentment, helplessness, indignation, are felt by the parent. The mother feels baffled and puzzled when her young child, once so accepting and dependent, begins to refuse her care and to assert his independence of her. She may react with counteraggression, or she may seek to prolong the child's dependence on her by becoming overattentive and overindulgent. A complex set of interrelated forces develops, with overreaction on both sides, so that the child's opportunity for normal maturation and development is seriously impaired.

Levy has pointed out that there is in the course of normal development a period, usually during the second year, when the child becomes excessively negativistic. He refuses to do what he is told, he wants to do things for himself, and his most frequent word is "No." Levy considers that it represents the child's initial efforts to establish himself as an independently functioning organism. Levy notes that its age of occurrence coincides approximately with the time when the mother would ordinarily be having her next child, and he considers that it may represent a kind of built-in behavior pattern which has had selective value in man's evolutionary history, enabling the child to achieve some independence at about the time that he will be supplanted by a newborn sibling.

The symptom which has here been called *social isolation* is actually a multiplicity of problems, all of which have the end result of a diminution of normal social experiences. A child exhibiting such a symptom may have no friends at all, or he may form a close attachment to another unhappy child. Occasionally he will attach himself to a group of delinquents, and frequently becomes the scapegoat. Some neurotic children play only with younger children; they thus avoid the problems of growing up and of having to demonstrate their right to consort with their peers. In this they are often encouraged by mothers who are unwilling to give up their "babies" to the cruel world. Some social isolates are, for various reasons, too preoccupied and too anxious to participate socially. These children are overtly unhappy. They are not welcomed into the company of peers, for they are recognized as being abnormal. They may be regarded with active dislike, or with suspicion, distrust, or indifference.

Depression in children is of two types. The first occurs in infants under 2 years of age, and results from separation from the mother or mother figure. This will be considered in the chapter on psychopathy (Chapter 11). The other type of depression is seen mainly in children of 6 years and older, and presents a picture of sadness, disinterest, and a general psychomotor diminution. In the neurotic child, depression seems to result when the child, finding no escape from his conflict, finally gives up the struggle. It may be in reaction to a variety of situations in the environment which the child views with hoplessness. Dynamically, as in adult depressions, it may represent the loss or threat of loss of a love object.

Depression in children does not appear as the chronic, intractible, disabling condition seen in adults. It is more transient or fluctuant, interspersed with periods of acting out or hyperemotionality. Its transient nature may be partly explained by the fact that the child is still in the process of growth. Depression in childhood has received remarkably little attention and investigation, and one might conclude from an examination of the literature that it is nonexistent or at least rare. Bierman and others reported in detail a case of depression in a 6-year-old boy with acute poliomyelitis. They reviewed the literature up to 1957, and observed "there is a noticeable gap in the knowledge about depressions between those in infancy and early childhood as described by Spitz . . . and the more numerous reports of adult cases." The fact that depression occurred in 6 of the 50 cases listed above suggests that it is not so rare as the literature would indicate. It is a serious symptom reflecting the child's helplessness in the face of his difficulties, and is an urgent indication for psychiatric help. In extreme forms it can result in suicide (Shaw and Schelkun).

Apathy and *lethargy* are akin to depression, and should perhaps be considered its subsymptoms. A notation that the child is apathetic suggests that the examiner was impressed chiefly with this aspect of his depression. Lethargy represents mainly the psychomotor component of the depression. The mother may say of such a child that "He just seems to lie around all the time," or "He just can't seem to get going."

The *somatic symptoms* in the four cases listed above were constipation, abdominal pains with vomiting, headaches, and, in the fourth case, a multitude of transient and migratory aches and pains. Such symptoms almost invariably occur in overdependent, aggression-inhibited children. The mechanisms which induce these symptoms are close to conscious levels and often include some conscious exaggeration and overconcern. The secondary gain from these symptoms is usually apparent.

Note that *conversion symptoms, compulsiveness,* and *phobias,* common in adult neuroses, are among the least frequent in the above list. The conversion symptoms occurred in an 11-year-old girl who was hyperemotional, extremely dependent, and infantile. The presenting symptom was weakness in both legs, so that she had been unable to walk for several months. The compulsiveness occurred in a 16-year-old boy who was effeminate, anxious, perfectionistic, and meticulous. Thus, both of these cases were in adolescents; such symptoms are rare in pre-adolescent children. The phobia occurred in a 10-year-old boy who had night terrors and often expressed a fear of death. Phobias of all kinds are not uncommon in children, and transient phobias often occur in perfectly normal children. It will be recalled that Billy S. expressed many phobias, and Francis, the schizophrenic boy in Chapter 6, had a chronic fear of buses and a transient fear of open spaces.

Other symptoms, including *enuresis, school refusal, fire-setting,* and *tics,* as well as other less frequently occurring symptoms, are discussed elsewhere in this book.

DIAGNOSIS

The diagnosis of childhood neurosis is a process of both elimination and synthesis. The major positive evidence is the demonstration, in one form or another, of anxiety. The major negative evidence is the absence of the usual signs of brain damage, schizophrenia, and primary language disorder. Additionally, in the history there is usually distortion of early experiences and of relationships to account for the disturbance. None of these factors alone is sufficient to make the diagnosis.

Diagnosis of the neurotic child, perhaps more than of any of the other disorders, must go beyond the mere attaching of a label. The psychodynamics must be clarified, the dynamic interrelationships between the child and his parents and between the various functions of the child's own personality must be explored and evaluated. It is sometimes difficult to say just when diagnosis ends, and it may continue throughout treatment. New facets may be continually uncovered, and as one learns in each session a bit more about the child, the diagnosis becomes more complete.

On the other hand, there is such a thing as too much diagnosis. The child is being seen because he needs help; he is not a psychodynamic specimen. Treatment begins the moment the child enters the therapist's office, for this is a meaningful experience and immediately begins its effect on him. Overconcern with diagnosis, with "working out" the dynamics, is an injustice to the child. The psychiatrist usually understands something of what the child's conflicts are about, that he resents his father's indifference, or that he feels inferior to his peers. Conjectures may be made about the origins of these feelings, but one must always be aware of what is conjecture and what is fact. The beginning student in psychotherapy is frequently so interested in working out the dynamics that he is in danger of overenthusiastically becoming convinced that his guesses are established facts. This seems particularly true if the student has been indoctrinated with too much theory which he attempts to apply to the child who, unfortunately, does not always fit the theory. Experienced therapists, whatever their background and training, avoid drawing conclusions and making interpretations in the absence of evidence.

DIFFERENTIAL DIAGNOSIS

Psychoneurosis may sometimes be confused with any of the other psychiatric disorders.

Personality disorder is perhaps most commonly mistaken for neurosis. In fact, the two conditions actually present a continuum, and the differentiation is sometimes arbitrary. In neurosis there is more anxiety, since the conflict has not become ego-syntonic. In the personality disorder, antisocial behavior is generally more chronic and there is less involvement in meaningful interpersonal relationships. In time, a childhood neurosis may develop into a personality disorder, as symptoms become fixed, defenses develop, and the child, unable to find comfort and security in relationships, becomes chronically distorted and damaged psychologically.

Brain damage may be mistakenly diagnosed in the neurotic child who is tense, restless, and driven by anxiety. A history of a disturbed environment does not assist in the differentiation, for, as noted earlier, such a history is common in the brain-damaged child with disturbed behavior. In practice, the distinction between the brain-damaged child with neurotic complications and a neurotic child who is congenitally hyperresponsive may be an arbitrary one, and the conditions undoubtedly merge. But most cases can be readily distinguished. Differentiation may be important because the therapy needs of the two differ in some respects. Both need ego support and help with impulse control. Additionally, the brain-damaged child is more likely to have special educational and training requirements.

Schizophrenia may be erroneously diagnosed in the severely disturbed neurotic child who is chronically anxious and who avoids social contacts. Such a child may be seclusive, shy, even autistic. He may present bizarre behavior: grimacing, peculiar mannerisms, silliness, inappropriate laughter. He may be obsessive, phobic, preoccupied, and prone to elaborate fantasies. The examiner may be hard put to ascertain whether such a child truly has disordered thinking or whether his behavior reflects his inability to cope with neurotic conflict. Again, differentiation is important, as treatment techniques are quite different. Such cases may require prolonged study. However, if studied too long, the child may spontaneously get better; then one never learns what he was dealing with, although it was probably not schizophrenia.

Perhaps the most difficult of the differential diagnoses is the decision as to whether or not the child is neurotic or normal. It has already been emphasized repeatedly that most of the symptoms of mental illness occur also in normal children. Some psychiatrists include an additional diagnostic category which has various names including behavior disorder, transient behavior disturbance, adjustment reaction, situational reaction, and others. These include the large group of children who are actually normal, or potentially normal, or only mildly and (hopefully) transiently upset, who are reacting to a "difficult" experience, and who are not considered sufficiently disturbed to be labelled neurotic. There is some justification for such a diagnosis, although the writer does not employ it, preferring instead to give the child the label of normal, sometimes with a qualification indicating that he is reacting normally to a particular situation. The distinction is based on whether the child has sufficient ego strength so that, if the environmental situation can be improved, the child will adapt adequately. This does not say, however, that the disturbance, although presently mild, is transient. It is potentially transient, but, too often, the causes persist. Parents may be "resistant" to change: The father may continue his drinking and his wife-beating, and the child's problem, at first mild and easily reducible, becomes chronic.

The psychiatrist looks for evidences of anxiety, and evaluates the child's capacity for relationship. These are perhaps the two best measures for deciding whether he is disturbed, and how much he is disturbed. The neurotic child invariably shows evidences of his anxiety. He overreacts to it in one way or another. He is ill at ease, or too much at ease. He is too outgoing, or too constricted. He is too fearful, or too bland. Yet almost every child brought to a psychiatrist's office because he is having some sort of trouble will feel anxiety, and only experience can teach one what degree of anxiety can be considered within normal limits in a particular situation. The therapist has to learn about himself, and how much anxiety his own personality and manner elicits in various types of children. Some psychiatrists deliberately seek to stimulate anxiety in order to evaluate it; others try to alleviate it and then judge how successfully the child is able to respond to their techniques. Some employ both techniques, depending upon the child and the nature of his problems.

TREATMENT

Treatment of the neurotic child is a highly individual matter, and may include anything from a single short talk with the mother to admission for many months or years for intensive inpatient therapy. The first decision is what kind of treatment is indicated. The second decision, then, is what kind of treatment is available. The two usually differ considerably.

The treatment may consist mainly of manipulating the child's environment, or making arrangements for him to live elsewhere: with a relative, in a foster home, in a group placement, or in a private school. It may consist of consulting with the school personnel, talking with the child's teacher and counselor, or arranging for special classes, an abbreviated course in school, or special-education teachers. It may consist of seeing the parents, having the father in, for one or several visits, to explain the child's needs, helping him to accept the fact that the child is emotionally sick and needs special care rather than punishment and rejection.

The decision as to what kind of treatment is indicated is usually a complex matter, and depends on many factors. A major one is whether the child should remain in his present environment or be placed in a different environment. In some cases the decision is obvious; the home may be quite adequate or deplorably bad. The decision will depend partly on the individual experience and feeling of the therapist. Some therapists are not willing, except in extreme cases, to remove the child from his home even temporarily. Others feel that it is not harmful so long as a good placement experience can be provided. This problem will be explored further in the chapters on inpatient treatment and special placement (Chapters 17 and 18).

Outpatient treatment of the neurotic child can be a satisfying and rewarding experience for both the therapist and patient. It can also be an extremely taxing and at times a harrowing experience. It is hard work, requiring continuous effort and attention to what is going on. Yet therapy can have its relaxed moments, it can be fun. It is always a very human, very individual process.

The formal, structured situation, still largely employed in adult analysis, in which the analyst obtains his material through the recollections of the patient, and in which he must at times carefully avoid "interfering with the associations" has little or no place in treatment of the child. This was quickly recognized by those who pioneered in child analysis: Hug-Hellmuth, Melanie Klein, and Anna Freud (1946b). The techniques of play therapy and the emphasis on the relationship, especially as developed by Anna Freud, are in no way distinguishable from the techniques of child therapy in use everywhere today, both by child analysts and child psychiatrists. As Lippman pointed out, therapy with most neurotic children does not consist in solving the underlying conflicts. In most cases, the conflicts are usually not even clearly understood. Therapeutic efforts are directed largely toward developing a relationship with the child, so that he develops some trust and confidence in the therapist and may find strength and support in the relationship.

Gitelson points to the "non-neurotic setting" of the psychotherapeutic situation as having major impact in treatment of the child. For the child reared in an atmosphere of distorted relations and reacting pathologically to the social pressures at school, the therapist's office may provide the child with his first opportunity for experiencing a reasonably normal relationship with a person who is interested in him and accepts him. Gitelson lists the functions of the therapist as follows:

1. Decrease the child's feeling that he is bad.
2. Introduce tolerance for feelings of hostility.
3. Supply information to the child.
4. Verify the actual conflict situation in real life.
5. Dispel old concepts of human relations engendered by the parents.
6. Point the way to compromises.
7. Differentiate feeling from acting out of feelings.

Treatment thus becomes a kind of combined experience in living and a process of re-education.

Margaret Gerard (1948) emphasized the flexibility of approach to child therapy. Noting that much modification and flexibility of the psychoanalytic method had recently developed in the analysis of adults, she observed, "For children, flexibility applies to an even larger number of problems than for adults; and the younger the child, the more directly can one approach the specific difficulty and thus shortcut the long process involved in the psychoanalysis of the total personality." By flexibility, Gerard includes all aspects of the treatment, including length and frequency of therapy sessions, attitudes and behavior of the therapist which are adjusted to "achieve corrective relationship for the child," variations in use of interpretation, the supplying of information, and in working with the child's parents, teachers, and other authority figures.

The principles of therapy outlined here for the neurotic child would in most cases apply as well to children with any of the other psychiatric disorders. However, for these other conditions, there are usually special considerations and techniques, with certain limitations of goals, as have been outlined in the chapters on those disorders. A common misconception is that in the treatment of neurosis one usually goes "deeper" into the problem, and works out with the child an understanding of the basic psychodynamics of the origins of the neurosis, thus enabling the child to "work through" his early distortions in the therapeutic relationship. In child neurosis this has little application. The child is not taken back through the early years of his development; the emphasis with the neurotic child as well as with those with other disturbances is mainly on the present and the immediate future.

A more detailed consideration of the techniques of psychotherapy appears in the chapter on psychotherapy (Chapter 16). Other therapies, including inpatient treatment, pharmacological treatment, and special schools, are discussed in Chapter 17, 18, and 19.

PROGNOSIS

Most of psychiatric theory, despite its many contradictions, disagreements, and points of view, finds general agreement on at least one major point, that mental disorder has its origins in the early life of the individual. Yet one of the largest gaps in psychiatric knowledge is the relationship between the emotional disorders of children and of adults. It is not known what percentage of disturbed children become disturbed adults, or how many disturbed adults were disturbed children. In treatment of adults there is usually evidence that the patient experienced considerable distortion of early relationships, but apparently in the majority of cases the disorder was not so severe as to require psychiatric attention during childhood.

Long-term follow-up studies are beginning to supply some of this vital information (O'Neal and Robbins) but these efforts are hampered by a lack of diagnostic standardization, with some disagreement between past and present diagnostic criteria. Extensive long-range follow-up studies have now been incorporated into the programs of a number of child psychiatry clinics and institutions, and it is to be expected that the next decade will see major advances in knowledge in this area. For the present, it must be conceded that not much is really known of what becomes of most of the neurotic children.

This does not mean that *nothing* is known about outcome of the neuroses, for there are many isolated cases who have been followed longitudinally. But the sample is probably biased. The tendency is to follow more closely the children who do not do well, who continue to come back for help. Those who improve and continue in relatively good adjustment are usually lost to psychiatrists forever.

It is possible to be both optimistic and pessimistic about the outcome of childhood neuroses. On the pessimistic side, it is certain that a large number of these children continue into adulthood highly disturbed and unhappy. On the other hand, there is no doubt that many improve greatly, and some even "get well." Because of this latter group, child psychiatry can be perhaps the most rewarding and satisfying of the medical specialties. We psychiatrists can see the fruits of our efforts, and can be assured that we are having a significant effect in altering the future course of a child from one of inevitable misery to one of reasonable happiness and productivity.

REFERENCES

Alexander, F. Fundamentals of Psychoanalysis, New York, W. W. Norton & Co., 1948.

Bierman, J., Silverstein, A., and Finesinger, J. A Depression in a Six Year Old Boy with Acute Poliomyelitis, Psychoanalytic Study of the Child, New York, International Universities Press, 1958, Vol. 13.

Chess, S., Thomas, A., and Birch, H. Characteristics of the Individual Child's Behavioral Responses to the Environment, Am. J. Orthopsychiatry, 29: 791, 1959.

Davis, E. R., Some Psychological Mechanisms Concerned in the Disorders of Childhood, The Nervous Child, 10: 283, 1953.

Erikson, E. Childhood and Society, New York, W. W. Norton & Co., 1950.

Fenichel, O. The Psychoanalytic Theory of Neurosis, New York, W. W. Norton & Co., 1945.

Finch, S. M. Fundamentals of Child Psychiatry, New York, W. W. Norton & Co., 1960.

Freud, A. The Ego and the Mechanisms of Defense, New York, International Universities Press, 1946a.

———— Psychoanalytic Treatment of Children, London, Imago Publishing Co., 1946b.

Fries, M., and Woolf, P. Some Hypotheses on the Role of the Congenital Activity Type in Personality Development, Psychoanalytic Study of the Child, New York, International Universities Press, 1954, Vol. 8.

Funkenstein, D. H. Norepinephrine-like and Epinephrine-like Substances in Relation to Human Behavior, J. Nerv. Ment. Dis., 124: 58, 1956.

Gerard, M. W. Direct Treatment of the Child, in Orthopsychiatry 1923–1948,
    ed. Lowrey and Sloane, New York, American Orthopsychiatric Association,
    1948.

—— The Emotionally Disturbed Child, New York, Child Welfare League
    of America, Inc., 1957, p. 13.

Gesell, A., and Amatruda, C. S. Developmental Diagnosis, New York, Paul B.
    Hoeber, 1941.

Gitelson, M. Direct Psychotherapy of Children, Arch. Neurol. Psychiatry, 43:
    1208, 1940.

Johnson, A., and Szurek, S. The Genesis of Antisocial Acting Out in Children
    and Adults, Psychoanalyt. Quart., 21: 323, 1952.

Klein, M. The Psychoanalysis of Children, London, Hogarth Press, 1949.

Levy, D. M. Oppositional Syndromes and Oppositional Behavior, in Psycho-
    pathology of Childhood, ed. Hoch and Zubin, New York, Grune & Stratton,
    1955.

Lippman, H. S. Treatment of the Child in Emotional Conflict, New York,
    McGraw-Hill Co., 1956.

Massermann, J. Behavior and Neurosis, Chicago, University of Chicago Press,
    1943.

O'Neal, P., and Robins, L. N. The Relation of Childhood Behavior Problems
    to Adult Psychiatric Status: A 30-Year Followup Study of 150 Subjects, Am.
    J. Psychiatry, 114: 961, 1958.

Rasey, M. Why Teachers? in The Nature of Being Human, ed. Rasey, Detroit,
    Wayne State University Press, 1959.

Shaw, C. R., and Schelkun, R. Suicidal Behavior in Children, Psychiatry, 28:
    157, 1965.

Tinbergen, N. The Study of Instinct, New York, Oxford University Press, 1951.

8

BRAIN DAMAGE

REPORT OF A CASE

Harry S. was referred to the psychiatric clinic at the age of 4 years because of chronic incorrigible behavior.

Harry had been a severe behavior problem since infancy. He would, without provocation, knock down smaller children. Once he beat a child so severely that minor surgery was required, and several times he had bitten little babies lying in their baby buggies. He could not be left to play outside without supervision, because of the possibility that he might hurt another child. His mother would sometimes let him play with other children in the back yard but she had to remain at the window watching, and would frequently rush out and intervene as he began to throw things or attack another child. While nursing, he used to bite his mother's nipples and he would still sometimes bite her on the leg or arm. He had always been highly excitable and hyperactive, and was never able to keep his attention on one subject for more than a minute or two.

When his parents tried to discipline him, either by reprimand or by punishment, he would become extremely tense and "keyed up," he would shake with rage and tension, and sometimes he would completely "fall apart," screaming, lying on the floor, and kicking.

Harry's mother said that Harry never really relaxed except when he was asleep. Even as a baby, he could not seem to relax when people were holding him, but would constantly squirm and kick so that he would have to be put down. He had even hurt people who were holding him, would reach up aggressively and scratch their faces or arms or try to bite them.

The mother said that Harry was "accident prone," and he would often hurt himself when playing or when running about the house. For about a year prior to referral Harry had been masturbating frequently. At times the parents were afraid he would injure himself because the masturbation was so vigorous. Recently they had begun to punish him for this, and the activity had diminished considerably.

PERSONAL HISTORY

Harry's birth was precipitous: to the best of the mother's recollection he was born within an hour after her first labor pain. Delivery was otherwise normal, he breathed readily, and had no cyanosis. There was never any motor paralysis. He was rather late in sitting up, and did not begin to walk until after 16 months. At about 18 months he began to talk a little, but at the time of referral, at the age of four, he did not yet speak in complete sentences. His speech had always been difficult to understand. Bladder training was late, and he still had nocturnal enuresis. He had severe colic in infancy, and screamed almost continuously for several weeks. Following this, he continued to be a feeding problem and could not tolerate solid foods until quite late.

FAMILY HISTORY

Harry was the middle of three children, having an older brother and a younger sister. The siblings were both normal: the brother an honor student and a very pleasant and likeable boy; the little sister a cute and appealing child, although at times quite impertinent to her mother and difficult to manage. The constant turbulence in the home created by Harry's disturbance made it difficult for the mother to give her younger child proper attention.

The parents were both school teachers, although the mother had stopped working at the age of 24 to raise her family. Both were warm, intelligent, and reasonably mature people. The father tended to suppress most of his feelings and gave the outward appearance of being well-controlled and stable. Mrs. S's emotions were patent. She was tense during the initial interview, cried readily, and spoke with obvious feeling about her frustration over Harry, and her anger at various doctors who had given conflicting opinions and advice. There was a desperate quality in her demeanor which reflected her long-suffering and intense concern over her child's disorder. While perhaps not ideal parents (are there any?), these two had certainly given their children an adequate amount of affection and care. It appeared from the history that Harry's disorder could not be explained as the result of his early handling, but rather that he had brought the disorder with him when he came into life.

PSYCHIATRIC EVALUATION

When he entered the psychiatrist's office for the initial interview, Harry was crying because he had slipped and fallen in the hallway and hurt his head. He was frightened of the office situation and was fearful because he sensed that the examiner was a doctor. In the office, he dashed back and forth from one parent to another, clinging to them and at the same time alternately biting and kicking at them. He also kicked at the examiner several times when he tried to interest him in a picture or in some toys.

Finally the parents were asked to leave the office, which they did with obvious misgivings. Then Harry was told very firmly that his behavior would not be tolerated, that he was to sit quietly and talk to the examiner, and was assured that although the examiner was a doctor, he did not give "shots" and that there was nothing to be afraid of. Harry's response was satisfactory; he was reassured, and immediately discontinued his aggressive behavior. However, he was unable to sit in the chair for more than a few seconds at a time, finding it necessary to get up and wander in a driven manner from one object of interest to another in the office. But he began to respond to my questions, and a friendly relationship was quickly established.

Harry was a somewhat dysplastic-looking boy with a large mouth and widely spaced eyes. Motor coordination was poor, and muscle tension was marked. He was extremely hyperkinetic, and gave the impression of never being relaxed. His respiratory rate was irregular, and occasionally he would appear consciously to take a deep breath, as if he had forgotten to breathe for a time. Speech articulation was impaired, and many of his words were not understandable. Language use was below average; he spoke only in short phrases or single words, never in complete sentences. He did not appear frustrated by the examiner's inability to understand a word, but would simply give up and change the subject. He was highly distractable, responding to every external stimulus. He would notice sounds of which the examiner was unaware, such as an office door shutting across the hall, and footsteps in the hallway overhead; these would interrupt his activity. Thus, he was constantly shifting from one subject or object of interest to another; he could sustain interest in nothing. As his initial apprehension diminished, he became warm and affectionate, and showed an excellent sense of humor. He responded to things which struck him as funny with loud laughter, and would sometimes clench his fists and shake them in a pleased and excited way.

PSYCHOLOGICAL EVALUATION

Psychological testing was a difficult and somewhat hectic session because of Harry's tension, distractability, and short attention span. However, the psychologist noted that he was cooperative and interested, albeit rather sporadically. On the Stanford-Binet he obtained a full-scale I.Q. of 91, and it was considered that the score accurately represented his potential. He was unable to perform the Bender Gestalt Test and figure drawing tests, he only scribbled. This was considerably below average ability for his age, and was partly due to his poor motor co-ordination.

DIAGNOSIS AND RECOMMENDATIONS

The diagnostic impression was that Harry had diffuse brain damage of moderate degree, possibly the result of birth injury. The disorder was complicated by the mother's overreaction, by her strong feelings of guilt and resentment, and by the frequent changes in techniques of handling which had resulted from the parents' uncertainty as well as from the conflicting advice they had received.

The parents were told of the diagnosis, were advised at considerable length as to Harry's special needs both in handling and education, and were assured that if these could be provided he would undoubtedly improve. It was pointed out that the process would be prolonged and at times difficult. The mother was advised that for the present she must continue to supervise him closely, as he could impulsively injure other children.

Harry was admitted to a special day school for disturbed children. His teacher was a woman with considerable experience who was expert at providing children with firm but warmly accepting control. Harry's improvement under her care was considerable. His improvement at home unfortunately did not parallel the school behavior. The mother was unable to discipline him as successfully as the teacher; she was too much involved, too overresponsive to his feelings and his outbursts. Nevertheless, the entire family situation improved, the other members were more relaxed and less apprehensive about Harry, and could tolerate him better.

After a year and a half at the day school, it was felt that he should be tried in public school. He attended kindergarten for two years, with limited success. It became obvious that, because of his impaired conceptual thinking and his impulsivity, he could not yet succeed either academically or socially. He was therefore placed at the age of seven and one-half in a small private boarding school for children with learning problems. Here he receives individual help with reading, and also whatever special controls and individual support he requires. His adjustment in this school has been excellent, he has developed warm feelings toward the staff, and has stimulated a like response in them. He is now an extremely appealing and talkative little boy, has an excellent sense of humor, has developed much self-control, and is interested in many things. He is beginning to learn to read, although it is likely that he will never read above a fourth-grade level. In other academic areas he is somewhat better, although still retarded.

PROGNOSIS

The outlook for Harry is fairly good. As his impulse control improves, as his speech and social skills improve, he should eventually be able to return home and function in society. His educational level will never be high, but there is every reason to expect that he will be able to work, support himself and perhaps a family, and become a reasonably happy and useful citizen.

The case of Harry is "typical" of brain damage, as much as any can be said to be typical. All are individuals, and show individual differences. Harry illustrates many of the common features of this disorder. His behavior is characteristic, with marked impulsivity and hyperkinesis. He has speech, language, and conceptual-thinking difficulties. Most importantly, he demonstrates that these children can be helped. The prevalent pessimism about brain damage is not always warranted, as the outlook for later adjustment is sometimes better than in the neuroses and personality disorders.

ETIOLOGY

Brain damage in children is seldom diagnosed on the basis of a history of damage to the brain. The disorder, when referred to the child psychiatrist, usually does not present gross neurological evidences of damage, such as motor paralyses and spasticity. Neither is there usually, in psychiatrically referred cases, mental retardation. The symptoms are largely manifested in abnormalities of behavior.

The justification for calling this group of children brain-damaged, in the absence of a history of brain damage and in the absence of the demonstration of pathological anatomy, is that the patients show the behavior which is known to occur in proven cases of brain damage, such as postencephalitic behavior disorder, and such as occurs following known severe cerebral anoxia at birth. They further present many of the symptoms described by Goldstein which follow head injury in adults, as will be described on page 164.

In the case of Harry, the precipitous labor may be regarded as possible corroborating evidence for brain damage. However, even in the absence of such a history, the diagnosis would not have been different. Just as tuberculosis is diagnosed on the basis of the present situation, that is, the presence of tubercle bacilli, rather than on a history of exposure to the infection, so brain damage is diagnosed on the present evidence, that is, "brain-damaged" behavior, rather than on the presence or absence of a history of trauma.

The grosser forms of brain damage resulting in readily measurable impairment of intellectual and motor functions of the nervous system have long been recognized. Pasamanick and Knobloch, from their epidemiological studies, postulated the existence of a "continuum of reproductive casualty" due to prematurity, complications of pregnancy, and paranatal injury causing various degrees and localization of damage to the brain resulting in "cerebral palsy, epilepsy, and mental deficiency through all types of behavioral and learning disabilities which are a result of lesser degrees of damage sufficient to disorganize behavioral development and lower thresholds to stress."

Brain damage in children may be caused by:

A. Prenatal factors
    1. Development defects
    2. Infections (especially German measles)
    3. Irradiation
    4. Nutritional deficiency
    5. Uterine pathology (premature separation of placenta, and so on)
B. Paranatal factors
    1. Premature birth
    2. Mechanical trauma to brain during delivery
    3. Cerebral anoxia from twisted umbilical cord, prolapsed cord, or apnea
C. Postnatal factors
    1. Central nervous system diseases, especially infections
    2. Any systemic disease with prolonged high fever
    3. Head injury

In addition to the brain damage which is caused by these various agents which produce actual injury to brain cells, the possibility exists that there are some children without actual brain damage whose "normal" brain function resembles that of the damaged brain. Just as there is a continuum of intellectual functioning in the normal population, so there is undoubtedly a continuum of such functions as perception of Gestalts, visual-motor coordination, ability to retain attention, and ability to control impulses. It is therefore probable that there are some children who are at one end of this continuum and who function much like children with brain damage. These factors are doubtless polygenically inherited, so that some children might be said to be hereditarily brain-damaged. A history of similar behavior in the parents (particularly fathers) of some such children has been noted, and is suggestive evidence of this variety of brain damage. Because of the lack of evidence for brain damage in many of the cases which present the clinical picture, some workers prefer to use other terms for cases lacking clear-cut evidence of organic damage. One term which has found some acceptance is *hyperkinetic impulse disorder* (Laufer and others). Other terms which have been suggested are *minimal brain damage* (Clemmens), and *minimal chronic brain syndrome* (Paine).

The nomenclature is not crucial so long as there is some agreement on what is meant by a term; the terms *brain injury* or *brain damage* are most used. The essential point is that it represents a specific type of defect in brain function which is present from early life and which has an organic basis. As diagnostic skills and techniques improve, clarification of etiology and differentiation of types of this disorder may be elicited. However, it is likely that the major concern will continue to be not so much with etiology as with the specific functional and behavioral manifestations, and with therapy directed toward their correction.

PSYCHOPATHOLOGY

A child whose brain performs adequately learns about himself and his environment through the following functions:
1. Perception
2. Memory
3. Conscious feeling
4. Organization and conceptualization
5. Controlled neuromuscular response.

The growing child learns to recognize patterns in his environment: He finds that feelings become familiar, and he learns to associate pleasant or unpleasant feelings with specific persons and with specific responses in himself. He learns how to use his own muscles and his own voice to gain satisfaction and to avoid unpleasantness; he learns self-confidence, and knows that he can obtain something by moving toward it or by asking for it in a particular way. There are consistencies in his life which are reassuring. He develops a stable self-percept and ego strength. He learns to delay gratification; he is assured that if he waits a while, satiation will occur. He learns the names of people and objects in his environment, learns thus to identify things by symbols, and the process of gratification is thereby enhanced; he is able to ask more definitively for what he wants. He learns about direction and time, he knows which way to turn in order to find his own room, he remembers that it has been some time since he last ate and that it is time to eat again. He has learned about the permanence of objects, that things which can no longer be seen, or heard, or felt, are not necessarily gone forever.

The perception of form and pattern are learned slowly over many months and years. And they are not a simple function of physical development of the brain. Senden (cited by Hebb) studied visual learning in adults who had had congenital cataracts surgically removed and who were thus able to see for the first time in their lives. The process of learning to see was a long and difficult one. It was many months before these patients could distinguish between simple geometric figures such as a square and a triangle. Then when they had finally learned to distinguish between dark figures on a light background and were presented with the opposite, that is, light figures on a dark background, they again could not distinguish them and further learning had to take place.

Thus, all the jumbled impressions received through all the sense modalities must be organized, and remembered, and ordered by the young infant, so that he is able to find consistencies and patterns in his own behavior and in his environment. He learns that the differences and similarities in things perceived occur in two fundamental parameters: space and time. He learns the relationship between these two, that impressions which occur in a series in time can be translated into a spatial concept. For example, glancing about his room, he sees first a portion of one wall, then the ceiling, then the other wall with perhaps a picture against it, and so on; after a while he is able to translate these originally unconnected temporally sequential impressions into a perception of the whole room. He learns that while he looks only at one wall the other walls are also present, and he expects that when he turns toward one of the others he will see it. Likewise he learns about people and other significant things in his environment. He learns to organize the impression of a particular group of sounds into the voice which signals the presence of his mother or father. He learns that when he sees this person from the side or from the back, from a long distance away, or from close up, against the background of the kitchen wall or the back yard, it is the same person.

In the normal child language soon intervenes to accelerate his learning. At first he learns the names of objects, and this is a profound advancement. This is the beginning of symbol formation, knowing that a particular vocal pattern represents a particular familiar object, such as "Mama," or "ball." Language quickly expands to express more abstract concepts, such as feelings and behaviors, like "hungry," and "me do it." Through language the child greatly enhances his knowledge about the world by adding the impressions of others to his own. He learns about the wants of others, the feelings of others; he learns quickly about social norms, so that his own egocentricities can be modified and he can learn to behave in an expected and accepted way. Through language he can learn vicariously, he can borrow from the experience of others. He thus avoids much trouble and acquires a greater peace of mind.

Concomitant with the understanding of relations and patterns is the conceptualization of causality. The child learns that there is some order in cause and effect, that when he pushes against a small object it will move in a particular direction, or that when he pushes against other objects, such as bigger children, they will push back at him. Later he learns more complex social causality, such as the things which he must not do lest his mother get angry.

Implicit in the above discussion of perception and concept formation is the notion that the behavior of the developing child, his response to stimuli, is somehow modulated and controlled. He exhibits differential responses, reacting in one way to one stimulus, in another way to another stimulus, sometimes responding little or not at all, sometimes with vigor and intensity. Out of the developing awareness of patterns and significances, he develops an ability to control his responses. He learns to sort out all the myriad incoming stimuli that impinge constantly on his various sensory organs, he learns to filter and modulate them, so that many of them never get beyond the lower levels of his central nervous system, and are channeled through reflex patterns which never reach conscious levels. Others are allowed entrance to higher centers, where they receive attention, or where they are stored for future use. The ways in which the brain handles, controls, and modulates these millions of consecutive impulses is as yet little understood. Neurophysiologists have learned in recent decades that much of this control is mediated through the reticular activating system of the brain stem, and relayed partly through the cortical projections of the thalamus. However, there is much still to be clarified, and what has thus far been learned about these systems has contributed little to our understanding of the psychopathology of brain damage. That neural correlates of such psychopathology exist must be accepted largely on faith, and must await development of new techniques and further studies seeking to correlate neuronal function with behavior, both in brain-damaged patients and in animals with experimentally induced brain damage.

All these functions are essential for the development of self-assurance and reasonable peace of mind. Any or all of these functions may be deficient when the brain has been damaged. It is not easy for those who have intact brains to understand fully the confusion and the disorganization of the brain-damaged child. He is not able to use his muscles in a smooth and relaxed way for locomotion, for exploring his environment and for obtaining the things he wants; the feelings that he experiences from muscle movement and from kinesthetic awareness are not reliable and reassuring. He literally does not know which way to turn, he is not sure which direction to go to find his own room or his friend's house. He lives in a disordered, perplexing, and frustrating world.

Not only is the brain-damaged child unable to modulate his responses to external stimuli, but the same holds true for those stimuli coming from within. He overresponds to his own feelings and thoughts. Thus he is constantly driven by impulse, unable to relax, unable to sort out the meaningful stimuli. Goldstein has called this condition "stimulus-bound," and these children are wretched indeed, driven constantly from one response to another. They seldom know real peace. Only when they are able at last to fall into an exhausted sleep at the end of each frantic day, can they find release. Thus their only relaxation comes when they are unconscious; relaxation is not a feeling which they ever consciously experience.

Bender (1949) has emphasized the intense anxiety of the brain damaged child. This is a diffuse, often overwhelming anxiety, not fixed to any specific situation or idea, as it is in the neurotic child. It comes from all their overstimulation and overresponsiveness, from their distorted self percept, from their disordered motility, and from their general feeling of perplexity and the realization that they are somehow different from other children.

Bender has further emphasized that children with brain damage have, from their earliest days, special needs for extra amounts of affection, attention, teaching, and control, and that, if these needs are met, the child may adjust reasonably well. She later pointed out (1956) that "children that have come to us with a behavior problem associated with an organic brain disorder have always other emotional and social problems in their life situation severe enough to account for their behavior disorder on a reactive basis alone." Some would not agree entirely with this statement, and it should be pointed out that Bender's case material was drawn largely from a social class of Manhattan's Lower East Side where neglect and poor upbringing of children were common. Nevertheless, there is no doubt that insufficient special care of brain-damaged children contributes importantly to their psychopathology, and a large proportion of those who develop serious behavior disorders would not do so had they received better care, with special attention to their particular needs.

Goldstein has noted certain parallels between the behavior of brain injured children and adults who have suffered recent brain trauma. He notes that the adult, when confronted with a problem which he could formerly solve, such as simple arithmetic, is not only unable to solve the problem, but "when he fails, he looks dazed, changes color, becomes agitated, anxious, starts to fumble and his pulse becomes irregular. A moment before, he was amiable; now he is sullen and evasive and exhibits temper or behaves aggressively. Because the patient's whole behavior is so disturbed we may call the situation catastrophic." Goldstein notes that an explanation of this reaction is not simply that the patient feels inadequate or unable to perform the task, as is demonstrated by the fact that the reaction complex does not follow the attempted performance but occurs simultaneously with it. Further, the patients are unable to adjust readily to changes in the environment. They "seek tranquility, and avoid company. Every readjustment is painfully difficult." They demonstrate a kind of rigidity in their personality. They show a perseveration of response, are unable to shift from one mental set to another. They continue trying to solve a problem in a particular way, even though the method has been found inadequate; or they tend to perseverate an emotional reaction, such as laughter or weeping. All of these symptoms may be seen in the brain-damaged child, and are discussed below.

SYMPTOMS

The major symptoms of brain damage in children are:

1. Hyperexcitability
2. Restlessness and hyperkinesis
3. Anxiety
4. Distractibility
5. Impulsivity
6. Aphasias—usually mixed, receptive and expressive types
7. Motor dysfunctions, involving muscles of:
   a. Posture
   b. Locomotion
   c. Respiration
   d. Speech
   e. Facial expression

Most of these symptoms are usually present in the brain-damaged child. The first five are almost invariably present, to some degree. The last two may or not be. The first five may be considered together as a group, as they all represent some aspect of uncontrolled response.

Excitability is usually described by the mother as having been present since early infancy. She may say that the child has always been easily upset, that he becomes excited and tense over things that would not disturb her other children. Associated with this are the restlessness and hyperkinesis. The child often gets more and more "keyed up" as the day proceeds. Sometimes the entire family becomes involved in a "vicious circle" in which the mother and other members of the family overreact to the child's tension and reactivity, their reaction produces more reaction in the patient, and the pitch of excitement mounts until it becomes unbearable. Such scenes are often described by the harried mothers of these children. Talking with them in the office, particularly if the child is present, one can feel the great strain and tension and can even become involved in it as the child wanders restlessly around and the mother reprimands him or shrieks at him. A half hour of such an interview can seem like half a day.

Hyperkinesis may be the most prominent symptom, and the mother will describe how the child is "always on the go," that he "can't sit still for a minute." Such children were usually very active babies, and are often described as having been "squirmy," unable to relax when held, always kicking and trying to get free. The symptom may escape serious attention until the child enters school. At this time the requirement for control in the group situation, the need to sit still for prolonged periods, emphasizes the patient's inability to do so.

The anxiety of a brain-damaged child is a complex symptom. Many factors contribute to it, both endogenous and exogenous; emotional conflict is involved, and the child has conflict over many things, over his interpersonal relationships, and over his own inabilities and frustrations. But there is a quality about the anxiety of brain damage which distinguishes it from the anxiety of the neurotic, and which is akin to the anxiety of the schizophrenic. Bender (1956) refers to it as "primary anxiety." She observes that "all organically disturbed children suffer profoundly from anxiety because of the disorganization, the difficulty in relating themselves to reality and the frustration in achieving normal maturation. There may also be difficulties in making articulate the anxiety that stems from unknown inner sources rather than a reality situation in the environment." These children look terribly anxious and they unquestionably feel anxious, but they cannot explain how they feel. They usually cannot point to a particular concern, and no amount of psychiatric probing can disclose the major underlying conflict, because it is not there. The conflicts which are present are obvious, and can be openly recognized early in treatment in conflict between child and therapist. But the "endogenous" anxiety remains, and the child can never understand it. In a sense, he is not even aware of it, since it has been with him always.

Distractibility means inability to fix attention, or overresponsiveness to stimuli not being directly attended to. All human beings are more or less distractible, so that a loud noise may take one's attention from the book one is reading. Normal persons are able to be selectively distractible. Thus, a mother sitting in the living room talking to friends may hear her baby cry from the bedroom while the others are unaware of it.

The brain-damaged child is unable to filter extraneous stimuli. He responds to everything. This is a function of his inability to perceive structure, to form the parts into a whole; he perceives the individual stimuli, and cannot retain the concept of a pattern, in which some stimuli have meaning and others do not. Thus, goal-directed behavior is diminished, and, having many small goals, the child ends by having no goals at all. He flits aimlessly from one small endeavor to another, and within the space of five minutes may take up and then discontinue five separate projects. In the examiner's office he may step to the drawing board and hastily sketch a few poorly executed lines, then drop the crayon, walk to the window and look out, commenting on the cars in the parking lot, then walk to the dart-board and throw a few darts, usually missing the board completely; he may hear some sound in the hallway which the examiner had not even noticed, open the door and look out, saying, "That kid down there just knocked over some blocks," and so on.

However, in a structured situation, he can be helped to maintain attention. If asked to sit down and perform a task, such as copying the Bender Gestalt cards, or drawing a figure, he can usually do so. It is helpful to give him close attention, and occasionally to draw his attention back to the task if he begins to wander. If he hastily sketches a face with two dots for eyes, one may say "now put in the rest of it," and he will continue the nose and perhaps a mouth. Then one urges him a bit further, saying "Now the ears," and so on. Thus coaxed, he may sit quietly, working very hard, for as long as five minutes. Moreover, he may actually enjoy it. These children are usually grateful for such attention, and, although perhaps not consciously, are relieved to be able to relax, to have their attention fixed, to be undistracted, for even these few minutes. This is in fact the key to their treatment. It is the approach through which they can be most helped.

Closely akin to the distractibility of the brain-damaged child is his impulsivity. Strauss and Kephart prefer the term *disinhibition*. The child reacts impulsively; he is unable to inhibit a response. This is another facet of his stimulus-boundness, and emphasizes the motor component of his response. It is most often seen as an aggressive act, because this is the part that gets him into the most trouble, and calls the most attention to him. Such a child is constantly getting into fights, and often it seems that he is the instigator of them and that there was no real provocation for his aggression. One often hears, in the history, that "he hits other children for no reason at all." Such a child may be walking along the hall apparently quite content and at ease, then, as he passes another child, he may suddenly strike at him or kick him. Asked why he did so, he may say that he doesn't know, or that he "just felt like it." Another child had the impulse, each time he saw an open door, to slam it shut, regardless of whether someone was standing in the way or not. Sometimes there may be some provocation, but the child's response is out of proportion. Such children, if reasonably verbal, may express the feeling that they are driven to these impulsive acts, that they want to prevent or avoid such behavior but are at times completely unable to control their response. And there is no doubt that this is true.

Aphasias of all kinds and of varying severity may be present in brain-damaged children. They probably occur to some degree in at least half of the encephalopathic children who are referred to the psychiatrist. These include various language disorders, particularly reading retardation, retarded use of language, and impaired number concept. There may be impaired conceptualization of time, space, and direction. These should be evaluated in the diagnostic examination of every child. Their presence is an indication for special educational methods, and often this approach to treatment can be the major contribution which the psychiatrist has to offer. These disorders will be described in detail in the chapter on language and learning disabilities (Chapter 9).

Motor dysfunctions of all kinds are seen. On the other hand, none may be present, and some brain-damaged children are excellent athletes. The usual motor disorders are diminished coordination, extraneous muscle movements, and a general lack of smooth and graceful movement. These are most apparent in locomotion: the child walks or moves awkwardly, and with a superfluity of motion. Sometimes most striking is the poor use of facial expression, so that expression does not always adequately complement emotion; there may be grimacing, exaggerated smiles and grins, and tic-like mannerisms. All these generalized faulty motor movements make up the appearance which is called "dysplasia." The dysplasia may also actually involve faulty body structure, and some brain-damaged children show considerable facial asymmetries or have abnormally shaped heads or other facial features.

Respiration is sometimes irregular, or the child may breathe in short gasps, sometimes with long periods of apnea. Some children appear to use more conscious control of respiration than is normal. This, together with impaired co-ordination of the tongue, oral musculature, and vocal cords, results in the dysarthric speech which is quite common in brain damage. The child may merely be unable to enunciate clearly. In severe form, he is unable to form certain of the basic sounds or phonemes, so that there may be serious inability at communication. This complicates the language problem, the aphasia (if it is also present), and even seriously impairs the child's motivation to language development.

In addition to those listed above, there are other symptoms which are not particularly specific to brain damage. Perhaps the most frequent of these, and indeed the one for which the child is probably referred more often than any other, is antisocial behavior. This may take virtually any form, and is dependent largely on the child's life experience, his modes of defense, his reaction formations, and the particular opportunities for acting out. Brain-damaged children are often socially delinquent; they may be fire-setters, sexual delinquents, vandals, the whole gamut of delinquency. Or they may simply be poorly behaved children, untrustworthy, dishonest, defiant of authority; they may disrupt the classroom, drive the teacher to despair; they may be the scourge of the neighborhood and the terror of the school. In such cases, by placing the child away from home, one is treating not only a patient but a whole community.

Some degree of mental retardation is not uncommon. The more severe retardations are, as noted above, not usually referred to the psychiatrist. These are often readily diagnosed early by the family physician or pediatrician. Other cases may have only moderate retardation, best measured by psychological testing. However, performance on psychological tests may be quite uneven, with low scoring in specific areas, so that a below-average total score may not be an accurate representation of certain of the specific capacities. Sensory disturbances are not uncommon, particularly auditory disturbances, and to a lesser extent, visual ones. On the other hand, these may be falsely diagnosed, and it is not unusual to find brain-damaged children who have been incorrectly labelled as partially deaf or as "needing glasses," when the difficulty is one of central perception, or of lack of motivation, or of inability to cooperate in the testing situation.

Epileptic seizures sometimes accompany brain damage. The most frequent is petit mal, and occasionally one sees the severe form of this, called pyknolepsy, with frequent brief petit mal attacks. Grand mal seizures seem to be rare in association with brain damage. However, this may be because such cases are referred to a physician primarily because of grand mal rather than because of their other symptoms, and are thus seen by the neurologist and treated mainly as epilepsy rather than as a psychiatric problem.

Psychomotor seizures, the so-called temporal lobe seizures, are also rarely seen in the child psychiatry clinic. They are perhaps overdiagnosed in some clinics, and this appears to depend largely on the examiner's particular interest in the disorder. Some suspect the presence of temporal lobe epilepsy in any case with frequent outbursts of anger or rage which the child is unable to explain to the examiner. If the case is accompanied by the presence of some "abnormal" discharges on the electroencephalogram, the diagnosis is "confirmed." Many of these cases are treated for years with anticonvulsants, usually without success, usually without proper attention to the child's real needs in the areas of learning and of help with patterning and control, and often to the extent that the child is in and out of drug toxicity during most of his childhood. This is maltreatment of the grossest type, and is obviously worse than no treatment at all. This is not to say that a trial of anticonvulsants is not indicated in a case which shows strong evidence of being a convulsive disorder, but such treatment, as in the case of any treatment of any epilepsy, should always include attention to the child's other problems, particularly problems of emotion and adjustment.

DIAGNOSIS

The major diagnostic criteria, listed in order of importance, are:
1. Clinical picture of brain damage
2. History of early maladjustment
3. Psychological tests characteristic of brain damage
4. History suggestive of brain trauma
5. Electroencephalography

The first three of these will contribute to the diagnosis in virtually every case. The fourth is absent more often than not.

By far the most important segments of the diagnostic evaluation are the clinical evaluation of presenting problems and examination of the patient. Most of the first five in the list of symptoms (mentioned above) will be found if carefully looked for, and these alone establish the diagnosis.

PSYCHIATRIC INTERVIEW

The diagnostic interview consists mainly in observing the child in the office. Brain-damaged children are generally among the easiest to evaluate, because much "material" is readily obtained; these children begin to "produce" the moment they enter the office. All one needs to do is watch them perform, as they dash about the office, or as they try unsuccessfully to sit quietly in the chair. The interview should usually begin with some conversation aimed toward establishing a relationship. A humorous approach is often helpful as it helps to alleviate the apprehension. Generally one should not attempt early to structure the situation, but should permit the child to relieve his tension by letting him wander. At some time in the interview, however, it is helpful diagnostically to see how long he can sit still, and also to see how long he can attend to a particular task such as drawing a picture both with and without close support and encouragement from the examiner.

In most cases, the child's symptoms should be openly recognized and discussed, or at least mentioned. One may point out that he seems quite nervous or that he seems unable to sit still, and one may ask him if he is aware of this, how long he has been this way, how he accounts for this trouble, and so on. A prolonged exploration of the subject is seldom indicated, but verbal recognition of it helps to set the therapeutic tone, and is also helpful in evaluating the child's feelings about himself. In brain damage, as in virtually every other disturbance in children, it is a mistake to act as if there is nothing wrong, and to pretend that the interview is just a friendly visit.

Sometimes, in an especially frightened and overcontrolled child, it may be helpful to stimulate him into activity in order to gauge the degree of his excitability and his inability to control his impulses. Verbal methods are often sufficient to stimulate him, through such techniques as making spontaneous jokes, silly remarks, laughing loudly, and the like. Another technique is the use of games which involve motor activity, such as building and knocking over a tall stack of blocks. Brain-damaged children may get wildly excited, and often are not able to stop when the examiner feels that it is time to call a halt. Obviously, the situation must not get out of hand, and, with experience, one can learn how far to proceed with such children, and how to interrupt the activity before the child becomes too excited. Sometimes considerable firmness is required, especially if the activity begins to be dangerous or destructive.

PERSONAL HISTORY

An accurate history of the child's early development and behavior will almost invariably disclose that his difficulties began early. The parents will describe the characteristic hyperkinesis, impulsivity, low frustration tolerance, and distractibility. The child is often described as having been difficult to manage from his first year, restless, difficult to hold as a baby, prone to outbursts of rage, always getting into fights, and frequently destructive of his toys and other objects. And through all of the story, through all of the parents' description and complaint of the chronic and continuous disorder and misbehavior, there runs a consistent thread of expostulation, implied or expressed, that somehow the child's behavior has been unreasonable, that it was more than the situation warranted, and, by inference, that the child's disorder comes from within. There is a vast difference between this attitude and the attitude of a mother who never wanted her child in the first place, and whose own rejection has induced his maladjustment and his misbehavior.

But differentiation is not always easy, and sometimes, of course, both problems are present. The presence of interfamilial psychopathology by no means rules out the possibility that the child's disorder may be intrinsic as well as extrinsic; as noted above, Bender feels that both are usually present in the brain-damaged child whose disorder is so severe as to come to psychiatric attention.

PSYCHOLOGICAL EXAMINATION

Psychological tests can be very helpful in the diagnosis of brain damage. However, as in all cases, the test results must be co-ordinated with the history and clinical findings. While it is sometimes possible for the psychologist to state unequivocally and with accuracy that this test performance is "organic," more often the test results will be only indicative or suggestive of brain damage. Psychological tests are most valuable in helping to evaluate the child's particular deficiencies and areas of difficulty, and thus aid in working out a more satisfactory plan of therapy.

Certain of the subtests of the Stanford-Binet and the Wechsler Intelligence Scale for Children have been found by psychologists to show particular patterns in many brain-damaged children. Most of these involve some aspect of perception, or perceptual-motor co-ordination, or the ability to conceptualize—to see the patterns in groups of similar things. For example, the block design and the similarities subtests on the Wechsler are often poorly executed by brain-damaged children. If symbolic processes, such as language and arithmetic, are deficient, then certain of the verbal scores will be lower, including the vocabulary and the arithmetic subtests.

The Bender Gestalt Test was developed by Bender and Schilder originally for the purpose of testing for defects of visual-motor coordination in organic brain disease. This test is now widely used and is considered by most psychologists to be valuable in eliciting evidences of brain damage in children. The test is administered by presenting the patient with nine cards, each of which contains a simple geometric figure. He is asked to copy the figures on a blank sheet of paper as accurately as possible. Administration and scoring of the test is described in a monograph by Bender (1952). This book and the test cards, obtainable from the American Orthopsychiatric Association, should be in the office of every child psychiatrist. If testing by psychologist is not a part of the evaluation, then the Bender Gestalt Test may be readily given by the examining psychiatrist. Administration of the test usually requires no more than five minutes, and is a most valuable part of the interview.

Findings in the Bender Gestalt Test most suggestive of brain damage are:

1. *Directional Confusion.* These include (a) rotation of figures so that they are drawn 90 to 180 degrees from the normal axis; (b) difficulty reproducing angles, so that angles are too obtuse or acute, or there may be little "ears" and other complex figures at the angle apices, indicating that the child was uncertain in which direction to go.

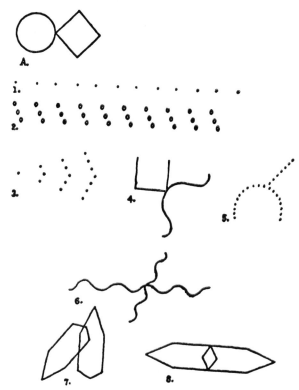

Fig. 1. Figures employed in Bender Gestalt test. Copyright, 1946, Lauretta Bender and American Orthopsychiatric Association, Inc. Reproduced with permission.

2. *Inability To Reproduce the Gestalts.* This graphically portrays the basic defect in brain damage, the inability to organize perceived parts into wholes, and the tendency to perceive them rather as separate, disunited fragments. This is most often elicited in the "Christmas tree" figure which is composed of a series of dots looking rather like a Christmas tree lying on its side. The child fails to perceive the figure as a whole, and produces simply a cluster of dots without any organization. Another common mistake is failure, in the first figure, to connect the diamond and circle, so that they are drawn as disunited fragments.

3. *Poor Organization.* The figures may be scattered at random over the page, sometimes overlapping one another, sometimes starting too near the edge so that they run off the page.

4. *Perseveration.* This is seen in the figures which consist of a long row of repeated figures, such as dots or circles. The child begins to draw the repetitious figure and continues until he comes to the end of the page.

Figure 1 shows Bender figures as they appear on the test cards, and

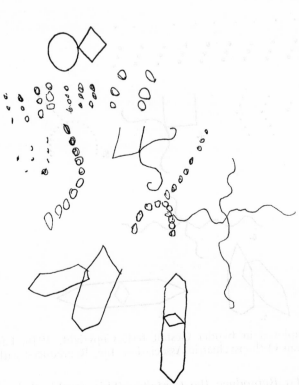

Fig. 2. Bender Gestalt drawings of 10-year-old boy with brain damage.

Figure 2 shows them as they were reproduced by a 10-year-old brain-damaged boy of average intelligence. Figure 3 shows Bender figures as drawn by two brain-damaged boys.

HISTORY OF BRAIN TRAUMA

It was pointed out earlier that such a history is not often obtained, and that it is not essential for the diagnosis of brain damage. When a good history of trauma is present, it may be regarded somewhat as a gratuity, as a piece of evidence which makes the diagnosis all the more conclusive. A careful inquiry into the circumstances of the pregnancy, delivery, and early postnatal period is therefore indicated. Unfortunately, obstetric complications are often concealed from parents to avoid alarming them. Thus, such complications as postnatal apnea or a twisted umbilical cord may have

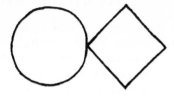

Fig. A

Fig. 3

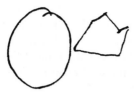

Same figures drawn by a 9-year-old brain-damaged boy.

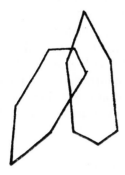

Fig. 7

Same figure drawn by an 11½-year-old
brain-damaged boy.

Fig. 3. Bender figures.

175

occurred without having been recorded, or at least without having been disclosed to the parents. A history of a severe illness during infancy with prolonged high fever is suggestive of brain damage, but is, of course, not conclusive. Evidences of behavioral changes immediately following such episodes are more strongly suggestive. A history of having received a blow on the head, or of having fallen on the head during infancy, is usually of no significance; probably no infant ever escaped at least one such injury. However, a head blow followed by protracted unconsciousness or by obvious behavioral changes may be important. A history of encephalitis is naturally highly significant, and Levy has pointed out that post-encephalitic behavior disorders are by no means rare. There may be other specific diseases which are the basis for the cerebral injury, and a thorough medical history and examination are indicated in all these cases. For example, the writer recently saw a 10-year-old boy with typical findings of brain damage, who was found on subsequent medical examination to have phenylpyruvic oligophrenia with average intelligence!

ELECTROENCEPHALOGRAPHY

An electroencephalogram is at present of little or no value in the diagnosis of brain damage in children. In most cases it should not be done, as it is merely an unnecessary expense for the parents. Electroencephalograms in children vary widely, and standardization is as yet unsatisfactory. Tracings which would be considered abnormal in adults, such as bursts of high frequency discharge, occur in normal children. Bradley has observed that "An abnormal electroencephalogram in the absence of organic behavior patterns of psychologic test performance is of little significance. . . . On the other hand, many children with convincing evidence that organic factors are influencing their adjustment will show normal tracings." Also, electroencephalograms have been shown to fluctuate with clinical changes in emotionally disturbed children who are apparently not brain damaged (Kennard). Electroencephalography is indicated in cases which are suggestive of epilepsy, and are specifically indicated in suspected cases of brain tumor or brain abscess.

DIFFERENTIAL DIAGNOSIS

Brain damage may at times be confused with virtually all of the other major psychiatric disorders in children. The child with neurosis, with personality disorder, with schizophrenia, or with specific language and learning disabilities, may, in certain cases, resemble the brain-damaged child.

The presence of a severely disordered and damaging life experience in a child is not a contraindication to the diagnosis of brain damage. The two often go together, and, as noted earlier, it is the children with brain damage who have also experienced emotional neglect who are most often seen in the psychiatric clinics. How many children there are with brain damage who, through excellent rearing, escape serious maladjustment is not known, but there are probably a considerable number.

The differential diagnosis between the child whose disturbance is caused mainly by his experiences and one with both brain damage and environmental trauma is not merely an academic one. Treatment requirements of the two are quite different. Both need attention to the environmental problems, with an aim of improving the child's present environment or transferring him to a different environment. Additionally, the brain-damaged child needs special attention to his specific disorders in the areas of conceptualization, language functioning, and so forth. The non-brain-damaged child, on the other hand, is more likely to benefit by individual psychotherapy directed toward his particular areas of conflict.

PSYCHONEUROSIS

The neurotic child who is highly anxious, tense, restless and fidgety, who exhibits a motor drivenness, who is too anxious to function well in school, too preoccupied to maintain attention, may be difficult to differentiate from a brain-damaged child. A good history of early infancy with evidence of characteristic early symptoms of brain damage is most helpful in the diagnosis. In the neurotic child, the perceptual and conceptual difficulties are usually absent, and some testing of these functions should be a part of the diagnostic evaluation. These include having the child estimate such things as the height of the examiner, the height of the ceiling, the relative distances between various objects, the time required for the child to come to the clinic, and the duration of the interview.

Psychological testing, especially the Bender Gestalt Test, usually shows evidences of brain damage which are not seen in the neurotic. Thought content expressing the emotional conflict is sometimes readily available in neurosis, and helps in the diagnosis, although the brain-damaged child who is anxious may also express similar content.

There is usually a difference in quality between the motor tension of the neurotic and of the brain-damaged child. This is difficult to describe, and best learned by experience. Briefly, it appears as a constriction of movement in the neurotic, as compared with a disorganization of movement in the brain-damaged. Yet, like all generalizations, this one has many exceptions, and the movements of a neurotic child can sometimes become rather wild.

PERSONALITY DISORDER

The remarks on psychoneurosis apply generally to this disorder. An additional difficulty in differentiation is presented by the chronicity, so that in this respect personality disorder more resembles brain damage. Another difficulty is that an accurate early history is usually more difficult to obtain, because the parents are usually more rejecting of the child, were less interested in him, and also are less likely to give an honest and careful story.

The disorganization of behavior in severe forms of personality disorder may resemble the behavior of brain damage to a remarkable degree. It is very likely, as a result of the chronic emotional conflict, of the lack of consistency in experience, of the constant shifting of stimulus-input, and of the inability to develop any persistent and sustained patterns of reaction, that brain function itself is disrupted and disorganized in these children, and that this disorganization is similar to that occurring where there is actual tissue destruction. Eisenberg has emphasized that the chronically disabling "experimental neuroses" produced in animals have demonstrated that severe brain dysfunction can be induced by environmental influences. Eisenberg observes: "Extrinsic influences have produced nervous dysfunction no less total than that which can be caused by intrinsic lesions." In such cases, differential diagnosis becomes a problem in assessing the extent to which extrinsic versus intrinsic factors have contributed to the child's disorder.

SCHIZOPHRENIA

Most cases of childhood schizophrenia are readily differentiated from brain damage, but some cases closely resemble one another. These are generally children with severe language dysfunction who have, because of lack of communication with the environment, made an autistic adjustment. A brain-damaged child of this type may be extremely inaccessible, may have developed bizarre mannerisms, and may have a language of his own which consists of meaningless, usually repetitive sounds. Such a child can be a real diagnostic puzzle, and differentiation from schizophrenia is difficult or impossible, especially in younger children.

LANGUAGE AND LEARNING DISABILITIES

Differentiation between these disorders and brain damage depends upon the demonstration of the other manifestations of brain damage as already described in this chapter. As noted previously, brain damage may be accompanied by various aphasias. Conversely, the aphasias may occur with little or none of the other dysfunctions seen in some brain damage such as disinhibition and the visual-motor dysfunctions. The aphasias may be caused by organic damage or by agenesis; some are genetically determined. There is thus considerable overlapping of these disorders. In many cases a clear-cut differentiation is not possible. Neither is it essential, and the important consideration must be to understand the extent of the child's difficulties in the several areas of function, including language, conceptualization, perception, and impulse control, and to provide him with the appropriate help.

TREATMENT

When parents are told that their child has brain damage, they invariably and understandably ask if anything can be done about it. By this they usually mean: can anything be done to restore the damaged tissue? The answer, of course, is "No." At the present time, except in the few rare cases in which a contracting scar or a localized mass of hyperdischarging nerve cells forming an epileptogenic focus may be surgically removed, there is nothing to be done directly for the damaged brain. However, the fact that such cases do exist may give promise for greater application of such approaches in the future. This is especially true if the basis of the disorder is the occurrence of groups of hyperirritable neurons. As neurosurgical techniques improve, and especially with the development of non-surgical methods for destruction or inhibition of such cells, by ultrasound, for example, or specific drugs, it may be hoped that "direct" treatment of brain damage may become more feasible. However, at present, treatment must remain largely in the hands of the pediatrician, the child psychiatrist, the teacher, and the parents.

The major approaches to treatment of the brain-damaged child may be classified as follows:
1. Treatment of the emotional and behavioral difficulties
2. Special education
3. Drugs

EMOTIONAL AND BEHAVIORAL PROBLEMS

These are approached in various ways, depending upon the specific indications, the child's particular home and school environment, the nature of the difficulties and the severity of the disorder. Treatment often involves manipulation of the environment, including working with the parents to help them understand the child's special needs and deficiencies, and, if indicated, placement away from home in a special school or institution. It may involve conferences and discussions with the child's teachers, arrangements for him to attend special classes or to have special attention or an individualized program within the regular school. Underlying all these arrangements and manipulations is the basic principle that the child needs individual attention, direct help with control of his impulses and maintaining his attention, and protection from distracting stimuli. These children invariably function better and learn better in small groups or in a "one-to one" situation. Thus, they may be benefited by private tutoring, and by a home situation where a parent or an older sibling can play with them periodically on an individual basis. At home they usually require rather close supervision, and while they should have some freedom of action and opportunity to socialize, mothers usually find it helpful to note when the child is becoming overly excited and to remove him from the situation for a period of quiet.

One of the paradoxes of treatment is that in a group setting such as the school classroom the brain-damaged child does best if the group is highly controlled, yet he himself cannot tolerate being too controlled. This requires that a teacher must be able to "keep the lid on" the class, yet must at times allow the brain-damaged child some opportunities for physical or verbal expression. Not all teachers are successful at this. The value of the child's having such a teacher can hardly be overestimated. The differences in adjustment which brain-damaged children are able to make with two different teachers is striking. If a teacher is unable to maintain order in the classroom, so that it is in constant turmoil, the child is seriously overstimulated, and no amount of psychotherapy or good care at home can overcome such a difficulty. Likewise a neurotic, rigid, or sadistic teacher can make him miserable, and, by her insistence on complete conformity to all the rules, can raise his tension to the breaking point and shatter what little remains of his hope and his self-esteem. The tragedy in many of these cases is that although what is needed is recognized, it cannot be obtained.

These are children with whom much effort must be expended. This requires that the psychiatrist should confer with the school, talk with the child's counselor, teacher, principal, whoever is interested, and whoever is sufficiently mature and intelligent to assist in effecting the required program. Most school authorities, if approached in the proper spirit, are willing to help the child.

The setting up of any treatment program requires that enough time be spent with the parents or parent figures to assure that they have some understanding of the child's deficiencies and particular needs. Almost without exception it is best to inform the parents immediately as to the diagnosis and nature of the problem. It might seem unkind to tell a parent that his child has brain damage. But the writer has seen many parents who have sought help for years from various clinics and agencies and who were never told the diagnosis, either because it was not made or because the therapist felt it better not to tell them. The implication is thus inevitably that the child's upbringing is the cause of his trouble, and much unnecessary guilt and self-recrimination ensue. Moreover, in such a situation, emphasis in therapy is usually in the wrong directions; since the child's needs are not understood, they can hardly be adequately met. Most parents are grateful, although understandably upset, when informed of the diagnosis. They often express such beliefs as "At least we know now what we're dealing with," or "I feel as if we are at last getting to the bottom of this thing."

Bradley has emphasized some of the problems in convincing parents and teachers of the necessity of special attention and special protection for these children. This may be especially difficult for a boy's father, who wants his boy to "learn how to take care of himself." Bradley notes "overprotection, which is so easily derided by those who cannot comprehend what a dependent child really needs, may be a necessity for such children, but many parents will need external support to enable them to follow their own urges in this direction. Approval of the child's need to be dependent, up to a point where he himself begins to seek emancipation, can and must be encouraged."

The parents' feelings about the cause of their child's problems must be explored, and their distortions and misconceptions straightened out. Mothers often wonder if they somehow caused the injury during their pregnancy, and they will dwell obsessively on some minor infraction, such as a dietary overindulgence, or an unnecessary automobile trip. Many parents, despite the diagnosis of brain damage, will continue to wonder if they were at fault in rearing the child, and if he would have "turned out" better under different care. Their feelings can be quite complex: They may resent the child bitterly, and in reaction formation feel excessively overprotective, or inordinately guilty.

Often the parents' distortions respond to simple reassurance. Sometimes they are deeper, and require psychiatric treatment.

SPECIAL EDUCATION

Special techniques in training and education relate to the language and learning problems which many brain-damaged children have. Education here includes both the formal academic training which has become a major subspecialty of the teaching profession, and the simple training and techniques which assist the child in learning such concepts as time, direction, and size, and which may be undertaken by anyone interested in helping him, including parents, siblings, and therapist.

The subject of special education is discussed more fully in the following chapter on specific learning disabilities, and will not be discussed here. This is a major aspect of the treatment of the brain-damaged child (Strauss and Lehtinen). Most of these children are strongly motivated to learn, although many are understandably discouraged and need much reassurance to convince them that effort expended will be rewarded. This is a problem for the therapist, and it should be approached in the initial evaluation. Throughout treatment, a major portion of the therapist's time is well spent in a consideration of the child's academic progress, and can even take the form of looking over some of his school work and helping him with a reading assignment or an arithmetic problem.

These children with special learning problems, because they do so poorly in school, often become convinced that they are "stupid." Such thoughts should be explored and discussed frankly early in the treatment program, and the therapist should try to explain that the child's learning defects are of a specific nature, and that his general intelligence is adequate. Such explanations are often highly reassuring, and can go a long way toward motivating the patient and raising his self-esteem.

DRUG THERAPY

The amphetamines have been extensively used in hyperactive brain-damaged children, and a proportion of such children respond favorably with reduction of their behavioral symptoms. Other brain-damaged children have been helped by various of the phenothiazine drugs. This aspect of treatment of the brain-damaged child is discussed more fully in the chapter on psychopharmacologic treatment (Chapter 19).

PROGNOSIS

There have not yet been sufficient long-term follow-up studies of brain-damaged children to warrant definite conclusions about prognosis. Undoubtedly, outcome varies greatly, depending on severity of disorder, continuing experience of the child, and opportunities for special education and treatment.

It is known that a large proportion of these children improve, and some improve tremendously. Laufer and others are generally optimistic about prognosis, noting that most cases spontaneously improve even to the point of complete cessation of symptoms. They observe that "in most children seen here, the manifestations of the hyperkinetic syndrome will disappear, with medication no longer needed, by the end of adolescence at least, and often before this." Most workers would probably not express so high an optimism, and it would certainly be a mistake to adopt the attitude that the condition will spontaneously "clear up," so that all one needs to do is wait for time to pass. If the child is in difficulty socially and academically, he must be helped, and the degree to which he can improve in the immediate future will determine, to a considerable extent, his adjustment for the more distant future.

REFERENCES

Bender, L. The Psychological Problems of Children with Organic Brain Disease, Am. J. Orthopsychiatry, 19: 404, 1949.
——— A Test of Visual-Motor Gestalt Functioning and Its Clinical Use, Research Monograph No. 3, New York, American Orthopsychiatric Association, 1952.
——— The Psychological Problems and Their Management in the Brain-Damaged Child—a Summary, in Psychopathology of Children with Organic Brain Disorders, Springfield, Ill., Charles C Thomas, 1956.
Bradley, C. Organic Factors in Psychopathology of Childhood, in Psychopathology of Childhood, eds. Hoch and Zubin, New York, Grune & Stratton, 1955.
Clemmens, R. S. Minimal Brain Damage in Children, Children, 8: 179, 1961.
Eisenberg, L. Psychiatric Implications of Brain Damage in Children, Psychiatric Quart., 31: 72, 1957.
Goldstein, K. The Brain-Injured Child, in Pediatric Problems in Clinical Practice, ed. Michal-Smith, New York, Grune & Stratton, 1954.
Hebb, D. O. The Organization of Behavior, New York, John Wiley & Sons, 1949.
Kennard, M. The Characteristics of Thought Disturbances as Related to Electroencephalographic Findings in Children and Adolescents, Am. J. Psychiatry, 115: 911, 1959.
Laufer, M., Denhoff, E., and Solomons, G. Hyperkinetic Impulse Disorder in Children's Behavior Problems, Psychosomatic Medicine, 19: 38, 1957.
Levy, S. Post-Encephalitic Behavior Disorder—a Forgotten Entity, Am. J. Psychiatry, 115: 1062, 1959.
Paine, R. S. Minimal Chronic Brain Syndromes in Children, Develop. Med. and Child Neurol., 4: 21, 1962.
Pasamanick, B., and Knobloch, H. Epidemiologic Studies on the Complications of Pregnancy and the Birth Process, in Prevention of Mental Disorders in Children, ed. G. Caplan, New York, Basic Books, 1961.
Strauss, A., and Kephart, N. Psychopathology and Education of the Brain-Injured Child, Volume II: Progress in Theory and Clinic, New York, Grune & Stratton, 1955.
——— and Lehtinen, L. Psychopathology and Education of the Brain-Injured Child, New York, Grune & Stratton, 1947.

9

SPECIFIC LEARNING DISABILITIES

REPORT OF TWO CASES

CASE 1—GEORGE B.

George B. first came to the attention of the juvenile court at the age of 6. His mother had asked the court for help with George's behavior, which consisted of "stealing, lying, assaulting classmates, swearing, destruction of household items, exclusion from school, and excessive masturbation."

When George was less than a year old his father was sentenced to five years in prison for larceny. Soon afterward, when George was 2, his mother obtained a divorce, and remarried. The stepfather had been previously married to an alcoholic woman, and had two children by his former marriage, a boy and a girl who were 6 and 4 years older than George respectively. The stepfather was a vast improvement over the mother's first husband; he was steadily employed, sober, and interested in his family. He was, however, a passive, somewhat ineffectual person. It was felt that he married the mother partly out of sympathy for her misfortunes and partly in the hope of providing a mother for his children. Unfortunately, she was a cold, domineering woman who resented all men. The home was thus not a happy one.

The court placed George for several months in a boarding home, hoping that a change of environment would help. It did not, and his behavior became worse. He was referred to a child guidance clinic, diagnosed there as an "adjustment reaction," and placed in an open institution for disturbed children.

George's behavior continued to be extremely disturbed; he was aggressive, negative, rebellious, and on two occasions he ran away from the institution. At the age of 10 he was admitted as a voluntary patient to the children's ward of a state hospital. At this time it was noted that his achievement was quite retarded, and he was referred to the psychiatric outpatient clinic for evaluation.

Reading tests showed that George was essentially a non-reader. His sight vocabulary consisted of five words. In the hospital school he had been doing third-grade arithmetic, and fifth- to sixth-grade geography and art, but all the written material had to be read to him. His verbal comprehension was adequate, and in normal conversation there was little evidence of language retardation. However, his language disclosed a rather concrete level of thinking. When questioned directly regarding such abstract concepts as time and distance, his defect became obvious. He did not know the number of months in a year, and when asked how many days in a month he guessed "66." He said the distance from Detroit to New York was 18 miles. When asked to name the months in winter he said, "Fall, September, and June." He could not print the word cat, and when he was told how to spell it he wrote the letter c backwards.

On the Wechsler Intelligence Scale for Children, George achieved a verbal I.Q. of 81 and a performance I.Q. of 115, a discrepancy of 34 points. The lowest subtest scores were in vocabulary and similarities. During the testing and the psychiatric interview he evidenced considerable anxiety and low self-esteem. His attitude toward authority figures was marked by resentment and distrust, but he was felt to have an adequate capacity for relationship. The psychiatric diagnosis was primary reading disability complicated by psychoneurosis.

It was arranged for George to attend the outpatient language clinic while remaining an inpatient at the state hospital. He made little progress at first, as he was in a group reading-therapy situation and continued to act out and be disruptive to the group. After six months, individual reading therapy was begun and his behavior and attitude toward reading improved dramatically. He became much more motivated, interested, and cooperative. He developed some phonic skills, and was soon able to sound out the simpler words by a phonic approach. But progress was slow and he never developed much sight vocabulary.

After 18 months in the outpatient reading clinic, George was admitted at the age of 12 to the residential treatment center. He continued to improve in his emotional adjustment; his self-esteem was greatly elevated, and peer relationships were for the most part excellent although he still had occasional problems with controlling his temper. He developed a great deal of personal insight, and some understanding and acceptance of his reading disability. At the time of discharge at the age of 13 he had a realistic appraisal of himself and plans for the future. He was transferred to Boys' Town, and continued to do well. At the time of discharge he was reading at about a second-grade level. He continued reading therapy, and it was expected that his eventual reading level should be about fourth-grade. He will thus not be able to complete a regular high school academic course, but will undoubtedly function well in a vocational course, and, with his high general intelligence, his vocational outlook is good.

CASE 2—ROBERT W.

Robert W. was referred to the guidance clinic by his school counselor because of academic failure, with special difficulty in reading. The referring letter stated that his difficulty was possibly due to "emotional block." At the time of referral Robert should normally have been in the sixth grade, but he was actually in the fourth, and was functioning far below this level. His teachers had long been puzzled by his inability to learn, as he was well-motivated, well-behaved, and "seemed to be an intelligent boy."

Robert's reading problem had been recognized soon after he started school. Special help had been sought, but with little success, as there were no reading teachers or tutors available in the area. The problem had been compounded by the family's having lived in another state for three years, during which time, when Robert was aged 7 to 10, he was seen intermittently at a guidance clinic and apparently had been considered neurotic. During this treatment, the parents had been "worked with" at some length, with much attention directed toward their own emotional adjustment and marital relationships. The chief effect of this had been to arouse doubt, confusion, guilt, and resentment in the parents, although they survived the experience well. Robert's reading remained unimproved.

At the second guidance clinic, the diagnosis of primary reading disability was made, and Robert was referred at age 11 to Hawthorn Center for evaluation in the language clinic. Outpatient testing disclosed that he was able to read at a low first-grade level. His sight vocabulary was almost nil. Speaking vocabulary was low for his age, but not nearly so low as the reading vocabulary, so that he could maintain a conversation, although his language use was quite concrete. In arithmetic, Robert scored at a third-grade level. On the Wechsler Intelligence Scale for Children, his verbal I.Q. was 87 and performance I.Q. 114, a discrepancy of 27 points. The lowest subtests were vocabulary, arithmetic, and information. The Bender Gestalt drawings were immature and poorly organized, but showed no evidence of directional confusion.

In the initial psychiatric interview, Robert was pleasant, friendly, and not unusually anxious or apprehensive. He expressed concern over his academic difficulties. When asked to estimate the examiner's height, he said "about 8½ feet." He did not know the present month. When asked what is the hottest month of the year he said "October." When asked what is the coldest month he said "Christmas—oh, I don't know."

The diagnostic impression was mixed aphasia with major difficulty in reading. Robert was placed on the waiting list for admission to the inpatient unit, but because of the number of applicants, he was not admitted until the following year. Meanwhile, arrangements were made for a private tutor in reading, and the tutoring was supervised through an arrangement by which the tutor and Robert were seen occasionally in the language clinic.

Robert was admitted to the inpatient unit at the age of 13. At that time he was still reading at only a first-grade level. Thus he could read with some facility: "The boy had a dog. The dog's face was black. He had no tail at all."

Because of his good looks, athletic prowess, and general friendliness and good adjustment, Robert quickly attained considerable status and prestige among his peers at the institution. He did well in most of his classes, as long as he could receive help with the written material. He progressed rapidly in arithmetic. He was highly motivated to learn the reading, and received an hour of individual reading therapy daily. Unfortunately, like George in the previous case, eagerness to learn was not enough, and progress was extremely slow. Some reading improvement did occur, and the technique which was most successful with Robert was the kinesthetic approach. In this method, the student traces out large letters with his fingers, and learns to perceive them through feel rather than visual perception. At the end of a year he had progressed one grade in reading. He was discharged to his home, and returned to public school. He continued to receive remedial reading from a private tutor. His reading therapist estimates that he will probably never progress beyond a third-grade reading level.

SUMMARY

These two cases are presented to contrast the behavior and emotional adjustment between two cases of primary reading disability, one of which had a good environment, the other a poor one. In both cases, the basic defect is the same: a mixed aphasia affecting all areas of language and conceptualization.

THE MEANING OF LANGUAGE

A dog can be taught that when he hears the sound of a buzzer he is about to receive an electric shock. The buzzer thus becomes a symbol: it represents or symbolizes that the shock is about to occur. Furthermore, the dog can learn that other, similar sounds have the same meaning, and he will respond to a different buzzer, of a frequency and intensity which he has not heard before. He has learned to *generalize*. Additionally, the dog can learn that another sound, say a bell tone, means that no shock is coming. He thus learns to *discriminate* between symbols; he does not react indiscriminately to all sounds.

The repertory of the dog's "language" understanding can become rather large. He can discriminate readily the sounds of a dozen or more verbal commands given by his master, all of which differ a little in pitch, volume, inflection, and duration. He can "roll over," "sit up," "heel," and so on. He can learn these complex signals so that other persons beside his trainer may, if they speak carefully, elicit the appropriate responses.

Can this be called language? Certainly, it contains most of the elements of a language: it is symbolic representation of a number of different meanings transmitted from one individual to another; it is systematic; and it is learned. The last point is an important one, as it helps to differentiate between true language and those instinctual signal systems employed by many of the lower animals, such as the "song" by which bees direct one another to flowers. The language of animals is a fascinating study, and many naturalists have become adept at analyzing and imitating the auditory signals of animals. The German naturalist, Lorenz, could "talk" to many of the wild birds around his Danube farm; he could call to a hawk as it wheeled high overhead, and could entice a jackdaw into his window with sounds suggesting to the unsuspecting bird that a lovely little mate was beckoning him. But these often complex natural signal systems can hardly be considered language, at least in the sense in which it is here used. They are a part of the built-in instinctual behavior of the animal, little modified by learning. Nor can the dog's understanding of his master's command be considered language; language implies a two-way communication.

LANGUAGE AS EMOTIONAL EXPRESSION

The chimpanzees may have a kind of primitive language. Certainly they have a rather large repertory of sounds. These appear to be subjective expressions of emotional states such as fear, alarm, and excitement (Yerkes and Lerned). The vocalizations of the lower primates probably represent the earliest form and use of language. It is likely that in primitive man language at first consisted of differential expressions of feeling.

Thus, language was originally not a system of communication but the vocal component of emotional expression. This remains one of its important functions. In the young child it is its chief function. Piaget has observed that much of the verbalization of nursery school children is simply expression of the child's feelings, and not intended to communicate with others. Piaget terms this speech "egocentric." For example, the child playing with his toys in a group of children may shout "Watch me," or he may say "It broke, it broke." These might seem intended to impart information to others, but on analysis one finds that the child does not really concern himself with an audience; he does not usually expect an answer. He is simply expressing what he feels and thinks.

LANGUAGE AS COMMUNICATION

The beginning of true language as a communication medium consists of the naming of objects. Here, a particular group of sounds represents a specific object. This is language at its most concrete. It is the language which infants first learn, and many nine-month old babies can say "ball" or "cup" when these objects are pointed to.

The next step in language development was undoubtedly the inclusion of verb forms, which indicate, to recall a phrase from grade-school English, "action or a state of being." This was a major development, involving a rather high level of abstraction. In terms of the intellectual level required for its attainment, it probably represents as great an advance in evolution as did the advance from the anthropoid stage to the stage of object-naming. As to time, it may have required half a million years. The human infant today accomplishes it in one year.

Higher language development proceeds as the child's intelligence and accumulated experience increase. Such abstract concepts as "good" and "bad," "love" and "hate," soon have meaning for the child as he learns to associate these words with parental approval or disapproval. Having experienced several episodes in which the word "bad" was applied, he soon is able to generalize, and understands that not only the episodes which he has experienced and remembered, but also other episodes which he might engage in would be designated as "bad." Along the way, certain confusions arise which have to be cleared up by later information. For instance, one mother would say to her child "hot" whenever he started to touch something that was forbidden, such as an expensive vase. For this child, the word "hot" did not refer to those things only which emitted heat, but to anything which he should not touch.

An amusing example of one child's concrete misinterpretation of an abstract word occurred on the occasion of the young child's first successful bowel movement accomplished on the toilet. The parents were praising and congratulating the little girl, and the mother, pointing to the stool, exclaimed "And such a *big* one!" On the next occasion, the child pointed proudly to her production and exclaimed "Big! big!" It was obvious to her, since she was still at the object-naming level of language, that the word "big" was here the name of an object, not the designation of a size category. This meaning was adopted by the family, and to this day, though the little girl is now an adolescent, having a bowel movement is called, in this family, "doing a big."

Higher levels of language abstraction are but elaborations of the original principle of generalization. Here, the variations in meaning among different individuals become more apparent. The meaning is determined not only by the conventional "definition" of the word, but also by the individual's own experiences which he has come to associate with the word. Take, for example, "art." The child is likely to meet the word first in his grade-school class, where "art" means drawing pictures and making things with clay. It also means, at this age, the total classroom situation, the presence of a particular teacher, the way other children conduct themselves during the art class, and the like. To the college sophomore pseudo-sophisticate, "art" still has as part of its meaning the drawing of pictures, but it also has many other meanings; it means, for example, something one must be able to talk knowingly about. To the artist and connoisseur, the word art has yet another level of meaning, and evokes a complex association of feelings and experiences. At this level, individual experiences and personality add greatly to the variety of meanings of the word. While these individuals could readily agree on some general definition of the word, they might also spend an entire evening arguing the question "What is art?"

LANGUAGE AS SOCIAL CONTACT

In addition to providing a means of emotional expression and of communication, language has a third important function: social contact. Revesz considers that it was the need for contact among social animals including man which was the basis for development of a true language. He thus considers the contact calls of lower animals a language. Certainly much of the conversation between people is a social experience, providing pleasure in the human contact. There is in such conversations no real need to transmit information; in fact, the participants can sometimes be seen to pause and scan their supply of information simply in order to "bring up" another subject to talk about. The writer's teen-age daughter, when asked, at the end of a one and one-half hour telephone conversation with her girl friend, what she had been talking about, answered, "Nothing." The answer was essentially correct. The essence of the telephone conversation had been not the content, but the social contact.

LANGUAGE AS ABSTRACTION

What is meant by abstraction? At an elementary level, the ability to abstract means to perceive the similarities in two or more things or situations. The capacity begins quite early, considerably before a baby's first birthday. When the baby sees his mother from the front and from the back, he sees two different images. But because of certain similar characteristics of these images (height, color of hair, characteristic motion, sound of voice, and so on) he knows that both images represent the same person. As his intellectual capacities improve, the child learns higher levels of abstractions. He is punished for playing with the sugar in the sugar bowl, and again, for playing with the raspberry jam. He soon perceives that it is forbidden to play, not only with sugar and jam, but with all food. This requires, of course, that he learn another generalization: which things are for eating and which are for playing with.

At higher levels of abstraction, the similarities may become obscure. An "abstract" painting is intended to evoke some emotion in its beholder. The association between the image and the feeling that it induces is often not definable but it involves perception of similarities between the painting and some previous experience. It is a personal and subjective matter. This kind of abstract experience is the basis for the Rorschach ink-blot test.

Roger Brown has pointed out that language even in its simplest and earliest form requires a capacity to generalize. The child must learn to perceive the similarities and to ignore the differences in each word which he hears repeated in many different situations and under varied circumstances. The word *no*, one of the first words a child learns, is never exactly the same sound on repetition. It comes to him from different distances and directions, and with varying volume and pitch. He must learn that a word has the same meaning when spoken in his mother's gentle, high-pitched voice and in his father's deeper, harsher voice. Having learned to identify, and recognize as familiar, a particular group of sounds constituting a word, the child must learn to generalize the meaning of the word. For example, he experiences on repeated occasions hearing the word *no*, each time something different happens. On one occasion his hand is removed from the sugar bowl, on another occasion he is picked up rather roughly from the muddy ground. After a few such experiences he begins to associate *no* with parental disapproval, with unpleasantness, and gradually he comes to understand that the word means that he is to stop whatever he is doing. A dog can learn the same thing. However, when the dog learns this he has about reached the limits of his capacity for understanding language; the child is only beginning.

Language is "completely" abstract. That is, the similarity between a word and the thing it represents (its *referent*) is usually entirely imaginary. The word has been arbitrarily assigned to its referent during the development of the language. Abstracting ability in the learning of language has been deliberately emphasized here. Its importance in understanding the patient with language disability can hardly be overestimated.

An understanding of the meaning of abstraction plays a central role in understanding language and its disorders. Inability to think abstractly affects not only a person's language function; it pervades his total personality, affects his entire life experience, and reduces his ability to function as a social being. The person with a language disability lives in a concrete, non-generalized world. Things occur for him as a series of unrelated episodes; there is little order and meaning to his life. The subtleties and nuances of social living are beyond his awareness. He has a vague sense of being isolated and lonely, but cannot understand why.

Not only does the learning of language require the ability to think abstractly; its use also aids in the development of conceptual thinking processes in the developing child. The Russian psychologists have perhaps investigated most extensively this function of language, although American workers have theorized on the subject for many years. Luriya cites several Russian studies which show that the rate of learning and generalization is greatly accelerated and strengthened by providing the child with verbal "hints." Most of these studies seem elementary, but their implications are of fundamental importance. For example, children were presented with a number of containers which were either red or green in color; the red ones contained a piece of candy, the green ones were empty. After some amount of trial and error, the child eventually learned the pattern. In the younger children (age 1 or 2) the learning was quickly extinguished, so that on the following day the child had to learn all over again. But when verbal aid was given, instructing the child to note the color of the container, learning occurred three times as quickly, and was virtually permanent. Even more interesting, the instructed child generalized easily to containers of different shapes.

Luriya emphasizes the importance which language plays in the developing child's understanding of himself and his environment. Through language, he is taught how to think logically. Through language he learns something of how adults think, he learns better to seek their help and to respect their capacities. Through language he strengthens his relationships with significant persons in his life. And through language he expresses himself: his feelings, his wishes, his likes and dislikes. He thus develops more fully a self-percept, an awareness of himself as a distinct and unique being. Learning what others think of him and how others respond to him, he is better able to control both himself and his environment.

SUMMARY

Language has been seen to have four principle functions:
1. To express emotion

2. To communicate
3. To effect social contact
4. To organize thinking

These functions are so interrelated that all operate simultaneously in informal language. Further, it was seen that the ability to understand and use language requires an ability to think abstractly.

Thus far only spoken language has been considered. In this the verbal symbols are sounds produced by the vocal apparatus and received by the auditory apparatus. However, spoken language has one important defect. It is transient. As soon as it is spoken, it is gone, leaving its traces only in the brains of its participants. The development of written language overcame this disadvantage, and through this medium man today knows what men "said" several thousand years ago.

THE READING PROCESS

Speech undoubtedly preceded writing in the course of man's development, but the origins of both are lost in history. The first graphic communications probably used pictures or more abstract symbols to represent specific things, persons, or events. The symbols were not phonetic representations, and could communicate much less information than can spoken language.

A major development in writing, and one which could be said to mark the beginnings of history, was phonetic language. Here, symbols represent spoken sounds. Since spoken words in any language consist of a finite and relatively small number of specific sounds uttered in varying combinations, alphabets logically evolved. In alphabet language, a written symbol represents a specific sound; rather, it represents a category of similar sounds, since the voices of no two persons are identical. With the development of alphabet writing, it became possible for anything which could be said to be written.

Children normally learn spoken language long before they learn to write. The vocabulary of a child is quite large before he has learned to read or write the simplest words: It is estimated that a child must have a vocabulary of the order of 2,500 words before he is "ready" to learn reading. One might wonder why a child should need to know this many words, including some polysyllabic ones, in order to be able to read the word "cat." What is actually required is that the child must have attained a particular level of intellectual functioning before he can learn to read, and his speaking vocabulary serves as a rough index of this capacity.

The reading process requires certain conceptualizations which are qualitatively different from those required for spoken language. Specifically, these are the concepts of spatial and directional orientation and the translation of the visual symbol into the spoken sound. All forms of writing have, by convention, a particular directional orientation, both for the individual symbols and for the ways in which they are assembled together. The English language has one letter, o, which is omnidirectional. All other letters have some orientation, either left to right, top to bottom, or both. The orientation is less critical for some letters than others. If an s is written backward, most people can recognize it. But a p printed backward becomes a q. In addition to the orientation of the letters, in English the groups of letters which are words are read from left to right, and the words are arranged in sentences also from left to right, beginning again at the left for each line.

In learning to read, the child usually begins by learning letters. It is known that left-right orientation develops slowly in children and is usually not firmly established until after the sixth year. This is a crucial, though by no means the only, factor in "reading readiness." It has already been noted that many functions operate in the learning of spoken language, and it is these plus the additional factors of visual perception and the concept of direction which are needed in understanding written language. These many and complex functions are not independent, isolated functions; they are interrelated. The concept of spatial orientation is an abstract function, just as the concept that the word flower refers not only to a particular object but to many similar objects is an abstraction. An impairment in one form of abstract thinking is usually accompanied by impairment in others. This will be discussed more fully below under Functional Pathology.

It was stated earlier that in an alphabet language, the words are represented phonetically by combinations of letters. This is true as a generalization; but there is a fly in the ointment. Languages are not "purely" phonetic. In English there are about 40 basic sounds (called "phonemes"), but only 26 letters with which to represent them. Obviously, some letters must serve double duty. An example is e, which has its long and short pronunciations. To make matters worse, certain phonemes are represented by more than one letter or combination of letters. For example, the sound of long e is indicated in various words by e, ie, ea, ee, and oe.

These complications add enormously to the task of learning to read. They require that the individual be able to look at the word as a "whole" rather than seeing it letter by letter, since a letter's pronunciation is often determined by the combination of letters in which it occurs. This has led Hermann as well as others to consider Gestalt functioning as an integral part of the reading process. As will be seen below under Psychological Testing, many children with reading disabilities evidence other impairment of Gestalt function.

READING DISABILITY

Reading disability is defined as a significant reduction in reading ability relative to general intelligence. Some definitions arbitrarily require that reading be a certain number of years or academic grades (usually two) below the individual's general capacity. Other definitions specify a certain percentage of reduction below average reading ability. However, these arbitrary figures have not found universal acceptance, and in practice, the crucial factor is that the child's reading ability be so impaired that he is unable to function adequately in school.

Note that the definition includes the phrase "relative to general intelligence." This means that the child's general intelligence must be higher than his reading ability. However, certain of the intellectual functions involved in reading ability also contribute to general intelligence, so that intelligence is itself somewhat reduced with the reading disability. Nevertheless, many children attain a full-scale intelligence score of average or higher, but are many grades below average in reading ability. Reading disability thus does not include most mentally retarded children.

Also not to be included are the considerable number of children who fail or who function at a marginal level academically in all areas and for a variety of reasons, including poor motivation, personality and emotional difficulties, and social factors such as overcrowded schools, overworked teachers, and frequent shifting from one school to another.

PREVALENCE

Figures on the prevalence of reading disability vary widely, and depend to a large extent on the particular definition. Vernon states that 20.3 per cent of 11-year-old children in England had reading ages of 7 to 9 years; 4.3 per cent of 15-year-olds and 2 per cent of 18-year-olds read at a 7 to 9 year level. Certainly the latter two groups would be considered seriously retarded in reading. Most authorities accept the figure of 10 per cent as an estimate of the prevalence of reading disability of all degrees.

The disorder is more frequent in boys than in girls, in the ratio of about 4 to 1 or higher. Vernon has reviewed the literature on sex differences in reading, and has found that in studies sampling the normal school population, about twice as many boys as girls are retarded in reading. In cases referred to clinics, which are presumably more severe, the predominance of boys is much higher, the ratios being reported from 4:1 to as high as 20:1. In the language clinic at Hawthorn Center, girl patients are so rare as to be almost an oddity, and the clinic director states that the male-to-female ratio is greater than 20:1. There is no satisfactory explanation for the sex difference. One suggested explanation has been that boys, being more aggressive, are more prone to act out and to call their problems to the attention of the authorities, while the girls simply sit in school and fail quietly year after year. It is unlikely that this accounts for more than a small fraction of the sex difference. Whatever its cause or causes, the sex difference is marked and real.

The ability to read varies widely in any large sample of the population. A graph of the reading scores of children at a particular age level would show a curve similar to that for general intelligence. That is, the curve would be a normal distribution, or Gaussian curve, except for some skew at the lower end. This skew represents the group of children with reading disability. Thus, while some children with reading disability may be considered as simply representing the lower end of the continuum, through having received particular combinations of the genes responsible for this polygenically determined capacity, there are additionally a considerable number who have specific pathology which results in severe reading disability.

TERMINOLOGY

A variety of terms are to be found in the literature to designate reading disability, with some resultant confusion in terminology. If one understands what is meant by each term, the confusion may be diminished. A frequent and acceptable term, *reading retardation*, is used interchangeably with *reading disability*, and will so appear in this volume. *Dyslexia* and *alexia* refer to specific types of reading disability; however, their meanings appear confused in the literature. Hermann indicates that *alexia* refers to an acquired disorder while *dyslexia* indicates the constitutional or congenital forms of reading retardation. On the other hand, Orton uses *alexia* to designate reading disability due to brain damage, whether congenital or acquired, and employs *word-blindness* synonymously with *alexia*. *Word-blindness* and *congenital word-blindness* sometimes appear interchangeably in the literature. Other authors have objected to these terms, pointing out that "blindness" is misleading, since the individual can see the word but cannot interpret it. Other terms used less frequently are *strephosymbolia* and *asymbolia*. The plethora of terms has not helped to clarify the problem of reading disability, and the present trend is toward simplification of terms. Most widely used in the United States at present are *reading disability* and *reading retardation*.

Much of the confusion in terminology has been over the question of which conditions are congenital and which acquired. Rabinovitch (1959)

has clarified this issue by differentiating three types of reading retardation:
1. Secondary reading retardation.
2. Reading retardation associated with brain damage.
3. Primary reading retardation.
Rabinovitch defines these as follows:

1. Secondary reading retardation—Capacity to learn to read is intact but is utilized insufficiently for the child to achieve a reading level appropriate to his intelligence. The causative factor is exogenous, a child having a normal reading potential that has been impaired by negativism, anxiety, depression, emotional blocking, psychosis, limited schooling opportunity, or other external influence.

2. Reading retardation associated with brain injury—Capacity to learn to read is impaired by frank brain damage manifested by clear-cut neurologic deficits. The picture is similar to the adult dyslexic syndromes. Other definite aphasic difficulties are generally present.

3. Primary reading retardation—Capacity to learn to read is impaired without definite brain damage suggested in history or on neurologic examination. The defect is in the ability to deal with letters and words as symbols, with resultant diminished ability to integrate the meaningfulness of written material. The problem appears to reflect a basic disturbed pattern of neurologic organization.

The majority of children with reading disability probably represent the primary type. Definite statistics are not available, but an estimate would be that these would constitute over 60 per cent of all cases. Because of current confusion regarding terminology and diagnostic criteria, it is unlikely that conclusive figures will be available for some time.

The remainder of this discussion on reading disability will, unless otherwise specified, pertain to the primary type.

ETIOLOGY

That lesions of the brain result in language defects has been known for over a century. Lordat (cited in Penfield and Roberts) in 1843 described his own loss of reading ability following a brain injury. The French surgeon, Broca, in 1861, showed that a specific region of the brain was specially concerned with speech. The aphasias are now well documented in medical literature, and the areas of the brain involved have been approximately mapped (Penfield and Roberts). The occurrence of reading and other language disorders in association with the syndrome of brain damage in children has already been mentioned. The case of Harry S. presented in the chapter on brain damage (Chapter 8) had a mixed aphasia involving both reading and spoken language.

An hereditary basis for primary reading disability has been postulated, and the evidence is strong that at least some cases are genetically determined. Hallgren investigated by history and in some cases by examination the near relatives of 212 children with reading disability; most of these cases appear to have been primary disability. In all but 13 families there was some reading disability in the parents and/or siblings, and in some cases the disorder could be traced back through three generations. Hallgren noted a high male-to-female ratio, but stated that this was not sufficiently high to demonstrate sex-linked inheritance.

It will be recalled from the chapter on genetics (Chapter 1) that the occurrence of a disorder in several members of a family is not *ipso facto* evidence that the disorder is hereditary. To reach such a conclusion, it must be shown that the condition was not induced by some environmental experience which the victims all shared.

What may be concluded, then, about the cause or causes of primary reading disability? First, it must be conceded that the available evidence is not conclusive. However, to the general but fundamental question of whether the condition is learned or inborn, the data points strongly to the latter. The major evidence lies within the nature of the basic pathology of primary reading disability. In the majority of cases this is clearly a neurological defect, identical with that seen in some cases with a known brain lesion, and it is difficult to conceive that such a defect could be a learned phenomenon. Those cases of reading disability which demonstrate a "learning block" induced by some neurotic overreaction to some aspect of the reading process do not show the specific neurologic defects found in primary reading disability. These defects will be considered in detail below under Functional Pathology.

While one may conclude with considerable assurance that primary reading disability is a "biologic" defect, the specific cause of the defect is, in most cases, not evident. That it does occur in families is unquestioned, and many cases have siblings, parents, or uncles with the disorder. However, this is true in considerably less than half the cases, and in the remainder no specific etiology can be elicited. The disorder occurs, probably inborn, and usually with no history of, or other evidence for, brain damage. It is unlikely that anatomic evidence of brain pathology can be found in most cases, at least by present techniques; nor would one necessarily expect that it should be, just as in mental retardation no anatomic basis is usually evident.

Much of the misconception regarding etiology of reading disability has resulted from overemphasis on the emotional aspects, with neglect of the neurological aspects of the case. Investigation of the psychiatric conflicts is an essential part of the evaluation, and will usually elicit interesting and important material; but one must be cautious in ascribing an etiological role to the conflict, and no diagnostic evaluation is complete without psychological and neurological examinations giving particular attention to conceptual thinking and spatial orientation. In the major literature concerned with the emotional aspects of reading and learning disabilities (Pearson 1952, 1954; Blanchard; Liss) the writers usually observe that some cases of learning disorder may result from neurological defect, but in most of the cases described there is little evidence that such neurologic defects were looked for. It is probable that the case material in these studies is a heterogeneous group consisting of both primary and secondary reading disabilities, perhaps some cases of brain damage, together with a large number of emotionally disturbed children who were failing academically in all areas.

Pearson (1952) observed that "more and more cases of learning difficulties are being referred to child psychoanalysts. This is a step in the right direction." Unfortunately, it has turned out in some ways to be a step in the wrong direction. While some cases can unquestionably benefit by psychoanalytic treatment, the total number of cases is so large that only a small fraction can possibly be seen by psychoanalysts. Moreover, the danger in emphasis on psychodynamics is that it induces persons charged with the care and treatment of these children to become overinvolved with the emotional problems and to neglect the child's needs for special education and training. There is a curious appeal and a satisfying simplicity in the notion that a child cannot learn to read, for example, because a particular letter appears to him as an animal with open mouth ready to bite him, activating his guilt over a repressed homicidal wish toward his baby sister (Blanchard). Much less exciting and more difficult to understand is the neurological basis of directional orientation, and the way in which a brain defect makes a child unable to determine whether a line turns to the right or to the left.

Much has been made of the "modern" teaching method as a cause of poor reading. This is the so-called "look and say" method, as opposed to the phonetic method: The child is taught to recognize each individual word rather than to "sound out" the word by a phonetic translation of the letters. This system of reading developed as a result of two formulations:

1. In written English there are so many different sounds for each letter that the child must learn the particular sounds with each word anyway; teaching him phonetic reading simply interposes an additional unnecessary step.

2. The child who must first sound out the word is more likely to become an auditory than a visual reader—he must translate what he sees into sounds, and reading by this method is invariably slower.

The "look-and-say" technique in the teaching of reading reached its height in the 1940's. The outcry against it was great. Parents began to complain that their children could not read, could not spell, and had little interest in learning how to do either. They were shocked that the child did not know what A sounded like, and were convinced that the country was raising a generation of illiterates. Teachers, too, were generally against the method; some accepted it reluctantly, others surreptitiously employed the old method. A popular book denouncing the "look-and-say" method became a best-seller (Flesch). Today, most schools teach a combination look-and-say and phonic method, with the child being taught certain of the basic and simpler words by visually encompassing the whole word, and at the same time learning the common phonetic sounds of the letters in order to analyze more complex and unfamiliar words.

How much the look-and-say technique contributed to the incidence of reading disability is impossible to determine. Probably it was not great. It is likely that some children who would have been poor readers anyway were made a little worse. The "naturally" good readers probably learned about equally well under either method. A child who is able to generalize readily will soon discover, whether it is pointed out to him or not, that when a appears as the middle letter in hat, man, and sad, it is likely to have a similar sound when it occurs in another word. Brown has ably discussed the question of phonic versus look-and-say teaching, and concludes that while "most children will make phonetic generalizations for themselves whether or not the teacher points them out, more of them would learn to read better and sooner with more explicit phonic instruction."

The relationship between handedness, or laterality, and reading disability has been the subject of much theory and investigation. The fact that a higher-than-average percentage of non-readers are left-handed and often show right-left confusion led many to postulate that reading disability may be caused by teaching techniques which required naturally left-handed children to write with their right hands. Others suggested that the left-handed children could not learn to read because the words are oriented from left to right and it was more "natural" for left-handed persons to read from right to left. Some non-readers were found to have "mixed dominance," being left-eyed and right-handed, left-footed and right-handed, or any other combination. Vernon reviewed the literature on laterality as it pertains to reading disability. She concludes that "the relationship to reading disability of incomplete lateralization and cerebral dominance is extremely obscure."

Actually, while the problem is far from being completely understood, it is not quite so obscure as all that. The "incomplete dominance," or directional confusion, when present, unquestionably contributes to the reading difficulty. The high incidence of left-handedness probably represents the presence of partial ambidexterity or incomplete lateralization. It is doubtful if requiring a left-handed person to use his right hand in writing is of major significance in the etiology of reading disability.

For many years it was considered that obscure visual defects might be etiological in the reading disorders, but it is now known that these are of minor significance. The child with reading disability, like any other child, should have regular opthalmological examinations; but correction of minor refractive errors will not help the reading disability.

FUNCTIONAL PATHOLOGY

The basic defect in primary reading retardation is inability to translate visually perceived symbols into words. The defect is fundamentally not one of *perception*, but of *conception*. The words are seen, but their meaning is not understood.

Primary reading disability probably consists of a heterogeneous group of neurological defects. Like all the aphasias, there are cases which are primarily receptive, others which are expressive, and a large majority which are mixed. There may be associated visual-perceptual difficulties, but they are not essential to the diagnosis. The perceptual impairment may involve difficulty in right-left orientation. There may also be inability to perceive Gestalts adequately; complex figures are perceived as unassociated fragments. The question of perceptual difficulty in reading disability is greatly in need of clarification. A recent study by Fuller and Shaw suggests that visual orientation is not impaired in primary reading disability, while it is moderately impaired in secondary reading disability and seriously impaired in reading disability associated with brain damage.

Usually, there are problems in other language areas as well as reading, together with impairment of conceptual thinking. Auditory as well as visual perception may be affected. Hearing is intact, but interpretation of sounds heard is interfered with.

The importance of abstract thinking in the child's development of a self-percept and his understanding of his environment has already been discussed earlier in this chapter. Impairment of this function is perhaps the most serious defect in the learning disabilities, and the symptoms secondary to it may affect profoundly the child's personality and his emotional adjustment.

SYMPTOMS

Symptoms of reading disability can be divided into two major groups:
1. Behavioral difficulties
2. Academic difficulties

1. *Behavioral Difficulties.* Bender has said (personal communication) that the single most common cause of juvenile delinquency is reading disability. This statement, though made informally and perhaps not the final and irrefutable opinion of its author, nevertheless makes a point. Reading disability is unquestionably a major cause of delinquency and behavioral disturbances of children. The percentage of children in the general population with reading disability has been estimated at between 5 and 10 per cent. The percentage of this group who present behavioral problems is not known, but it is undoubtedly considerable. Reading disability occurs in 16 per cent of all children seen at the Hawthorn Center outpatient clinic, and most of these cases are referred primarily because of their disturbed behavior.

The behavioral problems vary widely, and include virtually all those which a child can present. Most common are the acting-out forms, with incorrigibility, negativism, clowning, aggressiveness, and boisterousness. The acting out is generally worst in the classroom—this is the situation where the child has his greatest difficulty, and where he is most bored, restless, impatient, or angry. Outside of school, in athletics or social situations, he can often achieve as well as his peers. Here his language impairment and his conceptualization defects are less apparent; he can cover them up and fabricate so that others are hardly aware of them. However, as the years go by and his school difficulties continue, his maladjustment is likely to invade his total functioning, and in adolescence he often begins to get into serious trouble.

Sometimes the symptoms are internalized. The child may have real neurotic conflict. He may be depressed, or at least discouraged. There is often a sense of futility, a hopelessness; the future looks bleak, the child muddles listlessly through endless days of boredom or despair. Many children are baffled by their inability to learn what their classmates are learning; they feel an impotence, a frustration, and often they come to regard themselves as "stupid."

The conflict and the overreaction is often compounded within the family, as the parents feel disappointment in their child. They try everything and anything to help him or make him learn to read. They threaten, punish, offer rewards; many devoted parents work long hours every day tutoring the child, and become baffled, hurt, or angry when he learns nothing, or when he learns two or three words only to forget them the next day. Some are convinced that he does not want to learn, that he is being stubborn, or is deliberately trying to anger them. Some feel that the child is lazy, others accept that he is stupid, and often tell him so. One mother of a 7-year-old boy who had failed the first grade would often threaten, if he did not read a certain paragraph, that she would call the police, and once she actually did so. When this boy was seen by the psychiatrist at age 10 his neurotic overinvolvement with the reading process was deeply fixed.

The prominence of behavioral and emotional symptoms often overshadows the academic problems, so that there may be no mention in the referring complaints that the child has been failing academically. Or the referring agent may conclude that the academic difficulties are purely secondary, and consequently of little interest to the psychiatrist. Thus the psychiatrist has a responsibility to evaluate the reading ability, not only of those cases referred as reading problems, but of virtually all children with emotional and behavioral disorders.

2. *Academic Difficulties.* The academic problems begin early in the child's school career, and become progressively worse. It is quickly apparent that he is a "slow learner." However, at first the teacher does not usually become overly concerned, as many children progress slowly, and it is hoped that he will be one of those who begins to "catch on" in second grade. But he does not, and by the time he is in third grade it is apparent to all, including the teacher, the child, and his family, that he is in serious academic difficulty. By this time his inability to read is interfering with his achievement in all subjects, as the arithmetic and social studies involve some reading of text. Spelling and writing are generally as retarded as the reading. However, some children do surprisingly well in spelling, by rote memorization. It is astonishing to see one of these children spell aloud a fairly difficult word, then have no notion of what the word is when he sees it on the page of a book.

Arithmetic achievement is sometimes better than reading and writing, and it is not uncommon to see a fourth-grade child who reads at a low first-grade level but attains a grade score of 2.5 on the arithmetic tests. Numbers are, of course, abstract symbols, and it might therefore be inferred that the child with reading disability could not learn arithmetic. Upon investigation one finds that the child has little concept of the abstract meaning of the numbers—he has no "number sense." He can learn to read the numbers, since they are all rather unique figures (he may confuse 6 and 9). And he can learn to manipulate the figures in the routine operations of arithmetic; he can memorize the tables, that 6 plus 9 equals 15, 6 times 4 equals 24, and the like. But if he makes a simple mistake and gets an absurdly erroneous answer, for example finding that 3 times 25 is 775, he may have no awareness that the answer is ridiculously large.

DIAGNOSIS

The diagnostic evaluation in a suspected case of reading disability should include the following:

1. Psychiatric interview
2. Psychological tests
3. Special tests
4. Neurological evaluation

1. *Psychiatric Interview.*   Direct inquiry into the child's school functioning is an important segment of the psychiatric interview. Here one gets some feeling of the child's self-percept, the amount of his motivation and his discouragement, an understanding of his defenses, and what his explanations are for his inability to achieve. Most of these children want desperately to learn to read, although upon first inquiry many will deny it. Most of them are convinced of their stupidity, and a part of the initial interview should be devoted to explaining to the child the nature of his disorder, pointing out that his general intelligence is normal (if it is), and giving him some encouragement about his future achievement.

Attention to the child's speech will disclose that his use of language is limited. His vocabulary is usually small and the language is concrete. This is usually not so severe as to be obvious to other people in ordinary social situations, and the child is generally able to "get by." But his conversation is unstimulating, and if one tries to talk with him about his hobbies, or about what happened in school that day, the conversation becomes almost a monologue. It may go something like this: "Well, John, how was school today?" "O.K." "What did you do?" "Nothin'." "Certainly you must have done something—what about in gym?" "Played ball." "Did you get any hits?" "Nope."

And so the conversation goes. Each word has to be dragged out, and there are not many words available. There is always a feeling that the child is uncomfortable in a conversation; he is working hard, he cannot relax, and he is continuously wary lest his deficiencies become glaringly obvious. The child is constantly covering up; often he confabulates in order to conceal his deficiencies, hoping that he guesses correctly. In the interview he must be exposed, but as gently as possible. The examiner tests his deficiencies, and usually, because this is done in a clinical setting, the child can accept the exposure.

Conceptual thinking in the areas of spatial orientation, direction, time, and length, is usually impaired. These areas can be tested directly, and it is helpful if the examiner has a small store of routine questions, asking the child how far he drove in coming to the clinic, how high the ceiling is, how long the interview has been in progress, and things of the kind. It is fascinating how these children often will give an answer rather than admit they don't know. In the course of these inquiries, the writer's height has ranged from 3 inches to 65 feet. Often the child leaves out the unit word, giving a number. Thus, if one asks him how far away the lightpost outside the window is, and he answers "About 65," it is important to ask him "65 what?" He may say inches, thus ruining what was otherwise an amazingly accurate estimate.

2. *Psychological Testing.* Just as in other psychiatric disorders of children, there is no one psychological test or subtest which is absolutely diagnostic of primary reading disability. Perhaps the most helpful test presently available is the Wechsler Intelligence Scale for Children. Rabinovitch has emphasized the marked discrepancy between the verbal and performance portions of the Wechsler. He found in a series of cases that the mean discrepancy was more than 20 points, and in some cases more than 40 points. Rabinovitch feels that this discrepancy aids greatly in differentiating between primary and secondary reading disabilities. In both types, the verbal subtests, as a result of general verbal incapacity and academic retardation, are usually lower than the performance subtests; but in secondary reading disability this difference is seldom as large as in the primary cases. Differentiation is further aided by the fact that children with primary disability generally score lower on the subtests requiring abstract thinking (such as similarities, arithmetic, and block design) while the secondary cases do worst on those subtests reflecting social judgment (picture arrangement, comprehension).

The Bender Gestalt Test is also helpful in diagnosis: inadequate Gestalt function may be shown in failure to join parts of the figures, or a total failure to produce the form, especially on Figure 3 (the "Christmas tree" card).

3. *Special Tests.* During the initial clinical evaluation of any child, the psychiatrist should determine whether the child can read, and approximately at what grade level. Reading testing is not always necessary. If, in the course of the interview, one finds that the child enjoys reading, is conversant with many of the children's books, and is doing well academically, there is no need for a reading test. However, in over half the cases seen in most outpatient clinics this is not so, and in these cases a rough estimate of the child's reading level should be obtained. It is a matter of a minute or two to have the child read from one of the standard graded reading charts such as the Gray Oral. Although scoring this test is a rather elaborate process, involving a formula which incorporates elapsed time for reading each paragraph, and the total number of errors, an approximation of whether the child is seriously retarded in reading can be made simply by listening to him read the test and judging which is the most difficult paragraph he can read with reasonable facility.

The diagnosis of reading disability can usually be made from the information thus far obtained. But in order to assess more fully the child's deficiencies and needs for a reading therapy program, complete achievement testing is indicated. A battery of tests, such as those devised by Gates, requires from one to two hours and should be given by a trained person. These tests measure a variety of capacities. There are subtests of both silent and oral reading, with evaluation of such errors as omissions and additions of words, repetitions, mispronunciations, reversals within words, order of words, and the tendency to make most errors at the beginning, middle, or end of words. Oral and written vocabularies are measured, and the ability to blend letter sounds (k-o, n-a, e-t, t-e-x) is determined. Not only visual but also auditory perception is evaluated; for example, the examiner gives aloud two or more phonemes and the child is required to blend them into a phonogram (syllable).

Children vary widely in all the above functions, and the complex scoring from such tests is invaluable to the reading therapist. When the child's specific abilities and deficiencies are known, therapy is directed toward utilizing his strengths and overcoming his weaknesses through drill and training.

In addition to the reading tests, it is usual to evaluate the other academic functions, especially spelling, writing, and arithmetic. These too may be estimated during the psychiatric interview. Most non-readers can write their names. It is often highly revealing, however, when they are asked to write a line which the examiner dictates. Here again, the effort to cover up through fabrication is often striking, and the child will carefully inscribe a few words which have little resemblance to what was dictated or to any known language (Fig. 1).

How much retardation does one find on the reading tests? Rabinovitch and others (1956) found in a group of 20 children with primary reading disability, age range 10 to 16, that the mean discrepancy between mental age and reading age was 5½ years. The mean discrepancy in secondary reading disability was slightly less than 3½ years. Thus, children with primary reading disability are generally more retarded in reading than those with secondary disability.

4. *Neurological Examination.* In the absence, in the history and clinical examination, of other evidence suggestive of brain damage, there is little indication for complete neurological examination in children with reading disability. Rabinovitch and others (1956) found in their cases of primary reading disability "no evidence of abnormality in the routine neurological examination." However, in what they term the "expanded" neurological evaluation there were certain significant findings. These included a high incidence of right-left disorientation (elicited by a modification of Head's hand-eye-ear test), sensory disturbances revealed by a delayed appreciation of simultaneous double sensory stimulation, and a nonspecific, usually mild degree of motor clumsiness or awkwardness. It

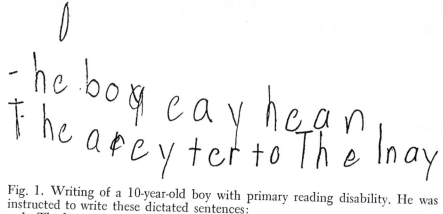

Fig. 1. Writing of a 10-year-old boy with primary reading disability. He was instructed to write these dictated sentences:
1. The boy came home.
2. The lady went to the store.

must be emphasized that the neurological findings are by no means always present. The right-left disorientation is not uncommon. The motor awkwardness is much less frequent; in fact, many of these children are skilled in athletics.

DIFFERENTIAL DIAGNOSIS

In addition to differentiating the three types of reading disability (primary, secondary, and that associated with brain damage), the following conditions may be confused with reading disability:
1. Acting-out behavior associated with neurosis or personality disorder
2. Mental retardation

In the first group, the error is more likely to be on the side of over-diagnosing the neurosis or the character disorder. Because the acting-out problems are more prominent and troublesome, the academic difficulties may be overlooked. Thus, the diagnosis of reading disability is missed chiefly because it is not looked for. Mental retardation may be erroneously suspected on the basis of the child's poor academic functioning or his low level of language use. His full-scale I.Q. may likewise be in the low-average or upper-defective range, having been depressed by his poor functioning on the verbal subtest. Thus a test should be employed which contains nonverbal items, such as the Wechsler, so that a more accurate estimate of his intellectual potential is available.

TREATMENT

All children with reading disability, whatever the type or the etiology, need remedial reading therapy. This is the first requirement—in many cases the major requirement—and it should be instituted as soon as possible. The sad fact is, however, that there are not nearly enough reading therapists available. Although recognition of this major need has been growing steadily, and many of the universities are increasing their training facilities for special education, at the present time it is simply not possible to provide remedial reading therapy for a great number of these children.

Sometimes arrangements can be made for private tutoring, with the tutor receiving supervision and instruction from a reading therapist. Many of the public schools now have remedial reading classes, and while group therapy is in most cases less satisfactory than individual therapy, it does accomplish something. At Hawthorn Center both group and individual techniques are employed.

Reading therapy should be given no less than three hours per week, and preferably five. With less, there is so little carry-over from one session to the next that little is achieved. Techniques vary widely, depending on the child's particular needs and capacities, and also according to the preferences and experience of the therapist. The important thing is that the therapy is geared to the individual child, so that he succeeds at one level before going to the next.

Progress varies greatly. Children with secondary reading disability generally progress more rapidly, since their basic functions are intact. The severe cases of primary reading disability and those associated with brain damage may show painfully slow progress, and can tax the patience of the best therapist. The visual or auditory memory of these children is often so impaired that they forget in a day or even an hour the one or two words that they may have spent an entire hour in acquiring.

A cardinal rule of reading therapy is that the parents should *not* give the therapy. Even with the most patient and understanding parents, there is too much emotional involvement; so much tension and exasperation develop that the results are often worse than no therapy at all. This should be explained to the parents, and they will usually accept and understand it. The parents' role should be, as with a normal child, one of support and authority, to see that the child is doing his homework, to give a little help when asked, but not to be directly involved in the work or to assume the role of tutor.

Treatment of children with reading problems requires close cooperation between the psychiatrist and the school. The teachers, counselors, and principal usually appreciate whatever help anyone can give them in management of these exasperating problems. They are often and understandably confused over what course of action to take with the child, whether to be firm or lenient, whether to give him extra homework or to give him less, whether to make him recite aloud in class or never to call on him, whether to pass him or fail him at the end of the year. The school authorities sometimes feel guilty over their management of the child, feeling that somehow they have failed; this guilt is often engendered by the attitudes of parents, who sometimes blame the school for the child's problems. All these misunderstandings and unnecessary tensions and resentment can often be relieved in an interview with the psychiatrist, either by telephone or in person, and the further cooperation of the school can be better effected in this way. Often special arrangements for the child can be made; he may discontinue those subjects in which he is completely lost, or attend certain of the classes for younger children, such as English composition and arithmetic. Such arrangements will pose other problems for the child, and these must be dealt with directly in psychotherapy.

Like the brain-damaged child, the child with primary reading disability needs special help with orientation. He should be drilled frequently in estimating such things as time and distance. He can learn, with practice, the order of the seasons, the months, the days, and so on, and while this is generally learned by rote rather than by true conceptualization, nevertheless it can serve to keep him better attuned to the affairs of his environment. He may even develop some concept of time, by attending to the approximate number of events that occur in an hour or in 10 minutes, and, with repetition, this sense can improve.

PROGNOSIS

In children with severe primary reading disability and that associated with brain damage, the outlook for learning to read is poor. It is rare for any of these to read beyond a fourth-grade level, and usually it is much less than this. Nevertheless, they should receive reading therapy, and it should be continued into adolescence. Reading at a third-grade level is vastly better than not reading at all. With this, children can function in many jobs which they could not otherwise hope to do. Obviously, their academic achievement will never be very high, and it should not be expected that they will graduate from a regular high school.

An accurate prognosis cannot be made until the child has had a considerable trial of reading therapy. The therapy itself often clarifies the diagnosis, and the most experienced child psychiatrist can be misled in some cases, mistaking the effects of disinterest and poor motivation for true conceptual impairment. Moreover, many cases of primary disability may initially appear more severe then they actually are, being aggravated by secondary problems.

Secondary reading disability is treated as are other neuroses or personality disorders, with the addition of reading therapy. The results in some cases can be most gratifying, and the child can make astonishing academic gains in a short time.

OTHER LEARNING DISABILITIES

The learning disabilities in addition to reading disability are disorders of:

1. Writing (agraphia, dysgraphia)
2. Spelling
3. Arithmetic (acalculia)
4. Spoken language (aphasia)
5. Speech (various types, including dysarthria, stuttering, lisping)

All of the above disorders may occur in greater or lesser degrees in association with reading disability, and most cases of primary reading disability will show some of them. An exception is the last category, the disorders of speech. These are usually of a different order of functioning, representing motor clumsiness of the muscles of articulation, or, in the case of stuttering, probably emotional conflict in relation to aggressive impulses. The other disorders are all dysfunctions of the symbolic process, and as such, are variants of the same basic disorder.

Penfield and Roberts have described the early efforts of neurologists to localize the specific symbolic functions, and drew a composite map indicating the centers for writing, naming, language formulation, and speaking. The authors conclude: "This was a good example of the hopeful effort which clinicians have made to recognize pure forms or subdivisions of aphasia, which really do not exist, and exclusively functioning centers of control, which also do not exist."

A possible exception to the lack of localization is seen in certain of the disorders of writing associated with directional confusion. These appear most often in children who are naturally left-handed and have been taught to write with the right hand. Many of these present the fascinating disorder of mirror writing. Orton described several cases of almost "pure" agraphia. Many of these children can read well; they also write correctly, but the writing is a painfully laborious and slow process, so that on writing tests their scores are reduced, mainly because they complete only a small portion of the test. Children with writing disorders who had been converted from left-handedness may be helped dramatically by reverting to the left hand and additionally given a brief period of specific writing training.

When cases of "pure" learning disabilities occur, they are usually of the secondary type; that is, they are a result of emotional overinvolvement with a particular aspect of the learning process. Rabinovitch (1959) cites the case of a nine-year-old boy who was specifically retarded in spelling. It was found that at the age of five he had been taught by an older boy to spell certain obscene words, and when he spelled these aloud at home his mother had punished him severely. Pearson has described a case of an 11-year-old girl with a specific inability to learn arithmetic. Analysis disclosed that she began to fail when the class started to learn to use the protractor in geometry. It was found that the protractor, through its resemblance to her older brother's slide rule, activated her conflict between jealousy and admiration of this older brother who was an excellent mathematician. Pearson's interpretation was that she equated slide rule with penis, and accordingly felt that girls lacked the equipment necessary for mathematics (an unsupported generalization).

SPEECH DISORDERS

Speech disorders, particularly poor articulation, are common in children with language disorders. Brain damage can produce both. In some cases, because the sounds do not have as much meaning to the child, he does not learn to pronounce them clearly. However, this relationship is not absolute, and many children with reading disability have excellent articulation, while many with serious speech problems have no language difficulty. Monroe found that 27 per cent of 415 children with reading disability had speech defects, compared to 8 per cent of 101 control cases.

Five per cent of persons in the United States aged 21 and under are estimated to have some speech defect (Bakwin and Bakwin). A report from the Mid-century White House Conference provides the following percentage figures for the various types of speech defects in all persons aged 5 to 21 years:

	Percentage
1. Functional articulatory	3.0
2. Stuttering	0.7
3. Voice	0.2
4. Cleft palate speech	0.1
5. Cerebral palsy speech	0.2
6. Retarded speech development	0.3
7. Impairment hearing with speech defect	0.5
TOTAL	5.0

The above table shows that over half of all speech defects are in faulty articulation. These include all degrees of severity. Some are only slightly handicapping while the more seriously interfere with communication and with the child's academic progress. The severe cases should receive speech therapy from a trained person. Where there is associated emotional disorder, psychotherapy is of course indicated. While accurate figures are not available, it is estimated that the majority of children with speech defects do not need psychiatric help.

An exception appears to be in the case of stuttering, where emotional conflict is usually present and is often an important part of the child's difficulty. There is little unanimity regarding the etiology of stuttering. Mixed dominance has often been implicated (Orton) but it is doubtful that this is fundamental. The cause-effect relationships between stuttering and emotional conflict remain obscure, but there is little doubt that the two are related. Psychiatric treatment as well as speech therapy is therefore frequently indicated. This may assist in the child's emotional adjustment, although it may not relieve the stuttering. This usually improves or disappears in adolescence or early adulthood, although residua may appear during moments of tension throughout life. Those cases which persist into adulthood are highly refractory to any current form of treatment (Karlin).

REFERENCES

Bakwin, H., and Bakwin, R. M. Clinical Management of the Behavior Disorders in Children, Philadelphia, W. B. Saunders Co., 1960.

Blanchard, Phyllis. Psychoanalytic Contributions to the Problems of Reading Disabilities, Psychoanalytic Study of the Child, New York, International Universities Press, 1946, Vol. 2.

Broca, P. Memoirs sur la Cerveau de l'Homme, Paris, C. Reinwald, 1888.

Brown, R. Words and Things, The Free Press, Glencoe, Ill., 1958.

Flesch, R. Why Johnny Can't Read, New York, Harper & Bros., 1955.

Fuller, J., and Shaw, C. R. Visual Orientation in the Three Types of Reading Disability, J. Am. Acad. Child Psychiatry, 1963.

Gates Reading Diagnostic Tests, Bureau of Publications, Teachers College, Columbia University, 1958.

Gray Oral Reading Paragraphs Test, Public School Publishing Company, Bloomington, Ind., 1955.

Hallgren, B. Specific Dyslexia, Acta Psychiatrica et Neurologica, Supplement 65, 1950.

Head, H. Aphasia and Kindred Disorders of Speech, London, Cambridge University Press, 1926.

Hermann, K. Reading Disability, Springfield, Ill., Charles C Thomas, 1959.

Karlin, I. W. Stuttering—a Problem Today, J.A.M.A., 143: 742, 1950.

Liss, E. Learning: Its Sadistic and Masochistic Manifestations, Am. J. Orthopsychiatry, 10: 123, 1940.

Lorenz, K. King Solomon's Ring, London, Methuen & Co., 1952.

Luriya, A. R. The Role of Speech in Child Development, in The Central Nervous System and Behavior—Selected Translations from the Russian Medical Literature, Washington, D.C., U.S. Dept. Health, Education & Welfare, 1959.

Mid-century White House Conference, Report on Speech Disorders and Speech Correction, J. Speech & Hearing Disorders, 17: 129, 1952.

Monroe, M. Children Who Cannot Read, Chicago, University of Chicago Press, 1932.

Orton, S. T. Reading, Writing and Speech Problems in Children, New York, W. W. Norton Co., 1937.

Pearson, G. H. J. A Survey of Learning Difficulties in Children, Psychoanalytic Study of the Child, New York, International Universities Press, 1952, Vol. 7.

—— Psychoanalysis and the Education of the Child, New York, W. W. Norton Co., 1954.

Penfield, W., and Roberts, L. Speech and Brain Mechanisms, Princeton, Princeton University Press, 1959.

Piaget, J. The Language and Thought of the Child, London, Routledge & Kegan Paul Ltd., 1952.

Rabinovitch, R. D. Reading and Learning Disablities, in American Handbook of Psychiatry, ed. S. Arieti, New York, Basic Books, Inc., 1959.

—— Drew, A. L., DeJong, R., Ingram, W., and Withey, L. A Research Approach to Reading Retardation, in Neurology and Psychiatry in Childhood, Proceedings of the Association for Research in Nervous and Mental Disease, No. 34, Baltimore, Williams and Wilkins, 1956.

Revesz, G. The Origins and Prehistory of Language, New York, Philosophical Library, 1956.

Stuttering in Children—a Symposium, The Nervous Child, 2: 85, 1943.

Vernon, M. D. Backwardness in Reading, New York, Cambridge University Press, 1957.

Yerkes, R. N. and Lerned, B. W. Chimpanzee Intelligence and Its Vocal Expressions, Baltimore, Williams & Wilkins Co., 1925.

10

PERSONALITY DISORDER

REPORT OF A CASE

Beverly J. was referred to the psychiatrist at the age of 11 by the visiting teacher because of fighting in the classroom, abusive language, and for telling outlandish stories which disturbed her classmates. The episode which precipitated the emergency referral was a fight with her arithmetic teacher in which Beverly scratched his face severely with her fingernails.

FAMILY HISTORY

Beverly's family consisted of her father, stepmother, an older brother and sister, two stepsiblings, and a half-sister, aged 2. Mr. J. worked intermittently as a truck driver, and was unemployed at the time of referral. He was a passive, ineffectual person, overwhelmed by his misfortunes and completely lacking in authority and control over his children. His feelings toward the children were ambivalent. He resented their lack of respect for him, and often seemed on the verge of tears when he discussed them.

The natural mother had been reared by foster parents since the age of 7, after her father committed suicide. She quit school at an early age, began to frequent neighborhood bars, stayed out late at night, and was flagrantly promiscuous sexually. She married at the age of 18 and for several years appeared to have "reformed," making an adjustment as a respectable housewife and mother. However, soon after Beverly's birth she became depressed, began again to visit local bars, leaving the children at home alone, and on many occasions was gone all night or was brought home late by various men. There were many violent arguments between the parents, often witnessed by the children. When Beverly was two, the mother failed to return home one night and had not been heard of since.

When Beverly was eight her father married a woman 10 years younger than himself. She had been divorced, and had two children younger than

214

Beverly. Her first husband had been an alcoholic and sexually promiscuous. She married Mr. J. in order to provide a home for her children. By this time Beverly and her brother and sister had been living for some time in various foster homes and institutions. It was decided that the entire family should be brought together, and this was quickly accomplished. The result was chaos.

PERSONAL HISTORY

When her mother left, Beverly went to live with a distant relative. She was then 2 years old. The first placement did not work out well because Beverly constantly misbehaved and fought with the relative's children. When she was about 3, she was placed with another family for prospective adoption. This placement lasted for six weeks and was terminated because Beverly refused to address the father as "Daddy." She was then placed in a church-operated institution for "homeless" children, where her older brother had been living for some time. Here, Beverly was a chronic behavior problem. She argued constantly with the staff, had many temper outbursts, lied, stole, and developed an amazing capacity to fabricate stories which she told to gullible children and adults for the obvious purpose of upsetting them and also of gaining status for herself. She lived at the institution for five years; then, at the age of 8, she returned home to live with her father and stepmother.

Soon after the family was brought together, mutual jealousy and distrust arose between Beverly and her stepmother, and within a short time this developed into open warfare. Beverly, already adept at manipulating people, developed this skill into a fine art in exploiting the triangle of herself, her father, and her stepmother. She aroused his suspicions of his new young wife by hints of male callers during his absence at work, and by veiled references to letters received by the wife addressed in a masculine scrawl. On at least one occasion, Beverly, a consummate actress, telephoned her father at his office, and, disguising her voice, assumed the role of an injured wife whose husband was consorting with Mrs. J. This deceit was not uncovered until some months later, and the damage which it meanwhile effected is not difficult to imagine. At the time Beverly was seen by the psychiatrist, Mr. J. complained with genuine feeling and not without reason that unless something was done soon, Beverly would "break up our marriage."

Despite her chronic misbehavior at school, Beverly had always done amazingly well academically. She attended at least six different schools during the first six grades, but had adjusted academically to each situation with apparent ease, and her grades were always excellent. Although she caused them much trouble, it is obvious from their reports that her teachers liked her and tried hard to help her. Her fifth-grade teacher wrote:

Beverly is a very emotionally disturbed child. It appears the child lacks love and attention at home and therefore is doing everything in her power to get it elsewhere. She is an intelligent child and she applies herself to the tasks at hand. Her one aim is to get attention and in doing so she becomes very persistent. Beverly has an idea that people don't like her. That is true when she is in one of her moods; otherwise she is one of the most enjoyable persons to be with.

As an example of Beverly's attention-seeking devices, when the class was discussing Christmas in foreign countries, Beverly announced that she had recently visited Italy and was prepared to tell the class about the Italian celebration of Christmas. The teacher remarked that "later during an individual conference Beverly reaffirmed her statement about her visit to Italy and informed me that she was born there." It was not clear from this teacher's report whether she actually believed this statement or not. As a matter of fact, except for one trip to Chicago, Beverly had never been outside Michigan.

At the time of referral the family situation had become chaotic. The older brother had recently been arrested for breaking-and-entering, and was on probation. There was some evidence that he had been sexually involved with the stepmother, although this was never confirmed. The home was the scene of constant quarrels, tension, and even physical violence, and, while the father denied it, the stepmother claimed that he beat her on several occasions. Engendered by this atmosphere of aggression, suspicion, and hatred, Beverly's emotional control, always tenuous, dissolved completely.

PSYCHIATRIC EVALUATION

When seen initially at the age of 11, Beverly was a thin, tense, but rather attractive girl. She was at first sullen and uncommunicative, but when asked why she was in so much trouble at school, she became histrionic, shrieked vituperations at her stepmother, and shouted that she would never go back home again and that no one could make her do anything she didn't want to do. When told that the psychiatrist's only aim was to help her, she began to sob dramatically and moaned, "It's no use, I'm beyond help." This was a sample of the dramatics with which the therapist was to become familiar in the ensuing months.

Psychological tests showed that Beverly was a bright girl, with a verbal I.Q. of 125, performance I.Q. of 110, and full-scale I.Q. of 119. The psychologist noted that Beverly obviously received much narcissistic gratification from the individual attention during the testing situation. She was strongly motivated to perform well on the tests, and often elaborated on her answers to impress the examiner.

The diagnostic impression was "personality disorder." Because of the extreme acting out and the defiance of authority, it was felt that Beverly would benefit by a period of treatment on a closed ward in the state hospital where the opportunities for manipulation of authorities were minimal. It was arranged for her to be admitted to a nearby state hospital, and after four months there she was transferred to the inpatient unit of a children's psychiatric hospital.

COURSE IN THE HOSPITAL

At the time of admission, five months after initial evaluation, the changes in Beverly were apparent. She was relatively quiet and subdued, and all the "fight" seemed to have gone out of her. However, her deep-seated suspicion and mistrust towards adults remained, and in the first therapy hour she expressed her anger at the therapist, for "getting me locked up in that awful place."

The calm lasted for two or three days, then the storm burst, not so furiously as before, but enough to have the girls and staff in her cottage in almost constant turmoil. Beverly loved the limelight, and would do anything to get it. For the first two months of her hospitalization she did have it almost constantly. Then the other girls began to "get wise" to her stories, no longer took her seriously, and largely ignored her, so that she became a social isolate.

Thereupon, Beverly began to work out her anger on her therapist, refusing his commands and defying his authority, and a power struggle ensued. After some months, the therapist won, and Beverly began to get better. Her ego strength increased and she was able, for the first time in her life, to experience a consistent, trustful, and meaningful relationship with another person.

She remained in the hospital for one year. Near the end of her stay, she began to develop some reasonably mature friendships with both patients and staff. She became especially attached to one of the younger staff women, sought her advice as to how to conduct herself socially, how to dress correctly, etc. Fortunately, she could be quite warm and appealing, and had an excellent sense of humor, so that it was not difficult to help her.

Because the situation at home had not improved, and had if anything gotten worse, it was arranged for Beverly to be placed in a small open-type institution where the children attended public school. Beverly continued to do well academically, and achieved a degree of acceptance by her peers at school and in the institution. That serious distortions in her personality persisted were evident: She remained highly narcissistic, argumentative, insistent on "having her own way," and manipulative of the staff. Today she has high ambitions, intends to go to college and to become a career woman. It is likely that she will achieve well in this area, but her outlook for happiness is not good.

Beverly represents one of the less severe cases of personality disorder. Her case illustrates that, contrary to wide belief, not every child with personality disorder is entirely hopeless. By contrast to many such children, she was not totally without motivation, she had considerable warmth and humor, and she was able to learn in the course of her therapy to feel some trust in others.

TERMINOLOGY

A variety of terms is used to describe this group of disorders. Some are virtually synonymous, others have slightly different meanings. *Personality disorder* and *character disorder* as used in the literature seem to be synonymous, and the two will be used interchangeably in this chapter. The term *character neurosis* also appears to have essentially the same meaning; however, because of possible confusion with *neurosis*, it will not be employed here. Some writers do in fact consider the present disorder to be a form of neurosis; but there are fundamental differences between personality disorder and neurosis, so that it seems preferable to consider them as separate conditions. Chess employs the term *neurotic character disorder.*

The terms *sociopath* and *sociopathic personality* as currently employed are not satisfactory. They seem to be a loose designation which may include any disorder in which the child exhibits antisocial behavior. *Character defect* or *characterologic defect* are other terms in common use, but appear more in the spoken than in the written language of psychiatry.

Psychopath or *psychopathic personality* is a widely used term and one over which there has been much confusion. It has, by convention, come to have a specific meaning, as will be discussed in a separate chapter (Chapter 11). Suffice it to say that it is not synonymous with the other terms mentioned here.

ETIOLOGY

More than any other of the emotional disturbances of childhood, personality disorder can be said to be a learned phenomenon. The disorder is mainly a result of the child's life experiences, and in the majority of cases the pathology in his environment is grossly evident. Despite much research into the problem of the so-called constitutional psychopath, congenital criminal type, and so on, evidence for a hereditary basis for this group of disorders is tenuous (Rees), while the evidence for an experiential etiology is quite strong.

These are Wednesday's children, children of misfortune, unwanted, unloved, brutalized, neglected. They come mainly from the lower socio-economic strata, but they may be found in any class and their number in the upper classes appears to be increasing. Many are the children of criminals, of alcoholics, of prostitutes; many of them have parents who are psychotic or severely neurotic. In this present-day culture with its emphasis on material gain and upward mobility, the "successful" parents are now contributing their share to the character disorders, and many of the children of the "country club set" easily qualify for admission.

The pathology in the child's environment may take many forms. But the single factor which appears common in the experience of every child with personality disorder is the absence of mature and consistent parental love. There may be love in some form, but it is invariably of a distorted kind, and may be expressed as a narcissistic overprotection, or sexual feelings, or an inordinate possessiveness, or any of the other varieties of pathological attachments which can come about between a parent and a child.

An important aspect of the etiology of personality disorder is the chronicity of the abnormal experience. The disturbed environment usually extends throughout the patient's childhood. We know that most children can survive, without permanent effects, brief episodes of psychological trauma. Trauma extending throughout childhood is another matter. The question of the "critical period" in early development was discussed in Chapter 2. The evidence for a critical period near the end of the first year is fairly conclusive, and the effects of deprivation at this period will be dealt with in the following chapter on Psychopathy. Whether specific periods in later development are important in the etiology of personality disorder is less clearly demonstrated. While variations in severity of trauma at the various periods of development may in part determine the particular form which the disorder takes, in most cases it appears that the disturbance is a continuously developing one, permeating the child's entire early life and involving all periods of psychosexual development.

Inconsistency in upbringing is frequent in the histories of these children. They are alternately caressed and beaten, given much attention or totally ignored. They never know what to expect, they become like the experimental animals who do not know whether or not they will receive the shock when they reach for food, so that they are chronically immobilized and without hope. One boy described how he got along better when he finally learned how to determine from the sound of his father's voice as he came home drunk whether he was going to be nice to the family or was going to beat them. Another boy hoped that his mother would get married soon because "some of the men that come home with her are nice to us, but some of them aren't."

Aggression is prominent in the experience of a majority of these children. Uncontrolled and unpredictable hostility is prevalent in their homes, and they are often witness to or victims of violent anger and aggression. Trapped, helpless and defenseless, some of them internalize their counter-aggression and become chronically fearful; others act out their counteraggression toward younger siblings or toward society.

Pathological sexual experiences are common in the histories of personality disorders. These may be overt relationships including incest, witnessing of sexual episodes between parents or other persons, experiences with older persons, and the like. One overgenitalized 11-year-old girl was seen by the psychiatrist following a series of sexual episodes with adolescent boys. Her genital orientation had developed at the age of nine when her father, a respected businessman, had, with the mother's approval, undertaken her sex education. This consisted of a series of lectures involving practical anatomical demonstrations in which she was allowed to manipulate his erect penis. In some cases the relationship is less overt, with only emotional overattachment between mother and son or between father and daughter. However, the effects of such an attachment can be as damaging as a more genitalized one.

A large percentage of children with personality disorders come from "broken homes." Many are illegitimate or born of forced marriages. Many, like Beverly, have lived in foster homes and institutions. Thus they have no real concept of the continuity of family life and of a permanence of identifications. To them, the word "parent" has quite a different meaning than it does to a normal child. One boy had two fathers living in his home at the same time. His natural father, an older man, had been relegated to the living-room couch. His stepfather (actually his second or third stepfather) slept with the mother when she was at home. On the nights when she was away, which were frequent, the two fathers slept together in the bedroom.

The specific etiologic factors and the examples given here have been mainly the overt, gross distortions in experience. These are not invariably present; rather, the distortions may be largely psychological. Nevertheless, they are usually extreme, and readily apparent to the psychiatrist in the course of a single interview with the mother and father. Behind the mask of respectability is readily perceived the narcissism, the chronic anxiety, the overwhelming tension of the severely neurotic parent; or the amused disinterest or resentment of the psychopathic parent; or the ineffectualness and preoccupation of the marginally adapted schizophrenic parent. Many of these parents try, in their own disturbed ways, to be good parents, and some even partially succeed. When they fail, their children come to the psychiatrist, or to the police.

Adelaide Johnson has described a particular type of character disorder the specific defect in which she has termed the "superego lacuna." Here the parent has unconsciously condoned and even stimulated the child's antisocial behavior, and receives vicarious satisfaction through identification with the child in his delinquent acts. The phenomenon should be looked for in any case of antisocial acting out in which the etiology is not grossly apparent.

COMPARISON OF THE ETIOLOGY OF PERSONALITY DISORDER AND PSYCHONEUROSIS

It was noted above that some workers consider personality disorder to be a form of neurosis, and employ such terms as *character neurosis* to designate this disorder. Below, under Differential Diagnosis, it will be shown that differentiation is sometimes difficult, as the two disorders actually form a continuum. The etiology of the two may likewise be essentially identical, consisting of emotional neglect or trauma in early childhood. Nevertheless, in the majority of cases, certain general distinctions in etiology exist. The important ones are:

1. Hereditary predisposition is probably more important in the etiology of neurosis than of character disorder.

2. The environmental pathology is generally more chronic and more severe in the history of character disorder than of neurosis.

Many cases of neurosis eventually become character disorders, as the child's symptoms increase in severity, as the struggle with himself and his environment persists and intensifies, and as the overreaction by his parents and other authority figures to his disturbance engenders greater counteraction in the child, until the distortions in his personality become so severe and so fixed as to constitute a personality disorder. However, this is not to say that all personality disorders were originally neuroses. It is obvious that in many cases the personality was seriously disordered in the earliest stages of its development.

PSYCHOPATHOLOGY

To understand the psychopathology of personality disorder, let us refer again to Erikson's eight stages of man. For, perhaps more than in any of the other disorders of childhood, the needs of these children have been unfulfilled at each stage and in all areas of functioning. It will

be recalled that in Erikson's formulation (see Chapter 2), the major
achievements in personality development at each stage, compared with the
major defects occurring if the child's needs were inadequately met, were as
follows:

1. Trust vs. basic mistrust
2. Autonomy vs. shame and doubt
3. Initiative vs. guilt
4. Industry vs. inferiority
5. Identity vs. role diffusion
6. Intimacy vs. isolation
7. Generativity vs. stagnation
8. Integrity vs. despair

Reading down the right-hand side of the above list we read the life
history of the personality disorder. Having been reared without love, or at
least without mature and consistent parental love, his personality has developed with serious distortions in:
1. His interpersonal relationships
2. His self-percept
His interpersonal relationships are characterized by any or all of the following: mistrust, suspicion, fear, anger, jealousy, scorn, and disinterest. These
characterize in greater or lesser degree his feelings toward all individuals.
His self-percept is characterized by: low self-esteem, uncertainty of identity
including sexual identity, self-hatred, and compensatory self-aggrandize-
ment.

The above distortions in his feelings toward self and others are the
basis for the abnormalities of emotion and social behavior which characterize this disorder. The child may act out his anger and resentment for others
in various ways, and he may act out his feelings of worthlessness and self-
hatred by seeking punishment or by avoiding the usual cautions against
personal injury. He may need to demonstrate his feelings of worthlessness
by failing in whatever he undertakes, or by getting into trouble with the
law. Whatever the symptoms, and the major ones are recounted below,
it will be found that their basis lies in one aspect or another of this fundamental psychopathology.

It is not always possible to uncover the underlying thought pathology
in these children. So completely do they sometimes resist the psychiatrist's
efforts to help them, so successfully do they refuse to disclose their feelings
and to verbalize their thoughts, that often we can only speculate on the
basis of the history and the disturbed behavior.

SYMPTOMS

As in neurosis, the symptoms of personality disorder can be classified into two groups:
1. Acting out
2. Internalization

The *acting out* includes delinquent behavior in all its forms and variations, and these need not be catalogued here. It also includes the so-called subdelinquent behaviors such as school truancy, negativism, disobedience, lying, cheating, and fighting. Then there are the less voluntary forms of acting out, such as temper outbursts, crying spells, surliness, and episodes of uncommunicativeness. Academically, these children are usually poor students; yet, as in the case of Beverly, some of the brighter ones find sufficient narcissistic gratification in school achievement to do remarkably well.

The internalized symptoms, though often less obvious and less dramatic, are at least as serious in their portent. Many such children are virtually immobilized by their conflicts over feelings of counteraggression, hatred, and self-denigration. They are depressed, silent, sullen, emotionally constricted. They are suspicious, fearful, mistrustful of authority, even afraid of their own occasional feelings of warmth and affection toward others because in the past such feelings have resulted only in crushed hopes and misery. It is sometimes said that children with personality disorder have no anxiety; yet some of them are literally driven by a chronic, free-floating anxiety which pervades all their functioning. This differs from neurotic anxiety, which is more directed and fixed to specific areas of conflict; the anxiety of character disorder, however, is no less intense.

If there are any symptoms characteristic of personality disorder, they would be not the various kinds of acting-out behavior; rather, they would occur within the child's expressions of his feelings about himself and about others.

DIAGNOSIS

It follows from the statement immediately above, that the diagnosis of character disorder cannot accurately be made from a report of the child's behavior. It requires those evidences uncovered in the clinical evaluation, in the psychiatric interview, in psychological tests, and in the past history. In the diagnostic evaluation, the therapist specifically looks for evidences of distortion in interpersonal relationships and in self-percept. The child with personality disorder is often excessively guarded and uncommunicative, which is in itself strong evidence of disturbed relationships.

Most children are initially apprehensive in a psychiatrist's office, but the experienced psychiatrist can, within a few minutes, provide enough reassurance so that the child will respond, if he has the capacity to do so. If the child does not, the evidence is strong that he has either personality disorder or schizophrenia.

The diagnostic interview with a child with character disorder is sometimes a turbulent and exhausting episode. When the child is sullen and unresponsive, a show of anger and firm authoritativeness is frequently required. The child may be told directly and strongly that he is here to be helped and that he is wasting the psychiatrist's time by sitting and doing nothing. However, an interview should never be ended on such a note, and whatever the child's response, the tactics should be changed at some point before the interview is over, and a tone of sympathy and reassurance employed. The therapist must not permit his own feelings of counteraggression to pervade the interview. Nor is this always easy: These children can be thoroughly exasperating.

To gauge the child's feelings for persons toward whom he should be expected to have some affection, such as parents and siblings, strong tactics are again often required. To ask a child with a character disorder if he loves his mother is often a useless question. He may reply with indifference, "Oh, she's all right"; he may say that he hates her and wishes she would leave, but these are not necessarily his true feelings. The therapist has to try to break down the child's strong guard, to stimulate genuine responses. One may talk with the child soberly and with feeling about the trouble he has caused his parents, about how his mother must feel over his being the way he is. One may berate him angrily, trying thus to stimulate his anger, which is genuine. One may insult his parents, saying it is no wonder the boy has turned out as he has, having a drunkard for a father. Such techniques seem harsh and they are not always indicated. But if the child should be hurt, the damage can usually be repaired. And if he cannot be hurt, this finding is significant.

The diffusion or uncertainty of identity which many of these children feel can often be strikingly demonstrated. One may ask a child who has lived in several foster homes, "How many fathers do you have, John?" Certainly an insulting and shocking question to ask any boy. But John, neither shocked nor insulted, begins to count on his fingers, and at length says "Four." "And which one was the best?" John mentions a man's name. "Why was he the best?" "He always bought me ice cream cones." One boy's preference was for the father who had whipped him only with his hand; the others used belts or sticks.

The child with character disorder is perhaps diagnosed as often by his appearance as by his verbalization. There is something about his whole demeanor: an air of emptiness, of hopelessness, of defeat; a total disinterest and absence of motivation toward anything. Many of these children have no spark, no warmth; humor is lost upon them. This is not true of all cases, of course, and some are still wonderfully combative and angry. These are probably the more hopeful ones.

DIFFERENTIAL DIAGNOSIS

It has been repeatedly emphasized in preceding chapters that it is the children who have had poor upbringing, no matter what their diagnosis, who most often need psychiatric help. Therefore, in order to diagnose the child as having a character disorder, one must determine that he does not have brain damage, or schizophrenia, or any of the other specific disorders. It is, of course, possible that the child may have more than one disorder, and a mixed diagnosis is quite justified, if it exists. However, the label is often a matter of emphasis: there may be no essential diagnostic difference between a child with mixed reading disability and character disorder, and a child with reading disability who has been badly mishandled.

Many children can be considered to have both neurosis and personality disorder. The differences between them are largely quantitative; the neurosis generally involves: more directed anxiety, less distortion of interpersonal relationships, less severe early mishandling, and a larger component of hereditary predisposition. Neurosis may eventually become character disorder, and at some time during the child's abnormal adjustment it may be difficult or impossible to come to a definite decision as to which it should be called.

Another difficult differentiation is between personality disorder and "normal" reaction to environmental stress. Some children resist amazingly well a chronically pathological environment. It is important to differentiate between those who have been adversely affected and those who, while showing some degree of misbehavior and distress, have sufficient ego strength and resiliency to adjust, if given the opportunity to do so. The diagnostic judgment is made largely on the basis of what one finds in the child's relationship with the examiner, and in his self-percept.

A severe character disorder can simulate schizophrenia. Such children may exhibit extremely bizarre behavior, may be socially isolated, silly, may laugh foolishly and inappropriately, grimace, shriek, weep uncontrollably, and verbalize meaningless phrases. Differentiation from schizophrenia can be difficult, and may require a period of observation in order to determine the presence or absence of dereistic thinking.

Psychopathy must be differentiated, and this depends on demonstrating an inability to relate. Psychopathy of milder degrees merges with character disorder.

PSYCHOLOGICAL TESTS

The child's performance in testing is often characterized by poor motivation, and this may reduce all of his performance much below his potential. His responses are desultory, he avoids involvement with the examiner, he is uncritical, satisfied with omissions and inaccuracies. Bender-Gestalt drawings may be poorly executed, again reflecting mainly disinterest and carelessness. Family drawings are primitive. The child often tries to "get by" with stick-figure drawings, which cannot be accepted. Intelligence, of course, varies widely, and some of these children, in moments of motivation, can achieve remarkably high levels. Tests reflecting social awareness, such as the Wechsler Intelligence Scale for Children subtests of comprehension and picture arrangement, are usually poorly done. Perhaps the most revealing test in this condition is the draw-a-family test. Here, the distortions in interpersonal relationship are often strikingly evident. Figures are stereotyped, widely separated from each other, perhaps distorted in size or configuration. The story which the child creates is equally pathological. Most often there is no story at all beyond a few stereotyped phrases. There is no particular pattern common to most of these children, but only pathology of all kinds in interpersonal feelings, usually with some degree of emptiness and uninvolvement.

Psychological tests are not often essential to the general diagnosis of personality disorder. That is, the test results seldom alter the diagnosis as obtained in the psychiatric interview. Tests are most helpful in disclosing the specific areas of difficulty, in eliciting the strongly suppressed feelings toward self and others which so many of these children have, and which are at times so difficult to uncover in the psychiatric interview. It is here that the projective techniques are needed, and these may be of inestimable value to the therapist in helping both with the planning and the carrying out of treatment.

TREATMENT

In this disorder removal of the child from his parental environment is very often indicated. The environmental pathology is frequently so severe that no amount of outpatient treatment and special education will help without altering the child's total life situation. Kanner has pointed out that while many of these children come from "broken homes," there are many who live in homes which are classified as intact, but which are so disturbed that it is the job of the psychiatrist to break them up himself.

The parents frequently refuse to let their children leave home. A mother who loves her child is usually willing to give him up temporarily if she is convinced that this will help him or that it will be the best thing for the family. Parents of children with character disorders will not place the children away from home for a variety of reasons. Many are threatened or angered by the suggestion that they are not adequate parents; many are strongly overinvolved with the child in a variety of pathological ways and are unwilling to have the relationship interfered with; some do not want the child to be helped and resent any outside interference; some are simply disinterested.

One of the most discouraging and at the same time most challenging aspects of child psychiatry is that often we know well what is needed to help the patient but are unable to provide it. This is most often true in personality disorders, and the psychiatrist often finds himself put to the test. His job is not finished when he has done the examination, made the diagnosis, and submitted a recommendation. The recommendation is no good to the child unless it is carried out. If the parents question or object to the psychiatrist's recommendation, there is nothing to be gained by an attitude of indignation, by saying "That's what should be done, do what you like about it." The parents' pathology is a part of the total problem, and as such, it is part of the concern of the child's psychiatrist. It is temptingly easy to work out one's counteraggression on the parents, but this can only harm the child.

There are many ways to deal with resistant parents, but the first step is to understand something at least about them and about the total family situation. This requires whenever possible, that both parents be seen and that communication be established. Many parents have distorted conceptions of psychiatry and psychiatrists, and are extremely threatened by these thoughts. One father of an adolescent girl would bring his daughter to the clinic for a weekly visit and would park his car in front of the office and watch through the window throughout the therapy hour. He refused repeated invitations sent through the patient to come in and meet me. Contact was finally established when I walked out to the car and introduced myself, and, thus reassured, the man was enticed into the office. He proved to be completely "unworkable," a hostile, suspicious old man, intensely jealous of any male who had any contact with his daughter; but at least he was no longer an unknown factor. In this instance the need for placement away from home was quickly established, and was effected through the use of strong threats.

The point to be made is that, in order to help our patients, we sometimes must work very hard. The psychiatrist is truly "involved" in mankind: he is not a dispassionate observer of the human scene. He must involve himself deeply at times with his patients and with their families, and the patients must know and expect that he is genuinely concerned with and for them. With these children, treatment cannot always be compartmentalized into one or two scheduled hours per week. The therapist must be on call at all times, he must be ready to meet whatever situation arises, and to proffer his help when it is needed. He must expect calls from the parents, school, patient, and police, and if he cannot discuss the matter at the precise moment, he must at least manage to do so within the hour. His sleep may be interrupted. One boy arrived at the clinic at two o'clock in the morning, having ridden his bicycle 20 miles through the rain after his parents had awakened and frightened him by their violent arguments.

The success of individual psychotherapy as a force in effecting improvement in personality disorder is determined chiefly by two factors:

1. The patient's ability to form meaningful interpersonal relationships, and

2. the amount of anxiety present. Of these, the former is by far the more significant; if present in adequate degree, it can be utilized to induce anxiety where little exists. Perhaps too much has been made of the prognostic implications of the presence or absence of anxiety in character disorder, and many workers have considered that if the symptoms are "ego-syntonic," then the child is perfectly content and has no motivation toward improvement. Certainly many of these children do not want psychiatric help, and are resentful and suspicious of any interference by an adult. But that they are genuinely content in their disorder, that the symptoms are truly ego-syntonic, is highly questionable in any case of personality disorder. Behind the thin structure of defense, the bulwarks of suspicion, resentment, cynicism, and aloofness, there are in great quantity anxiety, conflict, anger, self-doubt, and despair. These are not always readily displayed, and in fact can be kept hidden forever. But it is the task of the therapist, through persistence and through the developing relationship, to activate enough of the child's feelings so that he may be somehow motivated to change. This does not mean that in treatment of the character disorder one necessarily brings to the patient's consciousness his unconscious conflicts. This, the classic technique of psychoanalytic therapy, has little place in the treatment of most disturbed children (Lippmann). The child need never become aware of his unconscious conflicts and attitudes toward himself and others; he needs mainly to feel some respect. liking. and fear toward the therapist, and know that his behavior is being directed by that individual.

These principles of treatment will be discussed further in the chapter on outpatient therapy (Chapter 18). They are mentioned here to emphasize that individual psychotherapy has a place, often an important place, in the treatment of children with personality disorder.

PROGNOSIS

As in other disorders of children, there are not sufficient data on long-term follow-up studies to make reliable statements regarding the prognosis of personality disorder. The long-range studies thus far reported, such as that of Robins and O'Neal, while suggesting certain trends, are hampered by a lack of uniformity in diagnostic criteria, so that it is not possible to determine the diagnoses of the children seen many years earlier. There is no doubt that, as a group, children with personality disorder turn out more poorly adjusted in adulthood than a group of fairly normal children. However, it is also true that some do remarkably well when they grow up.

The question of reversibility of learned behavior is of fundamental importance to psychiatry and directly pertinent to the prognosis of personality disorder. Learning theory has demonstrated that there is wide variability in the rate of extinction of a learned response: Some learning is permanently retained while some appears quite transient. Many learning theorists object to the term *extinction* altogether, feeling, at least in higher animals, that the response is not extinguished, but that a new pattern of learning is superimposed, so that the original response is suppressed or otherwise superceded. This phenomenon has been amply demonstrated in man and is the basis for some of the major components of psychoanalytic psychology, especially ego psychology. Psychoanalysis has shown that much that was previously learned and long-since "forgotten" is still present and active in the individual's unconscious. It has also demonstrated major distortions in previously learned materials, so that everything which has been learned is not forever unchangeable or forever exerting the same influence as it originally did. Penfield's interesting findings of "flash-back" phenomena in patients given electrical stimulation in the temporal lobe have likewise demonstrated the permanence of certain long-forgotten experiences. Penfield observes that "The existence of the flash-back responses indicates that nerve cells and junctions employed in the preservation of the record retain 'increased excitatory efficacy' for a very long period—most of an individual's lifetime, in fact." Penfield's electrodes elicited only one or at most a small number of experiences in each patient. Whether all past experience is thus perfectly retained is questionable.

Do children ever really forget the experiences that happened in their childhood, good or bad, pleasant or unpleasant? Are the traces of a harsh and tragic rearing ever erased, or are they indelibly imprinted upon the personality? The answers to these important questions are, of course, complex and only a few fragments are yet available. It can be said that a child never totally forgets his early years; but experiences and recollections which once elicited much anxiety and anger no longer invariably do so. The gratifications which the child formerly felt in his pathological responses, in anger and aggression, in sadomasochistic strife, may be given up as the child grows older and as his way of life changes; the old reinforcements no longer function, a degree of maturity is attained, and the distortions in relationship that were once the personality disorder become diminished or erased. The effect which psychiatric treatment may have in bringing about this desirable outcome is in some cases considerable and in some cases minimal. We do what seems indicated and hope for the best. Sometimes it works out well, but there is no way of knowing how much we helped.

REFERENCES

Chess, S. An Introduction to Child Psychiatry, New York, Grune & Stratton, 1959.

Erikson, E. Childhood and Society, New York, W. W. Norton Co., 1950.

Johnson, A. M. Factors in the Etiology of Fixations and Symptom Choice, Psychoanalyt. Quart., 22: 475, 1953.

Kanner, L. Child Psychiatry, 3rd ed., Springfield, Ill., Charles C Thomas Co., 1957.

Lippman, H. S. Treatment of the Child in Emotional Conflict, New York, McGraw-Hill Co., 1956.

Penfield, W., and Roberts, L. Speech and Brain Mechanisms, Princeton, Princeton University Press, 1959.

Rees, L. Constitutional Factors and Abnormal Behavior, in Handbook of Abnormal Psychology, ed. H. J. Eysenck, New York, Basic Books, Inc., 1961.

Robins, L. N., and O'Neal, P. Mortality, Mobility, and Crime: Problem Children Thirty Years Later, Am. Sociological Review, 23: 162, 1958.

11

PSYCHOPATHY

REPORT OF A CASE

When Richard T. was born, the man who was legally his father had been overseas with the Army for a year and a half (his mother was not certain which of several men was Richard's natural father). The mother was sometimes away from home all night, and the neighbors could hear Richard and his older brother crying for hours at a time. The police were called on several occasions when the babies were left unattended, and finally, when Richard was six months old, a petition of neglect was filed. Shortly afterwards, the mother departed, and the children were placed temporarily in an institution operated by the county welfare department. After about one month, Richard was taken to live with a great-aunt.

When Richard was 18 months old his father was discharged from the Army and the family was reunited; however, the reunion was not a happy one. The father's drinking, always a problem, steadily grew worse. With some justification, he began to suspect his wife's fidelity, and, on many occasions, when she came home late at night he would berate and beat her.

In addition to the diffusion of maternal figures, Richard's early years were further marred by the punitive treatment of both parents and the inadequate emotional quality of the care he received. (One report from a welfare agent states that when he was 2 years old the mother sought to accomplish his bowel training by dunking his head in a tub of water whenever he soiled himself.) By the time he was 3, he was a severe behavior problem. He would totally ignore his mother's reprimands, and he fought constantly with his siblings, a younger brother and sister who were born after the father's return.

When Richard was 6, his mother was diagnosed at a psychiatric clinic as exhibiting "character neurosis with paranoid features" and it was felt that she could not be helped by psychiatric treatment. Soon afterwards the parents were divorced, with the children given into custody of the mother.

231

The father thereafter only sporadically provided small sums of money for the children's maintenance, and the living conditions in the home deteriorated further. At times there was nothing for the children to eat. The family periodically separated, the children from time to time going to live with their maternal grandparents or other relatives, and for a time Richard lived in a home for dependent children maintained by a church organization.

PRESENT ILLNESS

It is difficult to assign a definite age to the onset of Richard's disorder. It began early and progressed steadily. He was impulsive and aggressive, he had no sustained interest or motivation, he lied and stole; in short, he did very much as he pleased and never evidenced remorse or concern.

When Richard entered grade school his disturbed behavior became worse, as he was unable to accept the restrictions and controls imposed by the classroom situations. He caused frequent disruptions, and his entire school career was marked by limited academic achievement, with much punishment including several periods of expulsion. Remarkably, he did learn something, and many of the teachers' reports indicated that he evidenced an intellectual ability considerably higher than his grades might suggest.

When he was 11, Richard's disorganized behavior became even more noticeable. There were frequent episodes of silliness with outbursts of laughter and shouting; the teacher noted that when she sought to interrupt these outbursts he ignored her. Referred to the psychiatric clinic, Richard was soon thereafter, at the age of 12, admitted to the residential treatment center for diagnostic evaluation and treatment.

COURSE IN THE TREATMENT CENTER

It early became apparent that Richard was an emotionally empty, affectionless boy. Excerpts from the therapist's notes are as follows: "Throughout the entire stay in the hospital his motivation has been almost nil. His relationships with the other children are poor. He is basically an isolate. His lack of acceptance is caused by his untoward behavior, including stealing, and also the fact that he does not have much to offer the other children."

At the Center, when Richard's stealing or fighting got him into trouble, he usually accepted his punishments without apparent feeling but occasionally burst out in anger and several times attacked the staff. In the schoolroom, where the group was small and his teacher was able to control him and keep him at work, his academic work improved considerably during the seven months of hospitalization. However, there was little other improvement in any area. His therapist, who saw him for two or three hours weekly in addition to brief daily contacts, noted that after seven months there was no more feeling of warmth and relationship with Richard than there had been at the very first interview. The other staff members who had daily contact with him likewise reported that he was "cold," "distant," and that "you can't get close to him."

Diagnosis at the time of discharge was *psychopathic personality*. Richard was transferred to a closed institution for homeless children, where his behavior could be fairly well controlled. It was felt that further placement in a psychiatric setting was not indicated.

THE CONCEPT OF PRIMARY SOCIALIZATION

Animal breeders have long known that ewes . . . occasionally will reject their own offspring which have been handled and taken from the mother shortly after birth. Such rejected lambs are usually fed on a bottle and become strongly attached to human beings. To accomplish this under experimental conditions, we took a female lamb from its mother at birth and raised it on a bottle for the first ten days of life. After that we put it out in the field where other sheep were grazing. . . . The orphan followed an entirely different rhythm in its grazing pattern and had almost no contact with the flock, although they all stayed in the same small field. . . . Even after a period of several years this sheep displayed a great deal of independence from the rest of the flock, not running when they were frightened and staying away from them on most occasions (Scott).

This phenomenon of nonsocialization has been observed in a number of animals including the duck, dog, goat, and sheep. It is, by definition, confined to those species which are normally social animals, and develops when the animal, at a particular period early in its development, is separated from other members of the species. A special situation exists in the dog, which normally develops a social relationship both with other dogs and with man. Here, relationship with either one of these, or both, can also be prevented by separation during the critical period.

Does this phenomenon have a counterpart in the human animal? Most workers now believe that it does. While there is much controversy about the psychopathic personality, the controversy mainly concerns terminology, age of the critical period, degree of reversibility, and the importance of hereditary predisposition. Almost no one doubts that the phenomenon of nonsocialization occurs, that it is determined to a large extent by early neglect, and that it is extremely difficult if not impossible to treat.

EFFECTS OF EARLY NEGLECT

Pediatricians have long been aware of the seriously adverse effects of prolonged separation of an infant from its mother. Early in this century they began to become alarmed over the large number of deaths among infants being kept in institutions. Bakwin and Bakwin, reviewing the early reports on the condition which has come to be called "hospitalism," note that in some institutions such as foundling homes the mortality of infants who remained for a considerable period of time was as high as 100 per cent. For some time the condition was considered to be due to poor nutrition; then, when measures to overcome the undernutrition also met with little success, it was believed that infection might be the culprit. Intensive efforts to guard against cross-infection were instituted: the children were placed in separate cubicles, visitors were excluded, and personnel clothed in masks and gowns entered only for essential care and feeding. But the hospitalism worsened. Bakwin and Bakwin noted: "For many years thoughtful pediatricians suspected that the basis for hospitalism was in some vague way related to the infant's psyche." It was gradually discovered that when the institutionalized infants were given more individual attention and stimulation, they responded favorably, and the incidence of sickness and death diminished remarkably.

Psychiatrists, because of their interest in effects of early experience, quite naturally turned their attention to this phenomenon of hospitalism. Their interest has centered around three main areas: specific factors in etiology, age of susceptibility, and long range effects.

The work of Spitz has done much to clarify the etiological significance of early neglect. Infants reared in two different institutions, one a foundling home and one a nursery associated with a women's jail, were compared. In the foundling home the infants had minimal contact with humans, a single nurse being responsible for the care of about seven babies. In the nursery, the babies' own mothers were allowed to spend considerable time with them each day. Except for this difference, the two institutions were similar. Spitz reports profound differences between the two groups of infants. "The children in the foundling home showed all the manifestations of hospitalism, both physical and mental. In spite of the fact that hygiene and precautions against contagion were impeccable, the children showed, from the third month on, extreme susceptibility to infection and illness of any kind." Out of 88 children under age 2½, 23 died. In contrast, the children in the nursery were, for the most part, normal and healthy. Tests of development showed that the infants in both institutions, in their first four months of life, had normal developmental quotients, but by the end of the first year the foundling-home infants exhibited serious developmental retardation. Spitz concludes, "There is a point under which the mother-child relations cannot be restricted during the child's first year without inflicting irreparable damage."

LONG-RANGE EFFECTS OF EARLY NEGLECT (PSYCHOPATHY)

In the early 1930's, at about the same time that interest in hospitalism was developing, a number of child psychiatrists began to report cases of delinquent children who were highly resistant to treatment, who seemed to be lacking in feelings of human warmth and relationship, and who had histories of severe early neglect and deprivation. David Levy was among the first to describe the condition, and his original case report still stands as one of the best descriptions of this disorder. This was an 8-year-old girl, born illegitimately and cared for by a succession of relatives. She was brought to the psychiatrist by foster parents, because of chronic lying and stealing. When first taken to the foster home, at age 7, she showed no emotional response. The foster parents soon realized that the child showed no feelings of affection. The mother stated that she "would kiss you but it would mean nothing." Levy further reports:

The school teacher complained of her general inattention and her lack of pride in the way her things looked. However, she did well in her school subjects, in keeping with her good intelligence. She also made friends with children, though none of these were close friendships. After a contact of a year and a half with the patient the father said, "You just can't get to her," and the mother remarked, "I have no more idea today what's going on in that child's mind than I knew the day she came. You can't get under her skin. She never tells what she's thinking or what she feels. She chatters but it's all on the surface."

Bowlby, in a monograph which constitutes a major contribution to the literature of psychopathy, carefully reviewed the writings up to 1951 and concluded: "The evidence is now such that it leaves no room for doubt regarding the general proposition . . . that the prolonged deprivation of the young child of maternal care may have grave and far-reaching effects upon his character and so on the whole of his future life." Bowlby suggests that three somewhat different kinds of early experience may each produce psychopathic personality:

1. Lack of any opportunity for forming an attachment to a mother figure during the first three years

2. Emotional deprivation for a limited period—at least three months and probably more than six—during the first three or four years

3. Changes from one mother figure to another during the same period

The evidence that the above factors cause psychopathic personality, although strongly suggestive, is not conclusive. It is based mainly on retrospective data obtained from histories of children with the disorder. In the case of hospitalism, the evidence on etiology is more clear-cut; the direct cause-effect relationship between neglect and resulting disorder appears to be thoroughly validated. But it is less clear whether infants with hospitalism who survive later become psychopaths; and, if so, what percentage of them become psychopaths; and whether some psychopathic children did not have hospitalism as infants.

The problem is complex, and experimental and clinical data with a significantly large group of cases is difficult to gather (Casler). The measurement of neglect is not the least of the difficulties in such a study. There are degrees of neglect and various qualities of neglect. A mother who spanks her child whenever he cries is not neglecting him, nor is a mother who feeds him on a rigid schedule and ignores his cries in between. But the neglect associated with hospitalism appears to involve almost total isolation from human contact. Thus it is unlikely to occur in "pure" form in a child reared in a family environment, no matter how punitive or disorganized. Here, an infant receives much opportunity for human contact, as activities among the family and friends go on in the room about him. It is in the institutions and hospitals for infants that the affectionless children are most likely to be produced. Even today, despite current awareness of the importance of early human contact and stimulation, some of these institutions are so understaffed that it is impossible to give each child more than minimal care and attention.

Some of the evidence suggests that the important need of the infant is not merely for human contact, but for consistent contact with the same individual over a considerable period. Studies of infant development show that during the second half of the first year of life the child develops fear and avoidance of strangers and can only be satisfied by its own mother or mother-substitute. This may persist for a considerable time. Anna Freud and Burlingham found in their study of war orphans at the Hampstead Nursery that many of the younger children became less disturbed when each was assigned one staff person to become his mother-surrogate. Clinically, one finds in the histories of many psychopathic children that they were shifted frequently from one family to another with no opportunity for establishing lasting relationships.

THE CRITICAL PERIOD FOR PRIMARY SOCIALIZATION

A crucial question in the problem of psychopathic personality is: At what age must the child be isolated in order to be made psychopathic? or, to express it positively: At what age must the child experience human contact in order to develop the social relationship? An experiment designed to answer this question in one of the lower animals, the dog, is considered below.

Freedman and others raised puppies in such a way that these had no contact with humans except for certain specified periods. At various ages, each of the puppies was allowed a week's exposure to human handling. At the end of 14 weeks, all the puppies were tested for social response to humans. The authors concluded that the seventh week of age was the period in which the puppies were most receptive to socialization. However, all the puppies which had been handled scored higher on the socialization tests than did unhandled control animals, although the puppies exposed at age two weeks showed only a slight increase. The control puppies, which had not had any contact with humans during the entire first 14 weeks of life, apparently never overcame their subsequent avoidance of man.

In the above experiment, 34 "pure-bred" animals were used, and they were studied under conditions in which the environment could be kept relatively constant and controlled. The results represent a major step in clarification of the critical period in dogs. Yet, as the authors themselves suggest, "further work is necessary." For example, the duration of exposure might be varied; it would be important to know whether one day of handling by humans was as effective as one week or if a short period of human contact each day for a week was effective as the same total time given continuously on one day. One would like to know the importance of the quality of handling—whether a quiet, soothing experience has a different effect from a very active, stimulating experience, or if a painful experience administered by the handler counteracts the positive effects of the contact.

The above questions suggest the enormous complexity of the problem and indicate how difficult it is to reach definitive conclusion regarding the effects of a child's early handling on the basis of historical data that is retrospectively obtained. Each child's experience is unique. Casler, in a critical and comprehensive review of the literature on maternal deprivation, points out that:

The prodigious difficulties encountered in attempting to obtain representative samples of infants, along with the virtual impossibility of imposing experimental manipulations on human infants, have forced investigators usually to be content with reporting "natural" experiments whose variables are length of time in institution, age at separation, etc.

Casler concludes that, while the general concept that long-range detrimental effects result from early neglect seems valid, either the crucial factors involved or the periods of development which are critical, are far from being understood. Nevertheless, with the reservation that further confirmation is needed, most authors agree that the critical period for primary socialization in the average human infant is from about the seventh to the fifteenth month. The evidence is partly clinical, based on the histories of a large number of cases, and partly theoretical, based on extrapolation from data on animals.

This critical period coincides partially with Erikson's period for the development of a basic sense of trust, and also with the time when the infant is developing an awareness of self as differentiated from environment. These are not chance coincidences; socialization and individual development are parts of the same process and are intimately interrelated.

As with the puppies which varied in degree of social response, some humans relate more strongly than others. The development of a relationship capacity is not an all-or-none process, and the therapist must rely on a relative evaluation of a child's socialization. He sees children who have apparently no feeling for humans, some who have a minimal amount, some who have an average amount, and others who have more than average.

HEREDITARY FACTORS IN ETIOLOGY

There is only indirect evidence as to whether psychopathy may be affected by heredity. One notes, for example, wide differences in social response of different dog breeds. African Basenjis are aloof animals, and no amount of human contact has much influence on this aspect of their personality, while cocker spaniels, on the other hand, are friendly and responsive to humans. Observations of behavior of newborn and young babies disclose marked differences in their response to people. Whether these early responses are related in any consistent way to later sociability has not yet been adequately studied. It seems likely that relationship capacity in man is in part hereditarily determined, but until more direct evidence is obtained, this must remain conjecture.

TERMINOLOGY

In the years 1949 to 1951 a series of three round-table discussions were held at the annual meetings of the American Orthopsychiatric Association to consider the problem of psychopathic personality. These discussions under the title: *Child and Juvenile Delinquency*, and edited by Karpman appeared in monograph form. While much unanimity among the participants was evidenced over many aspects of the disorder, there was little agreement as to what it should be called. Many who employed the terms *psychopath* or *psychopathic* did so with reservation, as was indicated by their enclosing the words in quotation marks. Other terms included *affectionless, primary affect hunger, constitutional psychopath,* and *psychogenic acathexis.* As the disorder was considered to be more determined by environment than by constitution it was generally agreed to delete the qualification "constitutional"; however, consensus on terminology was not otherwise obtained.

The chief objection to the term *psychopath* was that it has been used indiscriminately. As introduced into psychiatric terminology early in the century, it was apparently applied to any person who exhibited chronic antisocial behavior, especially if the individual evidenced little remorse or guilt over his behavior. The category thus included persons with various psychiatric disorders, and, in fact, some children in each of the major diagnostic categories fulfilled the criteria. As diagnostic techniques improved, *psychopath* came to be recognized as too general and inadequate a term, and has largely fallen into disrepute in this country. Nevertheless, having certain advantages over its companions the term has persisted: it is brief, it is relatively euphonious, and, perhaps most importantly, it *sounds* like a good psychiatric term. For these reasons it is a word which is likely to stay; thus it becomes even more essential that unanimity be reached as to its meaning.

That the word *psychopath* continues to retain its early and more general meaning in certain areas and in other countries was indicated in 1960 by R. M. Mowbray. Mowbray cited a Royal Commission report which indicates that psychopaths are persons "whose daily behavior shows a want of social responsibility and of consideration for others, of prudence and foresight, and of ability to act in their own best interests. Their persistent antisocial mode of conduct may include inefficiency and lack of interest in any form of occupation; pathological lying, swindling and slandering; alcoholism and drug addiction, sexual offenses, and violent actions with little motivation and an entire absence of self restraint." Mowbray objects to this definition, as proposed by the Commission, since it is not a psychiatric one and would include a variety of disorders.

Fortunately, terminology is not crucial. What is more important is that there be general understanding and agreement regarding the nature of the disorder. As this develops, agreement on terms will undoubtedly follow. Meanwhile, each therapist will use the term he prefers, and hopefully will understand when he hears other terms that they have essentially the same meaning.

SYMPTOMS

Bowlby lists the following as typical clinical features of the psychopath:

1. Superficial relationships

2. No real feeling—no capacity to care for people or to make true friends

3. Inaccessibility, exasperating to those trying to help

4. No emotional response to situations where it is normal—a curious lack of concern

5. Deceit and evasion, often pointless

In addition, there are frequently, but not always, all the various forms of acting-out behavior, from mild negativism and temper outbursts to serious delinquency.

It is commonly considered that psychopaths are invariably severe behavior problems or delinquents. Perhaps this is true in the majority of cases; yet, surprisingly, some are able to avoid trouble for many years. One 15-year-old boy was brought to the clinic after hurting his mother rather seriously by hitting her over the head with a chair. The boy was found to be totally without concern or anxiety, and was, in fact, devoid of any feelings of interest or concern toward other persons. The diagnosis of psychopathy was made. The patient had been adopted at the age of two, and nothing was known of his history prior to adoption. The normal upper-middle-class parents had always sensed an absence of warmth and feeling in the child, but, by gratifying his physical needs and by giving in to him whenever his displeasure was strongly evidenced, they had managed to avoid crises, and had for 13 years maintained a superficial resemblance of normal family life. The blowup came when the father was out of town and the mother remonstrated with the boy for staying out too late at night. By good luck, he did not kill her.

The fact that the psychopath is without relationship feelings does not mean that he is without any feeling. He knows all the primitive emotions such as fear, anger, and pleasure. But the subtler and more exclusively human emotions—love, sorrow, joy, pity, loneliness—are beyond his comprehension. Yet, despite his lack of true interpersonal feeling, the psychopath is not ordinarily a social isolate. He may have a wide circle of acquaintances, whom he uses outrageously to advance his own ends. He sometimes possesses much attractiveness and charm—carrying an aura of recklessness, an indifference to insult and public attention, which is often the envy of those who are inhibited by caring what others think. He is thus the prototype of the hero in many detective novels and television Westerns —the tough guy, detached, aloof, calm in any argument, unruffled by his adversary's anger. But he does not welcome pain, and is not courageous. In the military, his successes are at the poker table rather than on the battle-front.

Any description of the psychopath, however clinical and dispassionate, usually succeeds in painting a picture of a thoroughly despicable character; and so he is. He inevitably outrages one's sense of justice and of human dignity. In no other disorder is it more difficult for the therapist to suppress his feelings of counteraggression. Fortunately, in this case, it does no harm to the patient, but it may become terribly distressing to the therapist.

In the earlier years in more extreme forms, severely disorganized behavior may occur. Bender has described such cases as follows:

Children who have been in institutions for the first two or three years of their lives without parents or other significant adults to visit them or take an interest in them frequently show a most severe type of deprived, asocial psychopathic personality deviation. These children do not develop a play pattern, and cannot enter into group play with other children. They abuse any child near them as frustrating objects to the satisfaction of their primitive impulses. They seek adults for constant contact and have temper tantrums when any impulse arising from their instinctive needs is frustrated or when any type of cooperation is expected from them which implies either interpersonal relationship or patterned behavior. They are hyperkinetic, distractible, short in attention span, and lack any concept of human relationship.

DIAGNOSIS

The diagnosis of psychopathy rests entirely on the demonstration of a diminished or absent capacity for relationship. It is not made on the basis of a history of chronic antisocial behavior or refractoriness to treatment; these, as has been shown, can occur in any of the psychiatric disorders. A history of early neglect is invariably present, except, of course, in adopted children where nothing is known of the first year or two of life. However, such a history is not per se sufficient evidence for the diagnosis—some degree of early neglect is common in children with other emotional illnesses, especially personality disorders, and it is not rare in normal children. That the neglect has been more severe and total in the psychopath may be inferred, but cannot always be conclusively proved.

Thus, the diagnosis of psychopathy becomes, more than in any other of the psychiatric disorders, a subjective one, involving to a large extent the "feeling" which the examiner experiences in his contact with the patient. Or, perhaps more accurately, it involves a lack of feeling, an awareness that nothing personal exists between patient and examiner; there is no warmth, no human spark. The diagnosis may not always be arrived at readily. Sometimes it takes much effort and time. One seeks in the usual ways to develop a relationship and to stimulate a response. All the usual techniques may be tried: threats, anger, reproach, all the ways one appeals to the child's "finer instincts." One must beware of interpreting his own exasperation and sense of helplessness as evidence of emptiness in the child, since children with neurosis or personality disorder sometimes induce these same feelings. But, once having known such a one, there is no mistaking a truly empty child.

The problem of diagnosis is complicated by the fact that there are degrees of psychopathy, and it is often found in association with personality disorder. Thus, both the "pure" psychopath and the "pure" personality disorder are relatively rare, and a much more frequent diagnosis is personality disorder with diminished relationship capacity, or mixed psychopathy and personality disorder. Most children neglected during the first year or two continue to be neglected in their later years, and the initial paucity of relationship becomes further distorted by subsequent experience. Relatively rare is the child who has suffered severe neglect in the first year with adequate care and attention through the remainder of childhood, as may be seen in the child reared in an inadequate institution, and then adopted into a good family.

DIFFERENTIAL DIAGNOSIS

Psychopathy is most likely to be confused with personality disorder and with schizophrenia.

The relation of psychopathy to personality disorder has been discussed above. Through development of their defenses, children with the latter problem may be so unable to enter into a meaningful interpersonal relationship as to present a picture of absence of capacity for relationship. Differentiation may be difficult, and can be made only after a considerable period of observation and treatment. The differentiation is important, as the development of a working relationship may be the only hope for treatment of the child with personality disorder.

Severely disorganized behavior and absence of relationship may cause confusion in diagnosis between psychopathy and schizophrenia. Bender (1956) has described a condition which she terms "pseudopsychopathic schizophrenia," in which the schizophrenic child, because of his tendency to act out antisocially and his aloofness from interpersonal relationship, is mistakenly thought to be psychopathic. Differentiation must rely mainly on evidences of disordered thinking in the schizophrenic child. Autistic behavior is unusual in the psychopath, and there is a different quality in the nonrelatingness in the two disorders: The schizophrenic is self-involved, the psychopath uninvolved. Additionally, anxiety is absent in psychopathy, although the disturbed, hyperkinetic behavior associated with the child's impulsivity and anger may at times be mistaken for anxiety.

The severe early form of psychopathic disorder described above by Bender offers the most difficult problem in differential diagnosis, as it may at times be confused with severe brain damage, primary learning disability, or mental retardation. Sometimes the diagnosis cannot be established until the child is older and better able to communicate his inner thoughts or the absence of thoughts.

TREATMENT

Strictly speaking, there is no treatment for psychopathy. Lourie has suggested, and this would seem to reflect the majority opinion, that if the disorder improves, then it was not psychopathy. Lourie states, "Even the most dramatic pictures of psychopathic behavior in young children are better described as psychopathic-like, particularly since most of them are reversible." Lourie further concludes that true psychopathic personality is relatively rare; with this the writer would agree, but with the condition that partial psychopathy, or a diminished but not absent relationship capacity, is not so rare.

Yet treatment of the psychopath is not necessarily a hopeless undertaking. If the goal of treatment is to develop a relationship feeling in the child, then treatment is indeed hopeless. But if the aim is to rehabilitate him to function without severe disharmony in society, then some successes may be achieved. The technique of treatment has been succinctly expressed by Rabinovitch: "Best results have come from placement, in the latency years, in a protective, non-punitive group environment, where the child can gradually learn to imitate the patterning of those about him." Here one utilizes the drive to emulate others which is as present in these children as in any, and which Bender (1953) has described as follows:

There is an imitative, passive, "as if" quality to the behavior of the older children. This is due to the inner drive for normality and the desire to behave like a human being. Whereas behavior in the normal child arises from internal mechanisms, such as identification processes, object relationship, anxieties and symbolic fantasy life, the psychopathic child has no such inner life though he still has the physiological and intellectual capacities to perceive and use symbols and patterned behavior. The psychopathic child, therefore, copies the behavior of other children, according to his maturation level, and ability.

Long-term treatment in a closely supervised and patterned environment is required. Psychotherapy is of little value. Best results are obtained if there is a minimum of opportunity for manipulation of staff; limits must be strictly set. It is preferable that individuals among the staff avoid too close involvement with the child, as this can lead to unfortunate complications and can be disturbing to the worker if he or she comes to expect much emotional return. If, upon being released into society, the patient manages to stay out of serious trouble, one may consider that the therapy has succeeded. It should not be expected that he become a loving husband and a pillar of the community, and it would of course be preferable that these patients never marry and reproduce. Unfortunately, many of them do.

IMPLICATIONS FOR ADOPTIVE PRACTICES

The knowledge that psychopathy cannot be cured but that it probably can be prevented is of profound import for child-adoption practices. The implications are clear-cut: adoption should wherever possible be permanently effected before the infant's fifth month of life, for at this time or soon thereafter the infant begins to avoid strangers and to develop an attachment to its mother or mother figure. To interrupt the association between mother and child following this time and throughout the remainder of early childhood can produce irreparable harm.

The practice of keeping the child in an adoptive institution or in a temporary foster home until he is old enough for various psychological and medical examinations for the purpose of "matching" him with the proper family is, in most cases, indefensible. There are, of course, exceptions, as in the case where the racial paternity is in doubt, or where there is suggestive evidence of such severe disorder as mongolism. Despite the slightly higher risk of the adoptive parents' getting an infant with some unrecognized physical defects, most well-managed adoption agencies have now accepted this principle and institute early adoption in the majority of cases.

REFERENCES

Bakwin, H., and Bakwin, R. Clinical Management of the Behavior Disorders in Children, Philadelphia, W. B. Saunders, 1960.

Bender, L. Aggression, Hostility and Anxiety in Children, Springfield, Ill., Charles C Thomas, 1953.

———— Schizophrenia in Childhood—Its Recognition, Description, and Treatment, Am. J. Orthopsychiatry, 26: 499, 1956.

Bowlby, J. Maternal Care and Mental Health, Geneva, World Health Organization Monograph No. 2, 1951.

Casler, L. Maternal Deprivation: A Critical Review of the Literature, Lafayette, Indiana, Child Development Publications, 1961.

Child and Juvenile Delinquency, ed. B. Karpman, Washington, D.C., Psychodynamics Monograph Series, 1959.

Erikson, E. Childhood and Society, New York, W. W. Norton Co., 1950.
Freedman, D. G., King, J. A., and Elliott, O. Critical Period in the Social Development of Dogs, Science, 133: 1016, 1961.
Freud, A., and Burlingham, D. Infants Without Families, New York, International University Press, 1944.
Levy, D. M. Primary Affect Hunger, Am. J. Psychiatry, 94: 643, 1937.
Lourie, R. S. The Irreversibility of Psychopathic-Like Patterns in Early Childhood, in Child and Juvenile Delinquency, ed. B. Karpman, Washington, D.C., Psychodynamics Monograph Series, 1959, p. 126.
Mowbray, R. M. The Concept of the Psychopath, J. Ment. Sci., 106: 537, 1960.
Rabinovitch, R. D. The Concept of Primary Psychogenic Acathexis, in Child and Juvenile Delinquency, ed. B. Karpman, Washington, D.C., Psychodynamics Monograph Series, 1959, p. 58.
Scott, J. P. Animal Behavior, Chicago, University of Chicago Press, 1958, p. 179.
Spitz, R. Hospitalism: an Inquiry into the Genesis of Psychiatric Conditions in Early Childhood, Psychoanalytic Study of the Child, International Universities Press, New York, 1945, Vol. 1.

12

MENTAL RETARDATION

REPORT OF TWO CASES

CASE 1—MARJORIE S.

Marjorie S., age 14, was referred to the psychiatric clinic by her school principal because of academic failure. Also, her behavior had recently become somewhat difficult both at home and at school; she was increasingly negative and disobedient, and had outbursts of anger.

Present Illness. Marjorie had been a poor student ever since the first grade. She was slow in learning to read, write, and do arithmetic. She was currently in the eighth grade, having failed only once to be promoted. However, her teachers reported that she was working nowhere near her grade level, and had little understanding of the work which the class was doing.

Marjorie had several girl friends in the school, whose company she enjoyed. She engaged in some social activities, but was not very popular and had little or no social contact with boys. Her immature and at times rather silly behavior tended to isolate her from most social circles. However, she was not an unhappy girl; at home she was quite content most of the time, watching television, playing with her younger sister, and helping her mother with the cooking.

Personal History. Pregnancy and birth were normal; birthweight was 6½ pounds, the baby cried spontaneously, appeared healthy, and ate well from the first day. She remained physically healthy throughout infancy and childhood. However, her behavioral development was slow. Marjorie did not sit up until about 9 or 10 months, did not walk until 2 years, and began to speak in single words or short phrases at about 3 years. Toilet training was likewise delayed, and the mother was unable to recall when bladder training was complete, as there had been several periods of regression after it had seemed that she was fully trained.

Mrs. S. felt that from the time Marjorie was about six months old she was "slow," because she was obviously less alert and responsive than her older brother and sister.

Family History. Marjorie was the third of four children. Her siblings were all normal, well-adjusted children, and above-average students. The father, age 41, had attended college for 2 years, and held a responsible position in the sales department of a large corporation. He appeared mature, friendly, and genuinely interested in his daughter. The mother had graduated from high school, and had worked as a secretary for three years prior to her marriage. She described herself as being "too nervous," and appeared somewhat apprehensive and anxious, but not excessively so. She said that she had always worried a great deal about Marjorie and had given her an extra amount of care. She felt that their family was a fairly happy one—they had many friends, and the children related well with their playmates. It was the examiner's impression that the family environment was generally healthy and happy.

Psychiatric and Psychological Examinations. In the psychiatric interview Marjorie was noted to be "a very pleasant appearing girl—she relates well and is quite warm and friendly. She was at first a little embarrassed, giggled frequently throughout the interview, and evidenced some apprehension." Speech was immature, with lisping and slurring of the *l*'s. She talked about her academic inadequacies, saying that she always had trouble with reading and arithmetic. She said that the children sometimes teased her about being "dumb," and this made her unhappy at times. Her thinking was concrete, her social judgment was fair, but there was little concern about the future and she was unable to discuss such abstractions as the requirements for being a good mother and the importance of newspapers. When asked what she would want her husband to be like, she giggled and said, "Be good lookin'."

On the Wechsler Intelligence Scale for Children, Marjorie attained a verbal I.Q. of 65, a performance I.Q. of 62, and a full-scale I.Q. of 62. The subtest scores were consistently low.

Diagnosis and Recommendations. The diagnosis was primary mental retardation with reasonably good emotional adjustment in a child who had been well cared for throughout her life.

The findings and diagnosis were discussed with the parents. They were assured that there was no indication for placement away from home, but that Marjorie would probably benefit by a special class for the educable retarded. The parents inquired about Marjorie's outlook for the future, especially regarding her social life and possible marriage. They were told that as she matured she would probably be included in the functions of the other adolescents and young adults—dances, movies, picnics, and so on, and that, since she was reasonably attractive and friendly, there was good reason to expect that she would find a husband. They were advised, however, that because of her poor judgment she should have more than the usual supervision and guidance during the courtship years.

The recommendation of a special class in public school was discussed with Marjorie. She understood the reasons for this, and was pleased with the idea, saying that she would like having school work which she was able to do. It was arranged with the school superintendent that she should continue the rest of that year in the same school, and then transfer to another school where a special class was available.

CASE 2—JOSHUA L.

Joshua L., age 11, was referred to the psychiatric clinic by a state adoption agency because of chronic misbehavior and academic failure.

Past History and Present Illness. Little was known of Joshua's infancy and early childhood. His mother was not married at the time of his birth, and the paternity was uncertain as she admitted to sexual promiscuity with a number of men. Joshua lived with his mother in his maternal grandparent's home until about six months of age, at which time the mother married a migrant farm worker. The family lived subsequently in a number of communities, usually in temporary quarters for the farm laborers. This continued for three or four years, during which time the mother had two more children. The parents then separated, following one of their frequent quarrels, and the mother returned to the home of her parents, who reluctantly took in their daughter and her three children. The mother soon left, following a quarrel with her father, and was found destitute, with the three children, in a bus station in a large city. The children were made wards of the court and were subsequently placed separately in foster homes. At this time Joshua was four.

Joshua's behavior early became a serious problem. He disobeyed the foster parents, was incorrigible, ill-tempered, aggressive, and unpatterned. He attended school irregularly, created constant turmoil in the classroom, and learned nothing. His language was often vulgar and abusive. Shortly before referral, on several occasions he had approached younger girls in the schoolyard, reached quickly under their dresses, pulled down their pants, and had then run away laughing. He had several times exhibited his genitals to little girls.

Joshua had been placed in a number of foster homes, and all placements had failed within six months. The agency made the referral because they wished the psychiatrists' advice regarding the feasibility of further home placements.

Psychiatric and Psychological Evaluation. In the psychiatric interview, Joshua showed complete unconcern about his past behavior, and was without apparent warmth or feeling. He was a cute-looking little boy and had a rather disarming grin, but this was patently superficial. When assured that the psychiatrist wanted to help him, and that he should discuss what was worrying him, he said, "I ain't worried about nothin'." This was obviously true. The psychiatrist noted that the interview revealed "emptiness, unconcern, motivation for nothing, and feeling for nothing; a great deal of id impulse without anything to control it."

On the Wechsler Intelligence Scale for Children, Joshua attained a verbal I.Q. of 71, a performance I.Q. of 63 and a full-scale I.Q. of 65. The subtest scores were consistently low. The psychologist noted the boy's extreme lack of concern and motivation. During the testing Joshua quickly became bored and disinterested, he was careless in his responses, impulsive, "gives any answer, responds minimally and temporarily to pressure or support." It was felt that the I.Q. scores represented his current intellectual functioning but that his potential was higher.

Diagnosis and Recommendations. The diagnosis was psychopathy with both primary and secondary mental retardation; the inherently borderline intelligence had probably been further reduced by early emotional deprivation and lack of stimulation. Because of Joshua's impulsivity, aggressiveness, and sexual preoccupation, he was considered potentially dangerous and unable to remain in the community. He was consequently committed to the state school for trainable retarded children.

These two cases illustrate the wide differences that occur in mentally retarded children. They suggest that emotional and social dysfunction do not inevitably accompany mental retardation, but that, as in children of normal intelligence, they are in large measure determined by early upbringing.

INTRODUCTION

The graph which represents the distribution of intelligence in the child population of this country is almost exactly a Gaussian or normal frequency distribution curve. It shows that 16 per cent of all children have I.Q.'s below 85, and 2 per cent have I.Q.'s below 70 (Kugelmass). An irregularity in the curve occurs at the extreme lower end, where there is a significantly greater number of severely retarded children than would be represented by a normal curve.

The graph indicates that in a normal population intelligence varies widely. The occurrence of mentally retarded children may thus be regarded as a "normal" phenomenon.

The definition of mental retardation is necessarily an arbitrary one. In general, it means diminished intelligence. The problem in definition becomes quantitative: Where is the line of demarcation? Tredgold (1947), reflecting the English point of view, defines mental deficiency not in quantitative terms, but in terms of the individual's total intellectual and social functioning. Tredgold states that the retarded person, or ament, has "a state of incomplete mental development" which is such as to make him incapable of adapting to his environment and of existing without external supervision or support. Such a definition, while admirable in its efforts to consider the individual's "whole" functioning, has certain drawbacks; it omits those mentally retarded persons who learn to support themselves, as many now do; likewise, it is lacking in specificity, and would perhaps include a number of persons of average intelligence who cannot function independently, such as certain schizophrenics and severe neurotics.

Most modern writings on mental retardation deplore the use of the intelligence quotient to define mental retardation. These often point out that the I.Q. fluctuates over time in most persons, and that a simple total of scores from the various subtests fails to reflect important differences among individuals. Nevertheless, the I.Q., as measured by psychological tests, remains the most important single criterion in defining retardation. Yet, as will be seen below under Diagnosis, it is by no means the only criterion, and must never be accepted uncritically.

The problem of defining retardation parallels the problem of defining intelligence. Everyone agrees that there is no wholly satisfactory definition of intelligence, and most agree that it is not simply that which intelligence tests measure. Beyond this, criteria begin to differ. Should intelligence include, for example, creativity? Many extremely bright and competent persons are totally lacking in creative capacities, while other highly creative and original thinkers perform with mediocrity in standardized situations. Memory or the capacity to retain learned information is an essential part of intelligence; but some persons have an amazing capacity for "total recall" yet are otherwise not remarkable intellectually. Number sense, mechanical aptitude, social judgment, a sense of rhythm, of musical pitch, a "feel" for beauty, alertness, high motivation, all these and many others are a person's personality and his intellectual endowment. Which of these should be measured in ascribing to him a particular I.Q.? Which are important and which irrelevant? Which are interrelated with the others and which are independent? Which are constant and which are affected by time, mood, recent experience, and all those other facets of his particular personality and the degree of his mental health or illness?

Yet, complex though the concept of intelligence may be, in most specific cases one is able with considerable confidence to make the generalization, and to say that a particular person is mentally retarded, or not. Moreover, one can usually quantify further, indicating that he is only a little retarded, moderately, or severely.

INCIDENCE

The incidence of mental deficiency depends upon its definition. It was stated earlier that 2 per cent of children have I.Q.'s below 70. In England, where the disorder implies a state of social dependency and where presumably many defectives who are self-supporting are not designated as retarded, the incidence is reported as less than ½ per cent (Tredgold and Soddy, 1956

The main concern here is with children who are sufficiently retarded to be educationally handicapped. This would include many in the I.Q. range 70 to 85, which constitutes 14 per cent of all children. What percentage of these require special help is not known, and the figures vary, depending on the area where the child lives and the facilities that are available. Certainly many of such children attend regular classes and function relatively well.

Retarded children make up the third largest diagnostic group referred to most psychiatric outpatient clinics. At Hawthorn Center, of 1,800 consecutive cases referred for diagnostic evaluation, 11 per cent fell in the retarded or borderline-retarded categories. Of these 8 per cent had primary mental retardation, and the other 3 per cent had secondary retardation. The mean I.Q. was 72, reflecting the fact that most retarded children referred to the psychiatrist are of the upper level. The majority of the referrals were from schools.

CLASSIFICATION

A variety of classifications have been employed to designate the degree of retardation. One of the earliest classifications used the terms *moron, imbecile* and *idiot*, defined by I.Q. (50 to 70, 25 to 50, and below 25, respectively). These terms are now little used in this country, largely because of the social opprobrium attached to them. Terms commonly used now are: *high-grade* and *low-grade defective; educable, trainable* and *untrainable;* and *borderline, moderate* and *severe.* These terms are not precisely definable—all are relative, and are used to approximate the child's level of functioning.

Perhaps the most meaningful classification is that of Penrose, which divides mental defectives into two major groups: high-grade and low-grade. Penrose shows that this natural dichotomy occurs, based on a number of criteria. The following table, adapted from Penrose, lists the major distinguishing features of the two groups. He cautions, however, that the dichotomy is not an absolute one, and that there is some overlapping.

TABLE 1

High-grade defective:
1. Relatively common—2 per cent of population
2. Rarely require institutionalization
3. Usually physically and physiologically normal
4. Usually fertile
5. Close relatives frequently high-grade defectives
6. Etiology:
    a. Hereditary factors: polygenic
    b. Environmental factors: cultural
Low-grade defective:
1. Relatively rare—0.25 per cent of population
2. Usually require institutionalization
3. Often have physical and physiological abnormalities
4. Usually sterile
5. Parents rarely defective; siblings occasionally low-grade defective, otherwise usually normal
6. Etiology:
    a. Hereditary factors: single recessive genes
    b. Environmental factors: organic central nervous system damage

The differences between the two major groups of retardation are not only quantitative, but also qualitative. In the low-grade, there is often gross physiologic or metabolic dysfunction. In this group are included the disorders with a known metabolic block such as phenylketonuria and galactosemia, chromosomal abnormalities such as mongolism, and children with severe tissue damage as in hydrocephalus and kernicterus.

Low-grade retardation is usually evident at birth or in early infancy (Kirman). Children with these disorders are properly the concern of the pediatrician and pediatric neurologist. Their care is mainly medical and custodial. Many of these children die early; most of those who survive remain institutionalized, and are not ordinarily referred to the child psychiatrist. These severe forms of mental deficiency will therefore not be considered in this book.

It is mainly with the upper-level or high-grade retarded that psychiatry is concerned. These children are, for the most part, physically normal, and their mental defect becomes gradually apparent during their early years. Special educational needs arise, together with a variety of emotional problems in their relationships with family and peers. Here, the child psychiatrist can help, both in planning for special education and in working out the emotional problems with the patient and his family.

ETIOLOGY

The various capacities which together make up intelligence are, for the most part, genetically determined. While all these functions are affected by experience, there are limits beyond which experience cannot alter them. No person who is tone-deaf can become a violinist, even if he practices the violin eight hours a day all of his life. Nor can a moron be made into a genius by any known learning process.

The cause of most cases of mental deficiency that are referred to the child psychiatrist, is, therefore, heredity. These children represent, for the most part, that portion of the normal population who are at the lower end of the continuum of intelligence. Their retardation represents the cumulative effect of a large number of genes, all of which are involved with the development and functioning of the brain, and which, in the particular combination present in that individual, has resulted in a brain which functions a little "slower" than most.

There may or may not be retardation in the child's family, although the probability that there is, is higher than in a child of average intelligence. These children, the majority of the high-grade retarded, are represented in most etiologic classifications as "idiopathic," meaning that there are no evident causes for the retardation. They are the group which Sarason refers to as the "garden-variety" defective. He states that these make up approximately 50 per cent of all defectives, with most of them in the upper intellectual level.

A significant number of trainable retarded children have symptoms indicative of brain damage, and in these, the retardation is considered secondary to the brain damage. Whether such an assumption is valid cannot often be determined; the intellectual capacities of brain-damaged children vary greatly, from extremely low to above average. Certain of the functions which are measured in intelligence tests are reduced in most cases of brain damage, especially conceptual thinking and attentiveness. Whatever the cause-effect relationships, the syndrome of brain damage with retardation is relatively common, and it presents problems in management not ordinarily encountered in "garden-variety" retardation.

A third important cause of retardation is cultural environment. Cases of this type are becoming less frequent in these days of compulsory education and consolidated school systems. Two decades ago, they were not uncommon in isolated communities such as small mining villages, or among Southern Negro communities where schools were not available. Rau tested the children in a primitive rural area in Devon, England, and found that over half were scored as mentally deficient. Rau concluded that the retardation was probably due to the high frequency of intermarriage. It is unlikely, however, that this is a major causative factor. While consanguinity is a frequent cause of low-grade deficiency, it is apparently not often responsible for the high-grade type (Penrose).

Mental retardation due to environmental experience is probably most often seen in this country today in association with other emotional disorders, especially character disorder. Such children have experienced chronic emotional neglect, have usually come from primitive and disorganized families, are unstimulated, socially ostracized, isolative, have never achieved in school, and are generally illiterate and uninformed. On psychological tests their scores are usually lower on the verbal than on the performance subtests, although their lack of motivation may depress all scores.

Retardation is also found in children with specific physical handicaps, especially sensory and perceptual defects. Deaf or partially deaf children, if undiagnosed for some years, may be significantly slowed in their intellectual development as a result of social isolation. Children with aphasias and other specific learning disabilities may lag in mental development.

The term *pseudo-retardation* has been used to designate those conditions in which intellectual functioning is retarded although intellectual potential is adequate. Chess defines pseudo-retardation as "a false impression of retardation in intellectual development." The term is not an entirely satisfactory one, as the retardation is quite real, and in some cases is as resistant to improvement as "true" retardation. At any rate, the designation *pseudo-retardation* should be accompanied by the diagnosis of the disorder which produced it; it is perhaps more accurate to employ the term *secondary mental retardation*, diagnosing the particular condition as, for example, "character disorder with secondary mental retardation."

SYMPTOMS AND PSYCHOPATHOLOGY

Retarded children, like those of average intelligence, vary widely in all areas of functioning and in total personality. Some show a general retardation of all development and learning. Others, especially the mildly retarded, show no gross evidence, and their deficiency is not suspected until they enter school.

How early the retardation is suspected often depends on the parents' perspicacity or willingness to accept the evidence that the child is not developing as he should. Often the mother notices that the child is slower than her other children. Sometimes visiting relatives or friends make the observation, although they do not always impart their suspicions to the mother.

Since Gesell's publications on child development, mothers have become aware of the so-called developmental norms, and measure their children's capacities against these norms. In some circles a reaction has occurred in response to warnings from various authorities that children vary greatly and that one should not be overconcerned if a child does not measure up to all of the norms at every age. Nevertheless, a reasonable and progressive rate of development is to be expected, and if the child is obviously lagging, then it is natural to be concerned and advisable to get professional evaluation.

At four to six weeks, most infants smile upon hearing their mother's voice, and show some attentiveness to her conversation. At two months they begin to vocalize spontaneously and to follow objects with their eyes. At three months the child should be quite interested in his environment, often clamors for attention and company, is able to control his head when held in an upright position, turns his head towards a sound, plays with bright-colored toys and other objects. If by this age the infant continues to be listless, lies supinely most of the time, is indifferent to people and sounds, one may suspect that he is retarded. But at this early age, it is difficult to be certain, and one can only wait for further development. Later the child may "catch up," or he may not. Continued retardation well into the second year becomes more conclusive. If, for example, by 16 months the child does not walk, cannot manipulate food into his mouth, does not explore and examine objects, is not able to indicate some of his wants; or if at 18 to 20 months he does not climb on things, does not scribble with a crayon or a pencil, then the evidence is growing that he is retarded.

Unevenness of development causes some difficulty in evaluation. In some retarded infants, motor development may proceed approximately at a normal rate, while speech and language are delayed; but this can also occur in a normal child. By the age of 3 or 4 years, if true retardation is present, it is clearly apparent. Language development is immature, abstract thinking is retarded, with impairment of comprehension, social awareness, and reasoning. The child is unable to keep up with his peers in learning the rules of games, remembering and understanding stories, etc. His playmates are aware that he is retarded, and may refer to him as "stupid" or "dumb."

Evidences of disturbed behavior may appear very early in the mentally retarded child. Early symptoms include hyperkinesis or motor restlessness, with excessive amounts of rhythmical motor play such as rocking and head banging. Irritability, listlessness, apathy and peculiar and unpleasant habits such as repetitive grimacing, nose-picking, and eating of inedible materials (pica) are more common in retarded than in normal children.

The majority of high-level retarded children, however, if their family environment is reasonably healthy, do not evidence emotional disturbances in their earlier years. The major emotional difficulties begin as the child grows older and gets out among other children. Here he often meets rebuff, derision, all the cruelties which any child experiences who cannot make the grade among his peers. While his level of comprehension may be inadequate, he is still able to perceive that he is, for some reason, not wanted. He may experience feelings of bafflement, sorrow, anger, and humiliation.

When he enters school, the problem is compounded. His incapacities are critically measured and publicly displayed. The educational system, geared to the average, either cannot accept him or must make special provisions for him. In either case, there are traumata, and the necessity for further adjustment.

The retarded child, like the normal child, develops defenses in response to his emotional conflicts. Reaction formations are common. To gain a degree of acceptance and status, the child becomes a clown, or he does reckless and foolish things. There are other reasons for such behavior: a masochistic orientation in reaction to low self-esteem or displaced aggression; self-blame for his disorder and for the trouble he causes his parents. Regression is frequent: The child retreats, seeks the comfort of his home and mother, wants to be cared for. Much of the ordinary conflict of growth and development which normal children successfully resolve is difficult for the retarded child. Sibling rivalries present extra difficulty, as the younger siblings overtake him, and as he fails to adjust to and comprehend the advantages and superiorities of older siblings. Siblings become understandably impatient with and resentful of the retarded child, and are often jealous of the extra attention he needs and receives.

Parental feelings and conflicts add further difficulties. Parents sometimes resent or are ashamed of the child. They try to deny his inferiorities, attempt to cover them up, and set impossible goals for him, hoping that the extra pressure and "training" will accelerate his growth. Or, what is perhaps worse, they neglect him, ignore him, fail to supply the extra care and attention he needs, fail to give him stimulation, to provide interest in his environment, to protect him. As a result, his level of retardation is often worsened and he becomes increasingly more apathetic and isolated.

Serious antisocial behavior and delinquency are frequent in the older children and adolescents. Studies of delinquency have shown that the incidence of mental retardation is considerably higher among delinquents than among the general population (see Chapter 13 on Delinquency). The delinquent retarded children actually constitute a heterogeneous group; many are "pseudo-retarded," with character disorder, schizophrenia, or language disability, and many come from primitive or deprived backgrounds.

On the other hand, a large number of retarded children make surprisingly good adjustments. The differences are striking between those who come from normal, healthy families and those who have been badly reared. A well-cared-for retarded child can be friendly, pleasant, happy, and responsive. Such children play contentedly with siblings and younger children, and find a degree of acceptance among their peers. These are not often seen by the child psychiatrist, or, if they are, it is mainly for advice in educational planning.

DIAGNOSIS

As in the other psychiatric disorders of children, the clinical interview is the most informative segment of the diagnostic evaluation. Here, one evaluates not only the child's general intellectual level, but also his social functioning, his motivation, and his emotional adjustment. To do this, the psychiatrist needs to know the average levels of functioning for each age. Additionally, he tries to judge whether the child is performing at his true capacity in the interview: Apprehension, constriction, apathy, and resentment may reduce the child's responsiveness and give a false impression of retardation.

While the general diagnosis can usually be made by the psychiatric interview, psychological tests and achievement tests are necessary for accurate assessment of specific capacities. These tests provide the basis for planning the child's program of treatment and education. The specific tests to be used are decided by the psychologist in consultation with the psychiatrist. The tests desired are mainly determined by the child's approximate mental age and by the particular preferences and training of the psychologist.

The most frequently used tests of intelligence for children are the Cattell Infant Intelligence Scale, the Merrill-Palmer Performance Tests, the Stanford-Binet, and the Wechsler Intelligence Scale for Children (Freeman).

The Cattell is designed for testing up to a mental age of 30 months (Cattell). It is largely a measure of neuromuscular development, and, while it can usually detect severe retardation, it is not considered highly reliable in the prediction of intelligence. Cronbach flatly states that it has no predictive value before the first birthday.

The Merrill-Palmer covers mental ages 1½ to 6 years and is considered highly reliable beyond the age of 3. Most psychologists feel, however, that it is less useful than the Stanford-Binet.

The Stanford-Binet (revised form) consists of groups of tests for each year from 2 to 14. It is a reliable test of general intelligence for most children. Its chief disadvantage is that in the older age groups it depends heavily on language function, so that poor language development results in a false indication of reduced general intelligence. For example, the six items for Year 10 are: 1. Vocabulary (defines 11 words). 2. Picture absurdities. 3. Reading and report (tells what he has read after reading a given story). 4. Finding reasons (tells why certain acts should be performed, and so on). 5. Word naming (names as many words as possible in one minute). 6. Repeating six digits.

The Wechsler Intelligence Scale for Children covers ages 5 to 16, approximately the same as the Stanford-Binet but it has the major advantage of testing separately the language and non-language functions. The WISC is divided into two main parts, the verbal and the performance sections. The performance subtests include such tasks as arranging colored blocks to copy a specific design, pointing out missing portions of a picture of familiar objects, and assembling pieces to form a familiar object. Such tests not only obviate language communication; they also have the advantage of maintaining the child's interest and attention much better than a question-and-answer session.

In addition to tests of general intelligence, school-age children who are considered bright enough for academic learning should have the appropriate diagnostic tests of academic capacities. These have been discussed in the chapter on learning disabilities (Chapter 9). They are essential for determining if the child is ready for reading, writing, arithmetic, and other subjects. In the younger children, predictions as to ultimate academic accomplishment should be made cautiously. Parents are understandably eager to know what to expect, but it is usually necessary to have a younger child return in six months to one year for repeated evaluations. The same is true to a lesser degree of older children, but with these, more accurate predictions are possible.

Diagnostic evaluation of the retarded child always includes interviews with the parents, and a careful history of the child's birth and early development. From these, one evaluates the child's environmental experience, the emotional tone in which he has lived, and, presumably, some notion of his rate of development. Additionally, one searches carefully for evidences of cerebral damage, both in the history and through neurological evaluation.

DIFFERENTIAL DIAGNOSIS

Primary mental retardation is to be differentiated from the several disorders associated with so-called pseudo-retardation, as has been discussed earlier. Probably the most difficult to distinguish is character disorder with secondary retardation. Often, there is no clear-cut distinction. A history of early severe neglect and emotional deprivation is helpful in the differentiation; however, many children with primary retardation may have suffered similar neglect. The intellectual defect in such character disorders is genuine, and may be severe. The disturbed behavior and distorted relationships of these children make treatment difficult, and special education alone is often unsuccessful.

Brain damage with secondary mental retardation is usually easily differentiated, as the other evidences of brain damage are present. These children, as do the character-disorder-with-secondary-retardation group, often have additional treatment needs, especially patterning and control, and many institutions for retarded children are reluctant to admit such children.

Many schizophrenic children function at retarded intellectual levels. Usually, however, their functioning is marked by unevenness and periodic fluctuations. As already noted, they often show changes in performance from one day to the next or even from one hour to the next. They demonstrate intratest variability on many subtests, often failing several easy tasks, then achieving a difficult one. Usually the differentiation presents little difficulty, and other evidences of schizophrenia aid in the diagnosis.

Specific learning and language disabilities must be differentiated from simple retardation. This is usually not difficult, since the child with these specific disabilities has average general intelligence. The error in differentiation is most likely to occur if one makes a diagnosis solely on the basis of the full-scale I.Q.

The deaf child may be mistakenly diagnosed as retarded. This is especially true in a child who has gone undetected for several years, has lagged markedly in language development, and has been generally neglected and unstimulated. The diagnosis need not be missed unless the examiner fails to think of deafness and to test for it.

TREATMENT

Treatment of the mentally retarded child is primarily a problem in education, and is thus the concern of the education profession. With the growth of special education and the development of programs and classes for "exceptional" children in public school systems, more and more of these children are receiving the care and training they need. Additionally, there is increasing understanding among educators of the emotional needs of retarded children. Writing on the education of mentally retarded children, G. O. Johnson states that there are three specific objectives in a public school program for the retarded:

1. Personal or emotional adjustment
2. Social adjustment
3. Economic adjustment

Johnson observes that: "The objective of personal or emotional growth and adjustment has been placed first because it is fundamental to the achievement of social and occupational competence. The entire program, in all of its various aspects, including placement in a special class, the curriculum, and the methods of instruction, is directed toward this end."

Many school systems have staff psychologists as well as special-education teachers, who are able to make their own diagnostic evaluations and placement recommendations. Such a system can care for the majority of educable retarded children, requiring psychiatric assistance only for those cases which present special difficulties in diagnosis or management.

The psychiatrist who sees a retarded child must determine both the educational and emotional needs. Until recently, there were usually only two choices in the matter of schooling: regular public school or an institutional training school. Today the psychiatrist must be informed as to which schools maintain special classes, and where there are special day schools for the retarded.

The psychiatrist must further decide whether psychiatric treatment or social casework is indicated. Whereas formerly, retarded children were not considered candidates for psychotherapy, it is now known that many can be benefited by individual or group psychotherapy. The more intelligent retarded children can relate meaningfully with a therapist, talk with him about their feelings and concerns, and express their anxieties, resentments, and conflicts. Many retarded children show a gratifying response to the individual therapeutic approach. Being understandably discouraged, frustrated, and depressed, they may, with the support and encouragement of the therapist, improve not only in emotional adjustment but also in intellectual and academic function. This is not to suggest that psychotherapy can "cure" mental deficiency. It can, however, help the child toward important gains in happiness, usefulness, and self-realization.

Working with the parent is an important part of the therapy. At the initial evaluation the parents should be informed as to the diagnosis, treatment needs, and prognosis. During this interview the parents should be allowed as much time as they need for asking questions and for working out the confusions and misconceptions which they may have about their child. Parents are understandably reluctant to accept the information that their child is retarded. Some go to several different doctors or clinics for evaluation, and may have obtained conflicting opinions and recommendations. Well-meaning but insufficiently informed diagnosticians, finding evidences of emotional conflict, may tell the parents that the apparent retardation is a "learning block," or that it is a "temporary lag." Sometimes, even when given correct information, parents are convinced that the diagnosis is in error. They often protest that the child cannot possibly be mentally retarded, then proceed to give examples of his performances indicating that he is a bright child. A mother may say, "But he remembers everything! He knows the names of all the streets in our neighborhood, and knows his way to the grocery store perfectly." One must point out to the mother that what she says may be true, but that the average child three years younger can do the same. One must explain that retardation does not mean a total absence of intellectual function, but a relative diminution.

The decision as to whether the child should remain at home or be placed away from home depends on a number of factors. If his behavior is seriously disturbed, with delinquency, aggressiveness, and sexual acting out, these are indications for institutionalization, just as they are in children of normal intelligence. Likewise, if the mental retardation is so severe that the child cannot be expected to function in a special class at school, placement is usually indicated soon after he reaches school age. Often the treatment needs are obvious, as in the case of an 18-year-old boy who made obscene telephone calls to women, and had the poor judgment to tell them his name and telephone number. He was quickly apprehended. The policeman who arrested him proffered the diagnostic opinion (correct) that the boy was "a moron with sex problems," and recommended (also correctly) that he be "locked up somewhere."

The parents' feelings and wishes regarding placement are of course an important factor. However, the decision should not be left entirely to them and their wishes. One must evaluate their feelings, then make a recommendation on the basis of the total picture, with the primary concern being the child's welfare. Following the initial evaluation and discussion with the parents, one usually suggests that they consider the matter for a time and return for a further discussion and later decision. The psychiatrist must recognize that the parents' feelings about the child are deep-seated, and have developed out of many months and years of living with and caring for the child. If they feel inordinately guilty for having produced such a child, or resentful, or so overattached and pitying that they cannot at the present conceive of having him live away from home, then one must endeavor to help them, like any other adult patient with emotional conflicts, and not expect that a few minutes of direct advice will be sufficient.

PROGNOSIS

The prognosis of mental retardation is, in most cases, continued retardation. Despite published case reports demonstrating significant improvements in I.Q. of patients in various treatment situations, and despite the evidences that cultural factors and early experience affect intelligence, the above statement holds.

The prognosis for improving intelligence is therefore poor. However, there are other important considerations. What is the child's outlook for learning to read, write, and do arithmetic? What are the probabilities that he will be self-supporting? that he will be reasonably happy? that he may marry and have a family? that he can become a useful citizen? For the upper-level and borderline defective child, the outlook is in many cases good. Kennedy (cited in Sarason), in a follow-up study of 256 children with I.Q.'s between 45 and 75, found, in comparing the retarded children with a group of normal children, that when seen at the time of follow-up (mean age 24 years) more of the retarded than of the normal persons were self-supporting (75 per cent vs. 68 per cent). The retarded were employed mainly in the laboring occupations (83 per cent vs. 56 per cent), but there was little difference in earning power between the two groups. On the average, the retarded held jobs longer than the normals. Kennedy concluded: "Our study reveals that morons are socially adequate in that they are economically independent and self supporting; and that they are not serious threateners of the safety of society, but are rather frequent breakers of conventional codes of behavior."

Each case is an individual. Prognosis varies with intelligence, emotional adjustment, background, degree of motivation, level of therapy, education available, and many other things. Whatever the outlook, one should usually be frank and realistic in discussing it with the parents. It is unfair and even cruel to create false hopes; moreover, it prevents their making realistic plans for the child. An intelligent treatment program requires that the parents know what is needed and why it is needed. They must then make their own adjustments to the situation. In a culture which overvalues intelligence and upward mobility, such an adjustment is not easy.

REFERENCES

Cattell, P. The Measurement of Intelligence of Infants and Young Children, New York, The Psychological Corporation, 1940.

Chess, S. An Introduction to Child Psychiatry, New York, Grune & Stratton, 1959.

Cronbach, L. J. Essentials of Psychological Testing, New York, Harper and Bros., 1960.

Freeman, F. S. Theory and Practice of Psychological Testing, New York, Henry Holt, 1956.

Johnson, G. O. The Education of Mentally Handicapped Children, in Education of Exceptional Children, eds. Cruickshank & Johnson, Englewood Cliffs, N.J., Prentice-Hall, 1958.

Kirman, B. Recognition of Mental Defect in Childhood, The Medical Press, 245: 10, 1961.

Kugelmass, N. The Management of Mental Deficiency in Children, New York, Grune & Stratton, 1954.

Masland, R. Sarason, S. B. and Gladwin, T. Mental Subnormality, New York, Basic Books, 1958.

Penrose, L. S. The Biology of Mental Defect, London, Sidwick & Jackson, 1954.

Rau, M. M. Mental Deficiency in Relation to Intermarriage, Child Development, 6: 213, 1935.

Sarason, S. B. Psychological Problems in Mental Deficiency, New York, Harper & Bros., 1953.

Tredgold, A. F. A Textbook of Mental Deficiency, Baltimore, Wm. Wood, 1947.

——— and Soddy, K. A Textbook of Mental Deficiency, Williams & Wilkins, Baltimore, 1956.

13

JUVENILE DELINQUENCY

Juvenile delinquency has been a major social problem in many cultures and many ages. References to "bad" children are frequent in the world's literature, both ancient and recent. One of the most celebrated of these, Mark Twain's Huckleberry Finn, would certainly qualify as a juvenile delinquent by current definitions. He never attended school, was responsible to no one, lived in an empty "hogshead" barrel in an alley, stole his food, and "could swear wonderfully." He was, according to his creator, the envy of every boy in the village. Fortunately for society, the other boys were not permitted to emulate their ideal; parents maintained some control over their children, and represented certain values and standards which their children incorporated.

Whether a delinquent like Huck Finn could exist in contemporary American culture is questionable. Such freedom would not be tolerated. Some well-meaning social worker, abetted by a child psychiatrist, would undoubtedly extract him from his hogshead, scrub him, "place" him in a home, and enroll him in a school.

DEFINITION

Most definitions of juvenile delinquency include any behavior by a person of juvenile-court age (usually under 17) which is in violation of a law or municipal ordinance. The distinction between delinquency and crime rests solely with the age of the offender. If he is beyond juvenile-court age, his illegal act becomes a crime. In some circles, including the psychiatric, the definition is usually extended to include all antisocial behavior serious enough to interfere with the rights of others, or to affect detrimentally the welfare of the community or the individual.

264

INCIDENCE

Accurate figures on the incidence of juvenile delinquency are impossible to compile. Definitions differ among the various states. Methods for obtaining the data vary, and are all, in one way or another, insufficient. Some communities are more lenient than others in apprehending and "booking" juvenile offenders. Populations are shifting at a considerable rate in many areas. Despite these difficulties in assessment, evidence is strong that juvenile delinquency is on the increase in this country. *Juvenile Court Statistics* compiled by the Children's Bureau in 1956 disclosed that the number of juvenile cases brought before the courts in the United States increased 70 per cent between 1948 and 1955. During this same period the child population (ages 10 to 17) increased only 16 per cent. It is estimated that, at the present rate of juvenile crime, about one boy out of every five will be involved in at least one act of delinquency serious enough to warrant the attention of the police.

The data are thus rather convincing that crime is increasingly becoming an activity of younger persons, and is consequently more and more the concern of those professional groups dealing with the young people.

Not only are juveniles becoming more active in crime, but they are committing it in different places: juvenile delinquency has moved to the suburbs. While large metropolitan areas continue to be the main scene of delinquency, its rate in less highly populated areas is increasing at an even more rapid pace.

There are important differences between boys and girls in the incidence, age of onset, etiology, and kinds of delinquent behavior (Ausubel). Many more boys than girls are delinquent; the ratio has been estimated at from four to seven times as many. However, the ratio was much higher at the beginning of this century, and appears to be steadily declining as more girls become involved. Age of onset is, on the average, younger in boys. This is partly because of the type of delinquent behavior—the most common delinquency in girls is sexual promiscuity, which does not occur until relatively late in adolescence. Another reason is that young adolescent girls are generally better supervised than boys. Aggressive and destructive types of behavior are more frequent in boys, and factors which stimulate such behavior play an important role in the development of male delinquency. On the other hand, overt sexual stimulation and emotional rejection play a more important role in female delinquency.

DELINQUENCY AND THE PSYCHIATRIST

Juvenile delinquency is the concern of many professional groups including law enforcement, criminology, education, clinical psychology, social work, sociology, cultural anthropology, and psychiatry. Each of these groups approaches the matter from a particular point of view, and there is sometimes little evidence that they are actually concerned with the same phenomenon. But no profession has a corner on the understanding and treatment of delinquency, and each can learn something from the others. Delinquency is a social problem; it is a problem in education, in epidemiology, and in law enforcement. It is certainly also a psychiatric problem.

Psychiatry now finds its services sought by many of the social agencies which deal with juvenile delinquents. Here the approach is usually at the individual level, since psychiatry, by tradition, treats the individual case. The psychiatrist is asked to evaluate the delinquent child and to make specific recommendations. Additionally, psychiatry has come to exert increasing influence in matters of policy in the operations of law-enforcement, educational, and social agencies, and the workers in these fields have become familiar with the psychiatric aspects of delinquency. Psychiatry thus has a major responsibility for carrying out careful research and providing improved theory in this area.

An important question is: What cases of delinquency are the proper concern of the psychiatrist? All children seen by the courts or apprehended by police cannot possibly be referred to the psychiatrist. On the other hand, many delinquent or predelinquent children seen by psychiatrists are never brought before the courts. What determines this? Is there a distinction between delinquency and emotional disturbance? In many cases the factors which determine whether a delinquent child receives psychiatric referral are not necessarily the most relevant factors. Availability of facilities, financial considerations, the orientation of the court toward psychiatry, and community pressures, are often more decisive than consideration of whether the child is likely to be benefited by psychiatric evaluation. Aside from these practical considerations, an intelligent appraisal of the delinquent child and of his needs must rest upon an understanding of the causes of delinquency. These will now be considered.

ETIOLOGY

Juvenile delinquency is not a specific syndrome nor a behavioral entity. Yet it is often so regarded in writings on delinquency; for example, the literature describes various classifications of the delinquent, such as maladaptive and adaptive delinquency, or considers in generalities the problem of the recidivist, the psychodynamics of delinquency, cultural determinants of delinquency, and similar matters. All such considerations are important and have some validity, but they lose much meaning without the condition that juvenile delinquents are psychiatrically a heterogeneous group. They have one thing in common: antisocial acting out. Yet it has been seen in the preceding chapters that certain children in every diagnostic category exhibit delinquent behavior. This is true of every kind of delinquent behavior—vandalism, fire-setting, stealing, truancy, murder, and the rest. All these have been committed by children of every diagnostic group—the brain-damaged child, the schizophrenic, the child with reading disability, and all the others.

But what about the proportions? Are most delinquents of the ordinary "social" variety, and only an occasional one emotionally disturbed? Accurate figures are not available, but it seems likely that the majority of delinquents are seriously disturbed. Bender has reported on a group of children who have committed murder and found that all of them have some psychiatric disorder, the most common being schizophrenia. Healy and Bronner reported that 91 per cent of juvenile delinquents suffered from major emotional disturbances. Sonntag observed that many juvenile delinquents are not overtly anxious or emotionally uncomfortable. He felt, however, that if one considers the social non-acceptability of their expressions of hostility and the fact that these expressions are extra-legal, one would be forced to classify them as sick children.

Some workers consider that the "social" delinquent is a more or less normal child who has been reared in a delinquent environment and is functioning compatibly with that environment. But the picture of a child who steals simply because he wants to, and without any notion of having committed an antisocial act, is a spurious one. Some children may experience no anxiety from such an act, but these children are in fact pathological. The fact that delinquency is not simply a "normal" response to a delinquent environment is pointed up in the question asked by Karpmann: "Why is it that, in the so-called delinquent environment, only certain children become delinquent while others seem largely unaffected?" Every child lives not in a single culture, but in a number of cultures and subcultures: his family, his neighborhood, his school, his church group, his city. Each of these cultures imposes varying standards of behavior and conformity. No child functions within a single culture in isolation from the others. It is possible to function in relatively good adjustment within each of the cultures. This is the usual normal state. If the demands of one culture induce serious conflict in another, distortions in interpersonal relationships inevitably arise, and the child must be considered to some degree emotionally disturbed.

Is it valid, then, to conclude that every child who commits an act of delinquency is emotionally disturbed? Definitely not. However, any child who is *chronically* delinquent is disturbed. What is more crucial to the present issue is whether every child who is seriously or chronically delinquent can be benefited by psychiatric help. The answer to this is an unqualified "No." Many delinquent children cannot be "reached," because they are psychotic, or because they have insufficient capacity to relate, or because their personality distortions are so fixed that they cannot be motivated to alter them. The decision as to whether or not a particular child is likely to be helped psychiatrically is often a difficult one, and can sometimes be answered only by a trial of psychiatric treatment.

Delinquent children are sometimes regarded as simply victims of circumstance, and this view is not without justification in certain cases. A 13-year-old Negro boy in a state mental hospital had killed another boy with a knife when that boy threw a rock at him. When asked why he had committed this crime, he said that it was "just bad luck." It was common in his neighborhood for children to carry knives, largely for self-protection, and knife fights were by no means rare. This boy had simply had the misfortune to thrust the knife into a fatal spot. He felt a normal degree of remorse over the incident, was by no means an empty or overly aggressive child, and while the diagnosis could not be considered as "normal," the degree of his mental disturbance was hardly sufficient to fit the crime of murder. The psychiatrist concluded that the boy had in fact accurately expressed his own diagnosis when he called it "bad luck."

The "causes" of juvenile delinquency are many and varied, with a complexity of interrelating forces in operation. Any classification of these forces is necessarily incomplete, and is largely determined by the point of view of the classifier. The following list indicates the variety of factors which have been implicated as causing delinquency.

A. Environmental
    1. Delinquent subculture:
       Poverty and unemployment
       Slums
       Neighborhood gangs
       Bad compaions
       Leisure time
    2. Family disorganization

     3. Social mobility:
        Restlessness
        Lack of community identification
  B. Psychological
     1. Mental deficiency
     2. Emotional conflict:
        Displaced feelings of resentment, aggression, inadequacy, rejection, jealousy
     3. Identification with delinquent ego ideal
     4. Impaired control of impulses:
        Sexual, aggressive
     5. Inordinate need for acceptance, recognition, love, status

Friedlander, whose approach is a dynamic one, indicates in her classification of delinquency that etiology is multi-causal. She asserts that the antecedent to delinquent behavior is, in the majority of cases, the presence of an "antisocial character," which develops out of various constitutional and environmental factors. The delinquent behavior may then be caused by the antisocial character formation alone, or by a lesser degree of antisocial character formation in combination with environmental or emotional stresses, or neurotic conflicts. In addition to these causes, Friedlander lists organic brain disturbances and the psychoses.

A combination of external and internal factors is invariably at work in any delinquent act. No child is delinquent only because he is, for example, schizophrenic. His disordered thinking and uncontrolled counteraggression are in part a reaction to external stimuli. Likewise, no child is delinquent only because of external factors—there is always some degree of personality distortion which reduces his internal control or which causes his hostility and counteraggression to become overwhelming.

Tables and classifications of delinquency are really of little aid in helping in the understanding of why a particular child is delinquent. The answers are to be found only in the child's individual history, and in his expression of his thoughts and feelings. This was what Healy meant when he spoke of "the individual delinquent." Seen individually, the psychopathology of a delinquent child is almost always easily apparent. We do not often need to speculate about it—the resentment, the loneliness, the sadism, the emptiness can be easily discerned.

Delinquency does not occur without a cause; nor does it arise suddenly and without premonition. A normal and well-reared child does not suddenly become delinquent. A girl does not, out of a clear sky, begin to be sexually promiscuous. A boy who has been happy and well-loved does not suddenly begin to steal, or go with a gang. All these developments have their antecedents, and they are neither subtle nor obscure. One needs only to look for them.

ADOLESCENCE AND DELINQUENCY

While delinquency is commonly associated with the adolescent years, premonitory symptoms are frequent before that age. Ausubel notes that the probability of delinquency in adolescence is much higher in the child who exhibits antisocial behavior before adolescence. It is estimated that two-thirds of delinquent adolescents actually begin their delinquent careers in preadolescence.

Serious delinquency in the preadolescent years does sometimes occur One boy, by the age of nine, had stolen and wrecked a truck, and stolen two cars and a horse. He was referred to the clinic by a desperate citizenry who sent with him a note labelling him "Public Enemy No. 1 of _____ County." Despite much psychotherapy, this boy went on to even greater heights of delinquent achievement: four years later his picture appeared in the newspaper, standing with his girl friend beside the remains of an airplane which he had stolen, flown 300 miles, and wrecked.

However, the above boy was unusual. Most children wait until adolescence to become genuine delinquents. There are two main factors which are considered to account for the upsurge in delinquent behavior with the coming of adolescence. These are:

1. The rejection of control by parents and other authorities.
2. The need for identification with a group.

The overthrow of parental authority is part of normal adolescence, as is also the need for other identifications, and most adolescents achieve this transition without becoming delinquent. Those in whom the need for counteraggression is great are able to express this when control by authorities is relaxed, or overthrown. In such children, the groups with which they identify are often delinquent ones. Many children with low self-esteem who have found little acceptance in healthy peer groups may find acceptance and gratification within delinquent groups.

Adults often feel that some degree of delinquent behavior is "natural" in the adolescent, and excuse him on the grounds that he is "sowing a few wild oats." Such an attitude among parents is most conducive to delinquent behavior, and unfortunately a high proportion of their children continue to sow their wild oats throughout life.

Josselyn; Redl and Wineman; and others who have written on the adolescent consider that in certain ways there is an increased rather than a lessened need for external controls. Nye, discussing the problem of discipline and control in the adolescent, observes:

We consider discipline to be related to delinquent behavior by affecting each of the elements of social control. 1. If it is extremely restrictive it may prevent the adolescent from meeting his recreational and associational needs in his peer group. 2. If it is absent or inadequate, he lacks a portion of direct control over his actions outside and inside the family. If parents make no demands or make no effort to enforce their commands, the child not only lacks external controls over his behavior; he also lacks a set of clear-cut parental expectations to which his parents obviously attach importance and which might be incorporated into his personality as internalized controls. 3. If it is unfair or if partiality is shown, it may be associated with an ambivalent or negative attitude toward the parent which reduces the indirect control that can be exercised by the parent.

These considerations, important during all stages in the child's development, are accentuated in adolescence, and parents are called upon to exercise acute judgment in the administration of their control.

Psychiatric treatment of the adolescent offers special problems arising out of the patient's need to reject authority. This will be considered in the chapter on psychotherapy (Chapter 16).

TREATMENT

The pioneering work of Aichhorn with juvenile offenders in Austria in the early part of this century demonstrated the efficacy of the psychotherapeutic approach to delinquency. Aichhorn's results, combining his own warmth, vigor, understanding, and long experience, with the application of psychoanalytic principles, furnished a guide and an inspiration to many workers, including psychiatrists in this country and abroad. The therapeutic approach to delinquency and crime has supplanted to a great degree the punitive debt-to-society philosophy.

Unfortunately, the therapeutic philosophy has a long way yet to go, and it is still too common to find sadistic and punitive attitudes among those dealing with delinquent children. Such attitudes not only fail in reducing crime, but actually effect its increase. Rabinovitch expressed the belief that:

One of the commonest causes of adult crime in America today [is] the punitive handling of children and adolescents at the time of their first delinquency. The delinquent act so often represents an expression of counteraggression by a child who feels he needs to strike back. The delinquent behavior may be the child's way of telling us that he needs help, that he is troubled and confused. If he is handled punitively at the time of his first delinquency, then his need for counteraggression will be reinforced and aggravated and we can expect further and more serious acting out.

The psychiatric treatment of delinquency consists of treatment of the underlying disorder. As in any psychiatric illness in children, the psychiatrist evaluates the child, makes the diagnosis, arrives at some understanding of the psychodynamics and the environmental situation, and recommends or carries out the specific therapeutic indications. Institutional placement is often indicated. Casework or psychiatric treatment of the family may be required. Outpatient psychotherapy, remedial education, all the various techniques in the therapeutic armamentarium, are utilized, as indicated and as available. External control is always indicated and should be instituted immediately. The psychiatrist may take a major role as the authority figure, and if the child is given psychotherapy, the psychiatrist's authority is an important aspect of the therapy. Other types of control may be utilized, including the extremes of the closed ward and pharmacologic control. Cooperative efforts with the school and law-enforcement personnel may require a major portion of the psychiatrist's efforts.

A reality which is sometimes disheartening reality, but which must be faced, is that, despite all the efforts and resources, therapy will often fail. It would be helpful if one could determine in advance those which would fail, but this is not always possible. The criterion considered most important in determining whether the delinquent child is treatable is the indication that he can relate meaningfully with the therapist. But even this criterion is by no means invariable, and a most depressing experience, and one which all who work with delinquent children inevitably experience, is to work long and hard with a child and to know that some feeling of mutual trust and respect has developed, then to be notified that the child has been arrested for stealing or carrying a concealed weapon, or some other crime perhaps worse than the one for which he was originally referred.

As in the psychiatric treatment of other problems in children, there are regrettably few controlled studies evaluating the results of treatment. Thus it is impossible to know how much effect the various therapeutic approaches are producing. A notable exception is the important study undertaken by Dr. Richard Cabot in 1937, now known as the Cambridge-Sommerville Youth Study, and published in 1951 as *An Experiment in the Prevention of Delinquency* (Powers and Witmer). This was not strictly a study of psychiatric treatment, but rather of individual casework. It endeavored to evaluate the results of a program involving treatment of the predelinquent or potentially delinquent child. Seven hundred such cases, all boys, were divided into two matched groups of 350 each. One group received casework counseling; the other did not. There were 19 counselors involved in the study, which continued for a period of seven years. Eight of the counselors were professional social workers, six were in social work training, two were group workers, two were psychologists, and one was a trained nurse. Therapy was of the relationship type, often largely unstructured and informal. It was thus of the type widely used in treatment of children both by psychiatrists and by other therapists; it could in no sense be considered intensive psychotherapy. Results of the Cambridge-Sommerville study indicate that by comparing the outcome of the treated and the control groups, 21 per cent of the treated cases were benefited by the treatment.

Most reviewers of the Cambridge-Sommerville study have considered the results disappointing, and point to them as an indication of the "failure" of the individual casework method in prevention of juvenile delinquency. This judgment seems unnecessarily harsh. Certainly any program which would deter from crime one out of every five potential criminals must be considered a major contribution. The delinquency problem must be approached from many points of view and must utilize many kinds of facilities; no single approach can be expected to contribute more than a small share to the results.

PREVENTION

Witmer and Tufts have analyzed the various delinquency prevention programs in the United States and have classified them into three types. The first are those which attempt major alterations in the child's social environment. The second are those which seek to identify the potentially delinquent child and to intervene before he gets into real trouble. The Cambridge-Sommerville project is of this type. The third type of preventive program involves work with the young offender, designed to reduce the possibilities of recidivism or to prevent his involvement in more serious crimes.

The most notable example of the first type of program is the Chicago Area Project, carried out by Shaw and his associates in the 1930's and reported by Shaw and McKay. This was a program designed to improve community living by encouraging residents in deteriorated neighborhoods to participate in community programs. A minimum of help from "outsiders" was employed, so that a spirit of neighborhood organization was created. The theory was that areas which lack social cohesiveness encourage delinquency, as the children have less sense of community identification and responsibility. The Chicago Area Project achieved a not-inconsiderable degree of success: Delinquency diminished in three of the four communities included in the project. Again, opinions differ as to whether the results should be considered encouraging or discouraging, but, as in the Cambridge-Sommerville Youth Study, some positive results were obtained, and indicate that this approach, too, can contribute to a reduction of the delinquency problem.

The third type of preventive program includes the work of all agencies involved with treatment and rehabilitation of the young offender—the courts, the casework agencies, psychiatrists, etc. There are few well-documented studies of the results of such work, and results undoubtedly vary widely among individual agencies and workers.

Witmer and Tufts conclude that, in general, there is little definitive knowledge on how to prevent delinquency. Progress is hampered by many factors: insufficient funds for adequate programs and a resulting lack of high-level trained personnel; inordinate enthusiasm for a particular approach, with lack of appreciation for the value of other approaches; and the orientation of the medical profession toward individual treatment with disinterest in preventive and social measures.

A general pessimism prevails among many professional workers dealing with juvenile delinquency. The opinion is often expressed that delinquency, like war, has always been with us and will continue to be. Others point to the deteriorating moral values of contemporary culture, with overemphasis on material gain and upward striving. The writing of the sociologist, Riesman, is often cited as evidence for the hopelessness of man's present situation, with the steady emergence of superficial values and the ascendancy of the "other-directed man." The nuclear bomb continues to receive a share of blame, and it is suggested that no society can expect to retain moral values when the threat of total destruction hangs continuously over it.

But the psychiatrist sees the children. They come to his office in an endless stream—unhappy, angry, defiant, afraid. They are not concerned about the atom bomb, and they rarely discuss slum-clearance projects. They talk about their friends and teachers and parents, with love and with hate. Not all of them are hopeless—they are still changing, still able to learn; and their anger and defiance can sometimes be dissolved.

REFERENCES

Aichhorn, A. Wayward Youth, New York, The Viking Press, 1935.
Ausubel, D. P. Theory and Problems of Adolescent Development, New York, Grune & Stratton, 1954.

Bender, L. Children and Adolescents Who Have Killed, Am. J. Psychiat., 116: 510, 1959.

Friedlander, K. The Psychoanalytical Approach to Juvenile Delinquency, London, Routledge & Kegan Paul Ltd., 1947.

Healy, W. The Individual Delinquent, Boston, Little, Brown & Co., 1915.

———— and Bronner, A. F. New Light on Delinquency and Its Treatment, New Haven, Yale University Press, 1939.

Josselyn, I. The Adolescent and His World, New York, Family Service Association of America, 1952.

Juvenile Court Statistics, Washington, D.C., Children's Bureau, Statistical Services, No. 37, 1956.

Karpman, B. Psychodynamics of Child Delinquency, in Child and Juvenile Delinquency, ed. B. Karpman, Washington, D.C., Psychodynamics Monograph Series, 1959, p. 151.

Nye, F. I. Family Relationships and Delinquent Behavior, New York, John Wiley & Sons, 1958.

Powers, E., and Witmer, H. An Experiment in the Prevention of Delinquency, New York, Columbia University Press, 1951.

Rabinovitch, R. D. Juvenile Delinquency: Considerations of the Etiology and Treatment, Pediatrics, 17: 945, 1956.

Redl, F., and Wineman, D. Controls from Within, Glencoe, Ill., The Free Press, 1952.

Riesman, D. The Lonely Crowd, New Haven, Yale University Press, 1950.

Shaw, C. R., and McKay, H. D. Juvenile Delinquency and Urban Areas, Chicago, University of Chicago Press, 1942.

Sonntag, L., Defenses in Delinquent Behavior, in Child and Juvenile Delinquency, ed., B. Karpman, Washington, D.C., Psychodynamics Monograph Series, p. 236.

Witmer, H., and Tufts, E. The Effectiveness of Delinquency Programs, Washington, D.C., Children's Bureau Publication No. 350, 1954.

14

PHYSICAL ILLNESS

The mind and the body are not separate entities, and dysfunction of one invariably affects the other. This chapter will consider their interaction through a discussion of children's emotional reactions to physical illness, and of the diseases commonly referred to as psychosomatic disorders.

EMOTIONAL REACTIONS TO PHYSICAL ILLNESS

When health gives way to illness, marked changes in feeling and awareness occur: pain, weakness, discomforts, vague changes in visceral sensation, alterations in daily routine. All these are strange, troubling, and often frightening, especially to a child, who is inexperienced, and who has not learned that these feelings pass. Transient physical illnesses are a normal part of life; their effects, however, are incorporated into one's personality and inevitably leave their mark. Usually the effects are not devastating. Most children "get over" the emotional effects of an illness, even a prolonged and serious one. Josselyn points out, however, that children with a serious or chronic illness have more emotional disturbance than do physically healthy children. Yet the majority of children with serious and chronic illnesses adjust remarkably well. Josselyn notes that she cannot offer a satisfactory explanation as to why the children who adjust healthily to their illnesses do so.

The psychiatrist is rarely consulted for physical illness in a child. Nor is this often indicated, provided that the pediatrician or other physician in charge understands and gives sufficient attention to the child's thoughts and emotions. Fortunately, the pediatric profession is, on the whole, highly cognizant of this area, and many pediatricians have familiarized themselves with the literature of child psychiatry.

The major emotional effects of serious or prolonged illness may be divided into two categories:

276

1. Those resulting from the interruption in the routine of living, especially separation from family

2. Those resulting from the child's thoughts and reactions to the illness itself.

The effects of institutionalization or separation from the mother were dealt with in the chapter on psychopathy (Chapter 11). The obvious hazards pointed out by the studies on very early separation should be avoided whenever possible, length of separation should be as brief as possible, and where prolonged separation is necessary, as in protracted surgical problems, paralytic poliomyelitis, and so on, a mother-substitute should be provided. Separation at a later age (after two years) while not having as profound effects, can nevertheless be terribly frightening and disturbing, and may adversely affect the child's reaction to illness. This is now recognized by many pediatricians, and in some hospitals, arrangements are made for the mother to remain with the child.

The emotional reactions and thoughts which the child may express as a result of medical illness are:

1. Anxiety
2. Fear of death
3. Guilt and wish for punishment
4. Anger and resentment
5. Regression and self-indulgence
6. Wish for and identification with normality
7. Lowered self-esteem
8. Feelings of helplessness

Dubo and others studied a group of hospitalized children with pulmonary tuberculosis. She found that despite a wide diversity of premorbid personalities, there was a remarkable similarity in the pattern of the emotional reaction to the illness. Outstanding was an intense anxiety, with much preoccupation with death. Dubo observes: "Their dreams, fantasies, and drawings are filled with morbid and threatening symbols. In interviews they talk frequently of death, expressing such fantasies as these: 'People with TB are half-dead and half-alive. When I grow up maybe I'll be dead. Sometimes when my feet are out of bed I think a ghost is pulling me and I'll be dead.' " Many of the children sought to deny fear of death. One 11-year-old girl said: "I don't believe in dying; I think they are going to think I'm dead and bury me alive. That's why I told my mother I only want to be buried one inch so I can get out." Dubo found much conflict between regressive wishes and wishes for normal growth. This made management difficult, as the children wanted to be babied and given much attention and at the same time they resented any unusual attention. Because of the necessity for isolation, and wearing of masks, many children had a feeling that the tuberculosis was somehow unclean and shameful. Many felt that they were somehow to blame for being ill, or that the illness was a punishment for vague wrongdoings.

Josselyn studied the emotional effects of rheumatic fever in a group of children in a convalescent home. There are important differences between the effects of tuberculosis and rheumatic fever. One is that the children with tuberculosis are virtually symptomless, so that the illness is much more of an abstraction, and the necessity for medical care is less apparent to the child. The rheumatic fever patient has, at least initially, severe illness with high fever and profound weakness. More important, there is the threat of a permanent handicap in rheumatic fever, which all the children become aware of in their contact with other cases. These children, too, are very aware of death. Josselyn found that the particular reaction pattern seemed strongly influenced by premorbid personality and the more severe emotional reactions occurred in those children who had been previously more unstable. Such children often exaggerate the effects of their illness, becoming overdependent and self-indulgent. Conflict over aggression became exaggerated in the rheumatic fever patients. This was possibly due to the imposed restriction on physical activity, so that normal expression of aggression was limited. Nevertheless, as noted earlier, Josselyn found that the majority of children made a remarkably good adjustment to this chronic and often debilitating illness.

Treatment of the emotional problems of medical illness is essentially the same as treatment of any emotional disorder in the child. It requires first of all that one spend some time with the child, talking with him, and establishing a relationship with him. This is usually quickly achieved with a sick child, as he is receptive of attention and accepting of the passive-dependent relationship. In fact, because of this, an intervening medical illness can be highly beneficial in the course of psychiatric treatment of a mentally disturbed child. This is especially true in older children and adolescents, who are resistant to relationship. When such a child develops any minor illness such as a common cold, so that he is bedridden, relatively helpless, and thus relieved of the necessity to appear mature and self-reliant, he can then more comfortably accept the overtures and the ministrations of his therapist. The therapist should exploit such an opportunity to the fullest, and the writer has on several occasions seen the treatment of a psychiatric in-patient markedly accelerated by some minor illness.

The child will usually talk readily about his illness, and in fact wants to do so. He should be led to express his fears and fantasies about the illness and should be questioned as to what he thinks caused him to be sick, why he got the disease while others in his family did not, and similar questions. He often blames himself for the illness, believing that he got sick because he went outside without his coat on, or because he didn't eat his meat when his mother told him to. His erroneous thoughts and fantasies should be dealt with directly, and reassurance should be given fully and frequently. His thoughts of death and of chronic debility should be explored and clarified.

Dubo found group therapy sessions helpful on the children's tuberculosis ward. The working out of thoughts and fears in the open group situation tended to relieve much of the obscurity which had surrounded these thoughts and fears; it also, because of the medical homogeneity of the group, improved the feeling of group identification.

The return of the chronically ill child to his home and community may be a critical time, as the adjustment to problems of imposed restriction can be trying. At such a time the physician or therapist must take care to maintain frequent contact with the child until the adjustment is proceeding satisfactorily.

Interviews with the parents of the chronically ill child can also be important to the child's emotional adjustment. Much unconscious resentment and hostility toward the child may exist. This may be a reaction in part to the financial burden of the illness, and in part due to feelings that the parent is responsible for the child's illness, either through imagined inadequate care or through the fact of having produced an unhealthy and inferior being. These problems must be explored and dealt with in a therapeutic manner, just like any other psychiatric problem. Obviously, the therapist's own feelings of resentment and reproach toward such parents cannot be a factor in his dealing with the problem, and casting insult and blame upon them can only be harmful both to the child and to the entire family.

PSYCHOSOMATIC DISORDERS

EMOTIONS AND ORGANS

The classic studies of William Beaumont on gastric functioning provide the first systematic demonstration of the influences of emotional state on the viscera. Wolf and Wolff confirmed and elaborated on Beaumont's studies, and showed that human gastric vascularity, motility, and secretions are increased during states of anger and anxiety, and are decreased during depression. There is now a vast body of evidence demonstrating that emotional state affects all the major organ systems. Among the more susceptible functions are blood pressure, heart rate, cardiac output, respiratory rate, intestinal motility, and tone of anal and urethral sphincters.

The brain exerts its influence over the viscera chiefly through the

autonomic nervous system and the endocrine system. A complex physiologic relationship exists between brain and other organs, with regulatory
feedback mechanisms involving the hypothalamus, the limbic system, and
the neocortex. The limbic system, termed by MacLean the "visceral brain"
appears to be closely involved in the subjective aspect of the emotions and
is strongly influenced by afferent impulses from the visceral organs.

To what extent the inner relationships and associations between emotional state and visceral function is learned and how much is innately determined is a problem that is but little understood. Certainly from the beginning of his life the infant's pleasures and discomforts are intimately
associated with the functions and dysfunctions of his digestive and urinary
systems. This fact profoundly influenced many of the major theories of
psychology, including psychoanalysis. It has also led to much formulation
regarding the etiology of certain of the psychosomatic disorders, but, as will
be discussed below, these theories are largely lacking in factual support.

THE CONCEPT OF PSYCHOSOMATIC DISORDER

Physicians have long been aware that the emotional state of a patient
may affect the onset, the symptoms, and the course of many medical illnesses. With the conquest of the major infectious diseases in civilized areas,
attention turned increasingly to the chronic and metabolic diseases. The
notion of multiple causation found wide favor, and with this came increased attention to the emotional aspects of illness. The term *psychosomatic* came to be applied to a fairly limited group of diseases in which
emotional factors were considered to play an important etiologic role.
These included peptic ulcer, ulcerative colitis, essential hypertension,
bronchial asthma, rheumatoid arthritis, anorexia nervosa, and hyperthy-
roidism. The concept of psychosomatic disease was generally accepted
quickly and with enthusiasm by all the medical specialties but particularly
by internal medicine. Co-operative efforts between medicine and psychiatry began to produce optimistic reports of successful treatment of many of
the chronic disorders. Nor was there a dearth of theorizing and research.

WHICH DISEASES?

As interest increased, investigators became aware that virtually any illness can be affected by personality factors and emotional state. Studies
appeared on the psychosomatic aspects of headache, dysmenorrhea, tuberculosis, diabetes, cancer, glaucoma, and warts. For a time it became fash-
ionable both within the profession and among the laity to designate as

"psychosomatic" virtually any symptom for which there was no obvious etiology. Some confusion arose over the distinction between psychosomatic disorders and conversion hysterias. Alexander (1943) helped resolve this dilemma by recommending that conversion symptoms be limited to those functions directly involving the motor or sensory cortex.

The term *psychosomatic* has now fallen into some disfavor. This is partly because of the multiplicity of meanings given to it, partly because etiologic relationships have not been adequately demonstrated, and partly because of disappointment in the results of therapeutic efforts. The future of the term is uncertain. However, most workers appear to feel that it will continue in use. Hopefully, as understanding of the cause-effect relationships between emotions and physical illness are clarified by further investigation, the word will come to be more specific and more meaningful.

THE PROBLEM OF ETIOLOGY

Any etiologic formulation for psychosomatic disease required that a demonstrable link should exist between brain and "target organ." This was readily at hand in the earlier studies on the autonomic and endocrine systems. But these studies had demonstrated only acute, transient effects. It was therefore hypothesized (Alexander, 1950) that chronic effects, sustained over considerable periods, would result in tissue changes. Such changes have been produced in experimental animals. French and others, using implanted electrodes, produced duodenal "ulcers" by electrical stimulation to the hypothalamus of monkeys over periods of from 30 to 86 days. Here the etiology appears clear-cut. Unfortunately, there is no way in which cause-effect relationships can be so clearly demonstrated in the patient.

Having tacitly accepted the fact that emotions were causative in psychosomatic illnesses, investigations began upon which emotions were involved and how they were produced. Two major schools developed. The first, headed by Dunbar, stressed constitutional factors and personality types. For example, the asthma type was a person who was emotionally insecure, narcissistic, with strong dependency needs and much drive toward external accomplishments; the peptic ulcer type was tense, socially striving, extravagant; the colitis type was orderly, obsessive, and greedy. The second or psychodynamic school, represented by Alexander and other psychoanalysts, investigated the emotional situation and the neurotic conflict. Here the nature of the conflict and the individual's way of handling the conflict were considered crucial in determining the involvement of a specific organ system. Certain of the analytic theorists considered the physiologic disturbances to be displaced unconscious symbolic expressions of repressed instinctual drives. Asthma, for example, was considered a displacement of the repressed cry of the infant for its mother.

Most psychiatric research in psychosomatic disorders has, unfortunately, been inadequately designed, with insufficient or no controls and with a too small or a biased sample. Many reports consisted of one or a very few cases with a particular disorder who were "studied" psychiatrically. Evidence was brought forth demonstrating an emotional or symbolic relationship between the involved organ system and psychological trauma in early life. Conclusions were then stated or inferred of some etiologic relationship between the early emotional trauma and the subsequent organ disease.

The problem of etiology is a vexing one. But the same can be said of virtually all medical diseases. Individual variability operates continuously, and one cannot determine why certain individuals get rheumatic fever, or poliomyelitis, or myelogenous leukemia, or ulcerative colitis or duodenal ulcer. Hereditary "predisposition" is certainly involved in all of these; exposure to specific infection is involved in some; a multiplicity of other unknown factors may also intervene.

Reiser and Bakst, discussing essential hypertension, have formulated a set of conclusions which might well be applied to the majority of the psychosomatic disorders:

While the literature is replete with observations which tend to implicate psychologic problems as contributors along with other factors in the genesis of the basic hypertensive mechanisms, such a role has not been finally demonstrated.

Regardless of the ultimate etiology, there can be little doubt that emotionally charged life situations may play a major role in affecting the time of onset and the clinical course of the disease process once it has been established in susceptible individuals.

Study of the life situations associated with precipitation of the disease, or its aggravation, demonstrate that these situations have specific emotional meaning for the individual patient by virtue of their relation to previous life experiences and unresolved conflicts and are conflictual for the patient because of these connections.

Most investigators now agree that there is no specific personality profile associated with the disease. In general, the data from various authors are in agreement with respect to the observation that the psychologic problems encountered with patients with hypertension frequently stem from early psychological trauma. This observation is in no way unique for patients with hypertension, but rather seems to characterize patients with all of the so-called classic psychosomatic diseases.

Altschule, discussing psychosomatic disorders of the gastrointestinal tract, suggests tentatively that emotional factors may play a primary etiologic role in hysterical dysphagia, irritable colon, spastic colon, and mucous colitis, but that in peptic ulcer and ulcerative colitis the etiologies remain unknown. He concludes, however, that emotions may have important influence on the course of any chronic gastrointestinal disease through effects on motility, spasm, and vascular flow.

SYMPTOMS AND EMOTIONS

The above comment regarding gastrointestinal disorders might well be extended to virtually all disease, and indeed Altschule observes: "There is ample evidence that emotion aggravates most disease." The literature is replete with instances of onset or exacerbation of symptoms following emotional stress. Chambers and Reiser found that in 75 per cent of patients admitted to the hospital with congestive heart failure, an emotionally stressful experience had immediately preceded the onset.

However, generalizations about the relationship between emotional state and severity or frequency of medical symptoms cannot be made. In neurotic patients, for example, symptoms of medical diseases are not invariably more severe or frequent, although the patient's reactions to his symptoms may be unusually intense. Moreover, while emotional stress may precede attacks of illness in some patients, in others there may be no such relationship. Additionally, cause-effect relationships are often obscure, so that it is difficult to know which came first, the symptom or the anxiety. Many patients have premonitory symptoms of an attack, vague feelings preceding the onset of the acute episode; these are not uncommon in asthma, ulcerative colitis, and migraine. The reactive anxiety may thus appear to precipitate the attack when in fact it results from it. Or the anxiety may intensify the attack. The interrelationships may thus become quite complex, and no one can determine with accuracy what actually occurs.

The other side of the coin is that many, in fact most, emotionally disturbed patients do not have "somatic" illness. Their symptoms are purely "psychological." Presumably, if they had any diseased organ they would, or might, overreact, and thus qualify for the label "psychosomatic." Can a psychiatrically normal individual have a psychosomatic disorder? Presumably not.

Viewed in the light above, the term *psychosomatic* must be limited to those situations in which there is both physical disease and some degree of emotional abnormality which is involved with that disease. There is thus no such thing as a purely psychosomatic disease. All or most medical diseases may, however, become involved in psychosomatic disorder.

CHILD PSYCHIATRY AND PSYCHOSOMATIC DISORDERS

The child psychiatrist sees a highly selected and unrepresentative sample of physical illnesses in children. Some are referred to him because the referring physician has been led to believe, correctly or otherwise, that the illness may be psychologically determined. Other cases are referred because they are unusually severe or intractible, and ordinary medical measures have failed. A third group are children with obvious emotional difficulties. The last is, in fact, the sole and specific indication for psychiatric intervention. The presence or absence of physical illness does nothing to alter this criterion. But the psychiatrist must help the referring physician in making this evaluation.

TREATMENT

Psychosomaticists deplore the "mind-body" dichotomy, and urge a monistic approach to the patient, meaning that the patient should be treated as a whole rather than a collection of disorders or dysfunctions (Editorial, *Psychosomatic Medicine*, 1957). Such an approach was perhaps feasible in the days when everything was treated by the general practitioner or the traveling medicine man. But today is the day of specialists, and the child psychiatrist can help the asthmatic child with his feelings of self-blame, even though he does not know the dosage or sometimes even the names of the modern drugs for relieving an acute asthmatic attack.

The dichotomy is a reality. It requires that the pediatrician and the psychiatrist work together, communicate with each other, and even understand each other to some extent. It does not mean that one can replace the other. Neither specialty must promise more than it is capable of delivering; likewise each must respect both the capabilities and limitations of the other.

The psychiatrist faced with a child with severe asthma cannot conclude a priori that the patient has severe emotional difficulties, nor that his family environment is seriously disordered.

Dubo and others in a careful and well-documented study, found no relationship between severity of asthma and degree of psychopathology in the child's family. They could find, however, as would be expected, a direct and clear-cut relationship between environment and emotional pathology in the child.

Thus each case must be approached individually, and the usual evidences of emotional disorder must be sought. If they are present, they are treated appropriately. Nor is psychosomatic disorder limited to the neurotic child; it may appear in any of the diagnostic categories, perhaps more in schizophrenia than in the others.

Psychiatric therapy in the psychosomatic disorders has not been marked by outstanding success. Indeed, failure to eliminate the symptoms has led to some disillusionment, and is regarded by some as evidence that psychologic factors are not pertinent to the disorder.

Special aspects of the treatment are as discussed above with regard to emotional reaction to medical disease. There may be morbid preoccupation, use of the illness for manipulation of family, regression, problems related to secondary gain, a kind of masochistic refusal to accept or cooperate in the necessary medical treatments, guilt over the inconvenience and expense caused the family. All these are to be dealt with as indicated.

Psychiatry is by necessity geared to the concept of improvement and amelioration of symptoms rather than cure, and this must frequently be the aim in psychosomatic disorders. As Lidz so succinctly put it, "Fortunately, effective therapeutic work with patients does not depend upon knowledge of how emotional conflicts are translated into physiologic malfunctioning, or upon resolution of problems concerning specificity."

REFERENCES

Alexander, F. Fundamental Concepts of Psychosomatic Research: Psychogenesis, Conversion, Specificity, Psychosomatic Medicine, 5: 205, 1943.
———— Psychosomatic Medicine, New York, W. W. Norton, 1950.
Altschule, M. D. Bodily Physiology in Mental and Emotional Disorders, New York, Grune & Stratton, 1953.
Beaumont, W. Experiments and Observations on the Gastric Juice and the Physiology of Digestion, Plattsburgh, N.Y., F. P. Allen, 1833.
Chambers, W., and Reiser, M. F. Emotional Stress in the Precipitation of Congestive Heart Failure, Psychosomatic Medicine, 15: 38, 1953.
Dubo, S. Psychiatric Study of Children with Pulmonary Tuberculosis, Amer. J. Orthopsychiatry, 20: 520, 1950.
———— McLean, J. A., Ching, A. Y. T., Wright, H. L., Kauffman, P. E., and Sheldon, J. M. A Study of Relationships between Family Situation, Bronchial Asthma, and Personal Adjustment in Children, J. Pediatrics, 59: 402, 1961.
Dunbar, F. Emotion and Bodily Changes, 3rd ed., New York, Columbia University Press, 1946.
Editorial: Monism and Psychosomatic Medicine, Psychosomatic Medicine, 19: 177, 1957.
French, J. D., Porter, R. W., Cavanaugh, E. B., and Longmire, R. L., Experimental Gastroduodenal Lesions Induced by Stimulation of the Brain, Psychosomatic Medicine, 19: 209, 1957.
Freud, A. The Role of Bodily Illness in the Mental Life of Children, Psychoanalytic Study of the Child, New York, Internat. Universities Press, 1952, Vol. 7, p. 69.

Josselyn, I., Emotional Implications of Rheumatic Heart Disease in Children, Am. J. Orthopsychiatry, 19: 87, 1949.

Lidz, T. General Concepts of Psychosomatic Medicine, Chap. 32 in American Handbook of Psychiatry, ed. S. Arieti, New York, Basic Books, 1959, Vol. 1.

MacLean, D. D. The Limbic System ("Visceral Brain") in Relation to Central Gray and Reticulum of the Brain Stem, Psychosomatic Medicine, 17: 355, 1955.

Reiser, M. F., and Bakst, H. Psychology of Cardiovascular Disorders, Chap. 33 in American Handbook of Psychiatry, ed. S. Arieti, New York, Basic Books, 1959, Vol. 1.

Wolf, S., and Wolff, H. G. Human Gastric Function, New York, Oxford University Press, 1943.

15

OTHER CLINICAL SYNDROMES

This chapter will consider a variety of children's disorders which have an emotional component. They are all fairly common, and have been the subjects of considerable attention and research. Because they have been accorded this attention, they have become, in a sense, regarded as distinct psychiatric entities or syndromes. This they are not. Rather, they are a part of the symptom complex of a variety of disorders. Most of them occur in every one of the major diagnostic categories, and may be present in association with virtually all of the other common symptoms.

The problems to be considered are:

Anorexia Nervosa
Enuresis
Fire-setting
School Refusal
Tic

ANOREXIA NERVOSA

CLASSIFICATION

Anorexia means loss of appetite. Anorexia nervosa is a disease entity characterized by refusal to eat and weight loss without demonstrable physical cause. This clinical syndrome was first described by Sir William Gull in 1868. While it is most common in females and associated with amenorrhea, Gull also noted the occurrence of the condition in males. It is often classified with the psychosomatic disorders, but differs from them by the absence of demonstrable anatomical changes. If one classifies it as a psychosomatic condition, as does Alexander, who calls it an organ neurosis, the gastrointestinal track is the target organ. Various symptoms referable to the gastrointestinal track, such as constipation and vomiting, may be seen, but no physiological changes occur. Alexander also describes the symptom as a manifestation of a neurotic disturbance of the total personality, and

287

this is a generally accepted view. Eissler differentiates symptomatic anorexia nervosa from anorexia nervosa as a disease entity. He distinguishes three degrees:

1. The anorexia is symptomatic and does not constitute a special therapeutic problem

2. The anorexia causes serious concern and reaches a dangerous degree

3. The disease entity anorexia nervosa as described by Gull.

The second and third of these categories could probably be combined. Eissler does not feel that the disorder represents an organ neurosis, nor that it can be adequately classified as a neurosis or psychosis. He calls it an "inhibitory state" in regard to the intake of food.

INCIDENCE

The disorder is not common, but exact incidence figures are not available. The two largest series in the literature, limited to children and adolescents, are those of Lesser and others, and Blitzer and others, each numbering 15. At Hawthorn Center approximately 3 per cent of a total of 700 inpatients hospitalized during the period from 1956 to 1965 had anorexia nervosa. Waller and others indicate that the syndrome usually occurs in girls between the ages of 12 and 21 but it may also occur later. Infrequently it is reported in young men. Falstein and others presented a study of four prepubertal boys whose pathological attitudes toward food resulted in clinical states revealing the classical picture of anorexia nervosa.

ETIOLOGY AND PSYCHOPATHOLOGY

Anorexia nervosa is one of the most graphic examples of a psychogenically induced neurotic symptom. In the families there is usually a history of undue emphasis on food and dieting. Conflicts are present between the child and the parents, as well as conflicts between the parents. Almost invariably patients with this disorder have displaced sexual impulses onto the act of eating, and have unconscious fantasies of oral impregnation and gastric pregnancy. Alexander feels that oral aggressive and receptive tendencies become erotized and connected with sexual fantasies. Thus the hunger drive is associated with sexual impulses. In describing anorexia nervosa as an organ neurosis, he implies inhibition of the gastrointestinal track through the autonomic nervous system by emotional influences, rather than the symbolic expression of psychological content as would occur in the voluntary and sensory-perceptive system in an hysterical conversion reaction.

Some authors stress that there is not true anorexia, but that the loss of appetite is a reaction of disgust toward food rather than an actual loss of appetite. Many patients with this condition are ravenously hungry but do not permit themselves to eat. Not infrequently the illness begins with the patient's fear that she is getting "too fat" (which may or may not be a realistic fear) and is followed by self-induced dieting which continues beyond propitious levels. The precipitating event may be the trying on of a too-tight dress or an innocent comment from a schoolmate. Most often a disturbed parent-child relationship has been present, and after the onset of the illness eating becomes the focus of conflict between mother and daughter. While some conflict between the parents and child is uniformly present, Dubo (personal communication) feels that underlying this is a more basic conflict between the two parents. The dinner table becomes the battleground for the family's neurotic interaction and thus the symptom becomes aggravated and more permanently fixed. Girls with this syndrome become extremely adept at clandestinely disposing of parts or all of their servings (sometimes after mastication) into their napkins and subsequently into the toilet. If these methods are thwarted the girls sometimes learn to regurgitate their food.

These patients appear to have an excess of energy; they frequently run instead of walking, they may stand in school instead of sitting, and are often found exercising vigorously in their rooms to avoid gaining weight. Cole and others presented the case of a 13-year-old girl who demonstrated a typical history, quite similar to that of many other girls with anorexia nervosa. She began dieting to lose weight, to reduce her waistline, after having been teased about her weight at camp. A precipitating event was her father's death. She began to withdraw, became irritable, and school performance dropped markedly. She became amenorrheic, showed increased sensitivity to cold, decreased perspiration, and constipation. On the psychiatric unit she poured food down the toilet and lied about the amount she consumed. She exhibited great energy and physical activity, including exercise when alone. She was greatly concerned about the food intake of other patients and showed much interest in feeding them. Interestingly enough, many of these patients spend most of their waking hours (and dreams) thinking and talking about food. The subject matter of their art work is food and they profess wanting to become dietitians and nurses.

Waller and others summarized the psychological circumstances surrounding the condition as:

1. Open conflict between the family and the patient, particularly the mother-daughter relationship

2. Often a preceding history of obesity and overeating, with dieting until cachectic

3. Peculiarities in the sphere of sex

4. Life adjustments of major psychological significance

5. Parental pressures

6. Family history of neurosis or psychosis, especially with an over-emphasis on eating

7. Importance of the secondary gain of the neurosis with frequent conscious attempts to divert the family notice from a supposedly more popular sibling.

Obsessive-compulsive features are frequently seen in patients with this illness. They are often fastidious, and have unusually high academic expectations for themselves. They are depressed and limited in their ability to display affects spontaneously. They are usually anxious and guilt-ridden. The degree of regression is marked.

The presence of underlying depression in anorexia nervosa cannot be overemphasized, and the symptom choice dramatically underlines the severity of the depression. A strong unconscious suicidal intent is present, and if the process goes unchecked, the patient will slowly starve herself to death.

DIAGNOSIS

Diagnosis is made on the basis of severe weight loss, refusal to eat, and amenorrhea or irregularity of menses in girls. Severe emaciation is the most striking feature, but physical vigor and strength are amazingly well maintained. Constipation may be present, and in severe cases secondary changes including dryness of the skin, intolerance to cold, and loss of hair may be seen. If the condition is prolonged without treatment other secondary changes due to malnutrition will be encountered.

DIFFERENTIAL DIAGNOSIS

The disease must be differentiated from several other conditions in which weight loss may be a prominent feature. This may be seen in schizophrenia and in primary depressions. The differentiation from schizophrenia may be difficult and in some severe cases of anorexia nervosa the denial of weight loss may reach psychotic proportions. If severe obsessive-compulsive features are present, the differential diagnosis may also be difficult, but the presence of a thought disorder should be demonstrated if the diagnosis of schizophrenia is made. Purposeful self-starvation to get out of an untenable home situation, and malnutrition due to environmental factors also are to be differentiated from anorexia nervosa. In both of these conditions the patient will begin to eat normally when removed from the home situation.

In the differential diagnosis, Simmonds' disease (panhypopituitarism) must be excluded. Usually this can be done easily because of the absence of other symptoms of endocrine dysfunction in anorexia nervosa. In questionable cases a determination of urinary 17-ketosteroids should be done; they will be reduced in Simmonds' disease while normal in anorexia nervosa.

PROGNOSIS

Kay and Leigh reviewed the natural history, treatment, and prognosis of 38 patients. Their group included patients in whom the onset was during adulthood. The group was not homogeneous and included, by the authors' own admission, patients with primary depressions which began during middle age. In this series, definitive symptoms persisted in half, and residual neurotic symptoms were the rule. Fifteen per cent of the patients died from the illness or its complications. In Lesser's group the prognosis was considerably better than in previously reported studies. The average follow-up period was five years after admission. The patients ranged in age from 10 to 16. Lesser and co-workers felt that the outcome depends on the nature of the conflict and the type of personality. Predominantly "hysterical" personality traits augur a better prognosis than predominantly schizoid or compulsive traits. In Blitzer's series the outcome of the illness was also related to personality structure. All of the patients with hysterical personalities recovered from anorexia. Sixty per cent became able to eat normally. One patient died. The others retained various eating disabilities. The most favorable situation was one in which the parents could allow hospitalization and enter a psychiatric relationship themselves while the child was receiving therapy.

TREATMENT

Anorexia nervosa is one of the few conditions encountered in child psychiatry which can lead to death. It must be considered a psychiatric emergency and calls for immediate hospitalization. Less energetic methods of treatment have usually been attempted before the psychiatrist is consulted and the weight loss has become severe. Hospitalization preferably should be in a residential treatment unit for children or, if not available, on a pediatric ward with close psychiatric liaison. Psychotherapeutic intervention alone before the weight loss is corrected is not successful, and can have dire consequences. First the weight loss must be treated; if necessary, by coercion. Supportive psychotherapy accompanies this treatment, but the dietary treatment takes precedence until the patient's weight reaches a safe level. It is explained to the patient that it is vitally necessary for her to gain weight, and that there can be no deviation from the program. In the hospital, average-sized portions are served to the patient and she is expected to eat them even if this requires her remaining at the table long after the other children have finished. A nurse, preferably the same one as often as possible, or, if necessary, the physician sits with the patient until her meal is completed. Many a patient at first creates a painfully drawn-out procedure out of meal time, lifting each tiny spoonful ever so slowly to her mouth. Chewing also appears to be in slow motion. All this may be accompanied by tears, whining and pleading, or hysterics. This is to be listened to sympathetically but the therapist must not permit himself to be manipulated into making bargains, or into deviating from the program. He must likewise be cognizant of the patient's many wiles and tricks through which she will attempt to avoid eating. This may necessitate the nurse's accompanying the patient at all times, including visits to the bathroom, to forestall regurgitation after meals. In some instances tube-feeding becomes necessary when refusal to eat persists. The life-saving necessity of this measure far outweighs any possible psychic trauma that this act may symbolically convey. Sometimes the threat of tube-feeding may itself induce eating. High-caloric dietary supplements such as ice cream or malted milks are often used in addition between meals or at bedtime. As weight gain occurs, supervision of the patient is gradually diminished.

If all other measures fail, if repeated regurgitation of food becomes fixed, and if weight loss continues unabated, suicidal outcome may be imminent. In such cases, as a life-saving measure, the use of electroconvulsive treatment may be indicated. This is one of the rare indications for ECT in child psychiatry. Schizophrenia should be highly suspected in patients in whom the illness becomes so grave even with treatment.

Psychotherapy and milieu therapy are necessary accompaniments of the treatment. A positive relationship needs to be established with the patient and, while she usually verbalizes resentment about the forced feeding, a close, strong relationship to the therapist is usually developed quite early. Art therapy is ideally adapted for use in the anorexic patient and through it dynamic conflicts are readily revealed. Interpretations should not be made early in the treatment and, even later on, should be made only with utmost care. An interpretation of oral impregnation fantasies should not be done during the acute phase of the illness, and interpretation of, for example, incestuous wishes toward the father should probably never be done with a child or adolescent. Instead, it is important to deal with conscious aspects of the patient's relationships with others.

The parents need to be worked with also before the anorexic child can return home. The type of involvement will depend upon the degree of their own disturbance.

A.R.L.

REFERENCES

Alexander, F. Psychosomatic Medicine, New York, W. W. Norton & Co., 1950, pp. 88–94.

Blitzer, J. R., Rollins, N., and Blackwell, A. Children Who Starve Themselves: Anorexia Nervosa, Psychosom. Med., 23: 369–383, 1961.

Cole, M., Straight, B., Robinson, M., and Lourie, R. S. Anorexia Nervosa, Clin. Proc. Children's Hosp. (Wash.), 14: 49–63, 1958.

Eissler, K. R. Some Psychiatric Aspects of Anorexia Nervosa, Demonstrated by a Case Report, Psychoanalyt. Rev., 30: 121–145, 1943.

Falstein, E. I., Feinstein, S. C., and Judas, I. Anorexia Nervosa in the Male Child, Am. J. Orthopsychiat., 26: 751–772, 1956.

Gull, W. W. Anorexia Nervosa, Clin. Soc. Trans., 7: 22, 1874.

Kay, D. W. K., and Leigh, D. The Natural History, Treatment and Prognosis of Anorexia Nervosa Based on A Study of 38 Patients, J. Ment. Sci., 100: 411–431, 1954.

Lesser, L. I., Ashenden, B. J., Debuskey, M., and Eisenberg, L. Anorexia Nervosa in Children, Amer. J. Orthopsychiat., 30: 572–580, 1960.

Waller, J. V., Kaufman, M. R., and Deutsch, F. Anorexia Nervosa: A Psychosomatic Entity, Psychosom. Med., 2: 3–16, 1940.

ENURESIS

Our ignorance about enuresis is possibly the most striking aspect of this puzzling symptom. Most children with enuresis are not seen by a psychiatrist; nor are most enuretic children who get to the psychiatrist brought primarily for that reason. Investigation into its etiology has been inconclusive and contradictory and most efforts at direct treatment have been unsuccessful. There is no general agreement as to whether it is a symptom of emotional disturbance; indeed, there is not even universal agreement that it is abnormal. The child psychiatrist usually operates under the impression that it is abnormal, because most of the enuretic children whom he sees are clearly disturbed. Unavoidably, his sample is a biased one.

INCIDENCE

Enuresis is one of the most common problems of childhood. Data on its incidence vary somewhat, since they depend frequently on the specific definition of the term. Table 1, adapted from Macfarlane and others, shows the incidence of diurnal and nocturnal enuresis at various ages in a sample of 252 apparently normal children.

TABLE 1

INCIDENCE OF ENURESIS IN NORMAL CHILDREN

Age	Diurnal (Percentage)	Nocturnal (Percentage)
21 mos.	52	74
3 yrs.	4	24
5 yrs.	2	10
14 yrs.	0	6

From Macfarlane et al. *A Developmental Study of the Behavior Problems of Normal Children between Twenty-one Months and Fourteen Years*, University of California Press.

Table 1 includes both boys and girls. There are significant sex differences, with considerably more boys than girls having diurunal enuresis at 21 months, and more girls than boys having nocturnal enuresis at 3 years. The final 6 per cent reported were all boys. In a study of 1,000 unselected children, ages 4 to 12 years, referred to a pediatric outpatient department, Bakwin and Bakwin found that 26 per cent had some enuresis, either diurnal or nocturnal. In a comprehensive survey of the literature, Michaels and Goodman concluded that approximately one child out of four had nocturnal enuresis after the age of 7. The studies of incidence, reported by Tapia and others, are perhaps the most significant of all. They evaluated the emotional adjustment of over 800 third-grade white children, through interviews with the teachers and from questionnaires administered to the children's parents. From information thus obtained, they assigned each child to one of four adjustment categories:

1. Well adjusted
2. No significant problems
3. Marginally disturbed
4. Clinically disturbed

Table 2, from Tapia and others, shows the incidence of enuresis in each of the four adjustment categories.

TABLE 2

| | Adjustment category | | | | |
	1	2	3	4	Total
Total subjects	167	425	164	68	824
Enuretic subjects	18	36	22	7	83
Percentage enuretic	10.8	8.5	13.4	10.3	10.1

Studies of emotionally disturbed children indicate about the same frequency of enuresis as occurs in normal subjects. For example, in 200 unselected cases seen in the outpatient clinic at Hawthorn Center, ranging in age from 5 to 16 years, 29 (or approximately 15 per cent) had some degree of enuresis. Over half of these were age 8 or less.

The incidence of enuresis, then, would seem to have no visible relation to emotional disturbance, a varying relation to sex, and an inverse relation to age.

ETIOLOGY AND PSYCHOPATHOLOGY

Opinions vary widely as to the cause or causes of enuresis: On the one hand, it has been considered psychogenic in origin; on the other, it has been thought to derive mainly from organic causes.

Gerard, reviewing literature on etiology, lists the following among the suggested organic causes: spina bifida, mental retardation, defective motor control of the bladder, defective bladder sensation, hypervagotonia, inadequate conditioned reflex development, thickened bladder musculature, and fatigue. Among the psychological causes, she mentions: poor training, regressive reaction to loss of parental love, unconscious expression of antagonism against parental domination, conduct disorder arising from the child's lack of responsibility, and various sexual aberrations, including direct erotic gratification in a character that is urethral, and expression of the passive sexual role in homosexually oriented males.

Gerard's well-known psychoanalytical study of enuresis, in which she investigated clinically and psychiatrically 72 children referred primarily for enuresis, concludes that in the majority of her cases the enuresis was one symptom of a syndrome which presented a clear-cut neurotic pattern of behavior. These cases, which Gerard calls "the common, garden variety of neurotic enuresis," all had nocturnal anxiety, many with nightmares and recurrent dreams, and both sexes admitted feelings of pleasantness during the act of urination. She found the boys to be passive, retiring, and self-deprecatory, while the girls were more physically active, aggressive, and competitive with males. In the boys, urination was considered as a passive act, without feelings of responsibility, and as a substitute for masturbation. Many of the girls had unconscious fears of seduction and regarded the sex act as an attack—their fathers being affectionate and sometimes seductive toward them, and usually favoring the patients over their siblings. Gerard assumes that the girls were unconsciously denying their feminine role.

Gerard's study, while an interesting report of the psychological meanings of enuresis in certain children, fails, however, to describe the sample from which the case material is drawn. Since her cases were described merely as having been "referred to the psychiatric service for wetting," it may be concluded that the sample was not truly representative (considering the reports of incidence among the general child population, most cases of "pure" enuresis never reach the psychiatrist). Moreover, no evidence is actually presented to substantiate the presence of neurosis in the subjects: Since the nocturnal fears, shared by all these children, is too little basis for a diagnosis of neurosis, the conclusion that enuresis is one symptom of a neurotic syndrome must presumably be accepted on faith.

Many psychiatrists and pediatricians express the feeling that most of the enuretics they see do not fit Gerard's classic description. Other studies suggest, moreover, that enuresis has no relationship with emotional state, and that it occurs as much in normal as in disturbed children.

In addition to their findings on incidence, which support this view, Tapia and others also determined the presence of a variety of symptoms commonly associated with emotional disturbance, such as tension, fearfulness, eating and sleep disturbances. They found that none of these symptoms occurred significantly more frequently in enuretic than in non-enuretic children. The authors conclude: "There seems to be enough lack of corroboration to justify questioning the traditional contention that enuresis is an emotional symptom. The fact is that several studies, including the present, actually contradict such a contention. It appears that enuresis is but an ubiquitous happenstance, the frequency of its appearance being more related to age cut-off point and to other statistical mechanics than to adjustment, other emotional symptoms, or future prospects of mental ill health."

While the cause or causes of enuresis are thus little known, the writer cannot concur entirely that it is merely "an ubiquitous happenstance." There is too much clinical evidence, at least in some cases, indicating that the disorder is not necessarily inevitable. Often the symptom does appear or disappear in response to environmental or emotional changes. For example, a 14-year-old girl, whose early toilet training had been uneventful, suddenly developed nocturnal enuresis when forbidden by her father to go on dates with a boy in whom she had become interested. The enuresis occurred every night she slept at home, but did not occur on the occasional nights when she stayed at the home of a favorite aunt. Following four sessions of psychotherapy, the symptom disappeared altogether. The "meaning" of the symptom in this case was never determined. That it was related to the girl's feelings of aggression and resentment toward her father is suggested by the fact that the psychotherapeutic interviews were concerned mainly with these feelings.

In most cases of enuresis, effects of environmental change are not so clear-cut as in the above example; nor are results of treatment often so successful. The fact is, it is not known why some children fail to achieve bladder training at the usual age. It is untenable to consider that enuresis extending beyond the fourth or fifth year is "normal"; neither can the conclusion be drawn that—simply because a child has this symptom—he is emotionally disturbed.

In the psychiatric evaluation of a child with enuresis, the cause-effect relationships are often obscure. That is, when there are associated with the enuresis other symptoms such as anxiety or dependence, it is usually impossible to determine what is cause and what is effect. Often, the enuresis becomes the focus of anxiety or of contention between child and parent or child and sibling. The enuresis thus comes to have heightened and pathological meanings to the child.

TREATMENT

In the face of present ignorance regarding this symptom, it is important to realize that any treatment program is empirical and can be judged only on pragmatic grounds. In other words, try it cautiously—and see if it works.

Most important is to undo the harm that almost certainly has been done before the child was ever referred to the psychiatrist. Kanner has indicated some of the kinds of emotional reactions resulting from mishandling of bedwetting. The child is often stigmatized, sadistically punished, exposed to extreme forms of humiliation and derision. Techniques of correction and "treatment" have involved almost unbelievable degrees of indignity and cruelty. It is quite common for a parent to press the boy's face or nose into his urine-soaked sheets. As a punitive measure, some children are made to wash out their bedclothes each morning. In many institutions, enuretic children are segregated from the others, sleeping in a separate area, and being designated by some colloquial title, such as "the untidies." Sometimes they are stigmatized by being required to wear some identification mark such as a strip of colored cloth conspicuously attached to their clothing, presumably for the purpose of aiding the institutional employees in their administration of special "treatment." Even well-intentioned parents may impart to the child the notion that his enuresis results from "weak kidneys," or a "weak bladder." In countless ways, the child is made to feel inferior, inadequate, and rejected by parents and peers. It is no wonder that one finds in the psychiatric examinations of enuretic children that much of their anxiety and other affects are associated with the enuresis.

Obviously, no treatment at all is to be preferred to vigorous mismanagement—and any error should probably be on the side of omission.

The first consideration in psychiatric treatment of the enuretic child is whether or not there is sufficient psychopathology to require treatment. If one decides that the child is reasonably normal, then some reassurance to the parents, coupled with advice regarding management, may be all that is indicated. If emotional disturbance exists, or if the family is overreacting to the enuresis, further psychiatric help is required.

The wide variety of direct-management techniques and treatments which appear in the literature or which are tried by pediatricians attests to the fact that no technique is very successful. Most treatments have not been evaluated in controlled studies, and most are probably worthless. Many physicians, finding that some of their cases improve after a particular treatment, are convinced that the method is a good one. Whether the child would have stopped wetting at that time spontaneously is, of course, not known. One technique which many pediatricians favor is to have a child drink fairly large quantities of fluids during the first half of the day, for the purpose of increasing his bladder capacity, then to restrict fluid intake in the afternoon and evening. An embellishment is for the parents to awaken the child and "drain" him at the time they themselves go to bed. This system may not cure the enuresis, but it almost certainly will reduce the volume of urine which is voided into the bed. Another favorite therapy involves "conditioning" by use of an alarm apparatus, which sounds a bell or buzzer when the sheet becomes moist. This is a bit like shutting the gate after the horse is stolen, but it has worked in selected cases and may deserve a trial. Drugs are often tried and success has been reported, especially with anti-cholinergic agents, such as belladonna, which is preferred by Bakwin and Bakwin. The temptation to use drugs is sometimes strong, but in most cases they are probably of little value. Further discussion of the use of drugs in enuresis will be found in the chapter on psychopharmacologic treatment (Chapter 19).

If the enuretic child is sufficiently disturbed to need psychiatric treatment, the enuresis should not be the focus of therapy. The subject should not be avoided; neither should it be overemphasized. Whatever questions, feelings, and conflicts the child has about his enuresis should be allowed free expression and exploration. In this way the secondary emotional effects can usually be alleviated. The symptom itself may or may not concomitantly improve.

Coupled with the child's therapy, there should, of course, be some time devoted to the parents' feelings and concerns about the problem. Some of their distortions of thinking about the enuresis may thus be alleviated, and their needs for expression of resentment toward the child may be reduced. The enuresis will probably continue at least for a time, but the family's capacity to live with it will usually be increased. This must be the chief goal of therapy.

PROGNOSIS

In general, the prognosis is good, although the symptom does occasionally persist into maturity. Macfarlane and others report a steady decline in the incidence as the age increases. Prognosis seems to be slightly better for girls than for boys, since the 6 per cent of patients who still had nocturnal enuresis at age 14 were all boys.

REFERENCES

Bakwin, H., and Bakwin, R. M. Clinical Management of the Behavior Disorders in Children, Philadelphia, W. B. Saunders Co., 1960.
Gerard, M. W. Enuresis: A Study in Etiology, Am. J. Orthopsychiatry, 9: 45, 1939.
Kanner, L. Child Psychiatry, Springfield, Ill., Charles C Thomas, 1957.
Macfarlane, J. W., Allen, L., and Honzik, M. A Developmental Study of the Behavior Problems of Normal Children between Twenty-one Months and Fourteen Years, Berkeley, University of California Press, 1954.
Michaels, J. J., and Goodman, S. E. Incidence and Intercorrelations of Enuresis and Other Neuropathic Traits in So-called Normal Children, Am. J. Orthopsychiatry, 4: 79, 1934.
Tapia, F., Jekel, J., and Domke H. Enuresis: An Emotional Symptom?, J. Nerv. Ment. Dis., 130: 61, 1960.

FIRE-SETTING

CLASSIFICATION AND DIFFERENTIATION

Bender classifies pathological fire-setting or incendiarism according to two types, which depend on the age of the child. In the preadolescent child, fire-setting is usually psychodynamically an act of aggression or revenge. In the adolescent, it usually has a sexual meaning.

Not all fire-setting is pathological, however. Fires set by children are often started because of curiosity, and such fires may occasionally get out of hand. It is common for small children, mainly boys between the ages of 4 and 7, to play with matches and to light small fires. They sit in the alley or a vacant lot watching the fire burn, and occasionally their fires spread out of control. The normal individual, at any age, is fascinated by fire, which is wonderfully destructive, powerful, all-consuming. But most people are satisfied to light only "safe" fires, which are kept under control and which are socially approved—such as bonfires and those set in fireplaces. Or they watch "other people's fires" when attracted by the fire engines and crowds. Most of us have felt the sense of exultation described by Walt Whitman:

I hear the alarm at dead of night
I hear the bells—shouts!
I pass the crowd—I run
The sight of flames maddens me with pleasure.

INCIDENCE

Considering the easy availability and destructiveness of fire, the wonder is that fire-setting is such a relatively infrequent symptom among emotionally disturbed children. Bender, who found only 60 cases out of 1,755
disturbed children aged 15 and under, notes that the juvenile courts of
New York City do not regard fire-setting as a major problem. The literature on this symptom is sparse, and data on incidence is hampered by the
fact that many fires that have been deliberately set, are unreported. Certainly, the brighter children are less likely to be caught—and since legal
and financial difficulties may be involved, parents are inclined to conceal
evidence of a child's having set a fire. Lewis and Yarnell, who studied the
reports of fires set by 238 juveniles under 16 years of age, state that incidence increases rapidly after age 12. Over 90 per cent of these young
incendiaries were boys.

ETIOLOGY AND PSYCHOPATHOLOGY

Among the earlier studies of fire-setting, the symptom was obviously
considered to be a neurotic manifestation. However, among more recent
studies, covering a large number of cases of all age levels, there seems to be
a variety of psychiatric disorders among children who set fires. Kaufman
and others have emphasized the various other symptoms associated with
fire-setting, pointing out that it rarely exists as an isolated symptom: In a
series of 30 children, they found that over three fourths had severe rage
reactions, two thirds showed chronic hyperactivity, and almost half were
enuretic. Diagnostically, not one child was considered psychoneurotic; over
two thirds were diagnosed as either psychotic or "borderline-prepsychotic."
In the pre-adolescent group, the most common diagnoses are personality
disorder and primary reading disability. In the adolescent group, many are
schizophrenic, and a considerable number are mentally retarded (27 of 95
adolescent boys apprehended for setting fires were reported by Lewis and
Yarnell to have I.Q.'s below 70). Bender also noted that, especially in
younger children, fire-setting was usually accompanied by other types of
antisocial behavior, including truancy, stealing, and generalized aggression.
There were frequent associated disorders, such as learning disabilities and
physical handicaps, which frustrated the children and impaired their social

adjustment. All the children showed acute anxiety and had frequent terrifying dreams and fantasies. The fires, which were set in or near the children's own homes, usually had caused little or no damage; and these were often set—with associated fantasies—to burn some member of the family who had withheld love from the children or who had been serious rivals for the parents' love.

Among adolescent fire-setters, the mechanisms and psychopathology are usually quite different. Many of these children tend to operate in pairs, usually consisting of an aggressive and a passive member. There is thus a strong homosexual tone to the relationship, which has been noted in most of the literature referring to this age group, although in Bender's cases there were no apparent overt homosexual episodes. The fires set by adolescents, frequently of a serious nature, are often planned in advance, and the culprits often remain in the vicinity to watch the fire and to enjoy the spectacle. Many express feelings of intense excitement, pleasure, and a sense of power. The adolescent group therefore resembles the neurotic adult fire-setter, or "pyromaniac," described in psychiatric and psychoanalytic literature. Adult incendiarism is classically regarded as a sadistically displaced sexual drive, mainly at the urethral-erotic level. Freud noted the occurrence of dreams about fire in association with reminiscences of childhood enuresis, and many writers have remarked on the frequency of bedwetting in children who set fires, regarding this as corroborative evidence that pyromania is a urethral-erotic experience. Unfortunately, all these studies have lacked adequate controls.

TREATMENT

Because of the severity of the disturbance, and also because it is potentially dangerous to the child, his family, and his community, fire-setting is often an indication for drastic treatment measures. Institutionalization is frequently required, the choice of institution depending on the diagnosis and other therapeutic considerations. Incarceration in a closed ward is by no means always necessary. Removal from the home environment to a therapeutic setting usually results in immediate cessation of the incendiary activities, so that an open institution is often satisfactory. In the writer's recollection, only one boy continued with his fire-setting after admission to the inpatient treatment unit. Following an argument with his therapist, he set a fire in a wastebasket. This created fine excitement, the ward was filled with smoke, and everyone had to go outside while the air cleared. But no harm was done and the incident was not repeated.

Not every child who sets a fire needs to be immediately removed from home. As in any case, the psychiatrist evaluates the total disturbance and seeks the cause of the episode. Sometimes the problem is minor, and brief outpatient therapy is sufficient. But it is wise to continue to keep in close contact, as a child who has set one fire is prone to set another.

REFERENCES

Bender, L. Firesetting in Children, in Aggression, Hostility and Anxiety in Children, Springfield, Ill., C. C Thomas, 1953.
Fenichel, O. Pyromania, in The Psychoanalytic Theory of Neurosis, New York, W. W. Norton & Co., 1945.
Freud, S. The Interpretation of Dreams, in Basic Writings of Sigmund Freud, ed. A. A. Brill, New York, Random House, 1938.
Kaufman, I., Heims, L. and Reiser, D. A Re-evaluation of the Psychodynamics of Firesetting, Am. J. Orthopsychiatry, 31: 123, 1961.
Lewis, N. D. C. and Yarnell, H. Pathological Firesetting, New York, Nervous and Mental Disease Monographs, 1951.

SCHOOL REFUSAL

CLASSIFICATION

The term *school phobia* is sometimes used interchangeably with *school refusal*, and there is much confusion in the literature over the two terms. Some writers use the latter to include all types, reserving *school phobia* for those cases with clear-cut neurotic psychopathology. Johnson, who first used the term *school phobia* in 1941, follows this pattern of classification. Because the preponderance of the literature on school refusal has dealt with this so-called classical type, the resultant overemphasis has perhaps caused psychiatrists to expect and to look for the classical psychodynamics in all cases of school refusal. More recently, it is coming to be recognized that a wide variety of disturbances can have the effect of making the child fearful of leaving home or going to school. There is no entirely satisfactory classification of the various types of school refusal, and any attempt to classify must recognize that many cases do not fit clearly into any specific type. Some authors, for example Coolidge and others, distinguish childhood and adolescent types. Kahn and Nursten, whose bibliographic review presents the group of disorders in excellent perspective, classify the types into three groups: the neurotic states, the character disorders, and the childhood psychoses. The various classifications, while at some variance, nevertheless make the point that there exists a variety of types, with differing etiologies, causes, and diagnoses; each case must therefore be judged individually if it is to be treated appropriately. The present discussion will follow the triple classification of Kahn and Nursten.

INCIDENCE

The ratio of boys to girls is about 1:1. Although more common in early school years, the more serious cases originate in or persist into adolescence. There are no reliable figures of incidence on a national scale, but in some child guidance clinics it occurs in 2 to 8 per cent of the total referrals. Obviously, only the more severe cases are reported and diagnosed—it is a rare child who has not fleetingly displayed some of the symptoms, without causing undue alarm at home or at school. The number of reported cases seems to be increasing; however it is impossible at present to determine whether this increase is the result of better recognition of the symptoms as relating to neurosis rather than delinquent truancy, or whether the increase is indeed clinically significant.

SYMPTOMS

A first attack may occur at any age in the child's or adolescent's school life, anxiety being the prominent and constant symptom.

The refusal to go to school may be directly expressed as an intense dislike for, or a fear of, school. More often, a particular aspect of the school situation is selected, such as a classmate toward whom the child may express fear or aversion, a teacher, or certain of the school subjects, assignments, regulations, and activities. Frequently, however, the child merely experiences somatic symptoms which prevent his going to school. These are mostly gastrointestinal symptoms (including pain, discomfort, nausea, and vomiting) although any organic system may be selected. These symptoms are genuine: The child looks miserable, and there is no doubt that he feels ill; his anxiety and apprehension are manifest. Only a heartless mother would force such a child to go to school, and since the majority of these mothers are far from heartless, the child is usually returned to bed, his mother hovering solicitously over him.

The onset of symptoms, whatever their nature, is usually on the morning of a school day, either when the child first arises or when it is almost time for him to leave for school. Symptoms are more likely to occur on Mondays or the day following a holiday.

School refusal must be differentiated from truancy or from parents' inability to accept normal social obligations required by regular school attendance. The normal child, too, may have very real reasons for dreading an encounter with the school bully, a sadistic teacher, or a school subject which is beyond his capacity. Truancy is defined as absence from school on rational (if not socially acceptable) grounds. The truant, who may be re-

belling against adverse school or home conditions, may be socially maladjusted, but he can be helped by social measures. It is significant in the
diagnosis of school refusal that, by the time it is recognized as a problem, it
has developed a chronicity and a pattern and that changing the teacher,
the subjects, or the school have managed to produce, at best, only temporary relief.

The symptomatology is similar in the three major types of school refusal:

1. In the neurotic and psychotic types, anxiety is usually more intense
and pervasive.

2. In cases associated with personality disorder there is more often
chronic argumentativeness, outbursts of anger, and disobedience.

The schizophrenic cases may assume a paranoid quality, with suspicions and accusations directed against schoolmates and school authorities.

ETIOLOGY AND PSYCHOPATHOLOGY

School refusal is basically a communication of distress. Once it has
been distinguished from truancy, the irrational basis of the distress may be
found to originate from several causes.

As in any neurosis, the etiology of neurotic school refusal involves
both hereditary and environmental factors. The biological predisposition
must be in the child, but in this disorder the type of environmental experience appears better understood than in most of the neuroses. The school
refusal seen in the neurotic child, and the type about which most has been
written, is basically a separation anxiety. Some authorities consider it a true
phobia, noting that the fear of separation from home and mother is displaced onto some aspect of the school situation. Waldfogel observes that
when the anxiety of school phobia is traced to its source, "it is invariably
found to originate in the child's fear of being separated from his mother."
There is remarkable agreement in the literature as to the psychodynamics
and basic etiology of this type of school phobia (Eisenberg, Johnson, E.,
Klein, Waldfogel). One often sees an intense interdependent relationship
between mother and child, with the mother being strongly identified with
the child. The mother, usually neurotic, anxious, overly concerned for her
child, and basically narcissistic, may be overpermissive and overindulgent
or excessively strict and controlling. Some mothers are both of these alternately. Because of the overdependence between mother and child, neither
is able to achieve the normal emancipation which usually occurs during
early latency. Waldfogel has stressed that, in looking for the cause of
school refusal, one rarely encounters a history of traumatic events in the
child's early life. He finds that the anxiety results not so much from early

trauma as from lack of opportunity to test the effects of traumatic experiences. Thus, he states: "the feelings of fear and rage come to assume overwhelming proportions and are associated with catastrophic expectations. There is no inner sense of being able to cope with these dangerous emotions independently, and when the child experiences these feelings, his inadequate ego requires the presence and support of his parents."

The school refusal associated with personality disorder usually appears as one of a complex of symptoms which mark a chronic distortion of interpersonal relationships. Although it commonly appears in late childhood or early adolescence, this symptom is preceded by a long history of personality disturbance. Coolidge and others consider that the disorder probably began in somewhat the same manner as the classic type of disturbance, but that chronicity of the total pathology has produced a more complicated situation. Weiss and Cain have described cases which they call "partially gratified," in which the parents, especially the mothers, throughout the patient's childhood would alternately supply and withhold emotional gratification from the children, at times openly rejecting them. Coolidge described cases in adolescence in which the mothers have imposed a prolonged dependency, so that on reaching adolescence the children, unable to meet the demands of an adolescent society, have refused to leave home. Kahn and Nursten regard this type of school refusal as due to a chronic failure of personality integration, with the symptoms finally appearing not so much as a crisis, but as an almost inevitable culmination.

In the schizophrenic child, school refusal, which is secondary to the basic ego defect, occurs as one symptom of a complex psychopathology. In this case, it results primarily from excessive need for close mothering and support, coupled with fearfulness of social contact and of changes in environment. Although the symptom may occur at any age, it is more frequently seen in adolescence, since the onset of schizophrenia is usually at this age or later.

TREATMENT

In treating a case of school refusal, probably the most important aspect of diagnosis is determining the severity of the underlying psychopathology. The simple fact of a child's feigning an illness and in other ways seeking to avoid going to school is by no means always a signal of serious disorder. Tom Sawyer exhibited a mild case of Sunday School phobia (a school-refusal variant) by feigning a complication in his sore toe, but his aunt, a good, sensible and notably unneurotic woman, suspected the ruse, and sent him off in his best Sunday clothes. Many unneurotic mothers cope just as successfully with abortive cases.

On the other hand, many cases of school refusal are serious, and some, particularly those of recent origin in younger children, should be regarded as psychiatric emergencies. In such cases, the consequence of prolonged absence from school may produce irreparable psychological damage. In such cases, too, the first step in treatment is to return the child to school immediately. This decision should be imparted to both child and parents during the initial interview, and usually must be adhered to unswervingly. Because treatment of school refusal involves not only a child, but the entire family, the therapist must involve himself in the family's complex of psychopathology. Often the most difficult and taxing aspect of treatment is dealing with the mother, her inconsistencies, her indecisions, her ambivalent feelings toward the child. The therapist often has to assume the role of egosubstitute for the mother, providing support at times of stress when the child is defiant, tearful, or retching with nausea.

The dictum that the child return immediately to school is, however, not invariable. It is usually tried, and more often than not it is successful, but the child's return is merely a good beginning, not the end of therapy. If the child's panic or anxiety at finding himself forced into the feared and hated environment threatens to become overwhelming, the physician must recognize this danger and allow a respite; therefore he must keep in touch with the situation constantly. School refusal cannot be treated on a schedule: The therapist must be prepared for and must encourage calls from the family whenever indicated—he can expect such calls most often in the morning.

In the neurotic cases, outpatient psychotherapy, often fairly long and intensive, is the treatment of choice. Combined treatment of the mother, with some involvement of the father, should be included and may be done either by the child's therapist or another.

In older children with personality disorder, the problem becomes more one of providing a consistent framework of discipline and external control, often impossible to accomplish within the home environment—in which case, placement away from home is indicated. Weiss and Cain have reported in a group of older children excellent results with residential psychiatric treatment. The symptom of school refusal invariably disappears immediately upon placement, with attendance at the residential school. Treatment should usually be continued throughout an academic year, followed either by return home or placement elsewhere, depending upon other pertinent factors. If any psychosis is involved, those in charge of the situation must recognize the child's limitations and tenuous control, since a forced return to school can precipitate panic and psychotic break. Some children of this type may never be able to return to school.

In treatment of the schizophrenic child with school refusal, a return to school must be attempted cautiously, with constant attunement to the child's fears and panics. A limited school program may be indicated, with attendance only in such classes as the child can best tolerate. School authorities should of course be advised of the child's special needs for support and protection.

PROGNOSIS

With early and consistent treatment, a majority of children with a short history of school refusal return to school and make a satisfactory academic adjustment. This is particularly true in the younger children; in the adolescent cases, the outlook for successful return to school is less favorable.

The outlook for future adjustment of a schizophrenic child with school refusal varies with severity, but is, in general, not good. Here the prognostic consideration is not whether the child will go to school and get an education, but whether he will survive in society. Thus, concern with the school refusal is subsidiary, and one must recognize that he is often safer, more comfortable, and more likely to survive if he remains away from school.

The prognosis for school refusal associated with personality disorder is likewise not good. The total disorder is chronic and firmly imbedded. One must expect frequent exacerbations, and treatment may be considered rather successful if the child continues school more or less regularly until the age at which he can legally withdraw. On the other hand, if residential treatment is accomplished, prognosis appears much better.

In the neurotic type, the prognosis for returning to school is heartening, although major improvement in personality adjustment is less likely. However, the outlook varies widely, requiring evaluation of family pathology and of the family's capacity to become involved in treatment. Not the least of the significant factors in prognosis are the therapist's own skill, motivation, and patience.

REFERENCES

Coolidge, J., Willer, M., Tessman, E., and Waldfogel, S. School Phobia in Adolescence: a Manifestation of Severe Character Disturbance, Am. J. Orthopsychiatry, 30: 599, 1960.

Eisenberg, L. School Phobia: a Study in the Communication of Anxiety, Am. J. Psychiatry, 114: 712, 1958.

Johnson, A. M., Falstein, E., Szurek, S., and Svendsen, M. School Phobia, Am. J. Orthopsychiatry, 11: 702, 1941.

Kahn, J. H., and Nursten, J. P. School Refusal: A Comprehensive View of School Phobia and Other Failures of School Attendance, Am. J. Orthopsychiatry, 32: 707, 1962.

Klein, E. The Reluctance to Go to School, Psychoanalytic Study of the Child, New York, International Universities Press, 1945, Vol. 1.
Waldfogel, S. Family Relations in the Development of School Phobia, Am. J. Orthopsychiatry, 27: 754, 1957.
Weiss, M., and Cain, B. The Residential Treatment of Children and Adolescents with School Phobia, Am. J. Orthopsychiatry, 34: 103, 1964.

TIC

Tic is a symptom, and may be the outward manifestation of a variety of disorders. Although it most often involves the face and neck muscles, it may occur in any part of the body. Tics sometimes consist of rather complex, co-ordinated motor functions and include a variety of behaviors, such as grimacing, sniffing, swallowing, coughing, wrinkling the forehead, shaking or nodding the head, or scratching the body with the hand. A vocal tic may consist of barking or the explosive production of a phrase or a short sentence.

CLASSIFICATION

Tic is sometimes classified according to the part of the body involved, but this would seem to have little diagnostic significance. Another classification depends upon whether the movements are simple and random or more complex and purposive.

Mahler considers that there are two major types of tic:

1. *Symptomatic tic*, which is one manifestation of a tension state or neurotic state

2. *Tic syndrome*, "an organ neurosis of the neuromuscular apparatus," in which the tic is an integral part of the disorder

The literature recognizes as an entity a type of tic which has been named, after the French physician who described it, *Gilles de la Tourette's disease*, or *maladies des tics*. This syndrome, occurring in childhood, consists of severe, chronic tics of the upper body, often including face, shoulder, and arm. It ultimately includes coprolalia, and may be accompanied by echolalia or echokinesis. Some authorities question whether this syndrome should be regarded as a specific entity; it would appear more reasonable to include it as a type of the disorder which Mahler calls the "tic syndrome."

DIAGNOSIS

Diagnosis of tic is usually obvious. Characteristic features of the tic movement are its quick, jerky quality and the fact that it is repetitive, involving the same muscle group and the same motion many times.

Some authorities include nail-biting, finger-sucking, nose-picking, and similar habits; however, these are more readily controlled by the patient than true tic, which is spasmodic, sudden, and involuntary. Ability to suppress tic movement does not rule out a diagnosis of tic, however, since the tiqueur is frequently able to restrain the movement when he consciously attempts to do so.

Tic must be differentiated from the following:

1. *Generalized Motor Restlessness.*   Here the movements are usually random, varied (consisting of fidgeting or constant moving about), and voluntary—such as tapping with the finger or swinging the leg. The restless, fidgety, overactive preschooler is sometimes confused with the tiqueur; however, according to Kanner, true tic rarely occurs before age six. The movements of the merely hyperactive child are not as consistently localized; they do not appear when the child is interested in something; and the restlessness may continue during sleep.

2. *Chorea.*   Choreiform movements, especially as seen in Sydenham's chorea, may be confused with tic. Typically, chorea consists of more generalized movements; the excursion is usually larger; and a variety of muscle groups is involved. There is often motor clumsiness or muscular weakness associated with chorea, which is often found in combination with rheumatic fever or cardiac involvement. Chorea varies irregularly, while tic is repeated constantly, in the same fashion.

3. *Athetosis.*   The athetoid movement is wormlike and continuous, and co-exists with other neurologic findings.

ETIOLOGY

While the cause of tic is not fully understood, there is fairly general agreement that it is a motor discharge of psychological tension. Psychoanalytic formulations generally consider that the tension results from repression of aggressive or libidinal impulses, and, clinically, it is usually possible to find evidence of much hostility or aggression which cannot be directly expressed. Fraiberg, for example, reports a case of tic which was symptomatic of a hidden homosexual conflict, its reappearance twice coinciding with the threat of overt contact. Tiqueurs often demonstrate various motor evidences of tension—including fidgetiness, hyperkinesis, and motor restlessness.

Mahler emphasizes the importance of constitutional predisposition in the etiology of tic; however there is little concrete evidence that the disorder is hereditarily determined. Organic factors are usually listed among the many causes, the evidence being based largely on the fact that tics frequently occur in the postencephalitic syndrome; however, psychologic factors may also be involved in these cases. Certainly, there is little data to warrant the conclusion, except in the most severe forms of tic syndrome, that tic is a symptom of organic brain disease, and in most cases the etiology must be sought elsewhere.

Most authorities report a background of emotional tension for the child with tic symptomology. That the symptom does not usually occur before the age of six suggests that repression of voluntary movements operates in the etiology. Prior to this age, children are usually permitted free expression of motor activity, but when they reach school age much restriction is imposed. Perhaps cultural differences operate in the etiology of tic, since the incidence of the symptom varies in different cultures. Tic was apparently more common among children in the United States early in the present century, when a prevailing attitude was that "children should be seen and not heard"; and Redl (personal communication) recently observed a high incidence of tic among Russian school children, where there is much regimentation and where expression of impulses is strongly forbidden in the classroom.

The individual tic symptoms, according to Kanner, have been known to arise from habitual repetitions of primarily purposive actions, from imitation of others, or from gestures which have been more or less customary for the child. Kanner states unequivocally that "no happy, secure child ever develops tics," and emphasizes the close correlation between intensity of movement and the severity of emotional strain. Although the strain may evolve from a specific event or situation, it more usually arises as a means of release from repeated emotional stress, through motor activity.

COURSE AND PROGNOSIS

It must be remembered that psychogenic tic is a symptom, and may be the outward manifestation of a variety of disorders. The course varies widely. Most cases show fluctuation, the tic varying from time to time in frequency and severity. It commonly shows exacerbation during periods of emotional tension.

Simple tic usually disappears spontaneously and rarely continues past adolescence. Tic syndrome and maladie des tics have a poorer prognosis. The earlier literature on the latter was uniformly pessimistic; however Eisenberg and others and Lucas and others report improvement in many cases. Kanner reports that tics of unquestionably organic origin which have been studied in post-encephalitic patients disappear spontaneously, although they may persist for years; these are often accessible to psychotherapeutic influences.

TREATMENT

Most of the literature reflects discouragement about the treatment of tic. It suggests that therapeutic intervention has little effect upon the course of the symptom and that the cases which improve do so spontaneously. However, it should be pointed out that no well-controlled studies of treatment have been reported.

Many of the suggestions for treatment consist of a number of admonitions against overtreatment. Kanner warns that "the more the child's attention is directed toward the movements, either in a therapeutic effort or otherwise, the less they are likely to disappear." Since the movements have probably brought about strong reactions of aversion and embarrassment, the parents usually must be warned to cease using any of the so-called corrective methods, such as having the child practice suppressing the movements, watch himself in the mirror, or exercise the involved muscles. Advising the parents of the nature of the disorder and assuring them that many tics spontaneously disappear can do much toward reducing their apprehension and the general family involvement in the child's difficulty.

It is helpful to relieve the situational difficulties in the child's background. For example, the schoolwork of the overburdened child may have to be lightened, the shy child may be helped toward greater participation, and medical difficulties can sometimes be straightened out. These measures help, primarily, by relieving the background of tensions.

The major therapeutic approaches have been psychotherapy and pharmacotherapy. While the use of drugs has in the past been discouraging, recent reports (Challas and Brauer; Chapel and others; Lucas) are more hopeful about the symptomatic treatment of tic syndrome with drugs of the butyrophenone and phenothiazine groups. However, psychiatric treatment should be, as in any disorder, directed toward the child's total constellation of problems rather than to the specific symptom alone.

REFERENCES

Challas, G., and Brauer, W. Tourette's Disease: Relief of Symptoms with R1625, Am. J. Psychiat., 120: 283, 1963.

Chapel, J. L., Brown, N., and Jenkins, R. L. Tourette's Disease: Symptomatic Relief with Haloperidol, Am. J. Psychiat., 121: 608, 1964.

Eisenberg, L., Ascher, E., and Kanner, L. A Clinical Study of Gilles de la Tourette's Disease (Maladie des Tics) in Children, Am. J. Psychiatry, 115: 715, 1959.

Fraiberg, S. H. Homosexual Conflicts, in Adolescents, ed. Lorand and Scheer, New York, Paul B. Hoeber Inc., 1961, p. 83.

Kanner, L. Child Psychiatry, Springfield, Ill., Charles C Thomas, 1957.

Lucas, A. R. Gilles de la Tourette's Disease in Children: Treatment With Phenothiazine Drugs, Am. J. Psychiat., 121: 606, 1964.

———— Gilles de la Tourette's Disease in Children: Treatment with Haloperidol, Am. J. Psychiat., 121: 606, 1964.

———— Kauffman, P. E., and Morris, E. M. Gilles de la Tourette's Disease: Clinical Study of 14 Cases, Amer. Psychiat. Assoc. Annual Meeting, Atlantic City, N.J., May 9, 1966.

Mahler, M. F. A Psychoanalytic Evaluation of Tic in Psychopathology of Children, Psychoanalytic Study of the Child, New York, International Universities Press, 1949, Vol. 3/4.

SECTION FOUR

TREATMENT

16

PSYCHOTHERAPY

It is the physician, not the prostitute, who sells love for a living. —HENRY SWAIN, M.D.

The above aphorism, most applicable to the specialty of psychiatry, is not facetious. There are some close parallels between psychotherapy and the love act. Relatively little of either can be taught, but in both one must apply behaviors both instinctual and individually learned through experience and experimentation. Something of the techniques may be learned intellectually: the various approaches, the cues, the symbols, the meaning of this or that reaction; when to tread cautiously, when to forge ahead boldly, when to remain passive, when to take the initiative. But, once face to face with a patient, one is entirely on his own, and there is little time for trying to recall memorized lessons. For here is a dynamic situation between two human beings. And in psychotherapy, as in the love relationship, the essence, the thing that really matters and that determines success or failure, rests inevitably on subjective phenomena, on the feelings and reciprocal relations of the participants. Psychotherapy has always been and must forever remain an intensely personal experience, a relationship of feelings between two people.

In this chapter something of the structure of psychotherapy will be described: the setting, the participants, the techniques. But the reader must realize that any such description can provide merely the skeleton, and that he must build onto that skeleton out of his own feelings, experiences, and personality, in order to form his own living concept of psychotherapy as he himself is to practice it. This comes gradually, and with experience. For the beginner, probably the best single principle is: Relax and do what comes naturally. This can only be done without supervision and without hidden microphones or one-way screens. There should be but two people, the patient and the therapist, sitting in a room together, getting acquainted.

315

WHAT IS PSYCHOTHERAPY?

Psychotherapy is treatment by psychological methods through direct communication between the patient and the therapist. Its aim is to improve the patient's life adjustment by diminishing disturbing symptoms and by freeing him of incapacitating internal conflicts. It implies a relationship between the patient and the therapist in which there is an interchange of verbal and nonverbal expression to further these aims. The term is often limited to treatment by a physician (psychiatrist) or psychologist. Other terms have been devised to designate the treatment relationship between other professional therapists and their clients: child analysis (by a medical or lay analyst), casework, and counseling. But in terms of what transpires in the treatment situation these designations are sometimes artificial. Many feel that the "type" of therapy differs among the professional groups; that the social caseworker practices chiefly superficial and supportive therapy, while the psychiatrist, and to even greater extent, the psychoanalyst engages in "deep, uncovering" therapy. There is some truth in the notion, particularly since the child analyst may select his cases and treat mainly those who are verbal, productive, and amenable to deep therapy. But in the majority of treatment cases the methods of all workers in the field are the same. "Good therapy" has much in common, regardless of the label. Redl (personal communication) has pointed out that experienced workers, regardless of the theoretical "school" to which they adhere, generally can discuss clinical cases on common ground. Nor is there any justification for a nonmedical worker's avoiding deep therapy, provided he has skill and experience. Fraiberg (1951) has expressed the opinion that it is not important who does deep or superficial therapy, but that deep therapy should be accompanied by "deep thinking."

The term *psychotherapy* will be here used to denote the direct individual treatment of the child, without distinguishing between particular theoretical orientations or the particular profession of the psychotherapist. Reference is made particularly to outpatient psychotherapy, but many of the same principles are equally applicable to children in a residential treatment setting.

WHO SHOULD RECEIVE PSYCHOTHERAPY?

There are few specific rules for determining which children to treat and how to treat them. However, the following generalizations usually apply:

1. The child with adequate relationship capacity will respond better than the child without such capacity. This eliminates the psychopath.

2. The disturbed child with anxiety is more treatable than the one whose conflicts are ego-syntonic, that is, not discomfort-producing.

3. If the parents are motivated and willing to become involved in the treatment program, there is more likelihood of success.

4. Children with personality disorder and schizophrenia are less treatable than those with neurosis; the distortions of personality of schizophrenic children are too severe to be affected significantly by an occasional hourly interview.

One important determinant of whether a child should be treated is the seriousness of his problem, the more severe cases presumably having priority. Every child clinic is beset with frequent requests to see a child who is in serious trouble. Many of these problems are urgent, and there is the feeling that we must see them and do what we can, no matter how unhopeful or difficult the situation. But the reality is that there are many patients for whom we can do little or nothing. Facilities are just not available, and, recognizing this, we are forced to give most attention to those patients who can be helped. Dubo and Rabinovitch point out:

> While guidance clinics have met many community needs, a high percentage of treatment failures occur because we have asked the clinic to do an impossible job; many severely disturbed children just cannot be adequately treated while they remain at home or in the community. The prevailing degree of trauma in their relationships or the level of personality disorganization is such that temporary separation for treatment is necessary. Direct psychotherapy is not sufficient to meet the needs of these children and a new gratifying living experience in a therapeutic milieu is required.

Nor, as will be seen in the following chapter on Residential Treatment is even total milieu therapy enough in some cases.

Selection of patients is partly a matter of the therapist's preferences. Some, for example, are most successful with adolescents, some do better with very young children. Preference may be for a diagnostic type. One therapist, for example, limits himself almost entirely to schizophrenic children. Some, particularly those with pediatric training, see a large number of children with psychosomatic disorders. Others are challenged by those children who are particularly recalcitrant or mute or negative, and with whom special techniques of communication such as art and play therapy are required. Most therapists, however, try to see children with varying pathology, and but few are masochistic enough to see only incorrigible acting-out children hour after hour.

In general terms those individuals whose symptoms are relatively mild and circumscribed, and whose ego structure is relatively intact will respond most favorably. To go a step further, those whose general adjustment most clearly approximates mental health are the best "candidates" for psychotherapy. These are the individuals least in need of treatment. Unfortunately no adequate controlled studies are available that answer the question, "Who should receive psychotherapy?" Sometimes the only way to decide whether a child is treatable is to treat him. If it works, fine; if not, only the time has been lost, and something may have been learned from the experience. But this is no justification for treating everyone indiscriminately. The therapist has a responsibility to try to understand, and to learn constantly through his experience and his reading, which children can be helped and how best to help them.

WHO CAN DO PSYCHOTHERAPY?

Psychiatrists are traditionally in charge of the clinic team, but this does not necessarily mean that they are the best therapists. Perhaps the three aspects of his training which best qualify the physician as a psychotherapist are:

1. An orientation toward care of the patient.
2. A diagnostic approach.
3. A sense of responsibility acquired through the experience of dealing with seriously ill persons and their families.

The medical student is thoroughly drilled in the principle that he must first find out the cause of the trouble, then, whether he can really help or not, he must do something. This orientation has its disadvantages: It leads to a tendency to "pigeon-hole" each case, and to a not entirely warranted sense of omnipotence, of a certainty that something, somehow, can always be done to help. However, as a generalization, these principles provide a good foundation for a fledgling psychiatrist.

In addition to his medical training the psychiatrist needs a body of knowledge of psychopathology as well as certain personal qualities to become a competent psychotherapist. These are personal maturity and a warm interest in the children he treats. Colby, listing the qualifications for a good psychotherapist, emphasizes technical experience which integrates theoretical concepts with clinical observations, intuition to empathically understand the patient beyond the face value of what he says, and awareness of the therapist's own inner wishes, anxieties, and defenses as these influence his therapeutic techniques.

It has been said that an emotionally ill person would be helped by the experience of talking regularly about his problems with any mature and interested adult. To some extent this is true, but some of the hazards inherent in dealing with mentally ill persons should place into medical hands the ultimate responsibility for determining the need for psychotherapy and for directing the treatment. These hazards include the patient's potential for suicide or homicide, the possibility of an impending psychosis, or the presence of physical illness complicating, or masked by, the emotional problems. As regards the psychotherapeutic process itself, professional training may be of less importance than personal inclination and intuition. Eisenberg estimated that in 1961 there were at least 2 million psychiatrically ill children in the United States, with only 250 physicians certified as fully qualified child psychiatrists—one certified psychiatrist for 8,000 children. Not all of these children are in need of individual psychotherapy, but obviously only a small fraction of those who are can be treated by a child psychiatrist. By 1966 the number of certified child psychiatrists has nearly doubled, but the demand for their services has increased even more rapidly than their supply. There are skilled and successful child therapists from a variety of backgrounds including social work, clinical psychology, psychiatry, and education. It may be recalled that in the Cambridge-Sommerville Study on the treatment of delinquency, the best therapist was a nurse, and she was the one person in the group without formal casework training.

Some persons are not emotionally qualified to do psychotherapy. Strong emotional responses toward the patient or his family impair the therapeutic relationship. The therapist cannot maintain a therapeutic attitude toward a person if he himself feels strongly resentful, hostile, unduly attached, or anxious; for he will then be acting out of his own conflicts rather than the patient's. All therapists have such feelings at times, but they must not allow themselves to be overwhelmed by them. As a general rule, anyone who has such difficulties in interpersonal relationships should not undertake psychotherapy, as he will thereby be doing a disservice both to himself and to his patient.

AGE OF THE CHILD

The child's age is important in determining the type and intensity of therapy. As a general rule, the younger the child, the more emphasis there needs to be on treatment or counseling of the parents; with older children and adolescents, emphasis is more on treatment of the patient, with relatively less contact with the parents. Gerard believes that in the young child the specific difficulty can be approached more directly and treatment can be shorter in duration. Certainly the symptoms are less likely to have been present as long, and defenses are less permanently established. The younger child is generally more closely tied to his mother, and effective treatment of his disturbance is contingent upon simultaneous work with the mother. Often the major therapeutic effort must be directed toward her, with a relatively shorter part of each hour being spent with the child. With the older child, particularly the older adolescent, it may be desirable or necessary to limit the contacts with the parents and focus the therapy almost exclusively on the child himself. Adolescence presents a special situation in psychotherapy and will be discussed on page 335.

The technique of therapy varies with the age of the child, too, and must be adjusted to his developmental level. The young child can be reached best through play, which is his most natural means of expression. Often he is unable to express his conflicts verbally, or is not even aware of them. With older children, verbal interaction can often be used successfully as the primary means of communication, but even with a highly verbal child it is wise to change the pace and intersperse verbal interviews with other activities.

At any age it is essential that there be at least some contact with the parents. They are entitled to know what are the goals and reasonable expectations of therapy, as well as what its limitations are. Moreover, the therapist needs their co-operation if the treatment plan is to be effective. Some therapists insist on treating even very young children in isolation. They feel that the therapy hour is "sacred," and avoid any intrusion in their relationship with the child, by refusing contact with parents, the school, or other interested persons. Such practice, needless to say, is to be deplored and may be very harmful to the child.

Fathers are often reluctant to take time off from their work, but this should be insisted upon, although not necessarily on a regular or frequent basis. If the parents need more intensive treatment for their own emotional problems, it is best to have them seen by another therapist, with the two therapists communicating with each other regarding progress and particular problems.

THE THERAPY SCHEDULE

The schedule includes such considerations as to what extent to involve the parents, how often to see the patient, whether to include special educational procedures or to work out a program with the school. A detailed and rigid program is not usually set up. Strict adherence to a schedule inevitably requires that things be done for the program and not for the patient, so that some flexibility is necessary in every case. However, a degree of order is also necessary and helpful. A fairly regular schedule can be decided upon, and the most usual schedule in outpatient treatment is one visit per week lasting approximately one hour. But this may vary widely; two to four hours a week are common, while some patients are seen but once every two or three weeks. Sometimes a p.r.n. schedule is best, and the mother calls whenever the situation requires it (obviously such an arrangement is not the rule, as every therapist needs to schedule his day). In some cases it is reassuring to the family simply to know that the therapist is available when needed, and he may have to be called upon only at long intervals.

The duration of treatment cannot be predicted with accuracy, and although parents often inquire about this it is not possible to indicate to them or the patient precisely how long it will continue. The therapist himself does not usually know, at the beginning of treatment, how long it will last. Some general guidelines can be stated, however, and parents appreciate having at least an approximate indication of what to expect. Usually therapy continues for a number of months. Exceptionally it may take years; there may be cases where one or two interviews are sufficient. In many clinics the period of therapy may correspond roughly with the academic year. The completion of a school year is often a suitable time for a child to terminate the treatment. This coincides also with the time of the year when there is greatest staff turnover, with psychiatric residents leaving and new ones coming. This is not to imply that a time for termination is to be or can be set arbitrarily or determined by external circumstances rather than by the child's emotional status. Certainly the patient may still be having trouble at the end of the school year and may have to continue with another therapist. However, most children who can be helped will have shown some improvement after a few months' time. It is most likely that those whose difficulties continue unabated after a year or two or three will not profit further from intensive psychotherapy and something else should be recommended.

There are some kinds of cases that need to be followed for many years, but not with intensive weekly psychotherapy. These are schizophrenic children, children with brain damage and severe learning problems, and some children with personality disorders. In these instances, the child and his family may need support from time to time, help with academic planning, or intervention at times of crisis.

Short-term therapy has become popular in the past decade, particularly as child analysts have discovered that success may be achieved in certain cases without going through the entire classical analytical process. Schmideberg has described experimentations with analytic technique, seeking to encourage early improvement and shorten the treatment period. She cautions that short-term therapy is not simply abbreviated, but, rather, is accelerated therapy, and concludes that this can be effective in some cases. Fraiberg (1954) likewise reports good results with short-term treatment, noting with "embarrassment" the excellent response from "a simple interpretation addressed to the mother's guilt, a comment to a little boy in an observational interview, some modest suggestion to the mother in an exchange of recipes."

TERMINATION

It is a rare therapist who knows when to terminate treatment. The indications should be obvious: The patient is either much better, or he is no better. And yet these two states are by no means always obvious. The therapist involved with the intricacies and complications of his patient's life is often in a poor position to judge that the patient should become disengaged from him. As this point would indicate, the tendency to err is on the side of too long, rather than too short, treatment.

In the physical diseases, the line between sickness and health is usually clear-cut. When the fracture heals, or the fever is gone, the physician is no longer needed. But in psychiatry, there is a multiplicity of problems, most of them ongoing, some improving, some getting worse. The patient may feel less anxious, but he is getting into more fights; he may be doing better with his schoolwork, but he is arguing more with his mother. And the psychiatrist is involved in all of this, in all aspects of the patient's life and his environment. The decision that the particular point in time has arrived when the therapist can be dispensed with is therefore often, one might add even usually, a very difficult one.

THE THERAPEUTIC PROCESS

In classic psychoanalytic therapy, unconscious conflicts are brought to consciousness, where they are "worked through." In the process, "transference feelings" toward the therapist are resolved. This is, of course, a gross oversimplification. To the treatment process with children this bears little resemblance, for neither is unconscious material often brought to consciousness nor is there true transference to be resolved. The therapist may be aware of, or at least suspect, specific unconscious conflicts in the child, but he often leaves them there, or even helps the child to bury them more deeply.

What actually happens in therapy? What are the factors which are at work in effecting significant changes in the child's thoughts and feelings? Why and how does therapy work? These are crucial questions, but they are difficult to answer with definitiveness, because the process of therapy does not lend itself readily to experimental verification. It is impossible to alter only one variable at a time, and to accumulate a sample of significant size involving the same or similar kinds of cases. Every case is different, each treatment course is incredibly complex, and no therapist can hope to understand all the factors which are going on.

Yet psychotherapy is by no means a matter of the blind leading the halt. A competent therapist has a considerable awareness of what he is doing, he knows what things are important in this particular patient's problem, and he usually has an accurate idea of whether or not the treatment is going to work. Therapy is more than simply a matter of spending time with a patient. Yet how many thousands of hours are spent yearly in which two persons sit together in a room, talking, or playing games, or building clay models, speaking mainly to avoid boredom, and neither having any notion of why he is there or what is happening—and all this in the name of psychotherapy.

Therapy is, first of all, a process in interpersonal relationship. This point has been made before, but it is significant and bears repeating. Relationship begins when therapist and child first meet. It forms a basis for all subsequent interaction and is the foundation on which all the complex processes of therapy are based. Through the relationship the child develops a feeling of trust and confidence in the therapist; he understands that the therapist is interested in him and is functioning for his best interests. He comes to expect and to know the confident feeling of a sustaining and consistent relationship, one that does not fail him, one that lets him know with assurance when things are right and when they are wrong. Often the therapy experience is the first time in a child's life when he has had the opportunity for a close and meaningful relationship with a mature person who is interested in him. It is impossible to overestimate the importance of such an experience for a child. It can literally change his whole life. The person who does psychotherapy with children unquestionably carries a grave responsibility. Yet this need be neither frightening nor anxiety-provoking. Indeed, it can be highly gratifying and enjoyable.

In the relationship, the child uses the therapist as a kind of sounding board—he tests himself, more or less consciously, on new ways of relating, on new patterns of aggression and nonaggression, of hostility and love. He learns that some people can be trusted, and that the world is not a totally hostile place. As Billy (the boy in the chapter on neurosis, Chapter 7) expressed it, "If I come to trust you, then later on I can trust other people, too." Billy was a highly verbal boy, and rarely in therapy does one hear the process expressed so beautifully; nevertheless, the process is usually in operation, and is a major part of the treatment process.

Another important operation in therapy is control of the child's behavior. The therapist effects control of the patient through two processes: first, through his status as an authority figure, and second, through his relationship with the patient. The therapist's authority status is considerable, and the child, especially a delinquent one, is acutely aware of this. If not, he should be made aware of it early. The therapist is "in league" with the school authorities, and can get directly in touch with the school principal merely by picking up his telephone. He is in communication with the law enforcement agencies, is a consultant and a confidant of the court, and the destiny of the offender is often in his hands. He is the advisor of the child's parents, who have come to him for recommendations. The child understands that in most instances the parents will carry out whatever the therapist suggests.

Thus, in a sense, the therapist's authority status is virtually absolute; and there are cases in which this authority is necessary, and should be fully utilized. It can be a mistake to relinquish this status too readily, and to let the child know too early that, in spite of his power, the therapist is after all not an ogre, and can really be quite a friendly chap. For the delinquent child, or one who is defiant of authority, an approach that is too friendly can destroy altogether the therapist's effectiveness. It is far preferable to let the illusion remain awhile, or even to enhance it. One's own feelings of counteraggression must, of course, be controlled, but there is no harm in the therapist's expressing a little honest anger. It will not hurt the child, and it is often highly effective.

The relationship, when one exists, is used for controlling the child. This operation may be largely nonverbal and the child may not be aware of it. The therapist imparts his approval or disapproval of the child's behavior in a variety of ways, and the child responds. The response is not always the desired one, but, with a little work, it may improve.

Control is important not only in the treatment of delinquent and acting-out children; it plays some role in the therapy of all disturbed children. With those who are mainly depressed, anxious, fearful, and constricted, the control is of a different quality, less severe, more in the nature of a directing and supporting function. But here, too, the child understands that the therapist is in charge of matters, that he is the authority, that he does what is best for the child, and that he will somehow straighten things out.

The third fundamental aspect of psychotherapy is that it must be a significant event in the child's experience. The child must understand that his coming to therapy has important meaning. For only in this way can it be an effective force in producing significant alterations in the child's functioning. This does not mean that every minute of treatment or every therapeutic session must be loaded with meaning. Nor is its significance necessarily imparted by direct verbalization. One need not remind the child (although it may sometimes be done), "You know, Johnny, these visits are very important to you." This information is usually imparted in other ways. The simple fact of the child's being kept out of school for half a day and brought to the office or clinic imparts a special meaning to the event. The obvious authority of the therapist, already discussed, provides impact. The making of major decisions, or the (palpable) evidence that they may be made, such as changing the child's school or classroom, having him take special tests, having him attend summer camp or be placed away from home, all these add meaning to the experience and assure that the therapy and the therapist have major significance for the child.

A fourth fundamental of psychotherapy is that it is hard work. Probably the oldest saw about psychoanalysis pictures the analyst seated in his easy chair snoozing comfortably while the patient on the couch drones on and on. While no one claims this to be good therapy, there is no doubt that it has happened occasionally. But it is doubtful that a therapist has ever gone to sleep while treating a child. In the first place, it could be dangerous. In the second place, child therapy is an active process, with the therapist a direct participant at all times. He sits facing the child, talking to him, or playing a game, or watching and commenting as the child draws or builds something or talks about himself. There must always and continuously be the feeling that the therapist is directing his interest to the child, and that the session is for the child's sake. This does not mean that one cannot relax. One should in fact be relaxed, be able to enjoy the games or the conversation. But, it must be an alert relaxation, with more or less constant attunement to the significance of the patient's activities and expressions.

A fifth characteristic of psychotherapy with children, and one which distinguishes it from treatment of adults, is that the child is usually living in the environment which contributed to his disorder. Thus, one does not often dwell on the past, and deal with the patient's recollections. Rather, emphasis is on the present, on current problems and relationships, on what happened today or yesterday at home and at school, what his father did to him last night rather than five years ago. Moreover, because his present environment is most significant, a major function of therapy is to deal directly with the environment, to manipulate it effectively, to talk with the parents and suggest changes in their functioning, to manipulate the school situation; in short, not only to help the child in his reactions to his environment but to help the environment to change itself.

Frederick Allen, whose name is inevitably linked with the relationship aspect of therapy, has developed masterfully the concept of psychotherapy as an immediate and present experience. In his chapter on the therapeutic process, Allen states: "Therapy emerges from an experience in living, not in isolation, but in relationship with another from whom the patient can eventually differentiate himself as he comes to perceive and accept his own self as separate and distinct." Allen emphasizes that the therapist provides:

a living symbol of the present world in which the patient is trying to find his place, a world often in strong contrast to that which the patient has built up. In the therapeutic hour the new and old meet. The patient may have to bring from his past a great deal of factual and emotional content before he can come to grips with the values he possesses in his present self, before he can use these for more effective living. To help the patient grow within the framework of this experience, the therapist must maintain his own realness and not be drawn back into dark recesses of the past to the exclusion of the here and now.

Too often patients in their therapy are drawn farther and farther from reality, dwelling within the troubled past, recounting to the therapist hour after hour episodes recollected from a nightmarish world, and steadily, as the months wear on, becoming sicker and more hopelessly involved. One such patient, an adolescent, compulsive boy, had been in outpatient therapy for a year, dwelling on the past, getting worse, failing in school despite superior intelligence, withdrawing more and more from social contacts. The therapist's case notes grew voluminous, recounting in detail all that the patient said about his early life, his father's unreasonableness and anger, his brother's favored position in the family, and so on and so on. The therapist finished his training at the end of the year and departed. The new therapist began their first interview by asking the boy about his family, the age of his sister, where his father worked, what his mother was like, and similar questions. The patient at length, and not unreasonably, complained, "But that's all in the notes. I've gone over all that before." The therapist explained, "I'm not interested in the notes, I'm interested in you." Angrily, the patient asked, "Do you mean I've wasted a whole year?" "Very probably," he was told. His anger and resentment continued through several sessions, during which he frequently threatened to quit therapy. But the anger was a real and present experience and it formed the basis for the beginning of relationship. As the relationship developed, and as the patient tried himself out in what Gitelson has called the "nonneurotic setting," his ego strength improved vastly. By being forced out of the unreal past, he gradually learned to live in the real present.

Allen has described the therapist's role as follows:

The only thing a therapist can do for anyone in a therapeutic experience is to help that person gradually to be himself, to help him gain a sounder

*evaluation of his own individuality and the consequent freedom to make
creative, responsible use of that individuality in the continuing realities of
his life, whatever they may be and wherever they may occur. This is the
measure of a healthy individual: free to live in each new present and to
borrow from previous presents the stuff that gives continuity to life; and
free from a past to which the neurotic is too highly bound.*

THE TECHNIQUES OF THERAPY

There are many ways to communicate with children. They depend on
a variety of factors: the age and personality of the child and his particular
interests, the personality of the communicator and his particular interests. Some people relate easily and naturally with children; others never
seem quite comfortable in a child's company. Some persons use special techniques which appeal to children: Hans Christian Andersen told
them stories; the Pied Piper of Hamelin played them sweet music. With
most children, special techniques are not necessary. All that is required is
that one be interested in the child, that one talk to him, and listen to him.

Probably the most difficult, and the most important aspect of child
therapy, is to convince the child that one is interested in him. To do this,
one must in fact *be* interested in him. This is a personal matter, and depends much on one's own personality, maturity, and level of training. It
may be especially difficult for the student, as he is necessarily overly concerned about doing well with the case, getting the right answers, trying to
remember what he has read and been told about interviewing, interpretation, psychodynamics, diagnostic criteria, and the rest. He is much too busy
to relax and enjoy the child. But to repeat advice given earlier, the most
important thing is to relax and to be spontaneous. Only thus can a relationship be established; only thus will the child feel that the therapist is
genuinely interested in him.

The classical technique of psychoanalysis requires that the patient lie
on the couch and say whatever comes to his mind. Children usually do the
latter without having to be instructed, but they are rarely able to lie on a
couch while fully awake for longer than five minutes. Psychoanalysts who
first began to apply analytic method and theory to child therapy, notably
Melanie Klein and Anna Freud (1946b), quickly recognized that modifications of the classical technique were required. Margaret Gerard described
the evolution of the various techniques in child analysis, beginning with
Hug-Hellmuth's play therapy developed in the first decade of this century.
Gerard emphasizes flexibility of approach to each case.

Flexibility includes such variations in technique as frequency and
duration of interviews, behavior and attitudes of the therapist regarding

corrective measures, controls, amount of interpretation, and amount of probing. It also includes such factors as how much and how often to see the parents, whether to have the parents enter into treatment themselves, special education techniques for the child, and school counseling. Gerard notes that in some of the minor difficulties, direct psychotherapy may not be indicated. She observes that

Environmental manipulation such as education of the parents in more wholesome training attitudes, arrangement for special tutoring or privileges at school, the use of special recreational facilities, etc., may give the child's developing ego sufficient opportunities to experiment with new methods of solving problems. The symptom, then, may be discarded because it is no longer the best solution which the child can achieve in the changed situation.

Psychotherapy of the child is indicated only when the above measures are insufficient. Often one first tries environmental manipulation, then if it does not help, one turns to psychotherapy.

Gerard notes that sometimes the therapist has little choice in the matter. For example, where the home environment is highly pathological, it is preferable to remove the child from the situation or to attempt to improve the situation by treatment of the parents. But the parents may refuse, in which case direct treatment of the child can help him adjust to his difficult environment; while it may not be the treatment of choice, it is better than nothing.

The use of "uncovering" therapy has been mentioned as well as the fact that this is less used in children than in adults. For clarification, here is an example of the divergent directions an incident in therapy may take, depending on the therapist's choice. A frail, depressed, neurotic 10-year-old boy, surrounded at home by three older sisters, had been acting out his anger at school. The father, an ex-football player with rather immature notions as to what constitutes manliness, was openly rejecting of the boy and markedly preferential toward the three girls. The mother was somewhat of a shrew, distressed over her vanishing sex appeal, contemptuous of all males, but expressing most of it toward the unfortunate patient. One day during the therapy hour, the boy weighted down by his cares, morosely and with real feeling lamented, "It seems like the world is full of women." Now, such a statement obviously is loaded with meaning, and one technique of treatment would be to question the boy at length about his feelings toward women. Such a session could be productive and helpful. In this particular case, however, the therapist found the boy's remark uproariously funny. He began to laugh. The boy, at first a bit startled, then pleased with the success of his remark and also perceiving the humor in it, began to laugh likewise. When the laughter subsided, the relationship between the child and adult had taken a step along the way toward mutual enjoyment and trust. And the therapist's response to the patient's deeply meaningful remark was: "Well, my boy, you're going to have to live with women all your life, and you might as well start learning right now."

INTERPRETATION

Interpretation means explanation of the psychological significance of the patient's thoughts or behavior. There are two phases to interpretation. The first is the psychiatrist's interpretation to himself, the second is the interpretation to the patient. For clarity, they will be considered separately below.

The psychiatrist's understanding of the psychopathological processes and his interpretation of them are part of the diagnostic process. The danger lies in inaccurate diagnosis. Great care must be taken lest interpretation be made on the basis of insufficient evidence. Characteristic of the inexperienced therapist, particularly one who has been titillated by having read some few case studies in psychoanalysis, is a willingness to interpret anything and everything on the basis of scanty evidence. Universal symbolism was discarded decades ago, and no experienced therapist any longer interprets every dream of being in a tunnel as the wish to return to the womb. Before interpreting every fear as a castration anxiety, one must at least have some evidence that the fear in question is concerned with self-mutilation.

It is understandable that the student should want to find the hidden significance in his patient's every word and act. He may be disappointed when his patients do not begin immediately to produce symbolic and meaningful material, for he has the mistaken notion that this is the essence of psychotherapy. The fact is that it is not the essence of psychotherapy. In most cases, in both children and adults, we seldom fully understand the meaning of anything, let alone of everything. We may have some accurate notions, and some more educated guesses. But for the most part, we understand only a little, deal with it as it comes along, and help the patient bolster his defenses or build new ones. We provide him with the opportunity for experimenting in the relationship with new or better ways of functioning socially, and hope that this will in the long run be of benefit.

Nor do we often interpret to the patient. Usually the patient is better off without such interpretations. In the first place, they may be incorrect. In the second place, they can be threatening to the patient who will seldom understand them, and who is likely to intellectualize them or to be upset by them. If one believes, for example, that the patient's anger toward the therapist is a reaction against his homosexual feelings, one seldom tells him so. There are exceptions, of course, and in deep or long-term therapy of a patient with developing ego strength, much interpretation can be and is done. But these are the rare cases. In child psychiatry they are exceptionally rare. Gerard has stated:

Direct interpretation is possible in some instances when the evidence is very clear, when the child's ego has become sturdy enough to face the anxiety which he could not face at the time of the onset of the symptom, and when his wish to get well is strong enough to give him courage to reveal facts about himself which he believes are unacceptable. This situation rarely occurs.

It might be added that when the situation does occur, the child usually no longer needs the interpretation or the treatment.

SPECIAL TECHNIQUES

Every man's work, whether it be literature or music or pictures or architecture, or anything else, is always a portrait of himself, and the more he tries to conceal himself, the more clearly will his character appear in spite of him.

—SAMUEL BUTLER

Many special techniques have been developed for use in the psychotherapy of children. These have an important place in child psychiatry and are useful both as projective methods for diagnostic evaluation and for communication throughout therapy (Bender). Projective methods are of great importance in all phases of work with disturbed children. In all of the special techniques to be described, projective methods help the child to express his conflicts, and consequently aid the therapist to understand these conflicts. Projective methods, as defined by Frank, are those which require the individual to project his own inner life or fantasies into a situation which has been structured to a greater or lesser extent by the therapist. Regardless of the medium or material used, the child projects upon it psychologically meaningful content. Because children, in contrast to adults, are rarely able to express their difficulties verbally either spontaneously or in response to direct questioning, special techniques are used.

These techniques include the following major categories:

A. Play Therapy
   1. Directed (structured) play
   2. Free play
   3. Dramatic play
   4. Puppets

    B. Art Therapy
       1. Graphic art
       2. Clay modeling
       3. Crafts
       4. Music and dance
    C. Creative Stories
    D. Humor

PLAY THERAPY

Play techniques with toys have been used by many child therapists but the term *play therapy* has probably been most closely associated with the child analysts Melanie Klein and Anna Freud. Both utilized this procedure as a substitute for free association and dream analysis, but differed in their theoretical view of the origin and meaning of its content, and in the method of interpretation. Klein tended to view most of the child's play as stemming from his sexual and aggressive drives while Anna Freud placed greater emphasis on the importance of current experience as influencing the child's play.

Many varieties of play therapy have been described, ranging from the highly formal and structured to the completely spontaneous and unorganized. They are all useful in the appropriate situations, and something can be accomplished and learned from all of them. D. M. Levy described what he calls "release therapy," which is a structured play situation using dolls to represent specific individuals. The therapist sets up a dramatic situation, usually related to the child's own family and involving his own particular problems, and the child is encouraged to "act out" the situation with the dolls. More commonly, dolls are used in a less structured way, and the child is given the opportunity to make his own identifications. Despert has described this technique of doll play, and notes that the freedom of action thus engendered results in more spontaneous expression by the child than would otherwise be obtained. Aggression may be successfully acted out, although it must not be allowed to go beyond certain limits. Despert points out that the technique of play therapy allows development of a relationship with the therapist largely through the act of sharing with him the child's pleasure. This point cannot be overemphasized. If therapist and child can play together, with mutual and genuine enjoyment, the natural gap between an adult and a child is bridged. There is thus attained a level of relationship that is unique in psychiatry: therapist and patient having a good time together.

Many therapists prefer the less formal varieties of play, and in general these are more fun for both patient and therapist. Most therapists like to have a variety of games in the office: a deck of cards, something like darts to throw, some sort of marble game, and so on. Most games have rules, but these can be broken. The therapist who is compulsive about rules may have a difficult time of it with emotionally disturbed children. Many of these children cheat at cards, and one's only defense is to cheat back. The game sometimes deteriorates completely, but little harm is done.

Therapy cannot be all play, and the therapist must never allow matters to get out of hand. He must be able to stop the game when it becomes too wild, or when the time has come for the more sober part of treatment Some children will "use" play to avoid discussing meaningful and threatening material. On the other hand, play can be an acceptable medium for aggressive expression. And it is often useful as a kind of vehicle for carrying the conversation. The significant portions of an interview may take place across the checkerboard. Many children can more comfortably talk about themselves and their families while playing than in the more formal situation, sitting in a chair facing the therapist across his desk.

Dramatic play has been used by Susan Isaacs and others to help children to work out their inner conflicts. J. L. Moreno has developed a special form of this, called "psychodrama," which is really a form of group therapy, allowing individuals to act out social situations.

The use of puppets has been found helpful by some to allow the child to express problems which he would be unable to verbalize if the focus were on himself.

ART THERAPY

Arts and crafts are used for the same general reasons as play therapy. These, too, depend partly on the orientation of the therapist, but to a greater extent on the capacities of the child. Some children are wonderfully adept at expressing themselves in drawing, painting, or crafts. In the therapy of depressed, constricted, or unusually apprehensive children, painting and drawing are especially useful in the early stages of treatment. They may, in fact, be used throughout treatment. It is fascinating to see the evolution of a child's art work as therapy progresses. The earlier drawings are usually stereotyped and unexpressive. As the child feels more comfortable in the situation, he develops greater freedom of expression. The art then becomes an important projective technique, and the patient is encouraged to talk about his pictures, to identify the figures, and perhaps to tell stories about the picture. Therapists who use this medium extensively may become quite skilled in helping the children express themselves and work out their conflicts through the medium of art. Margaret Naumburg, long a proponent of art therapy with children, complains that art as taught in the schools is much too structured and formal, and that the children thereby miss the experience of freedom of expression. She urges that in art therapy the child be allowed to do largely as he wishes, with little urging and suggestion from the therapist. Naumburg expresses the chief function of art therapy as follows: "Since the language of images is the speech of the unconscious, it serves as a more primitive and direct mode of personal expression than words."

Rabinovitch (personal communication) warns against premature interpretation of the art work to the child, as this often has the effect of stopping all further productions. Frequently the expression through art of the child's problems is in itself therapeutic, because, as Naumburg has pointed out, it is a method of communication.

Clay modeling has been used much like the graphic arts to help children to express themselves in therapy. Bender feels it is particularly useful in dealing with body-image problems, especially genital-anal ones.

A great variety of crafts materials can be used effectively with children, and the therapist and his patient are limited only by their ingenuity and inventiveness. Younger children often enjoy cutting and pasting colored construction paper. Scrapbooks may be made from magazine clippings. Many children enjoy making puppets which can later be used for puppet play. Making costume jewelry is an appropriate activity for most girls and plastic models provide an enjoyable activity for most boys.

Music and dance are art forms which have also been used, usually as a group-therapy technique in a hospital setting.

CREATIVE STORIES

Creative stories, either written or oral, may be used as a projective therapy technique in much the same way that art therapy is used. Often the two may be combined with the child telling a story about a picture he has drawn. Some children who are particularly resistive to direct interaction with the therapist have been able to compose lengthy stories when allowed to use a dictating machine or tape recorder. As in play therapy, the amount of structuring varies and the stories may be told or written by the child with little direction from the therapist, or the therapist may structure the situation by "setting the stage" for the story or even by telling part of the story himself, and then having the child continue at a given signal.

A twelve-year-old boy whose conflicts centered around the divorce of his parents, told a story about "Three Bears," by which he was able to verbalize indirectly his concerns about the divorce, and his hope for a reconciliation between the parents. The story was about "a bear who didn't want to leave his cub." In explanation to the therapist Don said that it was

usual for parent bears to send the baby bear up a tree when he was a certain age and old enough to leave the family. In the story the parent bears
really didn't want to send him away, but since it was the thing to do, they
had to. However, they both wanted the baby bear, and several times they
both came back to get him, but when the mama and papa bear saw each
other, they bared their teeth, snarled at each other, turned around, and
went away. But then, both of them came back at the same time and said,
"Why don't we take him home and keep him?" and lived happily ever
after. When Don was asked how the little bear felt when he was up in the
tree, he said, "It was pretty silly at first when they both started coming
back," and then added, "He didn't know which one to go with, but finally
they lived happily ever after."

A useful technique for children who are less creative involves the therapist's setting up hypothetical situations which he may make more vivid by
illustrating them with little sketches. Artistic talent on the part of the
therapist is not a requisite here, and stick figures will do. The therapist may
draw sketches of several boys to whom he assigns various attributes. With
an oppositional child, for example, he may draw three boys who say "No!"
The first boy says "No" all the time. The second one says "No," but
doesn't really mean it. The third boy says "No," but then he says "Yes." By
questioning the child about why each of the boys says "No," a great deal of
information may be gained about the dynamics of the child's own negativism. Although the child may know very well who the real topic of discussion is, by focusing on an anonymous boy on paper the situation becomes
much less threatening to his own integrity and self-esteem. This technique
may be tailored to fit almost any situation, and is particularly useful for
learning about the motivation for the child's interaction with others.

HUMOR

A fourth special technique widely used in child psychiatry is humor.
Since children are much more fun-oriented than adults, humor can be used
with nearly every disturbed child in both diagnostic and therapeutic ways.
Shaw observes that "For the child psychiatrist, humor is an indispensable
diagnostic and therapeutic tool. Some use it often, others seldom; some
employ it deliberately and with a careful awareness of its meanings, others
more spontaneously and intuitively." Like play therapy, humor is enjoyed
by the child, and it signals that the therapist is participating in and finding
genuine pleasure in the child's activities. Additionally, it is superbly fitted
to projective use. In a humor-oriented interview, the child can discuss subjects or express thoughts that he would not be able to approach directly. By
approaching a subject in a humorous context, there comes into existence a

kind of mutually understood pact that the subject, however forbidden or conflictual, is being treated lightly and in fun. The child may be quite aware of the significance of the interview, but is willing to go ahead under these conditions. He feels assured that the therapist will not hurt or disappoint him. It was perhaps with this aspect in mind that Freud (1953) asserted, "Humour possesses a dignity which is wholly lacking, for instance, in wit; for the aim of wit is simply to afford gratification."

The following illustrates the use of humor to explore and quantify a child's hostile-aggressive feelings toward members of his family. An eight-year-old neurotic boy was responding delightedly in a humor-oriented interview, and it was decided to explore the family dynamics. The therapist asked, "Listen, Jimmy, what are we going to do about this awful sister of yours?" "Let's drown her." "Where?" "In a river." Then (to quantify the hostility): "In a deep river or a shallow river?" "A deep river." (Huge delight) "And what about mother?" (Loudly and exultantly) "Drown her in a big lake!" "All right, and what about Dad?" "Oh, just put him in a little puddle." "A mud puddle?" "Yes." "And then push him over?" "No, just let him get his feet wet." Such an interview provides more accurate and meaningful information than asking a child directly which person he hates the most—sister, mother, or father. Also, it is much more successful in developing the relationship, and in enhancing the feeling of mutual trust between therapist and child.

While some therapists are more naturally facile in using humor than are others, nevertheless, everyone can learn something of the techniques. The way of all learning is to try to emulate one's teachers, and to correct one's errors. At the risk of losing some professional dignity, and perhaps at times appearing a little foolish, it may be possible to enhance the child's enjoyment of himself, and to share in that enjoyment. The enjoyment of humor is in fact a direct and primitive gratification of the pleasure-wish; it is a regression in which one gets a bit closer to childhood, and thus closer to the child. Freud (1938) said it best, when he observed that in wit, humor, and the comic, the adult is seeking, "the state of a bygone time, . . . the state of our childhood in which we did not know the comic, were incapable of wit, and did not need humor to make us happy."

TREATMENT OF ADOLESCENTS

Adolescence can be a delightful and wonderfully exciting age. Perhaps at no other time of life does the human being experience more excitement and pleasure, or more sorrow and misery. To the adolescent, everything has heightened meaning, every minute is important, and if a moment is not full of interest it is full of boredom. There are no neutral emotions, and there is little relaxation. To the parent and the therapist, an adolescent is a continually changing source of pleasure, pride, worry, and despair.

No one has described better than Anna Freud (1946a) the enigma and the paradox that is the adolescent:

> Adolescents are excessively egoistic, regarding themselves as the center of the universe and the sole object of interest, and yet at no time in later life are they capable of so much self-sacrifice and devotion. They form the most passionate love relations, only to break them off as abruptly as they began. On one hand they throw themselves enthusiastically into the life of the community, and, on the other, they have an over-powering longing for solitude. They oscillate between blind submission to some self-chosen leader and defiant rebellion against any and every authority. They are selfish and materially minded and at the same time full of lofty idealism. They are ascetic but will suddenly plunge into instinctual indulgence of the most primitive character. At times their behavior to other people is rough and inconsiderate, yet they themselves are extremely touchy. Their moods veer between light-hearted optimism and blackest pessimism. Sometimes they will work with indefatigable enthusiasm and at other times they are sluggish and apathetic.

Most of what has been said in this chapter regarding psychotherapy with children can be applied to adolescents, but it should be doubled or tripled. Relationship is all-important, and the therapist may expect to be drawn into active involvement in the adolescent's entangled life. Control is all-important, and the therapist must be able to rule with an iron glove encasing a soft and tender hand. Flexibility of approach is essential, and the harassed therapist must be ready to shift at a moment's notice from dealing with a young girl at the height of ecstasy and optimism to one shaken by sobs of grief and hopelessness. He must expect his help and support to be sought, implored, even begged for, only to find that suddenly he is not wanted, that his interest is not appreciated, indeed, that it is even resented as meddling and interference. It has been said of psychiatrists that one need not necessarily be a masochist to deal with adolescents, but it helps.

The excitement and heightened interest of adolescence are libidinal, biological, and diffusely directed. The adolescent is generally not seeking direct gratification. He or she does not usually know how. He simply has to do something, and he may do almost anything. He is not only full of excitement and drive, but he is in much conflict. The conflicts are of many kinds, but are usually, in one way or another, conflicts between wishes to become an adult and to remain a child. Thus, wishing desperately for independence and at the same time longing for the old, safe, dependent state, the adolescent has especial difficulty accepting the role of patient. He wants to respect and admire his therapist and at the same time he is contemptuous of him, convinced that the therapist is hopelessly out of touch with the new and important trends in society. Sometimes he may even feel a bit sorry for the therapist, and this is the unkindest cut of all.

Yet, they come to us for help, and this is one of the significant differences between treatment of children and adolescents. The adolescent may come on his own, or at least he will take some of the responsibility for getting himself there. He is beginning to be like an adult in that he recognizes his difficulties, and is sometimes motivated to do something about them. He is introspective; and this is the second unique factor in adolescent psychotherapy. He likes to talk about himself, think about himself, even philosophize about himself. He may become altruistic, which is a typically adolescent capacity, one which disappears altogether in the realism of adulthood, leaving its traces only in those adults who are forever immature or in those with a touch of greatness. The altruism of the adolescent is a displacement of libido onto "higher" endeavors, a kind of sublimation attending to the good of others. It is a defense which one respects most highly, perhaps even envies a little.

Another aspect which is emphasized in psychotherapy with adolescents is the sense of past and future. The adolescent, though he often denies it, is concerned with the roots of his past, and his prospects for the future. He has begun to be aware of himself as an individual in the adult world, in the world of work and responsibility. He is in the process of appraising his capacities and his weaknesses, and he can be benefited by mature counsel, by being helped to understand these parts of himself better, and thus in making reasonable plans. In the process of disowning the security of the past, he needs a sense of security for the future.

In general, good emotional adjustment throughout childhood will continue through adolescence, and the emotionally disturbed adolescent will usually be found to have had a disturbed childhood. But many of the children do not come to psychiatric attention until they are in their teens because the earlier symptoms were not severe enough. The exaggeration and intensification of affects and of acting-out behavior at this time demand intervention. Here, as in treatment of children, the focus is chiefly on the present. One deals mainly with present difficulties, and helps the adolescent through present relationships, rather than through recapitulation of his past traumas. This is true even of psychoanalysis with adolescents. Eissler, in a paper which should be read by all psychiatrists dealing with adolescents, has described the modifications of technique and aims of therapy in the psychoanalysis of adolescents. He emphasizes attention to present problems and the necessity for close involvement with the patient's daily difficulties, noting that the adolescent is not interested in recounting for hours on end recollections from his early life. Eissler comments, almost plaintively, that he has never been able to complete the analysis of an adolescent, adding that Aichhorn claims to have done so in one case.

Holmes emphasizes the importance of speaking with complete frankness and directness to adolescents, and uses the term *abnormal candor* to describe the conversational atmosphere in which the adolescent functions best. He stresses the need for departing from the conventional views of therapy when one is working with adolescents. Josselyn warns against overwhelming the adolescent by interpreting too deeply. She feels that rather than an intensive interpretive type of therapy the treatment of choice is one in which the patient is "protected from the external situations that excessively stimulate his internal drives" and one which gives him "an opportunity to sublimate his unacceptable primitive drives into socially acceptable, psychologically constructive paths."

They are a fascinating and frightening lot, these teenagers. To deal with them is no undertaking for the faint-hearted, or for the therapist who likes his fifty-minute hour on schedule and then on to the next case. Anna Freud (1958) has said that "the treatment of adolescents is a hazardous venture from beginning to end." But the work can be immensely rewarding, and there is immeasurable satisfaction in helping a potential hoodlum to become a happy and productive citizen. But don't expect him to be grateful; for as you watch, pleased with your success, he is on his way with scarcely a backward glance—he no longer needs your help, there are things to do, and the future is ahead.

THE RESULTS OF THERAPY

Of the patients who receive psychiatric treatment, some get better, some do not change significantly, and some get worse. Does the therapy have any effect on these results, and if so, how much? It is difficult to conceive of a more important question in psychiatry, yet the amount of investigation directed toward answering this fundamental question has been almost infinitesimal. In fact, Eysenck concludes from an extensive survey of the literature that there has been to date only one study of the results of psychotherapy from which important and valid conclusions may be drawn —the Cambridge-Somerville Study on the treatment of delinquency (Powers and Witmer).

It would appear almost as if psychiatrists do not want to know whether their work is of any value. Certainly it is more comfortable to carry on one's daily work under the assumption that something is being accomplished. To question this assumption can be unpleasant, and perhaps threatening. Besides, it entails extra work, and meanwhile there are more patients to be seen and only enough time for a fraction of them. Research appears to be a luxury, and the busy practitioner can little afford it.

Moreover, the question is not easy to answer, even if full time could be allotted to it. Ideally, the answer requires a research design in which the patients occur in matched pairs, one of whom receives therapy while the other does not. After a period of time (a year? ten years? a lifetime?) answers may begin to trickle in. Such a study is an undertaking of enormous proportions, far beyond the scope of any one psychiatrist, or of most institutions. The Cambridge-Somerville Youth Study, cited in the chapter in delinquency (Chapter 13), was a study of this type, encompassing a circumscribed segment of psychiatric disorders. But this has been called a courageous undertaking and was a rare event in research.

Besides the matched-pair technique, there is the method of follow-up study, usually done in a guidance-clinic setting, in which a group of treated cases are compared at follow-up with a group of more or less similar cases who for various reasons did not receive therapy. Sargent has discussed certain of the methodological difficulties in such follow-up studies. Major difficulties which she mentions are:

1. Accurate assessment of whether or not improvement has occurred is difficult.

   a. Effects of therapy may not appear until long after treatment, when they have been incorporated into ongoing patterns of growth and development.

   b. Criteria for improvement involve subjective judgments, and are highly complex, encompassing many areas of functioning.

2. Collection of data is often difficult or impossible.

   a. Following discharge from treatment, the relationship of the patient and his family with the therapist is altered. If no longer needing treatment, the family may resent the inquiry.

   b. Even when they are co-operative, patient and family may have selectively forgotten much of the previous difficulty and be unable to give valid comparisons between the former and the present state.

   c. The setting of follow-up studies is often other than the therapist's office, perhaps in the patient's home. Here, the relationship is likewise altered, and the therapist's impressions of the patients may be significantly influenced.

   d. Adequate follow-up requires information from sources other than the patient, but the family may be understandably reluctant to have relatives, neighbors, employers, and school authorities approached regarding the patient's follow-up adjustment.

Another difficulty is the problem of adequate controls. In those studies in which controls consist of patients who were seen for evaluation but were not treated, an important issue is the reason why they were not treated. This question is not usually explored, but one can assume a priori that in many cases, these reasons are of sufficient significance in the patient's life situation to make him unsuited as a control subject. If, for example, the parents are insufficiently motivated to bring the patient regularly to the clinic, then this patient cannot validly be compared with one whose parents are so motivated.

Heinicke and Goldman critically reviewed the literature up to 1959 on follow-up studies of psychotherapy with children, and evaluated the results of 17 reported studies. The combined results, obtained from a total of 4,010 cases, showed the following outcome:

    Successfully adjusted—45 per cent

    Partially improved—34 per cent

    No improvement—21 per cent

The authors point out, however, that the question of whether the same amount of improvement would have occurred without therapy has, in most cases, not been answered, inasmuch as control groups were not studied. They then reviewed more intensively two studies which did employ control groups, and, combining the data from these two studies, found the following results:

	Treated (Percentage)	Untreated (Percentage)
Successful adjustment	52	37
Partially improved	22	36
No improvement	26	28
Number of cases	393	160

The differences, in the above table, between the untreated and treated groups in successful and partially-improved results were statistically significant. Heinicke and Goldman concluded that the two best studies of follow-up results of outpatient treatment in a guidance-clinic setting indicate that the therapy was of definite value. Yet these results are far from striking. What they actually appear to show is that about 15 per cent of the children who did not receive treatment would have benefited by treatment, in that they would have shifted from the partially-improved to the successful-outcome category. These findings further imply that those children who did not improve without treatment would not have improved even if they had been treated. Surely, if true, this is an extremely important finding. It suggests that therapists need not feel too badly about treatment failures, but should make every effort to select in advance those cases which are potentially treatable.

Fortunately, there is another way to evaluate the results of therapy, and that is by using the individual patient as his own control. This is the familiar before-and-after technique, and has been honorably and satisfactorily employed in medical research for centuries. Its results have attested to the value of incantations, voodoo and the like, in almost any illness; of stump water in curing warts; and, more recently, of the sulfonamide drugs in coccal infections. Obviously, the significance of the results varies with the interpreter. But the technique can produce results which are scientifically beyond reproach. The course of pneumococcal pneumonia was well known and documented. When the first case of pneumonia to receive sulfanilimide showed an immediate and marked deviation from the classical course, it could have been attributed to chance. When the second case did likewise, only the most skeptical could have been unmoved. By the fifth case, all doubt was removed, and a new era in medicine had begun.

In psychotherapy, results as convincing as the above are sometimes achieved. The boy mentioned earlier in this chapter, the one who thought the world was overpopulated with females, had been chronically negative, failing in school, morose, miserably unhappy. He had been getting progressively worse for at least three years. Following two interviews, in which he ventilated his feelings about his selfish sisters and his rejecting father, as well as an interview between the therapist and the father in which the latter was instructed explicitly in the many ways in which he was damaging the boy, and also a long talk with the school principal and teacher regarding management of the boy's aggression, the entire situation shifted dramatically from the negative to the positive. The boy suddenly felt that things were good, that the future was hopeful, that he was not a failure, that he had been right all along about his father's being selfish (he was), and that the therapist was interested in him and would continue to help him. The mother reported "It's the first time in three years I've seen him really enjoying himself."

Naturally, the above case was not "cured" in two weeks. But the early gains were maintained, and after three months of weekly visits, in which the boy continued to develop his ego strength and to consolidate his defenses, treatment was discontinued, with the case being kept "open" so that the mother could occasionally phone or at least know that the therapist was available in case there was need.

Could such a result have happened "by chance?" The answer is "No." Statisticians may argue ad nauseam that nothing can be learned from a sample of one. But it can. From a sample of one, one can learn that when a pin is stuck into a balloon, the balloon bursts. In the above case, it is known that the treatment effected the improvement, because the processes of the therapy were intimately linked to the course of the improvement. Also, much of what happened is known: what the child did, what he felt, what he thought, the responses that he made to the changes in his thinking. The therapist knows that a relationship existed between himself and the child, he experienced it, and he felt the depth of its meaning to the child. He knows that this relationship was a significant factor in the child's subsequent functioning.

This is not to say that we know everything that happens in treatment, or even that we necessarily know what all the critical factors are. But the therapist senses when there is a genuine relationship in the therapy, and when the therapy is significant in affecting the patient's life. The honest therapist also knows that this by no means always occurs, and that, no matter how hard he tries, he often fails. But he cannot state with precision that a certain percentage of his cases improve to this degree, another percentage to that degree. Human happiness and misery are not thus measured.

Psychotherapy is no panacea; the best therapist in the world can help only a limited number of problems. An important task of the therapist, and of psychiatry, is to learn better which cases are amenable to psychotherapy and which are not. Nolan Lewis, speaking on the future of psychotherapy, remarked: "There will probably come to be a greater recognition of the limitations of psychotherapy, and a greater awareness of the fostering and retarding effects of the social environment on its results." To which the writer would add that the child's psychotherapy must be, not isolated from, but a significant part of, his social environment.

REFERENCES

Allen, F. H. Psychotherapy with Children, New York, W. W. Norton Co., 1942.

Bender, L. Child Psychiatric Techniques, Springfield, Ill., Charles C Thomas, 1952.

Colby, K. A Primer for Psychotherapists, New York, Ronald Press, 1951.

Despert, J. L. Play Analysis in Research and Therapy, in Modern Trends in Child Psychiatry, eds. Lewis and Pacella, New York, International Universities Press, 1945.

Dubo, S., and Rabinovitch, R. D. Child Psychiatry, in Progress in Neurology and Psychiatry, ed. S. Spiegel, New York, Grune & Stratton, 1953, Vol. 8.

Eisenberg, L. The Strategic Deployment of the Child Psychiatrist in Preventive Psychiatry, J. Child Psychol. & Psychiat., 2: 229, 1961.

Eissler, K. Ego-Psychological Implications of the Psychoanalytic Treatment of Delinquents, Psychoanalytic Study of the Child, New York, International Universities Press, 1950, Vol. 5.

Eysenck, H. J. The Effects of Psychotherapy, in Handbook of Abnormal Psychology, ed. Eysenck, New York, Basic Books, 1961.
Fraiberg, S. Applications of Psychoanalytic Principles in Casework Practice with Children, Quart. J. Child Behavior, 3: 175, 1951.
———— Counseling for the Parents of the Very Young Child, Social Casework, 35: 47, 1954.
Frank, L. K. Projective Methods for the Study of Personality, Springfield, Ill., Charles C Thomas, 1948.
Freud, A. The Ego and the Mechanisms of Defense, New York, International Universities Press, 1946a.
———— The Psychoanalytic Treatment of Children, London, Imago, 1946b.
———— Adolescence, Psychoanalytic Study of the Child, New York, International Universities Press, 1958, Vol. 13.
Freud, S. Wit and the Various Forms of the Comic, in Basic Writings of Sigmund Freud, ed. A. A. Brill, New York, Random House, 1938.
———— Humour, in Collected Papers, London, Hogarth Press, 1953, Vol. 5.
Gerard, M. W. Direct Treatment of the Child, in Orthopsychiatry 1923–1948, eds. Lowrey and Sloan, New York, American Orthopsychiatric Association, 1948.
Gitelson, M. Direct Psychotherapy of Children, Arch. Neurol. Psychiatry, 43: 1208, 1940.
Heinicke, C. M., and Goldman, A. Research on Psychotherapy with Children: A Review and Suggestions for Further Study, Am. J. Orthopsychiatry, 30: 483, 1960.
Holmes, D. J. The Adolescent in Psychotherapy, Boston, Little, Brown and Co. 1964.
Hug-Hellmuth, H. On the Technique of Child Analysis, Internat. J. Psychoanal., 2: 287, 1921.
Isaacs, S. Childhood and After, New York, International Universities Press, 1949.
Josselyn, I. The Adolescent and his World, New York, Family Service Association of America, 1952.
Klein, M. The Psycho-Analysis of Children, London, International Psycho-Analytic Press, 1932.
Levy, D. M. Release Therapy, Am. J. Orthopsychiatry, 9: 713, 1939.
Lewis, N. The Future of Psychotherapy, Am. J. Psychotherapy, 15: 184, 1961.
Lippman, H. S. Treatment of the Child in Emotional Conflict, 2nd ed., New York, McGraw-Hill Co., 1962.
Moreno, J. L. Psychodrama, New York, Beacon House, 1945.
Naumburg, M. Fantasy and Reality in the Art Expression of Behavior Problem Children, in Modern Trends in Child Psychiatry, eds. Lewis and Pacella, New York, International Universities Press, 1945.
Powers, E. and Witmer, H. An Experiment in the Prevention of Delinquency, New York, Columbia University Press, 1951.
Sargent, H. D. Methodological Problems of Followup Studies in Psychotherapy Research, Am. J. Orthopsychiatry, 30: 495, 1960.
Schmideberg, M. Short Analytic Therapy, The Nervous Child, 8: 281, 1949.
Shaw, C. R. The Use of Humor in Child Psychiatry, Am. J. Psychotherapy, 15: 368, 1961.

17

RESIDENTIAL TREATMENT

Traditionally, psychiatric treatment of children required that the child be brought to the clinic or office for individual therapy. If he was too disturbed, or if his home was too disturbed, he was placed in a foster home or incarcerated at a mental hospital, detention home, or jail. Here he might occasionally be seen by a psychiatrist, but not often enough to be considered in psychotherapy.

It became apparent that, for some children, the advantages of these two treatment approaches could be combined into a setting away from home which would provide the child with a therapeutic environment, psychiatrically oriented, and with sufficient external control to prevent his getting into trouble with society. Dubo and Rabinovitch wrote, in 1957:

> Over the past ten years we have noted . . . the development of interest in the field of inpatient treatment for emotionally disturbed children. Experience and evaluative research in our guidance clinics have shown that a good many children cannot be treated successfully while they remain at home; a totally planned treatment program, emphasizing the living experience, has been shown to be necessary for these severely disturbed youngsters.

The idea of providing the child with a therapeutic environment is perhaps not altogether new, but its realization is fairly recent. Prior to 1940, intensive treatment inpatient units for emotionally disturbed children existed at perhaps no more than a dozen centers. Among the first to be established were the children's ward of Bellevue Hospital in New York City and the Child Guidance Home in Cincinnati, both in the 1920's. The Children's Bureau in 1952 compiled a list of residential treatment centers for children. The total number in this country at that time was 36. Since then, more have been established, others are in the planning stages, and it appears likely that the number of such institutions will continue to increase. In 1961 the Children's Bureau listed 80, but it is doubtful that all of these

344

institutions meet the criteria of a true residential treatment center. Hylton, under the auspices of the Child Welfare League of America selected 21 residential treatment centers and 2 day care centers for a detailed study, and in 1964 published her report of these centers from the viewpoint of the kinds of children served, the program, the staff, and the costs.

Residential treatment centers vary widely in size, philosophy, aims, and methods, and because of their recency, there has not yet been time for much evaluative research. It cannot be stated with certainty that this or that approach is better, that a particular staff-patient ratio, size of patient group, daily schedule, and so on, are optimal. In some cases, the criterion for success has been simply that the institution has continued to operate. Some have not met even this criterion, and Dubo and Rabinovitch warn: "In the absence of any proven tradition, there has been much trial and error, and a significant number of projects have foundered."

In the discussion below, much of the material represents the writer's opinion based on personal observation and experience. It is not claimed that the particular type of inpatient program here outlined is the only feasible one, but by current standards it is a reasonably successful one.

TOTAL MILIEU THERAPY

The concept of total milieu therapy implies that the child's entire daily environment be so ordered and conceived by the professional staff as to provide a therapeutic experience. Thus, the inpatient unit is much more than a place where the patient lives in order to be away from his family and to be available to his therapist for an occasional scheduled hour of psychotherapy. Alt states that the treatment philosophy to be effective in influencing the child must be "expressed in every phase of the milieu (and) incorporated in attitudes of adults in the design of living, and in specific methods of child management and therapy."

Redl notes that there are many different levels of milieu therapy. These range from the most primitive, which Redl characterizes by the philosophy, "Don't put poison in their soup," to the highest level, which he calls "re-education for life." He points out that, while the therapeutic milieu is usually talked of in vague generalities, it is in actuality as real a part of the child's surroundings as the room in which he sleeps. In a therapeutic setting, the attempt is made to understand the milieu, and to control it to the advantage of the child. The milieu consists of people: children, professional staff, janitors and cooks, visitors. It also consists of buildings, the rooms where the child works and plays and sleeps, the outdoors. It includes the child's possessions, books, television, letters from home, telephone calls, and sometimes a dog or the animals in the science room. For each child, his milieu is the constellation of stimuli that is impinging upon him at each moment, and it is changing continuously. While it cannot be expected that everyone involved understands all that operates in the milieu, there is a great deal of it that can be understood, and much of it can be determined and controlled.

The therapeutic milieu is in large part determined by the director of the institution. His personality, teachings, and philosophy will influence every aspect, and the success or failure of the institution rests almost exclusively upon him. He not only controls the physical environment, the staff, and the program, but he is the one who sets the whole tone of the institution. He does this in countless ways: by selection of his staff and by removal of those members whom he does not want; through the rules and regulations which he orders; most importantly, through his own values and attitudes which he imparts consciously and unconsciously, directly and indirectly, by approval and disapproval, example, teaching, and supervision. The children's treatment center, like any institution, is a representation of the personality of its director. Consequently, every institution will be unique. There are, however, requirements which each must meet in order to be therapeutic. These will now be considered.

All-important is the tone of the institution. To be therapeutic, the tone must include personal warmth and maturity. There must be among the staff a sense of responsibility and of interest in the children, together with some spontaneity, a feeling that the worker may do within reasonable limits what it is his nature to do, and without the continual need for caution against "making a mistake." The tone often includes a sense of humor, and an appreciation of the humor in children. It includes a flexibility of approach, with the capacity for adapting to new situations in new and spontaneous ways. The therapeutic tone cannot operate in the presence of excessive feelings of counteraggression and hostility among the staff; yet, it recognizes that everyone has these feelings, and that to experience and express them occasionally is not a crime. Nor can the therapeutic tone encompass too strong a feeling of attachment to children, too much need for love and for the expression of love; for the motivation to help would then represent only the pathological need of the staff member. Also, the children's institution cannot stand too much on professional dignity, or on an inordinate need for professional status. A hierarchy, if it is to exist, must develop naturally, based on genuine skills and capacities.

THE THERAPEUTIC PROCESS

Redl has said that milieu therapy is re-education for life. The process of therapy is then a process of education, or rather, of re-education. Old ways are changed—old patterns are replaced by new ones.

The child who comes into the treatment center comes from an environment which somehow fostered his disturbance, or at least sustained it. The new environment, inevitably a major alteration in the child's experience, is bound to effect changes in him. Many of these will, a priori, be therapeutic, for they represent removal of those very factors which have operated to perpetuate his disorder. Some symptoms vanish suddenly and miraculously, even symptoms which had been severe and chronic.

Thus, the night terrors of Billy (the boy in Chapter 7) disappeared on the day he entered, along with his school phobia. Some children, oppositional, defiant, and stubborn at home, become compliant and respectful of the staff the moment they cross the new threshold. But not always, and not always permanently. Often the change is transient, or the old symptom is replaced by a new one. But learning inevitably occurs, and the aim of therapy is to influence the learning process wisely, and to avoid interfering with it where it is progressing well.

Seen in terms of learning theory, the treatment process is a complex kind of reconditioning. Many of the old stimuli are no longer being applied, and the old responses are extinguished. Thus the school phobic, no longer faced with the issue of being separated from his mother each morning, ceases to experience the displaced fear when he enters the schoolroom. Likewise, the old reinforcements no longer operate. The staff do not respond to the child's behavior as, for example, his mother did. His aggression fails to incite the same counteraggression, his panic does not awaken the old responses of anxiety and overconcern.

Sometimes the changes come slowly. Deeply ingrained processes are not always readily altered. Moreover, the child's reactions to the new and unfamiliar, to the frustrations that often accompany the failure of old and gratifying defenses, can themselves create new problems and new conflicts.

There are countless facets to the treatment process, and the needs of every child are different. These needs involve such things as his specific skills and capacities, his tolerance for change, the degree of his warmth, his motivation for improvement, and his anxiety. They require a consideration of the child's past, the way he has formerly been treated by people, the amount of his trust or mistrust. They are concerned with environmental realities: What will his parents do? Where will he go next? Should he be allowed to visit home? All these and many other needs and questions are constantly reconsidered and re-evaluated by those involved in the child's treatment, and, prescription-like, the changing needs are met in ways that are hopefully therapeutic.

In the residential treatment center, the child finds an environment that can tolerate more from him than can the community. Likewise, the center is better able to control and direct him, its authority is more certain, it is less reactive to his temperament.

Greater tolerance, firmer control, consistency, and the association with adults who are warm, mature, and interested in him—these are among the ingredients that the treatment center provides. No child can be wholly unaffected by the experience. Even against his will he responds. He responds to the people who are "nice" to him even though he sees himself as bad, useless, and a failure. Inevitably, his self-percept is altered.

It is a form of brain-washing, the therapeutic process. The child is a captive, and, like most brain-washed prisoners, he succumbs, at least to some degree. The changes in him may be profound and lasting. For, unlike the adult, the potential for change is considerable in the growing child. It is this which provides the high chances for success in therapy, and which also makes so great the therapist's responsibility to treat wisely and well.

THE STAFF

Inpatient institutions for total milieu therapy of disturbed children are still very much in the experimental stage, and opinions vary as to the number and kinds of professional workers which, ideally, should constitute the staff. While the specialties presented in the following discussion are, for the most part, included in the programs of the majority of inpatient centers, it must be recognized that specific representations are based mainly on the writer's personal experience.

The staff includes the following:
1. Psychiatrists
2. Clinical psychologists
3. Psychiatric social workers
4. Psychiatric nurses
5. Special-education teachers
6. Language therapists
7. Occupational therapists
8. Child-care workers

In addition there may be group therapists and recreational therapists, although these are often included among the child-care workers.

GENERAL FUNCTIONS OF THE STAFF

As a member of the therapeutic group, each staff member has a responsibility to function in a therapeutic manner in his relationship with the children. This requires that he or she should have a certain knowledge and understanding of the principles of psychiatry and abnormal psychology. Additionally, it requires that he have some knowledge of the individual child. Emphasis must be on a diagnostic orientation. While we may generalize about the needs of disturbed children, saying that they all require understanding, acceptance, and control, the needs of each child must be met individually. For example, a child's expression of hostility toward a teacher may have many different mechanisms: It may represent an exaggerated adolescent need for independence; it may be a displacement of hostility toward a punitive father; in a brain-damaged boy, it may be partly an impairment of impulse control; in a neurotic child it may be a reaction to chronic rejection by all authorities; it may be an attempt to test the strength of a teacher's feelings of concern for the patient, or it may be a reaction to feelings of guilt and self-blame over his parents' divorce, or even chronic illness, or any number of things, all of which result in a wish for punishment.

Each staff member who has any sustained and meaningful contact with a child must have some understanding of the mechanisms of the child's psychopathology, the explanations for his behavior, and an awareness of his specific needs in the relationship. Thus, the masochistically oriented child will interpret the teacher's efforts at control as punishment and rejection. He is likely to respond better to a sympathetic and individualized approach. The brain-damaged child functions better in a well-controlled environment; a hyperactive, stimulating group excites him and drives him to further tension and acting out. He may respond better to a brief period of isolation from the group, or to an approach which imposes firm restrictions both on his own acting out and that of the group. With experience, professional staff develop their skills and knowledge about the various kinds of psychiatric disorders, and learn to individualize their approaches to the children.

In a therapeutic milieu, where the tone is as described above, staff members recognize mutually that working with disturbed children is at times difficult, and they can feel able to ask for and to accept whatever assistance they need in helping the children. Among a group of trained and professionally-oriented workers, there is mutual respect and recognition that each member can help the other. The psychiatrist recognizes that the contributions of the other specialists are as essential as his own. Moreover, he must be able to accept without feeling unduly threatened that the other workers may have a better understanding of the child's functioning in certain areas, and may in fact contribute more to the total therapeutic experience than does the therapist. At the same time, the other members must accept the fact that the therapist prescribes the treatment program.

There is a major distinction between the functions of the therapist and those of the other members of the therapeutic group, and this must be recognized by all. Briefly expressed, the therapist does therapy while the other staff members provide therapeutic support and education. As an illustration, when a child gets angry at the teacher, throws his book on the floor, and shouts, "I hate arithmetic," the teacher deals with the situation in the appropriate way; perhaps he takes the child aside and suggests that they try the problem again, or that the child work on something else, or perhaps sends him back to his room, or calls his therapist. He does not take him to his office and ask probing questions about the child's feelings about arithmetic, or ask why he feels in a bad humor today, or suggest that the reason he is angry at himself is because of his feelings about his roommate or about his mother, or the like. This is the therapist's job, and should be dealt with as part of the individual psychotherapy. The therapist should be informed that the child is having problems that day. He may wish to talk with the child at that time, or later at the regularly scheduled interview, or perhaps not at all. Inexperienced staff members, particularly those in training for higher professional levels, are often interested in and intrigued by the possible meaning of a child's behavior, and cannot resist the temptation to probe his psyche. This is understandable, but it must be discouraged. At the same time, the staff's interests in the child need not be rebuffed, lest they feel unnecessarily discouraged or frustrated in their efforts to help the children.

COMMUNICATION AMONG THE STAFF

It is impossible to exaggerate the importance of good communication. The operation of the treatment center is as dependent on its lines of communication as is the operation of an army, and if the communications break down, the entire operation flounders. If the child's treatment is to succeed, the program must be an integrated one. Everyone involved in a child's treatment must know what his program is: its aims, the functions of the other staff, the child's progress, and the modifications which so frequently occur. If, for example, the child's therapist decides that he needs to be handled more firmly, and not allowed to act out his aggression so much, then everyone directly involved with the child must know of the altered programs: his teacher, the charge nurse, the child care workers, the occupational therapy worker, and, sometimes, the child himself. To communicate this information, a variety of channels may be used—scheduled staff conferences, written memos, informal contacts by telephone or in the hallways or the coffee room—it makes little difference where, so long as the information is transmitted.

Another kind of information which is essential is a daily report to each concerned staff member on each child's activities and behavior of the previous day. This may be done in the daily morning meetings, or by the use of staff notes in each child's chart. One efficient and effective method is to compile notes from the previous day and evening, selecting those items of particular significance and interest, and to mimeograph from these a report of the entire patient group. When the staff member arrives in the morning, he finds on his desk a one-page summary of the significant happenings of the previous day and evening. It is not necessary to include each child, only those whose behavior warranted some comment. Thus, if a therapist glances through the daily summary and does not find the names of any of his patients, he can assume that his children were exemplary. If, on the other hand, there are numerous references to his charges, he knows he is in for a difficult day.

The daily summary is valuable not only for apprising each therapist about his own patients. A quick perusal imparts a general feeling of what the day was like, its whole emotional tone, whether it was a quiet day or a noisy one, whether the group was reasonably controlled or "high." The director, reading the summary, knows whether he can relax at his desk and dictate letters, or whether he must march sternly forth to battle.

Following is a sample copy of a daily patient report:

Day report, Monday—Ward:
John G. needing frequent bed restrictions, much talk about syringes. Joe P. seeking favors from staff, sent from class for disruptive, profane behavior. Fred talking about his placement, aggressively playful with little boys. Donna hostile toward Betty G. Quite stimulated by Jean M. Betty G. clinging, hyperactive, very aggressive in gym with equipment, sent back from class for fighting with peer. Melanie Raymond admitted at 3:00 p.m. (age 11, schizophrenic, Dr. Scott).

Evening report, Monday—Ward:
Jean F. transferred from cottage #2, a little stimulated by the activity of moving but settled well. Betty G. often silly and loud. Dave M. blew up in gym area at supper and sent to quiet room. Ronnie was unable to settle down, became very negative, defiant, and went to quiet room where he ripped off his clothing and threw it through hole in door, needing constant staff support to complete evening without further incident. Melanie R. asked a lot of questions about rules and limits, volunteered a lot of information about herself, had no apparent anxiety. Joe P. often negative, using a lot of profanity.

Midnight report, Monday—Ward:
Melanie R. would not settle down and go to sleep. Extremely agreeable but very bizarre in her comments. Seconal, 100 mg, at 11:30 p. m. but sat on edge of bed and did not lie down until 2:00 a.m. Jean F. up frequently between 4 and 6 a.m. Boys slept well.

Day report, Monday—Cottage #5:
Tone in A.M. very poor with boys being negative, whiny, hostile. Bennie upset over his watch missing and cried when he had to turn in money. Mike S. soiled in early morning. Bert A. teasing, provoking peers. Alan G. moody.

Evening report, Monday—Cottage #5:
Mike S. soiled once. Bill L. had difficulty in gym (see chart). Stuttering improved with help from staff. Bert, Fred, and Don rather high.

Midnight report, Monday—Cottage #5:
Good night although Tommy was unable to sleep and appeared anxious. Seen by Dr. D. at 11:45 and reassured; went to sleep shortly and slept for remainder of night.

So ends another routine day, with the children asleep and untroubled.

THE THERAPIST

Each child should have a therapist, and should receive from two to five hours of individual psychotherapy per week. Traditionally, therapists are either psychiatrists, clinical psychologists, or psychiatric social workers (or trainees in these three professions). However, formal training is not necessarily a prerequisite for doing good therapy. At Hawthorn Center, one of the most accomplished therapists is a man whose official position is on the administrative staff, and whose professional training was in the military. Trainees, whether in psychiatry, psychology, or social work, should be supervised in part by a psychiatrist. The amount of supervision may vary, but obviously should be sufficient for the supervisor to discuss the progress of each of the therapist's patients every week. Two or three hours weekly is usual, depending upon the case load and the amount of supervision available. This may be entirely with one supervisor; in the case of psychology and social-work trainees, it should also include some time with a senior person in the trainee's particular specialty.

The child's therapist inevitably becomes an important and meaningful person to the child. The children often become rather possessive of their therapists; however, feelings of rivalry over the attributes of different therapists do not often develop, and the children mutually respect another child's attachment to his own therapist. The therapist is usually referred to by the child as his "Doctor." A social-work student may thus find upon first coming to work in the institution that she has suddenly and gratuitously been awarded the doctoral degree. This may afford some early discomfiture, but most people readily make the adjustment. The first-year psychiatric resident may feel, with some justification, resentment that he thus receives no extra recognition for his hard-earned M.D. degree; but this is his problem, and again, the adjustment is usually made readily. If not, he had best not remain in child psychiatry.

The therapist may play a minor role in the therapy of some inpatients; in other cases, his role is of major importance. This depends on the relative needs of the child for individual relationship, support, and opportunity for exploration of his problems. With those children who are most benefited by the opportunities for social experience and for special education, the therapist must be able to accept his minor role, and not insist on the patient's involvement in psychotherapy. Nevertheless each child should continue to have a therapist, even though the contacts may be abbreviated almost to the point of disappearance. The child needs the status associated with having his own therapist, and, furthermore, he must know that, although the contacts may be few and brief, the therapist is always available if needed.

The latter point expresses an important aspect of therapy in the inpatient setting. That is, the therapist is available when situations arise which require his intervention. The therapist can see the child at critical times, say during a temper tantrum, or in a moment of deep anxiety or depression. Such a contact can be of more value to the child than a dozen scheduled interviews. At such a time the therapist may learn a great deal about the child, can observe the intensity of his feelings; moreover, by being available when urgently needed, a stronger relationship and dependency feeling can be developed. The child may at such times, or following the experience of such contacts, feel inclined to relate to the therapist in ways which he would otherwise never consider. The case of Billy, in the chapter on neurosis (Chapter 7), is a case in point. Here, the therapist, told by the counselor that Billy seemed depressed and agitated, visited him in his room, and there followed a long and highly meaningful interview which marked the beginning of Billy's recovery. In another case, a 16-year-old boy, hostile, defiant toward all authority, got into a rather serious fight with another boy. His therapist was called, managed, with help, to break up the fight, then took the boy for a walk to help him "cool off." The boy was fearful of punishment, but prepared to face it with indifference and scorn. When, instead of an angry and punitive approach, the therapist began to inquire sympathetically about the fight, the boy spoke about his father, contrasting the father's attitude with that of the therapist. It was the first time in the four months of his treatment that the patient had mentioned his father or permitted any expression indicating relationship. Once the door was opened, his feelings poured out in a flood. The relationship developed quickly and strongly following this interview. The boy was eventually discharged, greatly improved, and subsequently enlisted in the Air Force, still owing the therapist not only his mental health, but $15.00 which he had borrowed. But his gratitude, which was genuine, was sufficient repayment.

THERAPIST'S CASELOAD

Six to eight inpatients is enough for any therapist. With a larger caseload, sufficient attention can not be given to each child. Each patient will occupy an average of about five hours per week. This includes three hours of individual therapy plus the time required in morning rounds, brief contacts with the child's teacher, child-care workers, and other staff members. This does not include the time spent in formal staff meetings discussing the child. Presumably, the therapist will have other duties such as evaluation and treatment of outpatients, attendance at teaching conferences, supervisory interviews, and the like. Thus, a caseload of six emotionally disturbed children plus the other various duties will provide a full and strenuous week's work.

THE SCHOOL

One might suppose that highly disturbed children would not be able to function academically, and that opportunities for continuing academic education while in a mental hospital could not be utilized to any advantage. Quite the contrary is true. David found that a group of inpatients in an intensive treatment center showed a mean over-all academic improvement of approximately one-half a grade during a six-month period. This was only about one-tenth of a grade less than the mean improvement of children in a regular public school. Some of the disturbed children showed improvement of two grades or more, and some who had fallen behind academically in the public school were able to "catch up" during a year's inpatient treatment.

The school is an integral part of the intensive treatment center; indeed if one were to select the single most important segment of the total program, it would probably be the school. Some inpatient units provide for the children to attend a nearby public school, either in regular classes or in special classes which are set up by an arrangement worked out jointly between the school and the institution. However, for severely disturbed children, attendance at public school is usually not desirable, and an institution which presumes to treat them adequately needs to provide its own special school.

The size of the class is smaller than in regular school. A group of six is considered ideal by most special-education teachers, and eight is certainly a maximum. A larger group of disturbed children is unmanageable even by the most experienced teacher. Moreover, a small group permits the individualization of teaching which is so essential to success with these children.

Experience has shown that grouping of children in the school is best done according to approximate academic level, so all the children in the group will be working at about the same level. The groups are preferably heterogeneous as to sex, psychiatric diagnosis, personality, and degree of disturbance. Hence, factors other than academic achievement must be considered in organizing a group or in assigning a new patient. A group should not consist entirely of highly active, aggressive boys. Neither should it include only passive, unmotivated, unstimulated children. The personality and the experience of the teacher are important factors in assigning groups. Some teachers are more skillful at controlling difficult children, others are more successful at stimulating unmotivated ones.

The amount of time which each child attends school varies approximately with his age. Younger children, ages 6 to 8, can tolerate no more than about three academic hours daily. Adolescents can attend up to five hours per day. For the older children and adolescents, it is best to provide a "department" type of program, in which different subjects are taught by different teachers. Especially successful with most children is a science program, and even the younger children enjoy the collection of animal specimens, building of space models, etc.

THE TEACHER

The most important single factor for success in the teaching of disturbed children is the teacher's personality. No special aptitudes are needed, and, generally speaking, a teacher who works well with normal children will do well with mentally disturbed children. Like all persons working with such children, chief qualifications are emotional maturity, capacity for empathy and insight, a reasonable amount of intelligence and common sense, and the ability to control a situation. The teacher must expect that there will be difficult times, and must be able and willing to ask for help when it is needed. The help most often required is the sort known as "moral support"; it is always reassuring to know that one's fellow teachers have periodically had as difficult a time. However, in a well-organized inpatient school, the moments of turbulence are surprisingly few. Visitors often express surprise at the spectacle of groups of disturbed children bending studiously over their books or participating in a classroom discussion. The remark is often heard that most of the children appear quite normal. And so they do, much of the time.

In addition to these general qualifications, at least some of the teachers should have had formal training in special education. Degrees in special education are now available in many universities, and this rapidly-expanding professional group is assuming more and more importance in the treatment not only of emotionally disturbed children, but also those with educational and physical handicaps. With a background and an orientation in the psychological and psychiatric aspects of educational dysfunctions, the special-education teacher is better able to co-operate with the psychiatrist and clinical psychologist in organizing and effecting treatment programs for handicapped children of all types. The importance of this group in future developments in preventive psychiatry can hardly be over-estimated.

Morse, discussing the problems and the techniques in education of the mentally disturbed child, emphasizes the necessity for individualization of approach, for diagnosis as the basis of therapeutic teaching, and for the integration of the special-education teacher as a member of the therapeutic team. He cautions against overemphasis on academic achievement, noting that the primary concern of all involved in the child's program must be for emotional growth and development. At the same time, success in any area is important, so that each child may be encouraged and supported to achieve at a level commensurate with his capacities and problems, while at the same time the teacher avoids a punitive or reproachful attitude in the face of the child's failures.

The majority of children coming to an inpatient center have had chronically unfortunate and unhappy experiences in school, and have understandably become negatively conditioned to the academic situation. This experience has often been in part engendered by attitudes of teachers who were uninsightful, resentful, often overtly punitive and at times even cruel. All these factors provide an ever greater challenge to the special-education teacher entrusted with the treatment of such children. The child's relationship with his teacher is often the most crucial single factor in determining the course of his therapy, and a positive experience at the inpatient school can effect a readjustment in his later relationship toward schools and teachers which will be a major benefit to his entire subsequent life experience.

THE LANGUAGE CLINIC

A large number of the children in an inpatient treatment center need reading therapy. The number varies with the type of caseload, but in most institutions it is of the order of 50 percent of the patients. These include both children with specific learning disabilities and those who are retarded academically as a result of their emotional disorder.

Both individual and group therapy may be employed. As a generaliza-tion, those children with more severe degrees of emotional disorder as well as language disability require individual therapy, while less severe cases benefit equally well from small-group therapy. Many language therapists feel that certain children do better in group situations, being more moti-vated by the competitive atmosphere. Groups are ideally composed of from four to six children. In a larger group, each child does not receive sufficient individual attention, and problems of group control become insurmounta-ble. All members of the group should be functioning at approximately the same level, in order that they can participate in the group discussions. Some therapists employ a combined group-individual technique in which the children receive part of their therapy in the group, then have addi-tional individual sessions.

Each child with reading retardation should ideally receive four to five hours of reading therapy per week. With less than this, there is insufficient carry-over from one session to the next. Language therapy is, in most cases, in addition to the regular school program. Co-ordination between language therapist and teacher is essential.

OCCUPATIONAL THERAPY AND CRAFTS

Occupational therapy or O.T. is a term borrowed from the adult set-ting, and is perhaps not an appropriate term for the children's setting. Nevertheless, since trained O.T. workers are used for this function, it is usually known by this term in the children's hospital. Most of the chil-dren have no notion of what the term O.T. actually means, but they enjoy the therapy anyway.

O.T. serves an important function in the total program. Each child attends for about an hour each day. Its value to the child varies considera-bly, as do all the other parts of the program. For many children, it is the only area in which they can function at a significant level of achievement. Making things with their hands, learning to use tools and to manipulate materials in an organized and constructive way, is often highly meaningful and a source of real satisfaction to many of these poorly motivated and chronically deprived children. A patient and understanding O.T. worker may sometimes be the first person with whom the child has ever been able to experience a consistent dependent relationship.

The O.T. shop should be relatively small and the group should like-wise be small. In this somewhat confined and enclosed environment the child is less stimulated to act out, he feels more secure and better con-trolled. At the same time, external controls must not be too severe; some amount of aggression can be tolerated here. Freedom of expression is encouraged, provided it does not include such things as breaking windows or hitting other children with a hammer.

In the O.T. shop, individual work rather than a group project is the rule. Most children attend to their own projects and are seen busily sawing away on a piece of wood or punching holes in a piece of leather, for the most part oblivious to the activities going on around them.

Attendance at O.T. is, for most children, compulsory. Some may at first be disinterested, and prefer to wander out of the shop into other areas. Much ingenuity is required to stimulate their interest in a project, but an experienced O.T. worker can usually find something to engage them. Some children become very involved in one project and see it through to completion. Others may start a half-dozen different projects without finishing one. The primary consideration is the child's emotional needs rather than a finished product. Observing the disorganization usually present in the O.T. shop, one might wonder whether any project is ever finished. But surprisingly many are, and the therapist's office eventually becomes cluttered with a variety of more or less recognizable objects d'art.

THE NURSING STAFF

Psychiatric nurses contribute in an important measure to the professional and medical orientation of the children's psychiatric unit. Trained to assist the physician, they function in both a supervisory and patient-care capacity, and are best employed in positions of authority, usually in charge of the wards and cottages. Additionally, they are directly charged with care of the children. As ward supervisors, the nurses have charge of the child-care workers. They arrange the scheduled activities and various ward programs. They administer the drugs which have become an important part of the treatment program in most inpatient units, and they keep the daily ward records and patient-progress reports.

The nursing staff, in comprising the "hard core" of permanent, responsible, professional personnel directly involved in patient care, have to a large extent pre-empted many of the functions formerly carried out by house parents. Many administrators have found that house parents, who are for the most part older persons, usually couples permanently living in the cottages, do not provide the kind of therapeutic and flexible care which severely disturbed children need. Such persons, often somewhat rigid in their attitudes toward children, are unable to accept and cope with the behavior of aggressive, defiant, and profane children. The strain of living 24 hours a day with such children is too much for anyone, so that house parents have been largely replaced by employees living away from the institution and working on eight-hour shifts. Konopka and others have discussed the changes in philosophy of the residential treatment program, and note that one of the most significant changes of the last decade has been the replacement of house parents by nurses, child-care workers and other staff employed on a regular-shift basis.

THE CHILD-CARE WORKERS

The child-care workers or counselors constitute the largest single group of personnel in the residential treatment center. Their number should ideally be such as to provide a ratio of approximately one worker for each one and one-half patients. By working on three eight-hour shifts, this ratio becomes about one counselor for every five patients. However, the ratio is not constant throughout the 24-hour period, since during certain times of the day there is relatively greater need for individual care, while during the hours of sleep one worker may be in charge of as many as a dozen or more children.

The times of greatest activity and need for closest supervision are mealtimes, times of arising in the morning and preparing for bed at night, and the activity periods in late afternoon and after supper. These hours present rather peculiar problems in arranging work time, being concentrated in the early morning and late afternoon and evening. It has been found that these hours coincide nicely with the times when college students are available for work, and many residential treatment centers employ college students almost exclusively as child-care workers. This obviously requires that the institution be located in the vicinity of a college, and, in fact, this may be mentioned as an important criterion for determining the location of a contemplated institution.

Just as the nursing staff have taken over certain of the functions formerly carried out by house parents, so also have the child-care workers taken over others of those functions. They have direct and continuous contact with the children, being responsible for getting them up and dressed, getting them to meals, seeing them off to school or to other organized activities, and finally tucking them into bed at night. They also are available for almost anything which may be required: breaking up fights, retrieving lost articles, supervising or participating in sports or games, taking the children on hikes, to the movies and bowling, into town shopping, and for whatever semi-organized, organized, or disorganized activities may constitute part of the child's total therapy program.

The child-care workers are an integral part of the therapy, and as such are included in the meetings and discussions regarding the child's diagnosis and treatment. Here their comments and observations about the children constitute a major source of information.

The chief requirements for a good child-care worker are, like those of the other staff members, a reasonable amount of intelligence, maturity, warmth, and common sense. Their college courses need not be in fields allied to psychiatry, such as clinical psychology, social work, or premedicine. In fact, it is generally found that students training for other types of careers make better child-care workers. Students in engineering, chemistry, physical education, home economics, mathematics, and literature have all been excellent child-care workers. Their work with the children is thus not a part of their career training; it is regarded more as a job, chiefly for making money, but additionally one which most of them find interesting and challenging. They are less likely to be overinterested in the theoretical aspects of the child's psychodynamics, and retain more spontaneity and objectivity.

While the counselors must be able to accept without strong negative reactions the acting-out behavior of the children, it is implicit that the behavior of the counselors themselves be at all times exemplary. The profane language which inevitably fills the air at any institution for disturbed children should come only from the mouths of the children. Moreover, the foul language and other forms of misbehavior must in no way be condoned or encouraged by the staff. While it is not feasible to reprimand a child every time he swears, neither must the impression be left that these things are quite acceptable. The profanity, by being forbidden, retains its value as a vehicle for aggressive acting out. Should it become acceptable, there would no longer be any "kick" in it. Thus the child would be in the frustrating position of one depicted in a recent cartoon: The setting is a "progressive" nursery school, and in the background are children engaged in various destructive activities, driving nails into the floor, slopping paint onto the walls, hurling blocks at each other, and the like; one forlorn-looking boy, holding a saw in his hand, is confronting the teacher and asking her, in what must be a desperate tone of voice, "Isn't there *anything* we mustn't do?"

There are of course many things which the children mustn't do. They will do them anyway; but they must know that these things are not acceptable. A major function of the child-care workers is to teach the children acceptable modes of behavior. This they do largely by example. They impart in their own daily living with the children a high standard of values, a system of living which includes principles of individual equality, human dignity, and a sympathetic regard for the feelings of others. Living from day to day in close association with such persons is a new experience for most of the children in a residential treatment center. The values which they learn from this association constitute a major aspect of their therapy. It is an important reason why the children usually enjoy their stay at the institution, and why many of them afterward have pleasant recollections of that time. For many of them, it becomes the only bright spot in an otherwise unhappy childhood. Some of them keep in touch long afterward, and come back for visits, like old grads.

RECREATIONAL THERAPY AND GROUP WORK

Certain of the organized activities, such as athletic events, group games, parties, outings, and so on, may be supervised by professional workers trained in these areas, the recreational therapists and group workers. These specialties are assuming increasing importance in the programs of treatment institutions. However, qualified persons in these fields are relatively scarce, and such functions are often performed by the nursing and child-care staff, who have particular interests and talents along these lines. The recreation counselor need not be a good athlete, and in fact those qualifications that are usually associated with the physical culture enthusiast or the professional coach would be contraindications for working with disturbed children. Athletic performance is largely de-emphasized, as the level of expectation must remain low. Some of these children can scarcely pick up a ball, let alone catch one. The main thing is that they be encouraged to participate, and to have fun, and to act out some aggression.

WHO IS ADMITTED?

Criteria for admission to the intensive treatment center is an important matter of policy, and one which should be early clarified. If the institution is to fulfill its functions, the first rule is that the director and his staff make the final decision as to what children are admitted. If this decision is partly in the hands of the courts and other agencies, the community pressures will be such that only those children will be admitted who are a danger or a disturbance in the community.

The first criterion for admission should be that he is likely to be helped by the treatment, not that a child is a problem to the community. This does not mean that the director should refuse to help with emergent problems, but it must be understood that the institution is not an emergency hospital and should not be so considered. Otherwise, the beds will soon be filled with children with severe character disorders and psychopaths upon whom psychotherapy would be largely wasted. Facilities for such emergency problems are important for every community, but they can be provided elsewhere at a much lower cost than at an intensive treatment center.

What kinds of children are most likely to benefit from inpatient treatment? The first requirement is the same as that for outpatient psychotherapy: relationship capacity. Additionally, the child should come from an environment which is in some way pathological, and one from which he may be removed with benefits. The child then experiences his change in environment as a positive and desirable experience. Some institutions have the policy of admitting only those children whose parents can be "worked with," in order to assure that the home setting will be better when the child is ready to return to it. However, such a policy means refusing admission to many children who could be most helped by the inpatient treatment. The goal is not necessarily to return the child home. Many children should not return home at all, and are later, following discharge from the psychiatric center, placed in open-type institutions or special schools.

There are few rigid rules or criteria for admission. One is that the child be of average or high intelligence. There is no indication for admitting mental defectives, as they benefit little from a program geared to the child of average intelligence. Likewise, psychopaths are for the most part not admitted. They may benefit to a limited degree, through the experience of prolonged patterning and environmental control. However, the ultimate gains realized in working with psychopaths are so limited as to make their admission untenable and uneconomical. Nevertheless, some are invariably admitted, largely because of difficulties in diagnosis. As has been noted, diagnosis is by no means easy in many affectionless or relatively affectionless children, and admission for a period of diagnostic study sometimes is the best solution.

Severely schizophrenic children are not often admitted. The degree of their disturbance is such that they are unable to function in the program, their bizarre behavior is often upsetting to the other children, and they may themselves be made worse by the high level of stimulation and activity taking place about them. Such children usually function better either at home, in small private institutions, or in the closed wards of mental hospitals. Some of the less disturbed schizophrenic children may improve in the intensive treatment center. Those who have some degree of ego strength, and who are in communication with their environment, may make remarkable strides in the inpatient school setting and may develop some social skills through participation in the daily ward program.

The best candidates for admission are children with neurosis, personality disorder, brain damage, language disabilities, or the milder forms of schizophrenia, who are able to relate to some degree, and who would be benefited by being removed from their present environments. All of these are represented in the populations of most residential treatment centers. All or most of these should be represented, as it has been found that there is advantage in having a heterogeneous population. The children should vary as to diagnosis, symptoms, degree of acting out, age, and sex. With such a population there is better opportunity for a child to experience a variety of social relationships. Also, such a population is more interesting for the staff. The more active children provide some stimulation for the passive; the quiet ones help to keep the noise level tolerable. A population composed of all aggressive, acting-out children would be impossible to control. A population of all schizophrenics can be rather pathetic, depressing, and discouraging to work with. Opportunity for group experience is one of the major therapeutic benefits of a treatment center, and in order for group processes to operate, heterogeneity is essential.

DURATION OF INPATIENT TREATMENT

The length of time which a child remains in the treatment center varies greatly. In theory, this should coincide with the length of time in which he will receive benefit from treatment, and should end when placement elsewhere is indicated. In practice, the time has been found usually to be a relatively short period, in most cases of the order of 6 to 18 months. If the child is going to be benefited by the treatment, it will have occurred in this period of time. He is then ready for return to the community or placement in a less intensive setting. If he has not so improved, further intensive treatment is unlikely to help, and it is not justifiable to keep his place occupied when a new patient would be more likely to benefit.

As already noted, many residential centers gear their programs to the academic year, discharging old patients and admitting new ones during the summer. This has many advantages. One is that it fits in with the programs at other institutions where some of the discharged patients are to be placed. Additionally, it permits the children to return to school at the usual time. Also, it has the effect of reducing the inpatient population during the summer months, to coincide with staff changes and vacations.

Many placements cannot be arranged on a precise schedule, since the other placement institutions have to wait for their vacancies to occur before taking new cases. The situation is not unlike the game of musical chairs, with the additional complication that new participants are continually entering the game while others are leaving. And, unfortunately, there is always an excess of those waiting to enter and an insufficiency of places for those waiting to leave.

Despite the advantages of admitting and discharging patients between academic school years, these considerations must not be allowed to outweigh the primary one, namely, the child's individual needs. If a child is not emotionally ready for discharge, or if a satisfactory placement cannot be found, he should not be discharged. Likewise, if a child is urgently in need of admission, and a place is available at that time, he should be admitted. Records at Hawthorn Center indicate that approximately 60 per cent of the patients are admitted during the summertime, with the remaining 40 per cent scattered throughout the rest of the year.

DISPOSITION OF PATIENTS

The children who improve and who have reasonably intact homes usually return home following inpatient treatment. Contact should be retained, and usually these children are seen as outpatients for a time thereafter. Casework with the parents, initiated during the period of inpatient treatment, may also be continued. Newman has emphasized the importance of contacting the public school where the child will be attending and when possible effecting the child's enrollment in a school and class which is sympathetic to his needs.

Alternatively, the case may be referred to a local agency, perhaps the guidance clinic which made the original referral. No case should simply be dropped at the time of discharge. Further help is always needed.

Many patients do not return home upon discharge. This number will vary widely, according to the types of cases in treatment, the placement facilities available, and the treatment philosophy of the institution. At Hawthorn Center, about one-third of the children return directly home on discharge. An integral part of the program of the residential treatment center is an intimate knowledge of, and good working relationship with, other placement institutions and agencies in the area. Many of the inpatients may have improved considerably, but not enough to return to their home communities. These are best placed for a time in an open-type institution, perhaps one which permits attendance at a public school, and where less strict environmental controls are imposed. The kinds of such institutions available will be dealt with in the following chapter.

Some children get worse. Others retain a significant level of disturbance, making their return home or placement in an open institution untenable. For these, institutionalization in a closed setting is usually indicated. It is desirable for the residential center to have a reciprocal working relationship with a state mental hospital, preferably one which is located nearby, and which has a children's program. A child who becomes excessively disturbed, or one who truants regularly, may be transferred on short notice to the closed ward. The reciprocal aspect of this arrangement is that, in exchange, the treatment center may admit patients from the mental hospital who are considered good candidates for intensive treatment.

RESULTS OF INPATIENT THERAPY

Strictly speaking, the results of intensive inpatient treatment are not known. Adequately controlled research designed to answer this question has not been done, and probably can never be done. Such a study would require that a group of control patients be selected to "match" the inpatients, that these controls not have any inpatient treatment, and that they be followed for a sufficiently long period so that conclusive data could be obtained. The theoretical and practical difficulties involved render so complete a study unfeasible.

Follow-up studies on patients discharged from treatment centers, while falling considerably short of the ideal research design, nevertheless provide important information as to which kinds of cases make a good adjustment and which do not. Such information is important in planning a treatment program, and also in policy decisions regarding what cases should be admitted. Additionally, general knowledge about the "normal" course of the various emotional disorders of children, while admittedly far from complete, can provide at least suggestive information as to which kinds of cases seem most benefited by intensive treatment. Current thinking about this subject has already been outlined earlier in this chapter.

As in the evaluation of outpatient psychotherapy, the best evidence as to whether or not the treatment helps the patient is the therapist's knowledge of the individual patient. Here, the patient serves as his own control. Major changes observed in the child's personality, involving his interrelationships with other children and staff, are often so marked as to be irrefutable, and a matched control is not necessary. In the case of Billy, for example, the little boy described in the chapter on psychoneurosis (Chapter 7), important changes occurred the day Billy was admitted to the institution. His night terrors, present for a long time, ceased immediately. Further important changes occurred as Billy's relationships with staff and therapist developed, and these changes involved his feelings about the staff. While one could not state with certainty that Billy would not have improved had he not been given inpatient treatment, one can say with conviction that he would not have improved as readily, or in the same ways, and probably not to the same degree. It is very likely that he would have gotten worse, but this, of course, can never be known.

As a generalization, one can state that the majority of children in well-run treatment centers show improvement, some only to a moderate degree, some to a great degree. But this is hardly more than should be expected. Cases are admitted on a highly selective basis, the chief criterion being, as already emphasized, that the case is likely to be benefited by the treatment.

The question is often asked as to whether the intensive treatment center is "efficient" enough to justify its expense. There is no denying that it is an expensive operation, both in terms of money and in the number of skilled professional staff expended per child. The answer is impossible to give statistically. One cannot say, for example, that if the same amount of staff and money were spread out to treat four times as many children, then more children would be helped, or perhaps less children would be helped. Nobody knows. One can say with certainty that if the patient population at an inpatient treatment center were quadrupled while the staff remained constant, no child would receive what could properly be called intensive treatment. Some of the children would undoubtedly improve, but others would not, and many would probably get worse. There would be insufficient control of the group, there would be less individualization of treatment, and the program would not function as it should.

The point is that there must be many different types of treatment situations. The intensive treatment center is only one of these, and it would not be justifiable to treat all children in such an institution. A major justification for the intensive treatment center is its functions as a center for training and for research. Having a large and experienced staff, it provides training opportunities not available in those institutions where the staff is relatively small, and where most of their time and effort must be directed toward patient care. As for research, the first requirement is that the worker have time during the regular working day in which to do research. Equally important are the availability of sufficient well-diagnosed clinical material and the opportunities for close association and communication with a competent and stimulating clinical staff. These requirements can only be met in full in the intensive treatment center.

THE PHYSICAL PLANT

There are many and varied opinions about the requirements for a good physical plant to house a residential treatment center for children. Most agree, however, that personnel are far more crucial, and that a really good staff could operate successfully in an old barn.

Nevertheless, there are certain desirable features for the physical plant, and probably the two most important ones are:

1. Enough space for active play, both indoors and out.

2. A sufficient number of relatively small separate indoor areas to contain small group activities.

Architectural style is not of great importance, although an aesthetically pleasing environment helps the morale of the staff and is beneficial to the children. The trend is away from prison-like, solid-looking structures and toward more open-type, light, colorful buildings. The notion that the buildings should be made as indestructible as possible has been shown to be unwarranted, as relatively little damage occurs in an adequately staffed center.

The controversy of cottage plan versus closed ward is one to which there is no specific answer. There are advantages and disadvantages to each. A combination of the two is probably best: It permits using cottages for the more amenable children and the closed ward for those who require more containment and environmental security; it also provides more flexibility in the management of children whose needs for containment undergo change during the course of their treatment.

A seclusion room (also called "isolation room," "quiet room," and a variety of other names) is extremely helpful for children whose acting out gets beyond control. It may not be required often, but its presence provides a wonderful sense of security both to the staff and to certain of the children.

The school area, staff office area, and children's living area should be separated, but not so widely that communication is impeded. And somewhere, preferably at a location central to these areas, there should be a staff conference room and library, where the staff can meet both formally and informally, and talk over the current problems of their children.

These are but general recommendations. The requirements for the physical plant have been considered in somewhat greater detail in the Report of the Conference on Inpatient Psychiatric Treatment for Children (1957). This report cautions, however, that every residential treatment center is unique, and its physical plant must be determined by its particular aims, treatment philosophy, size of staff, size of patient population, and, inevitably, fiscal considerations.

REFERENCES

Alt, H. Residential Treatment for the Disturbed Child, New York, International Universities Press, 1960.
Children's Bureau. Residential Treatment Centers for Emotionally Disturbed Children, a Listing, Washington, D.C., U.S. Department of Health, Education, and Welfare, 1952.
———— Child Welfare Statistics 1961, Statistical Series No. 66, Washington, D.C., U.S. Department of Health, Education, and Welfare, 1962.
David, W. J. A Study of Educational and Intellectual Growth of Inpatient Emotionally Disturbed Children, thesis submitted for the degree of Master of Arts in Education, University of Michigan, 1958.
Dubo, S., and Rabinovitch, R. D. Child Psychiatry, in Progress in Neurology and Psychiatry, ed. S. Spiegel, New York, Grune & Stratton, 1957, Vol. 12.

Hylton, L. F. The Residential Treatment Center, New York, Child Welfare League of America, 1964.

Konopka, G., Kamps, F., Wallinga, J., and Hovda, P. Implications of a Changing Residential Treatment Program, Am. J. Orthopsychiatry, 31: 17, 1961.

Morse, W. C. The Education of Socially Maladjusted and Emotionally Disturbed Children, in Education of Exceptional Children and Youth, eds. Cruickshank and Johnson, Englewood Cliffs, N.J., Prentice-Hall, 1958.

Newman, R. The Way Back: Extramural Schooling as a Transitional Phase of Residential Therapy, Am. J. Orthopsychiatry, 30: 588, 1960.

Redl, F. The Concept of a "Therapeutic Milieu," Am. J. Orthopsychiatry, 29: 721, 1959.

Report of the Conference on Inpatient Psychiatric Treatment for Children, Psychiatric Inpatient Treatment of Children, Washington, D.C., American Psychiatric Association, 1957.

18

OTHER THERAPEUTIC MEASURES

The preceding two chapters have described two types of treatment for emotionally disturbed children: psychotherapy and intensive residential treatment. These two, however, by no means exhaust the treatment possibilities, and are, in fact, prescribed for a relatively small number of cases. Of the approximately 1,100 new cases seen at Hawthorn Center annually for evaluation, less than 10 per cent are admitted for inpatient treatment, and about 20 per cent receive outpatient psychotherapy either at the Center or elsewhere.

Yet it is important in every case that something be done. The psychiatrist who has seen a child for diagnostic evaluation has a responsibility to make a potentially therapeutic disposition. It is indefensible to tell the parents that one is unable to be of any help in this case, and thus disavow further responsibility. Some recommendation, or at least a referral to another agency or therapist, should always be made. Occasionally, nothing is indicated beyond a brief discussion with the parents, which includes the assurance that the child will probably adjust well or will otherwise improve spontaneously. Obviously, one should be reasonably certain that such is the case before making such a forecast.

Usually, more than this is needed. The following table lists a number of measures besides psychotherapy and residential psychiatric treatment which are used for treating an emotionally disturbed child. These are the subject of this chapter.

A. Child Remains at Home
    1. Day school
    2. Special program or class at public school
    3. Individual tutoring
    4. Psychotherapy or counseling for parents
    5. Group psychotherapy
    6. Family therapy

B. Placement Away from Home
  1. Boarding home
  2. Open institution
  3. Closed institution
     a. Mental hospital
     b. Juvenile detention home
  4. Boarding school
  5. Summer camp

THE CHILD REMAINS AT HOME

THE SPECIAL DAY SCHOOL

The modern trend in mental hygiene is away from large mental hospitals. These are being replaced by smaller community-type institutions, both for inpatient and for day care. This trend is also developing in the field of child mental health, and the special day school is rapidly becoming an important segment of the program. Approximately 5 per cent of the new cases seen at Hawthorn Center enter the day-care program.

Some of the important advantages of a special day school for emotionally disturbed children are:

1. Patients continue to live with their families, and thus retain the advantages of close family identification.

2. Children with educational handicaps and academic retardation need not experience the traumata and frustrations of attending school with normal children.

3. Cost per patient is much less than in a residential treatment center.

4. The parents may be more actively involved, since the child is living at home, the parents are in touch with his daily behavior, and, if they drive him to school, there is in addition frequent contact with the teacher.

The day-school program is especially beneficial for younger children, ages four to seven, particularly those who have behavioral disturbances but who, because of their young age, are more likely to be traumatized by continuous separation from home.

Day schools vary widely in their programs and in the degrees of pathology which they can tolerate and treat among the children. Many day-school programs designed for normal children may be able to accept a few moderately disturbed children, and such programs should be considered when one is seeking placement for a mildly disturbed nursery-school-aged child. Here, the chief advantage is that the child is away from home for several hours each day, socially involved with normal children and with a reasonably mature teacher.

For the most part, however, disturbed children need special day-school experiences. Such schools should have therapeutically oriented personnel, special-education teachers, and, hopefully, psychiatric and psychological consultants. As in the inpatient school program, the day-school groups for disturbed children should be relatively small, and the children should be placed approximately according to their level of academic functioning. The group sessions should, where possible, be supplemented by individual psychotherapy (Alpert).

Results of treatment in the special day schools have not been adequately assessed, and they undoubtedly vary widely, depending on the skill of the teachers and the types of cases treated. Nevertheless, a surprising number of children improve, following a year or two of such treatment, and many are able to enter regular school and to make reasonably successful adjustments there. On the other hand, there is also a considerable number who remain seriously disturbed, and many of these, as they get older, require institutionalization.

The day school associated with a psychiatric facility may be utilized for diagnostic study also. By admitting a child for a week or two, where he is under continuous observation by the day-school staff and is available for frequent interviews by the psychiatrist, a more accurate impression of his functioning may be obtained than in regularly scheduled outpatient visits.

SPECIAL PROGRAM AT THE PUBLIC SCHOOL

Special programs or classes for physically handicapped and mentally retarded children have long been available in most of the larger public school systems. These have included classes for the blind, the deaf, children with speech defect, crippled children, and children with chronic medical problems. Some school systems have also given special consideration to children with unusually high mental ability, as well as to the trainable mentally retarded. Only recently, however, have programs begun to be developed for children with emotional disturbances or with specific learning disabilities.

In general, classes for disturbed children in the public schools are organized along the same lines as those described in the inpatient treatment center (Chapter 17). The two major requirements are that the group be small, and that the teacher be capable. Teacher training in special education is desirable, but not essential. Most important, as Berkowitz and Rothman emphasize, is that the teacher be mature, warm, insightful, and skilled in dealing with disturbed children. Educators reading this list of criteria may smile wistfully and wonder where such teachers are to be found. Every school principal knows that good teachers are at a premium and that the shortage of skilled personnel is the most serious dilemma facing the education profession today.

Morse has described the pitiful inadequacy of facilities in the public schools for emotionally disturbed children. He notes that for every child enrolled in a special class or school, there are about 20 more who should be in such classes but who instead are attending regular classes. The inadequacy of available facilities is all too apparent to the child psychiatrist to whom the schools refer their problem children. In the majority of these cases, the psychiatrist can make an adequate diagnosis, and can determine that the child needs to be in a special class. But the class is simply not available. Some of the schools try to handle such problems in their classes for "slow learners," but this is a far from satisfactory arrangement. The result is usually that the disturbed child creates such turmoil in the classroom that all the pupils suffer and nobody benefits.

The hopeful note is that educators, the public, and legislators are coming to recognize the urgent need for special facilities. Also, special-education teachers trained to work with emotionally disturbed children are increasing in number.

Short of having special-education teachers and classes for disturbed children, there is much else that the schools can and sometimes will do in response to recommendations from the child psychiatrist. Many schools have counselors or teachers who give individual help to the student. Sometimes an individualized program can be arranged for the child, wherein he is allowed to attend those classes in which he can function best. Sometimes it is helpful for the child to be transferred to a different school, where the teachers may be more accepting of his behavior and better able to provide adequate controls, and where he can "make a new start." In working out such recommendations and arrangements, it is essential that the psychiatrist familiarize himself with the conditions at the school, talk with the principal and perhaps the teachers, and make a recommendation based on a sound understanding of the child's needs and situation. It is obviously useless to make a recommendation simply for the sake of doing something or of providing a change.

INDIVIDUAL TUTORING

There are two specific indications for the use of a private tutor for an emotionally disturbed child. One is that the child is unable to function in a group setting, or at least in any of the group settings that are available in his area. The second is that the child needs special education, and that none is available in the school system either on an individual or a group basis.

Having a tutor at home because the child cannot function in a group should be only a temporary arrangement. No child should continue in this way for any prolonged period, as, while his educational needs may be adequately met, his social needs are not. The latter are at least as important, and some solution should be sought which will enable him to be in a group: a special class, institution, or whatever is indicated.

Quite another matter is the indication for special education in a child with specific learning disability. Here, a private tutor may be profitably utilized throughout the entire period of the child's education. Generally, the hours spent with the tutor supplement the child's regular education, although in some cases arrangements may be made whereby they replace certain of the school hours. Obviously, the tutor should be trained in the subject he is teaching, and also, hopefully, in special education. This matter has already been discussed in the chapter on learning disabilities (Chapter 9). Unfortunately, good tutors are hard to find and are relatively expensive. Nevertheless, money thus spent may be the best investment the parents will ever make.

The parents should not attempt to function as tutors themselves. This, too, has been discussed in the chapter on learning disabilities, but it bears repetition. A parent may sometimes successfully tutor a normal child. An emotionally disturbed child is altogether another problem. The parent is too much involved emotionally with the child's difficulties to work with him in a therapeutic manner.

PSYCHOTHERAPY OR COUNSELING FOR PARENTS

It is a truism that the parents of a disturbed child are often more in need of psychiatric treatment than the child himself. However, when it is the child who is brought to the psychiatrist, it is not often that one can say to the parent, "You're the one who needs the psychiatrist." Occasionally it is possible to be as direct as this. An 11-year-old boy was referred by the school because he had become highly emotional, wept easily in class, and seemed troubled and depressed. When the mother was interviewed she became distraught, began to weep, and said that her husband had recently become emotionally disturbed. He was suspicious that she was being unfaithful whenever she was away from home for even a few minutes, and he would have terrible rages directed at her and the children with little provocation. She and the children had become deathly afraid of him. Arrangements were made for a social worker to visit the home that same afternoon. The husband, although resentful, agreed to come in immediately to see the psychiatrist, and when interviewed he, too, became quite tearful and emotional, described his unwarranted suspicions of his wife, said that he was afraid that he would hurt his family, admitted to having frequent suicidal thoughts, and begged the psychiatrist to help him. A diagnosis of paranoid schizophrenia was made, and the father was admitted to a mental hospital on an emergency order that very night.

But such cases are rare. Usually, the parents are "worked with" during several interviews, with the child's difficulties as the initial focus. Then, as a working relationship is established, the parents' own involvement with the child and their own personal difficulties may assume increasing prominence in the discussions. In some cases, more than this is not indicated. In others, it may be decided mutually between therapist and parent that the parent should have further counseling or psychotherapy. This can be administered by the child's own therapist, or by another therapist either in the same clinic or elsewhere.

In treating the parents, the child must not be lost sight of. To conclude that the child's difficulty results from his parents' disturbances may be quite correct, but it does not necessarily follow that by treating the parent the child will automatically improve.

GROUP PSYCHOTHERAPY

Group psychotherapy is a method of treatment which was used first with adults and then adapted for use with children and adolescents. One of the early applications of group therapy was in large hospitals where the method aimed to reach a larger number of patients than was possible with individual therapy. With children it has had a variety of applications, and the added dimension of group dynamics has aroused considerable interest in recent years. It has been successfully used with groups of parents whose children are in psychiatric treatment. It is desirable, when forming a therapy group, to have a reasonable degree of homogeneity in the group with respect to age, diagnosis, type of problem, and social and cultural background. With older children and particularly adolescents it is preferable to segregate the sexes. Four to eight patients make a satisfactory number. If there are as many as 10 or more, the group becomes unwieldy. There may be a single therapist or two therapists in the group but if there are two it is usually best to designate one as the "leader" and the other as an observer or recorder. To function effectively the group should be relatively "closed," that is, the membership of the group should remain fairly constant throughout the period of treatment.

Group therapy may be used in addition to or in place of individual psychotherapy. One of the advantages of this type of therapy is that group behavior and problems in interpersonal relationships, such as sibling rivalry and disrespect of authority figures, can be observed first-hand, and the child has the opportunity for developing and testing new ways of relating with others.

Many methods and approaches to group therapy have been described. Dreikurs, who has reviewed these, lists two distinguishing factors: the verbal vs. nonverbal approach, and the directive vs. nondirective approach.

Innumerable degrees and combinations of these have been described by their proponents. Much pioneering work in group therapy with children was done by Slavson (1943) in New York in the 1930's. He developed the "activity group therapy" through which children from disturbed home situations were allowed to enjoy a new type of experience with other children and with the therapist who did not react to their misbehavior in the punitive way to which they had been accustomed. The groups functioned much like a club, and the activities involved such pleasurable experiences as games, field trips, and eating, with much of the planning done by the children themselves. Slavson described the process by stating that "Emotional reorientation comes from the very fact that the child experiences actual situations, lives and works with other children, comes into direct and meaningful interaction with others, and as a result modifies his feeling tones and habitual responses."

Later, Slavson (1950) differentiated activity group psychotherapy from analytic group psychotherapy. Activity group psychotherapy was intended for school-age children and did not utilize discussion of problems with the therapist or interpretation by him. The therapeutic value was in the activity itself and in the lack of restrictions by the therapist. Analytic group psychotherapy included various types of therapy groups, some revolving around an activity and others relying more on verbalization, in all of which the aim was to develop insight through interpretation. Specific types included group play psychotherapy for preschool children, activity-interview group psychotherapy for more disturbed latency-age children, and interview group psychotherapy for adolescents.

FAMILY THERAPY

A special type of group therapy is family therapy, espoused mainly by Ackerman. Here, all members of the family, including the patient (who is presumably the most disturbed) are encouraged to express themselves freely in the family group, with the therapist making interpretations. The families to be so treated must be carefully selected and the technique should not be undertaken by someone who has not been specially trained in it. The method can be effective in improving communication among a family unit, but within a pathological family group it could have serious and even dangerous repercussions.

PLACEMENT AWAY FROM HOME

A natural reluctance to recommend placement of a child away from his home is widespread among workers in the field of child psychiatry. In this present-day family-oriented culture, a high value is placed on maintaining the family unit. Unfortunately, value judgments of this kind often interfere with therapeutic considerations.

In general, any child will adjust better in a good placement than in a poor home environment. Nonetheless, removing a child from his family is always a serious step, and not one to be taken lightly. The decision must be based on careful evaluation, with a clear understanding of the meanings of the family to the child, and the degree to which the family psychopathology contributes to his disorder. The indications for placement are usually obvious. If there is much doubt, it is better to temporize, continuing to see the child and the family, and to re-evaluate the situation periodically.

In most cases, placement is recommended as a temporary measure. Even though one feels that in the home the environment is such that the child can never safely return to his family, one seldom verbalizes such a prediction at the outset. Few parents, even the most rejecting, will consent to giving up their child "forever."

The specific type of placement depends on a variety of factors. Most of these involve the child's pathology, the degree of his acting out, the requirements for environmental control, and his capacity to function in a relatively normal social environment. Specific indications will be dealt with below in the discussion on the various types of placement.

BOARDING HOME

Theoretically, a boarding home would seem to offer the most satisfactory type of placement for most children. Here the environment is of the "normal" type, as it provides a regular family group, usually mother, father, and other children, living in a house or other single-family quarters, and in a neighborhood setting. In practice, boarding-home placement occupies a minor role in the treatment of emotionally-disturbed children. While boarding-care services are an important and generally successful aspect of community service for many types of "homeless" children, they are for the most part ill-suited for the care of disturbed children. Most children requiring psychiatric services are unable to function well in such a benign and relatively uncontrolled environment. Boarding parents, however good their intentions, and however mature and intact they may be, are seldom able to cope with the disordered behavior of these children. Most boarding parents expect, and rightly so, a certain degree of compliance with the usual rules of conduct, and, more important, they need some return of affection and warmth. The disturbed child is usually unable to enter readily into a meaningful relationship with anyone at a reasonably mature level. The boarding parents are too often baffled, disappointed, and hurt by the lack of normal response to their care. The result is that a child, sensing these negative reactions, finds his own conflicts and pathological feelings intensified, and the placement soon fails.

Failure of placement does not, of course, always occur. But the risk is often too great to take. Failure of a placement can produce more serious damage to the child's psyche than was already present. Naughton observes that "the all important consideration common to every foster child is his need to be protected against replacement. With a child who has experienced repeated failure it is essential that all possible precautions be taken to avoid continuation of the traumatic pattern."

Thus, only rarely does the child psychiatrist see a case in which he can reasonably make the recommendation of boarding-home placement. The exception may be the child who has reacted emotionally to an acute situation, whose ego is intact, and who has experienced relatively normal family relationships prior to the acute situation. Another case may be the one in which the psychiatrist is consulted specifically for the problem of determining whether a child in need of placement because of external reasons is sufficiently intact emotionally to adjust in a boarding home.

THE OPEN INSTITUTION

The term open institution includes a variety of institutions in which the physical environment permits the child relative freedom to come and go more or less as he wishes, and in which he usually has some social contact with the surrounding community, especially for school and for recreational pursuits. Institutions vary widely in their degree of openness. Some consist of small groups living in a neighborhood community, often in a converted dwelling house, with the children attending local schools, and playing with other children in the neighborhood. Others are larger group settings, housed in large buildings in the city or in a rural setting, having a more organized type of internal structure, perhaps with more specific rules regarding the times when the child may be away from the institution grounds, but still not "closed," in the sense that there are not barred windows or a surrounding barbed wire fence. Such an institution may be of the mixed open and closed type, perhaps with its own campus school for the more disturbed children, while the less disturbed children attend the community schools.

The variety of open institutions is virtually infinite, depending on the aims and purposes of the particular institution. They are supported and operated by a number of different types of agencies. Many are run by church groups, others by philanthropic organizations, some by the local communities, some by various agencies at the local, state, or federal levels.

Some are well-endowed financially, providing the finest of physical facilities and a large and well-trained staff. Others operate on a limited budget. The level of care provided and the results of treatment are not necessarily correlated with the wealth of the institution, and some of the poorest financially have the most devoted and successful workers.

The child psychiatrist should become personally familiar with the institutions in his area. He should have some personal contact with the directors and their staffs, so that he is in a position to know which are best suited for particular types of disturbed children. In arranging placement for a patient at one of these institutions, he must not only have a reasonable expectation that the child will be benefited by the placement and that he will adjust relatively well there; he must also represent to the director of the institution frankly and honestly what the child's problems are. Otherwise, he may find that, after one or two placements, his patients are no longer accepted there.

Many open-type institutions whose programs are primarily organized for normal children may nevertheless be able to accept a few disturbed children. Such an arrangement often requires that the referring psychiatrist keep in touch with his patient following placement, providing such advice and assistance as may be indicated in the management of the child. Some such institutions maintain their own medical, psychological, and psychiatric consultants, in which case these consultants should be conferred with prior to placement of any child.

The need for special education is often an important consideration in placing the child in an open institution, and those which maintain on-campus schools or provide tutoring services are much better placements for children with educational problems.

The open-type institution has an important function as an interim placement for gradual transition of a disturbed child from a closed institution to final return to his home and community. Many children, following treatment in an intensive treatment center, may be successfully placed for a year or two in an open institution before returning home.

THE CLOSED INSTITUTION

There are several types of closed institutions for children. Some are primarily for the care of the mentally ill, some are for mentally retarded, others are concerned with the various forms of antisocial behavior, pre-delinquent, delinquent, and criminal. These institutions vary widely in size, in organization, and in therapeutic orientation. Some are purely custodial, and function only to keep their inmates separated from the outside world. Others have active programs designed to train, re-educate, rehabilitate, and treat the patients, and hopefully to return them to society. Some of these institutions are privately maintained, some are public institutions, either municipal, county, state, or federal.

Closed institutions have an important place in a mental health program for children. While the confinement of a child in a locked building may seem unnecessarily harsh, in certain cases it is the treatment of choice. On the other hand, probably more children than should be are thus treated, simply because no other facilities are available.

Closed institutions for children will be discussed under two major headings:

1. The mental hospital
2. The juvenile detention home

1. *The Mental Hospital.* Private mental hospitals are usually relatively small, and seldom have facilities for children. Most of the mental hospitals which do admit children are the large public institutions operated mainly by the state or county. The inadequacy of many of these institutions is so well known as to require little discussion here, except insofar as it pertains to the treatment of children.

The number of children admitted to mental hospitals has increased steadily over the past two decades. Reasons are not entirely clear, but an important one is the increased recognition that many acting-out children are emotionally disturbed and should be appropriately treated rather than confined in jails and detention homes. Most of the older hospitals are not designed for the care of children, and have had to introduce makeshift arrangements which have usually been far from satisfactory. Some just admit the children to a regular adult ward, finding that two or three children on a ward of 250 adults do not pose serious management problems, and often the less disturbed adult patients help care for the children. Needless to say, living with a group of mentally-ill adults is scarcely a therapeutic experience for any child. Some hospitals have set aside a ward, or part of a ward, for a children's program. This necessitates an increased number of personnel, as a group of children are more active and demanding, requiring more supervision than adults. Additionally, if there is to be any semblance of a therapeutic program for the children, special staff are needed, such as teachers, group workers, and others. The mental hospitals, understaffed and underbudgeted, are seldom able to provide enough special personnel or facilities, so that such programs for children are usually minimal. The result is that only a few of the children are able to participate in therapeutic programs, or else all participate infrequently.

While most of the children's services at the mental hospitals probably need some improvement, there is a limit beyond which such improvement cannot be justified. A program of the intensive-treatment type is not indicated because of the restrictions on therapeutic aims imposed by the nature of the pathology present in the majority of children admitted to these institutions. The mental hospitals are usually commitment-type institutions, and the hospital staff do not make the decision as to which patients to admit. The importance of this policy in the management of an intensive treatment center was emphasized in Chapter 17. It is also important, however, that there be hospitals of the commitment type; if there were not, many of the children would never be hospitalized. But, by the very nature of the system, the result is that the commitment hospitals receive, to a large extent, those children whom nobody else wants to treat.

The child population in a mental hospital usually consists of the most severely and chronically disturbed cases, of whom over one-half are character disorders, the remainder being mainly schizophrenics and children with brain damage, usually complicated by character disorder. Most of these children have been badly mishandled all of their lives. Most come from extremely disturbed homes, have experienced severe distortions in their relationships, and their capacities for relationship are usually impaired. The result is that the outlook for improvement in many cases is poor, and it is difficult to undertake a therapeutic program with a great deal of hope or enthusiasm. The staff become understandably discouraged with their work. Resident psychiatrists training exclusively in these institutions get a somewhat distorted experience in child psychiatry. The opportunities for meaningful relationships with such a child population are seriously limited. This was exemplified when a visiting child analyst was planning a teaching seminar at such a hospital. He asked the staff in advance to have a case available for his discussion, the criteria for selecting the case being that the child should be no older than 12, reasonably verbal, and with some anxiety and relationship capacity. Out of the population of over 50 children age 12 and under, not a single child could be found who fulfilled these requirements.

Yet, the outlook for children in the mental hospitals is by no means hopeless. One might expect that most of them would remain in the institution the remainder of their lives. On the contrary, three-fourths are discharged, and the average duration of hospitalization is between three and four years. True, the ultimate adjustment of many of those who are discharged is far from good, and some join the ranks of the lowest elements of society: criminals, prostitutes, chronic alcoholics, and the like. On the other hand, a considerable number return to their communities, go back to school, and appear to be on the road to becoming normal adults and productive citizens. Statistical data on follow-up studies are not yet available, as the mental hospital programs for children are too new to provide a sufficient sample of long-term follow-ups.

Thus, the mental hospital can provide a therapeutic experience for certain disorders. The children most benefited are those with personality disorders who have some degree of ego strength and who have been engaged in a kind of running battle with life. These children, with their uncontrolled aggression and with their distortions in relationship, often improve in the mental hospital. The major therapeutic factors are:

1. The children are removed from the environment which nurtured their disorder.

2. They are in an environment where their acting out is to no avail; aggression is little tolerated and seldom satisfying, since counteraggression does not result.

3. Their days are for the most part spent in idleness, boredom and misery—there is just nothing to do, they become apathetic, listless, and wearily unhappy.

Two or three or four years of such a "flattening" experience is a true learning experience for these children. A kind of deconditioning occurs, in which the old responses and behaviors, no longer finding reinforcement, gradually drop out of the patient's repertory. Returning to society, they no longer get into so much trouble. On the other hand, such an experience is not therapeutic for some children and may even be damaging.

The child is further helped to normal adjustment if during his hospitalization he has some relationship with mature adults on the staff, and also if he can receive individual counseling and psychotherapy. This is often not possible because of the high patient-to-staff ratio; the contact between child and professional staff member may consist of a few words spoken in the hallway, or at best of a brief office interview every month or two. Many of these children are pathetically desirous of attention and relationship, and are sometimes seen following the social worker or psychiatrist down the hall or ward, begging for attention, asking some small personal favor or special privilege, and turning away in despair as the locked door closes between them. Most of the staff of the children's services are devoted, hard-working, and genuinely regretful and resentful that they have so little time available for the individual child.

Inglis and Marsh have discussed the need for improved children's programs in the state mental hospitals. Describing the situation in Connecticut, they found that during the five-year period preceding 1956, 143 children entered the three state mental hospitals, despite the fact that these hospitals did not have specially designated children's services. There was little communication between the state hospitals and other community facilities, and no over-all planning program which involved the use of the mental hospitals as part of the total program for the care of disturbed children. Inglis and Marsh conclude:

Mental hospital use for children points to the need for the community to review its resources and its problems, to bring programs inherited from the past in line with present knowledge of human behavior. We may have many worthwhile individual programs. However, they must be coordinated in a community-wide effort to meet the full range of children's needs. Until this is done, those who are not provided for may continue to be found in places never meant to serve them, such as the state mental hospitals.

2. *The Juvenile Detention Home.* The last sentence in the above quotation may well be extended to include the detention homes. These institutions, usually maintained by the city or the county, are often little more than children's jails. Intended mainly as facilities where the court may temporarily house juvenile offenders, they are too often used for the containment of the dangerous or potentially-dangerous mentally ill; moreover, many children remain there for as long as a year or two, because there is no other place for them.

The budgets of the detention homes, or "youth homes" as they are sometimes euphemistically called, are often inadequate, staff is minimal, and, because the pay scale is low, many of the staff workers are hired not because they are suited for the work, but because they could not find employment elsewhere. Treatment of the children is often excessively punitive, even cruel. Frequently in detention homes the younger delinquents learn advanced techniques in crime from the more experienced, and are exposed to much aggression and immorality. The philosophy of operating the detention home is often effected or determined by an ill-informed police force whose approach to delinquency is largely a punitive one, and by a judge whose knowledge of child psychology and of criminal psychodynamics is limited.

Most of the detention homes maintain a school where attendance is semi-compulsory, but the teachers at such schools are frequently ill qualified for working with disturbed children, and their time is largely occupied with preventing fights and attempting to maintain some semblance of order.

Gill observes that one of the most widespread and dangerous misconceptions in criminology is that crime prevention is primarily the function of the police. He points out that many police departments have assumed broad powers in developing programs aimed at prevention of crime and delinquency, and, as a result, other agencies which should be directly involved in these activities are either blocked in their efforts or are inclined to shift their responsibilities to the police. Gill notes that this prevents the development of "an intelligent and organized program of crime prevention —both juvenile and adult—which is the responsibility of the home, the school, the church, and those other character-building organizations of society which are especially trained and qualified (as the police notoriously are not) to undertake the work of prevention of development of criminal and antisocial tendencies in individuals." Gill concedes that the police have an important part in such programs, but that they must not accept "a responsibility which calls for the training, wisdom, and experience of parents, teachers, ministers, psychologists, and many others not to be found on the police force."

The situation is, however, not all bad. There are police officers who are well qualified, both personally and professionally, to deal with emotionally disturbed children. There are probate judges of wisdom and insight. Many courts employ trained social workers, psychologists, and psychiatrists, to help in the proper disposition of each case. Nevertheless, many detention homes continue to provide an environment which would be harmful to a normal child, not to mention a mentally disturbed one. An example is the case of a 13-year-old, bright, frail, neurotic boy who was socially inhibited, shy, and given to daydreaming. He occupied himself alone much of the time, reading science fiction, and became interested in chemistry. He set up a chemistry laboratory in the basement of a deserted house in the neighborhood, and spent many hours there mixing concoctions, making dyes from the roots and leaves of plants, and similar things. A curious neighbor, suspicious of the boy's comings and goings at the old house, called the police. The police, questioning neighborhood children, elicited vague rumors to the effect that the boy was a "saboteur," and that he was manufacturing explosives. He was arrested and taken to the detention home. Two days later, after several frantic telephone calls by the father, it was arranged to have the boy brought to the psychiatric hospital for evaluation. He was brought to the ward in handcuffs, accompanied by two uniformed policemen. In tears, he described his terror while at the detention home, bullied and derided by the children there. A more harmless-looking and unhappy child could not be imagined. Yet he had been treated as a desperate and dangerous criminal.

The needs are clear. A variety of facilities are necessary. Additionally, there must be early evaluation by competent personnel, so that each child receives the kind of treatment he needs. Peck and others summed up the present state of affairs by stating that: "All too often, a court appearance brings the wrong person to the wrong place to see the wrong person at the wrong time." Out of their experience in an experimental research project attached to a New York City court, grew the following recommendations for the planning of court services to juvenile offenders:

1. The consultation of professionally qualified clinicians from physical and psychiatric medicine, psychology, and social work should be made available to the judges.

2. Psychosocial histories and clinical data should be made available for all children coming before the court, regardless of the seriousness of the offense.

3. A court intake service could integrate the work of the professional diagnostic team, the court administrative departments, and the probation department.

4. The court must study the population it serves to gain perspective and coordinate its efforts with existing services for children in the community.

BOARDING SCHOOLS

The boarding school, called in England the public school, is not a highly popular educational institution in America. For one thing, it costs money. For another, it connotes a type of class distinction which is distasteful to most people. But perhaps the major reason why boarding schools are so little used is the general high level of public education in this country. As a result of this, the boarding school's original reason for being, which was to send the child away to a good school because there was none in the vicinity, no longer exists in most areas.

Nevertheless, there are many fine private boarding schools in the United States, and some of these provide an excellent opportunity for satisfactory placement of moderately disturbed children whose chief therapeutic need is to be away from their home environment. *Sargent's Private Schools* lists over 500 private boarding schools in this country. The heaviest concentration of such schools is in the East and South, but there is also a fair number in the Midwest and far West. These schools vary widely in type: Some have high academic and social standards; many are military-type schools; others are oriented in whole or in part toward pupils with learning problems, and these provide some special education. A few are of the vocational-training type, frankly intended for children who cannot be expected to achieve much academically. Another resource particularly useful to the child psychiatrist is the *Directory for Exceptional Children* which lists 2,000 programs for the training and education of children with special problems such as aphasia, brain damage, various physical handicaps, and emotional disturbances.

Most private schools are, by average standards, rather expensive. Thus, sending a child to such a school will impose some financial burden on middle-income families. However, the cost is, for many families, not prohibitive, so that if the indication for the child's attending the school is strong, the family can often, by making certain sacrifices, manage it.

A good, well-run military-type school can be a highly successful therapeutic experience for a moderately acting-out boy whose needs for pattern-ing and control cannot be met at home. Such cases are frequently seen in families in which the father is passive and ineffectual, or perhaps even grossly neurotic or psychotic and unable to function as a figure of authority and an adequate masculine identification. Yet a school where the discipline is too rigid and military-like is not good for disturbed children. In fact, it is probably not good for any child. A possible exception is the psychopath, particularly the overindulged type often seen in higher-income families. Such a boy may function surprisingly well in a strict military school where little is expected of him in terms of relationship, and where rigorous pat-terning is imposed.

SUMMER CAMPS

Summertime can be a period of heightened difficulty for the emotion-ally disturbed child. Forced to spend many additional hours every day with his family, tensions and frictions which were kept in abeyance throughout the school year may get out of control. Many parents look forward to the end of the school year with justifiable apprehension. Their concern is usually imparted to the child, and as a result their worst fears are often realized. Summer camps are an ideal solution to such a problem. Plans for a patient's summer should be made well in advance, as good camps are scarce, and their rolls are often filled by early spring. There are a variety of camps, private, church-operated, Y.M.-Y.W.C.A., Boy and Girl Scout, and the like. Most are primarily for normal children, but can tolerate a few marginally-adjusted. Some are designed for children with specific problems, physical handicaps, learning difficulties, even emotional difficulties. The University of Michigan, for example, maintains a large summer camp for emotionally disturbed boys. Counselors are University students, mainly in training for various types of children's work. The service which such a camp renders to families, to communities, and to the children themselves is inestimable.

The summer camp may serve not only as a temporary relief measure to get the child away from home; it can often be a true therapeutic experi-ence, perhaps providing the child the first real opportunity of his life for a close and consistent relationship with a mature and interested adult.

REFERENCES

Ackerman, N. W. The Psychodynamics of Family Life, New York, Basic Books, 1958.

Alpert, A. The Treatment of Emotionally Disturbed Children in a Therapeutic Nursery, Am. J. Orthopsychiatry, 25: 826, 1955.

Berkowitz, P. and Rothman, E. The Teacher and the Disturbed Child, in The
    Disturbed Child, New York, New York University Press, 1960.
Directory for Exceptional Children, 4th ed., Boston, Porter Sargent, 1962.
Dreikurs, R., and Corsini, R. Twenty Years of Group Psychotherapy, Am. J.
    Psychiat., 110: 567, 1954.
Gill, H. B. Correction's Sacred Cows, Arch. Crim. Dynamics, 3: 237, 1959.
Inglis, D., and Marsh, E. J. Use of State Mental Hospitals as a Resource for
    Children, Am. J. Orthopsychiatry, 28: 689, 1958.
Morse, W. C. The Education of Socially Maladjusted and Emotionally Dis-
    turbed Children, in Education of Exceptional Children and Youth, eds.
    Cruickshank and Johnson, Englewood Cliffs, N.J., Prentice-Hall, 1958.
Naughton, F. Home Care Following Residential Treatment, Child Welfare,
    36: 1, Dec. 1957.
Peck, H. B., Harrower, M., and Beck, M. B. A New Pattern for Mental Health
    Services in a Children's Court, Springfield, Ill., Charles C Thomas, 1958.
Sargent's Private Schools. Boston, Porter Sargent, 1956.
Slavson, S. R. An Introduction to Group Therapy, New York, International Uni-
    versities Press, 1943.
——— Analytic Group Psychotherapy With Children, Adolescents and Adults,
    New York, Columbia University Press, 1950.

19

PSYCHOPHARMACOLOGIC TREATMENT

Alexander R. Lucas, M.D.

In treating adult disorders, the psychiatrist has at his disposal two somatic therapies: convulsive therapy and the psychoactive drugs. However, in the therapy of disturbed children, electroconvulsive and insulin-coma treatments have virtually no place. Rarely, in life-threatening situations such as acute suicidal reactions or severe anorexia, which have not responded to other forms of treatment, convulsive therapy may be indicated. Most of the conditions formerly considered indications for convulsive therapy are now treated more successfully and safely with the "tranquilizer" drugs, and these, together with the antidepressives and certain other formulations, are the somatic therapies preferred by the child psychiatrist.

For many reasons, determining whether a child will receive benefit from a given drug can be an extremely vexing problem, and a survey of the literature gives the reader a confusing and often contradictory view of a territory that is sparsely mapped and constantly changing. Moreover, once a given drug therapy is embarked upon, it is often difficult to determine what benefits, if any, the child is receiving.

To begin with, relatively few studies of drug therapy have been done on children, and even fewer of these are controlled studies. Most of the clinical experience has been obtained from adult patients, and the more potent drugs have had their greatest usefulness in the adult psychoses and endogenous depressions. The majority of studies on children have dealt with mentally retarded children, rather than with emotionally disturbed ones.

Even the most objective therapist, attempting to evaluate a drug's effect on emotionally disturbed children, will be likely to run afoul of several hazards—particularly, the phenomenon of suggestion and a host of confusing variables.

387

Suggestion often plays a decisive role in the success or failure of drug therapy. This is not to decry the use of suggestion in treating the patient—if a therapist gets good results by combining drugs with suggestion, so much the better. On the other hand, this approach provides little understanding of the drug's specific effect. Most investigators consider the use of placebo controls to be the best technique for evaluating drug effectiveness, but even this method is fallible and combines several disadvantages. One of these is that the child may experience subjective disturbances from the sudden alteration in his psychological state when he is shunted from drug to placebo or vice versa. Another defect in the technique is that the use of suggestion in conjunction with the drug treatment cannot operate if placebos are used, since therapists tend to be more cautious or "objective" when their patients are drug-study subjects. Bender (1959), in defending the use of non-placebo-controlled drug studies, has observed:

I have seen well-controlled research that was very bad therapy and that also, since it was research concerned with pharmacotherapy, was bad research. I cannot conceive of how one can treat a human being in distress and call it research, and try to leave out the interpersonal relationships, and not control the drug dosage, and not know what is going on in the individual that is being researched.

Variables which must be taken into consideration involve the child himself, the therapist, and the environment. Since all children fluctuate periodically in their behavior and adjustment, it is often difficult to determine what effect a given therapy is having on the child at a given time— not to mention the individual differences which complicate the comparison of effects on different children. The individual therapist represents another variable, since some psychiatrists tend to be more "drug-oriented" than others and thus may be overenthusiastic about the benefits of this or that particular drug.

The third variable is most pronounced when the child under treatment is an outpatient. Observations on the child's adjustment and behavior are subjective, and when these come, in the main, from the parents and the school, such information is often sketchy and unreliable. With outpatient treatment, there may also be inadequate supervision of drug intake, so that it is impossible to know if the patient is actually receiving the prescribed dosage. In many cases, parents voluntarily change the dose, omit giving the tablets, or fail to keep accurate records. In other cases, the child himself forgets or omits the medication. Another problem inherent in outpatient treatment involves a reluctance to prescribe as large a dose as can be safely administered in a more controlled environment, with the result that many outpatients never receive therapeutic doses.

Despite the difficulties in evaluation, drugs are beneficial in selected cases in both inpatient and outpatient therapy, and they do have a definite place in the treatment plan. In time, one can expect further research to clarify some of the issues and make evaluation more reliable: For example, it is now possible to determine whether a patient is receiving phenothiazine drugs by means of urinary tests (Forrest and others) which estimate the dose of the drug ingested.

The main requirements for proof of direct drug action have been summarized by Grant:

1. Accurate, consistent, reliable, and objective measures of those aspects of behavior that are being assessed as to change.

2. Use of sufficiently large groups to allow statistical control and confidence in the results.

3. Random assignment of cases to drug or control group.

4. Elimination of contaminants such as changed environment or concurrent therapy to only one of the groups under comparison.

Drugs useful in the treatment of psychiatric disorders fall into two major categories: the tranquilizers and the antidepressives. Others used to a lesser extent are the barbiturates, other anticonvulsants, and some experimental psychotomimetic drugs. The following classification is used:

A. Tranquilizers
    1. Phenothiazine derivatives
    2. Butyrophenones
    3. Rauwolfia alkaloids
    4. Diphenylmethane derivatives
    5. Substituted propanediols
    6. Benzodiazepine compounds
B. Antidepressives
    1. Amphetamines
    2. Monoamine oxidase inhibitors
    3. Iminodibenzyl derivatives
    4. Miscellaneous structures
C. Other Drugs
    1. Barbiturates
    2. Anticonvulsants
    3. Experimental psychotomimetics

TRANQUILIZERS

The term *tranquilizer* has met with some objections among medical etymologists, since certain of these drugs have other therapeutic effects besides their calming or tranquilizing actions. Other terms proposed have included *ataraxic*, *phrenotropic*, and *neuroleptic*; however, the term *tranquilizer* has been most widely adopted and appears destined to remain in use.

Soon after the introduction of the tranquilizer drugs in the early 1950's, there occurred the usual wave of overreactions, both positive and negative, which have historically followed the introduction of any major therapy. There were forecasts, mostly in the lay press, that the mental hos-. pitals would soon be empty, as well as, on the other hand, dire predictions that wholesale use of the drugs to alleviate every minor anxiety would rob the population of its moral fiber and make this a nation of placid, pill-swallowing automata. Neither of these predictions was realized, and today, seen in the perspective of a few years' experience and research, it is accepted that the tranquilizer drugs are an important addition to the therapeutic armamentarium of the child psychiatrist. The use of tranquilizer drugs, particularly in a residential treatment center, can be an important adjunct in the treatment of selected cases. However, it cannot replace the other forms of therapy, and its chief function is in enabling the children to participate better in the total treatment program. The real danger is that the drugs may be overused for the convenience of others, so that the patient is too tranquilized, too sedated, and spends most of his day sitting or lying listlessly about. Occasionally, use of massive doses of a drug is indicated for brief periods in a child during an episode of excessive agitation, but then only rarely and only temporarily. Redl has aptly characterized the overuse of tranquilizer drugs as "chemical warfare against the unruly child."

The use of drugs for alleviation of tension and anxiety is, of course, not new: Alcohol has probably been employed for such purposes since prehistory. However, tranquilizer drugs are unique in that they are not general anesthetic agents. They do not act by depressing all central nervous system activity, and there is a wide margin between therapeutic effect and the production of unconsciousness. Actually, a concise definition covering the entire group of tranquilizer drugs is not available. Berger, noting that tranquilizers are "usually described as substances that reduce excitement and agitation without clouding consciousness," points out that this definition is unsuitable for at least two reasons, first, there other drugs, such as scopolamine, which may have these same results, and which are not ordinarily considered tranquilizers. Second, tranquilizers sometimes do much more than reduce excitement and agitation: "They may facilitate social adjustment, eliminate delusions and hallucinations, or make mute patients communicative."

The drugs most commonly referred to as tranquilizers include:

1. The phenothiazine derivatives

2. The butyrophenones
3. The rauwolfia alkaloids
4. The diphenylmethane derivatives
5. The substituted propanediols
6. The benzodiazepine compounds

PHENOTHIAZINE DERIVATIVES

The first of the phenothiazine compounds to have extensive clinical use was chlorpromazine. Since then, numerous derivatives have been synthesized, some more powerful in action and producing fewer side effects; nevertheless, chlorpromazine continues to be used in greater amounts than the other derivatives. While much has been learned about the pharmacological action of the phenothiazines, their mode of action in producing therapeutic effects is by no means clearly understood. They are known to have powerful effects on the hypothalamus and the limbic system, and produce some alteration of the activity of the reticular formation. In therapeutic doses they have little or no effect on cortical structure. In experimental work, the phenothiazines have shown a dramatic ability to transform ferocious animals into tame and placid creatures. Olds and Travis found that when animals which had been placed in the brain-self-stimulation apparatus were injected with chlorpromazine, the rate of self-stimulation was markedly reduced, in some cases almost to the point of total disappearance.

Despite a vast and growing body of information on the pharmacology of these drugs, clinical application still rests on observations obtained from empirical usage. As the most potent of the tranquilizer drugs, the phenothiazines are usually needed when pharmacotherapy is required in children with severe disturbances of behavior. Rather than altering the basic psychopathology in either severe or milder disturbances, these drugs modify certain behavioral symptoms, and thereby improve the child's functioning or his responsiveness to psychotherapy. Motor excitation and hyperactivity are the symptoms which respond most favorably to the phenothiazine drugs. Severe anxiety is also often diminished, and there may be improved behavioral organization.

Shaw and others have reported the results of a four-year study of tranquilizer drugs at a residential treatment center, using the placebo-control technique. They found that for the child inpatients, all of whom were moderately to severely disturbed, only the phenothiazine drugs (Mellaril, Prolixin, Stelazine, and Vesprin) were of significant benefit. The most beneficial effect of the drugs was to make the patient more amenable to external control. Additionally, the children were able to function better in social situations, to react with less anger and aggression, to participate more in the treatment program, and to tolerate better the aggression of others. The authors found that the patients most likely to benefit from these drugs are those who exhibit the following symptoms:

1. Anxiety and tension   4. Aggressiveness
2. Hyperexcitability   5. Impulsiveness
3. Oppositional behavior

Diagnosis did not correlate with amount of improvement. Thus, the indications for use of the drug are specific symptoms rather than diagnosis. The drugs were not given to patients at random. Rather, cases were selected for the study as being ones which were considered, on the basis of previous experience, to be likely to benefit from the drug. Of 74 children who received complete trials of one of the phenothiazine drugs, 50 (68 per cent) showed some clinical improvement.

The phenothiazines vary in their potency and in the severity of side effects. Their therapeutic results are generally similar if appropriate dosages are used. In individual children, however, there may be selective responsiveness to certain of the drugs, as well as varying susceptibility to side effects, not always dose-related. Thus, it may be necessary to try several drugs before finding an effective one. This should be done systematically and each drug should be given an adequate trial for at least two weeks. The dosage should be increased gradually until the desired effect is obtained, or until side effects, usually drowsiness, are encountered.

Side effects from the phenothiazines are common. In the above study, transient drowsiness and lassitude appeared in over 60 per cent of the patients—usually disappearing within three to six days if the dosage level was maintained. Occasionally, reduction of dosage was required. Dosage adjustment is sometimes difficult in children, and tolerance appears to fluctuate in some cases. Moreover, the margin between therapeutic and toxic dose is often small. Extrapyramidal dysfunction, reported in 31 per cent of cases, ranged from mild tremors to a full-blown parkinsonism. Most of these effects were promptly relieved by anti-parkinson drugs. Occasionally, a more severe side effect occurred, consisting of a rather sudden onset of muscular rigidity, usually involving neck or upper-extremity muscles. This syndrome has been termed *dyskinesia*. It may include torticollis, dysphagia, or aphonia. Sometimes the respiratory muscles are involved, although complete apnea has not been reported. The reaction is frightening to both patient and physician, and prompt treatment measures are indicated, with quick relief being obtained with an anti-parkinson drug. Because of dysphagia, the patient may be unable to swallow tablets; therefore a parenteral preparation should be kept on hand. Rarely, blood dyscrasias may occur. Recent reports indicate that if blood dyscrasias occur, they will do so early in treatment; thus it is advisable to do weekly blood counts for the first three months of phenothiazine therapy.

Because of the problems of dosage adjustment, and the number of toxic effects, phenothiazine drugs present more difficulties when used with outpatients. However, if the physician understands the difficulties involved, and keeps in close communication with the family, these drugs may be very successful in an outpatient program. (Sometimes the results are better if the parent rather than the child receives the drug!) In many brain-damaged and schizophrenic children, hyperactivity and anxiety may be reduced to such a point that they are able to function adequately in public school. If the family situation is stable and additional psychotherapy is not required, the child may be seen by the family physician or pediatrician for regulation of the medication and for blood counts when necessary. Not infrequently it is possible in fairly severely disturbed children to obviate hospitalization through the use of these drugs.

Table 1 summarizes the dosages and specific indications for the phenothiazine drugs which have been most used in children. The information is drawn from the reports of Freedman (1958), Bender (1961), and Fish (1960), as well as from the writer's experience. For an approximation of dosage, for children under five years it is calculated on the basis of weight from information supplied by the drug manufacturer; above age 12, adult doses are used.

TABLE 1

PHENOTHIAZINE DRUGS: DOSE AND INDICATIONS

Drug	Daily Dose Range	Frequency of Administration	Remarks
1. Chlorpromazine (Thorazine)	75–300 mg.	t.i.d.	Indicated in severe anxiety, agitation, hyperkinesis
2. Promazine (Sparine)	75–300 mg.	t.i.d.	Same as above
3. Prochlorperazine (Compazine)	15–30 mg.	t.i.d.	Indications as above. Rather frequent extrapyramidal side effects
4. Triflupromazine (Vesprin)	30–100 mg.	t.i.d.	Useful in severe disturbance. May be helpful in tic syndrome, Gilles de la Tourette's disease (Lucas, 1964)

TABLE 1 (*continued*)

PHENOTHIAZINE DRUGS: DOSE AND INDICATIONS

Drug	Daily Dose Range	Frequency of Administration	Remarks
5. Thioridazine (Mellaril)	30–300 mg.	t.i.d.	Wide range of disorders, including tic syndrome. Much used in outpatients
6. Perphenazine (Trilafon)	2–16 mg.	t.i.d.	Same indications as chlorpromazine
7. Trifluoperazine (Stelazine)	2–20 mg.	b.i.d.	Especially useful in schizophrenia
8. Fluphenazine (Permitil, Prolixin)	1–7.5 mg.	q.d. or b.i.d.	Most potent phenothiazine. May have a stimulating effect in apathetic children. Useful also in slowing the hyperkinesis of encephalopathy
9. Promethazine (Phenergan)	15–100 mg.	t.i.d. or h.s.	Unique among the phenothiazines: main effects are antihistaminic and sedative. Useful for bedtime sedation

BUTYROPHENONES

This new group of potent compounds, including haloperidol (Haldol) and triperidol, has been widely used in Europe and Canada in adult psychotic patients. Chemically the butyrophenones are unrelated to the phenothiazines, but their pharmacologic actions are very similar. Their usefulness in disturbed children is yet to be established through controlled studies, but haloperidol appears to have a markedly palliative effect on certain tics, particularly the vocal tics of Gilles de la Tourette's disease (Challas and Brauer; Chapel and others; Lucas, 1966).

RAUWOLFIA ALKALOIDS

Rauwolfia serpentina was used hundreds of years ago in India as an antipsychotic drug. As reserpine (Serpasil), it was first used in psychiatry in 1954. Along with the phenothiazines and the butyrophenones the rauwolfias constitute the "major tranquilizers" because of their usefulness in psychosis. Pharmacologically, reserpine probably acts by reducing brain serotonin levels. Bender (1961) has found it useful in autistic and in disorganized organic children. Other studies have reported variable success. With adequate doses, severe lethargy, nasal congestion, weight gain, and other disturbing side effects are often encountered. In some children it is of definite value and should be utilized for the same general indications as the phenothiazines. It has been used in dosages of from 0.5 mg to 8 mg daily, given in divided doses.

DIPHENYLMETHANE DERIVATIVES

Diphenylmethane derivatives and the following two categories of drugs, because of their indication in milder psychiatric disorders, have been termed the "minor tranquilizers." These drugs have their chief use in the outpatient treatment of disturbed children, although results of outpatient treatment with tranquilizer drugs have not been so well documented as treatment of inpatients.

The diphenylmethanes include several drugs which have antihistaminic properties: Among those used in children are hydroxyzine (Atarax, Vistaril), azacyclonol (Frenquel), benactyzine (Suavitil), captodiamine (Suvren), and diphenhydramine (Benadryl). Azacyclonol, benactyzine and captodiamine probably have little or no effect in disturbed children. Hydroxyzine has a tranquilizing effect in mild anxiety. Freedman (1958) found it useful in anxiety states, night terrors, reaction to somatic difficulties, and school phobia. It has been used fairly extensively in pediatric practice and in psychosomatic conditions. Dosage ranges from 50 mg to 150 mg or more daily in divided doses. Diphenhydramine has been used extensively in child psychiatry and some are enthusiastic about the results. It was used at Bellevue Hospital in New York before the introduction of the tranquilizer drugs, and has been recommended for use in disorganized younger children, in impulsive children, and particularly in those with overt anxiety. Fish (1963) notes that its effectiveness drops markedly at puberty. Dosages from 30 mg to 400 mg daily have been used. It is generally given three times daily.

SUBSTITUTED PROPANEDIOLS

Of greatest importance in this group is meprobamate (Equanil, Miltown). In certain situations it is definitely beneficial, but because of the difficulties of evaluating drugs in outpatients, and the lack of controlled studies, most knowledge concerning its value is still based upon clinical impressions. In severely disturbed hospitalized children, Shaw and others found the results discouraging. In relatively mild disturbances, in transient anxiety states, and for bedtime sedation, meprobamate has been useful. Daily dosage in children ranges from 600 mg to 1,600 mg or more, given in divided doses.

BENZODIAZEPINE COMPOUNDS

Chlordiazepoxide (Librium), like meprobamate, is useful in relatively mild disorders, particularly anxiety states. Children's dosages have not yet been established, but the starting dose is generally 5 mg or 10 mg, three times daily. Related to and more potent than chlordiazepoxide is diazepam (Valium). Although studies in adults suggest that it has a powerful antianxiety effect, sufficient data are not yet available to evaluate its importance in the treatment of disturbed children.

ANTIDEPRESSIVES

As with tranquilizers, various terms have been suggested for psychoactive drugs which have an excitatory or stimulating effect upon the central nervous system. These include *psychic energizers, central nervous system stimulants,* and *psychoanaleptics.* The most widely accepted term is *antidepressives* because of the primary indication for these drugs; that is, the depressive illnesses of adulthood. Whether the newer antidepressive drugs will find a place in the psychopharmacologic armamentarium of the child psychiatrist is not yet established.

Within this group, the drugs of greatest interest to child psychiatrists are the amphetamines, which were among the first drugs used in child psychiatry. Classifying the amphetamines under "stimulants" is somewhat misleading for the child psychiatrist, however, because the rationale for using them in disturbed children has been not to stimulate but to diminish the children's hyperactivity. The antidepressives, then, include:

1. The amphetamines
2. The monoamine oxidase inhibitors
3. The iminodibenzyl derivatives
4. Antidepressive drugs of miscellaneous structure

AMPHETAMINES

Early use of amphetamines has been reported since the 1930's, when Bradley used amphetamine (Benzedrine) and later dextro-amphetamine (Dexedrine) in children with behavior disorders. These drugs were used by such researchers as Bradley and Bender (1942) in children having a wide variety of behavior problems. Later, Ginn and Hohman—noting that many of the children in whom the drugs were effective evidenced a common syndrome characterized by excessive restlessness, short attention span, impulsiveness, and emotional lability—postulated that these children were evidencing diffuse brain damage. In another study, Laufer and others found that children with a "hyperkinetic impulse disorder" had an abnormally low photo-Metrazol threshold which suggested a functional disturbance of the diencephalon. This low threshold was raised to normal levels by amphetamine administration. These authors theorized that amphetamine acts by raising the level of synaptic resistance, altering the function of the diencephalon in such a way as to keep the cortex from being flooded by streams of unmodulated sensory impulses which stimulated the reticular activating system. Controlled studies are lacking, but in some encephalopathic children, the effects of dextro-amphetamine on the classical symptoms of brain damage are so dramatic and sudden as to be incontrovertible; however, there are no criteria for identifying which children among the hyperactive brain-damaged ones will respond to this drug.

Treatment is usually initiated with 5 mg daily in the morning and is increased, if necessary, to 10 mg or 15 mg, or occasionally more, taken in the morning or in divided doses twice a day. When improvement occurs, it will usually do so within a few days, often after the first dose. Some children require higher doses, but if there is no discernible change in symptoms after two weeks the drug should be discontinued as ineffective, and another drug, usually one of the phenothiazines, should be tried. Somewhat less than half of the children with the classical syndrome of hyperactivity, short attention span, impulsiveness, and restlessness respond to this drug. When effective, the medication may be continued for years without adverse effects. It is usually no longer needed when the child approaches puberty.

Side effects are usually lacking, but because of occasional insomnia, the drug should not be given in the late afternoon or evening. Rarely, in children, anorexia is an accompaniment of treatment with this drug. The dextro portion of the drug appears to have the desired activity in encephalopathic children and therefore is the drug of choice. If racemic amphetamine is used, the dosage should be doubled.

Additional use of the amphetamines has been suggested by Fish (1963) to stimulate overly-inhibited neurotic children and she and Bender (1956) found them especially useful in prepubertal children with excessive sexual preoccupations and fantasies, and in those with school phobia.

MONOAMINE OXIDASE INHIBITORS

This and the next group constitute the newer antidepressives whose effectiveness in the severe depressions of adulthood is now well known. Pharmacologically, through their inhibition of the enzyme monoamine oxidase, the MAO inhibitors exert a protective action on serotonin and norepinephrine. Iproniazid, the first of the MAO inhibitors used in psychiatry, but no longer marketed because of its toxicity, was administered by Freedman (1958) to a group of autistic schizophrenic children. He found that they showed an increased awareness of their surroundings and some of them employed a greater use of language. Nialamide (Niamid) and phenelzine (Nardil) have been used by Bender (1961) in similar situations, as well as with withdrawn, depressed adolescents.

IMINODIBENZYL DERIVATIVES

This group, differing chemically but resembling the MAO inhibitors in clinical action, includes imipramine (Tofranil), amitriptyline (Elavil) and nortriptyline (Aventyl). Bender (1961) reported using imipramine in autistic children who became more alert, made attempts to speak, and began to relate. Quite a different indication has been reported by MacLean, who found imipramine useful in alleviating enuresis in children. Results of several subsequent studies have been contradictory but in the writer's experience many children have completely ceased wetting when treated with imipramine, 25 mg to 75 mg given at bedtime. Related drugs appear to have a similar action. That imipramine is significantly more effective than placebo has now been adequately confirmed by Alderton, and Poussaint and Ditman in double-blind studies.

Lucas and others (1965) reported a placebo-controlled study of amitriptyline in a group of inpatients with symptoms of depression. These were children and adolescents ranging in age from 10 to 17, more than half of whom showed significant improvement, as compared to placebo, in some of the symptoms relating to their depression. Dosages used ranged up to 75 mg daily.

ANTIDEPRESSIVE DRUGS OF MISCELLANEOUS STRUCTURE

Methylphenidate (Ritalin) has been effective in some hyperactive brain-damaged children exhibiting the same symptoms which respond to amphetamine. It has also been found useful in stimulating some apathetic depressed children, particularly adolescent schizophrenics. Dosages used are generally 10 mg or 20 mg daily. Pipradol (Meratran) has been used in child psychiatry, but not sufficient evidence is yet available to evaluate its effectiveness. Deanol (Deaner) has been reported to stimulate learning and control behavior; however, controlled studies (Kugel and Alexander; Shaw and others) have not demonstrated its superiority over placebo.

OTHER DRUGS

Medications which do not readily fit into the categories of tranquilizer or antidepressive drugs, but which have found some application in child psychiatry are:
1. Barbiturates
2. Anticonvulsant drugs
3. The psychotomimetic drugs (to a lesser extent)

BARBITURATES

The barbiturates, long a mainstay in the pharmacologic management of psychiatric patients, now have little place in child psychiatry. Infrequently they are indicated for the sedation of acutely agitated patients, but most such situations are now better handled by injectable preparations of the phenothiazines. Barbiturates are sometimes useful for nighttime sedation when given orally, but chloral hydrate and some of the tranquilizers are often effective for this purpose, with fewer undesirable side effects. Chronic administration of the barbiturates, except in convulsive disorders, is no longer tenable, since, in children, confusion, disorientation, and increased agitation are often produced.

ANTICONVULSANTS

The convulsive disorders require specific drug therapy. Medical management of the convulsive disorders is not considered properly within the realm of the child psychiatrist, and is best done by the pediatrician or pediatric neurologist. It is most important that an accurate diagnosis be made, as it is a serious error to treat a child with episodic behavior disorder as an "epileptic equivalent," when he is in fact an acting-out emotionally disturbed child. The opposite error is, of course, equally serious. At one time there was some enthusiasm about treating children whose behavior disorders were accompanied by diffuse EEG abnormalities with anticonvulsant drugs, but this is no longer in vogue and is not indicated unless an actual convulsive disorder can be demonstrated.

EXPERIMENTAL PSYCHOTOMIMETICS

The psychotomimetic drugs, including lysergic acid diethylamide (LSD-25), sernyl, mescaline, and psylocybin, because of their unusual properties and sometimes unjustified therapeutic claims, have of late received much publicity in the lay press and in the professional literature. However, the efficacy and the safety of these drugs is still uncertain and their use in therapy is not recommended. These drugs have thus far had only a limited experimental use in children—Freedman and others (1962), for example, reported negative results in their attempt to produce increased speech in autistic schizophrenic children given LSD-25.

SUMMARY

Psychoactive drugs have now achieved status as important tools in the treatment of the psychiatric disorders of childhood, but the day when they can replace psychotherapy has not arrived, nor is it in the foreseeable future.

REFERENCES

Alderton, H. R. Imipramine in the Treatment of Nocturnal Enuresis of Childhood, Canad. Psychiat. Assoc. J., 10: 141, 1965.
Bender, L., and Cottington, F. The Use of Amphetamine Sulfate (Benzedrine) in Child Psychiatry, Am. J. Psychiat., 99: 116, 1942.
——— and Nichtern, S. Chemotherapy in Child Psychiatry, New York State J. Med., 56: 2791, 1956.

Bender, L., and Faretra, G. Organic Therapy in Pediatric Psychiatry, Dis. Nerv. Syst., 22: Suppl., p. 110, 1961.

———— Discussion of paper by L. Eisenberg, Basic Issues in Drug Research with Children, in Child Research in Psychopharmacology, ed. S. Fisher, Springfield, Ill., Charles C Thomas, 1959.

Berger, F. M. Classification of Psychoactive Drugs According to Their Chemical Structures and Sites of Action, in Drugs and Behavior, eds. Uhr and Miller, New York, John Wiley & Sons, 1960.

Bradley, C. Benzedrine and Dexedrine in the Treatment of Children's Behavior Disorders, Pediatrics, 5: 24, 1950.

Challas, G., and Brauer, W. Tourette's Disease: Relief of Symptoms with R1625, Amer. J. Psychiat., 120: 283, 1963.

Chapel, J. L. Brown, N., and Jenkins, R. L. Tourette's Disease: Symptomatic Relief with Haloperidol, Amer. J. Psychiat., 121: 608, 1964.

Fish, B. Drug Therapy in Child Psychiatry: Pharmacological Aspects, Comprehensive Psychiat., 1: 212, 1960.

———— Pharmacotherapy in Children's Behavior Disorders, in Current Psychiatric Therapies, New York, Grune & Stratton, 1963, Vol. 3.

Forrest, I. S., Forrest, F. M., and Mason, A. S. A Rapid Urine Color Test for Thioridazine, Am. J. Psychiat., 116: 928, 1960.

Freed, H. The Chemistry and Therapy of Behavior Disorders in Children, Springfield, Ill., Charles C Thomas, 1962.

Freedman, A. M. Drug Therapy in Behavior Disorders, Ped. Clin. N. Amer., 5: 573, 1958.

———— Ebin, E. V., and Wilson, E. A. Autistic Schizophrenic Children, Arch. Gen. Psychiat., 6: 203, 1962.

Ginn, S. A., and Hohman, L. B. The Use of Dextro-Amphetamine in Severe Behavior Problems of Children, South. M. J., 46: 1124, 1953.

Grant, Q. R. Psychopharmacology in Childhood Emotional and Mental Disorders, J. Pediatrics, 61: 626, 1962.

Kugel, R. B., and Alexander, T. The Effect of a Central Nervous System Stimulant (Deanol) on Behavior, Pediatrics, 31: 651, 1963.

Laufer, M. W., Denhoff, E., and Solomon, G. Hyperkinetic Impulse Disorder in Children's Behavior Problems, Psychosomatic Med., 19: 38, 1957.

Lucas, A. R. Gilles de la Tourette's Disease in Children: Treatment with Phenothiazine Drugs, Am. J. Psychiat., 121: 606, 1964.

———— Lockett, H. J., and Grimm, F. Amitriptyline in Childhood Depressions, Dis. Nerv. Syst., 26: 105, 1965.

———— Gilles de la Tourette's Disease in Children: Treatment with Haloperidol, Amer. J. Psychiat. In press.

MacLean, R. E. G. Imipramine Hydrochloride (Tofranil) and Enuresis, Am. J. Psychiat., 117: 551, 1960.

Olds, J., and Travis, R. Effects of Chlorpromazine, Meprobamate and Morphine on Self-Stimulation, in Drugs and Behavior, eds. Uhr and Miller, New York, John Wiley & Sons, 1960.

Poussaint, A. F., and Ditman, K. S. A Controlled Study of Imipramine (Tofranil) in the Treatment of Childhood Enuresis, J. of Pediatrics, 67: 283, 1965.

Redl, F. Discussion of paper by L. J. Borstelmann, Populations, Behaviors, and

Situations; some Ecological Considerations in Child Drug Research, in Child
Research in Psychopharmacology, ed. S. Fisher, Springfield, Ill., Charles C
Thomas, 1959.
Shaw, C. R., Lockett, H. J., Lucas, A. R., Lamontagne, C. H., and Grimm, F.
Tranquilizer Drugs in the Treatment of Emotionally Disturbed Children: I.
Inpatients in a Residential Treatment Center, J. Amer. Acad. Child. Psy-
chiat., 2: 725, 1963.

SECTION FIVE

PERSPECTIVE

20

CHILD PSYCHIATRY:
RETROSPECT AND PROSPECT

In the days when Tom Sawyer went to the old one-room schoolhouse in Missouri, a guiding principle of education was "spare the rod and spoil the child." If Mark Twain's accounts are to be credited (he has been suspected of exaggeration), children went to school grudgingly, hated it heartily, and envied Huckleberry Finn, son of the town drunk, who remained free. In those days, children who were temperamentally or intellectually unsuited to attend school, or who were needed to help support the family, simply stayed home. Today, if a child does not go to school, his parents can be legally prosecuted.

There are a number of landmarks in the history of child psychiatry, but perhaps the most significant was the passage of compulsory education laws. The requirement that all children attend school had a number of sweeping effects. One was to demonstrate and at times to aggravate the multitude of mental and emotional problems among the juvenile population. Another was to force attention and effort to the care and treatment of these problems.

It is thus no coincidence that the beginning of compulsory education coincided closely with the beginning of child psychiatry, both of which occurred around the onset of the present century. Leo Kanner, who is perhaps best qualified to speak on the subject, has said that: "When the twentieth century made its appearance, there was not—and there could not be—anything that might in any sense be regarded as child psychiatry."

Prior to 1900, there had been a number of significant contributions to knowledge and understanding of the emotional and intellectual development of children, but these could be considered no more than breaking the ground. In the latter part of the nineteenth century, educators in Europe and America, influenced by the writings of Rousseau and Pestalozzi, and by the teachings of William James and his pupil, John Dewey, had begun

405

to attend to the individual capacities and needs of children. Before that time, education was conceived mainly in terms of moulding the child to fit the form. Emphasis was on curricula rather than on pupils, and the teacher's aim was to see that the pupil learned a certain amount of Latin, of mathematics, of rhetoric, and so on. The child was expected to behave. If he did not, he was punished. If he did not learn at a sufficient rate, he repeated the grade, or was expelled.

The mental disorders of children, in the late nineteenth century, were described largely in the same terms as those of adults. Witch-burning was by then a thing of the past, but psychotic children were still regarded with revulsion and mistrust, and were labeled "demented." Etiology was expressed in such terms as overwork, excessive study, and moral degeneracy.

Perhaps the area of greatest advance in the treatment of problem children prior to the present century was with the mentally retarded. In the early 1800's a French physician, Jean Itard, had become interested in a "wolf boy" who had been found living in a woods near Aveyron. After trying with little success for five years to teach the boy language, Itard concluded that he was mentally defective. While the results of Itard's efforts were not promising, they nevertheless demonstrated that the feeble-minded could be improved by intensive training. A pupil of Itard's, Edward Seguin, developed methods for the training of "idiots." In 1848 Seguin came to the United States and helped establish several schools for the mentally retarded, the first of which was in Massachusetts. These schools were originally intended as temporary educational centers, from which the child, after training, could be returned to his home; but it was soon realized that custodial care, often of a permanent nature, was sometimes required.

It was not until the 1930's that facilities for mentally ill children were first provided at psychiatric hospitals. Thus, the inpatient care of the retarded preceded by some 80 years that of the mentally disturbed child.

THE PRESENT CENTURY

Beginning in the early 1900's, a number of major developments, directly or indirectly influencing child psychiatry, appeared in rapid succession. These include:

1. Psychological testing
2. Child psychology
3. Juvenile courts
4. The study of delinquency
5. The mental hygiene movement and guidance clinics
6. The visiting-teacher program

7. Special education
8. Dynamic psychiatry and psychoanalysis
9. Psychiatric treatment of children

Each of the above developments will be reviewed below in historical perspective, with a consideration of their current status and their significance to child psychiatry. Much of the historical material has been obtained from the excellent article by Roberta Crutcher.

PSYCHOLOGICAL TESTING

Early work with the mentally retarded had produced some efforts to measure and classify the intellectual capabilities of children. But it was not until 1905 that a standardized and systematized psychometric test was developed. Binet, at the request of the Minister of Public Instruction in France, undertook an extensive study of "backward" children for the purpose of devising methods of teaching. It became apparent to Binet that a major problem was to define backwardness, and to differentiate retarded children from those who were poor students for other reasons. He devised a test composed of a series of questions of gradually increasing difficulty. In the subsequent five years he revised it into a form which consisted of groups of questions arranged according to age level, the "average" child of a particular age being expected to answer all questions at that age level.

Terman in the United States further improved and standardized Binet's test, employing a larger and more adequate sample of the general population. His revised form, known as the Stanford-Binet, is still in wide use today.

The concept of measuring psychological performance soon attained wide popularity. A major development was the use of the so-called nonverbal tests, which measure capacities not based on an understanding of language. A nonverbal test used by Seguin in the previous century had consisted of a board containing cutouts in a variety of geometric patterns into which the subject was required to fit wooden blocks of the appropriate shape. The Seguin Form Board is still used as a part of some psychological tests for children. Wechsler, at New York's Bellevue Hospital, devised a test for older children and adults which combined many of the best features of both verbal and nonverbal tests. The Wechsler-Bellevue was later revised and divided into two tests, one for children and one for adults. The Wechsler Intelligence Scale for Children (WISC) and the Wechsler Adult Intelligence Scale (WAIS) are perhaps the most widely used psychological tests in this country today.

Another development in psychological testing was the concept that the subject's responses to a standardized test situation could reveal much about his personality and inner life. Known as the projective technique, this was successfully applied by the Swiss psychologist, Hermann Rorschach, whose ink-blot test is today one of the most important and popular of the projective tests. The projective aspects of all psychological tests are now well appreciated, and are often valuable to the psychiatrist in his diagnostic evaluation.

CHILD PSYCHOLOGY

Studies of child behavior and development had been made as early as the late eighteenth century in the observations of Rousseau, and again in the middle and later nineteenth century in the detailed notes of Charles Darwin and Preyer on the behavior of their own children. However, the systematic study of child behavior on a major scale began with the work of G. Stanley Hall in the 1880's (Watson). Hall theorized that the mental development of the individual occurred in a series of stages more or less corresponding to the levels attained by early man and his prehuman ancestors in evolution—a psychological application of the biological principle that ontogeny recapitulates phylogeny. Hall accumulated a great body of information about child thinking and behavior, mainly through the use of questionnaires which he developed for parents and teachers to apply to their children. Among the topics which he investigated were appetites, fears, punishments, dreams, memories, toys, early sense of self, prayers, crying and laughing, perceptions of rhythm, and motor abilities. Hall's studies have been criticized as lacking scientific merit and statistical validity. The content of his studies was probably of little value, but he stimulated interest in the systematic study of children, and thus laid the foundations of child psychology.

During the first two decades of the twentieth century, psychology as a scientific discipline was emerging from a slow start into a period of vigorous growth. The major technique for obtaining data on mental processes was still the introspective method, in which the subject was asked to report his thoughts and feelings in response to certain questions or stimuli—a technique poorly suited to young children. John Watson's work marked the next advance. By relying on objective observations and measurements rather than on introspective reporting, Watson was able to study the emotional responses of infants and young children as well as animals. He applied the conditioning techniques of Pavlov to human subjects. In a number of now-famous experiments, Watson showed that young children do not have an inherent fear of animals, but that they can be readily conditioned to fear a small animal, or any other object, if presentation of the object is accompanied by presentation of an unpleasant stimulus, such as an electric shock. Watson founded a major school of psychology, the behaviorist school, the contributions of which have been of fundamental importance in understanding human behavior.

With the general growth of interest in children as objects worthy of further understanding and investigation, child psychology has developed rapidly into a discipline that shapes many areas of contemporary culture. By studying the normal child, it has provided child psychiatry with a foundation for the understanding of the abnormal child.

JUVENILE COURTS

Until the end of the nineteenth century there were no special courts for children. Any child who committed an illegal act, including such minor offenses as school truancy and vandalism, was arrested and brought before the same court as an adult offender. While the attitudes and punitive measures of the police and courts were generally more lenient toward children, nevertheless an encounter with the law was seldom a therapeutic experience. Because the law made no provision for special handling of delinquent children, a magistrate could actually impose long terms of imprisonment for repeated offenses.

In 1899, the states of Illinois and Colorado passed laws providing for the establishment of juvenile courts. The other states quickly followed suit. This step both reflected and further stimulated changing attitudes toward the antisocial behavior of children, and greatly facilitated the enlightened study and treatment of delinquency.

THE STUDY OF DELINQUENCY

In 1908, the juvenile court of Chicago, on the recommendation of Adolf Meyer, invited William Healy to come to Chicago to undertake an investigation into the causes and treatment of juvenile delinquency. Healy and Bronner describing the original conception of the study, point out that one central and major weakness had been noted in the juvenile court proceedings:

The individual before the court, given at most only a physical examination, was not in the least known with regard to his essential nature. Nor was anything known as to why he was a delinquent. Nevertheless, judgment was passed and the type of penalty of supposed treatment that a court can order was prescribed. How, observers argued, can a judge or anyone else, laboring under such a handicap, possibly prescribe wisely for the individual who, if placed on probation, needs some special form of treatment, or incentive to help him mend his ways; or should have some particular type of institutional training or segregation?

It was to the causes of delinquency that Healy turned his full attention. Experienced as a neurologist and a physician interested in children with behavior difficulties, Healy approached each delinquent child individually, interviewing him, investigating his background, endeavoring always to understand him rather than to judge him. The results of Healy's work at Chicago, and later at the Judge Baker Foundation in Boston, profoundly influenced thinking about the disturbances of childhood, and led to major developments in the fields of criminology, sociology, education, and social work. While Healy's own work was directed toward etiology rather than therapy, it formed an important basis for the later development of the guidance clinic movement. The publication in 1915 of his book, *The Individual Delinquent,* is considered a milestone in the understanding not only of delinquency but of all of human behavior.

Healy's pioneering work led to the formation of the Juvenile Psychopathic Institute of Chicago, now called the Institute for Juvenile Research, which still carries on studies in the causes and treatment of delinquency. It was at the Institute for Juvenile Research that a group of psychiatrists met in 1924 to form the American Orthopsychiatric Association, and in June of that year Healy was elected its first president.

MENTAL HYGIENE AND GUIDANCE CLINICS

With the great advances in bacteriology and public health that occurred early in the twentieth century, it was natural that the preventive medicine movement should spread to include other forms of disease in addition to the infectious. The original impetus for the mental hygiene movement was largely the work of Clifford Beers, a young law student who had been hospitalized for depression. Following his recovery, Beers began to devote his energies to improving facilities for the care and treatment of the mentally ill. He enlisted the aid and advice of a number of prominent people. Among the most enthusiastic of these was Adolf Meyer, who is credited with suggesting the term "mental hygiene."

In 1909 Beers founded the National Committee for Mental Hygiene. The original purpose of this Committee was to promote improvement in the care of "the insane" and to educate the public to a better understanding of the nature of mental illness and the need for preventive measures. Gradually, the scope of the Committee's work broadened to include delinquency, neurosis, and mental retardation.

With the emergence of child psychiatry after World War I, the mental hygiene movement began to shift its attention from adults to children. The National Committee for Mental Hygiene quickly espoused the child guidance movement, first through the effort of its Division on Prevention of Delinquency, and later through the succeeding Division on Community Clinics (Stevenson).

The concept of the child guidance clinic had first arisen out of the work of Healy and his associates at the Juvenile Psychopathic Institute in Chicago. While Healy's primary aim was to investigate the causes of delinquency, the experience gained from working as a team in a community clinic indicated that this was a logical therapeutic approach to the treatment of disturbed children. The first guidance clinic, called the Boston Habit Clinic, was opened in 1921, and was soon followed by others in various cities. The movement was greatly aided by the Committee for Mental Hygiene, with the financial assistance of the Commonwealth Fund. Communities were aided in organizing their own clinics by the setting up of "demonstration clinics" by a traveling team of psychiatrists, psychologists, and social workers. The guidance clinic movement was further stimulated by the formation in 1924 of the American Orthopsychiatric Association, already noted. This organization, which embraces many professions, including psychiatry, clinical psychology, social work, education, probation work, and psychiatric nursing, has become a major force in promoting and developing the multidisciplinary approach to preventive and child psychiatry.

THE VISITING TEACHER PROGRAM

The education profession, steadily giving increased recognition to its responsibilities for problem children, has developed the subspecialty of special education, and the visiting-teacher program.

The visiting-teacher movement originated in New York City, when the Public Education Association in 1907 employed several workers who combined a knowledge of social work and classroom teaching (Krugman). However, the movement was apparently premature, as for some years it struggled along with little recognition or success. It required the growing public acceptance of the mental hygiene movement of the 1920's for the visiting-teacher program to attain some importance. Even then, growth was relatively slow. Kanner notes that in 1921 there was a total of 91 visiting teachers in 28 communities of 13 states; by 1927 this had increased to 205 visiting teachers in 78 communities in 34 states. Growth of the movement was rapid following World War II. Current figures are not available, but visiting teachers would now certainly be numbered in the thousands, and they are found in virtually all schools in the larger communities, and in a number of the smaller ones.

The training and background of visiting teachers varies considerably, and there is as yet no standardization of requirements for this function. Many are regular teachers who have developed special skills and interests in working with problem children. Some are social workers, and a few are psychologists, while a growing number are trained in special education. The function of the visiting teacher is chiefly to act as a consultant for the school in the management of children with particular behavior or learning problems. Usually, the school principal together with the classroom teacher makes the decision that a child should be referred to the visiting teacher. The latter then sees the child individually, investigates his family background and school history, and determines what specific measures are indicated. Often the visiting teacher carries out case work with the child's family, either in the home or at her office. The child may himself be seen for regular interviews, which can be primarily oriented toward academic problems, even, at times, taking the form of tutorial sessions, or the interviews may be primarily of a psychotherapeutic nature.

The visiting teacher often requests psychological and psychiatric evaluation of the child, and this may constitute the largest referral source of a child psychiatry clinic. Following referral to the psychiatrist, the visiting teacher usually continues with the case, sometimes as the therapist receiving supervision from the psychiatrist, sometimes acting as liaison between the psychiatrist and the child's teachers and family.

SPECIAL EDUCATION

The profession of special education was originally concerned with the physically handicapped and the mentally retarded, and these continue to be two of its major areas of emphasis. The Rev. Thomas Gallaudet is generally credited with founding the movement (Cruickshank); as early as 1817 he began a program for the education of deaf children in his Connecticut parish. The following several decades saw much activity in the establishment of special programs and boarding schools for the blind, the deaf, and the mentally retarded.

A lull in progress then set in, characterized by a kind of public and professional apathy toward the problems of the handicapped. Institutions continued to operate, but the general philosophy was one of keeping the handicapped in the institutions rather than attempting to educate them to function in society. Then, soon after the turn of the century, developments in special education occurred as a part of the general movement in public health. Much impetus was gained through the effects of the two world wars and the resulting need for rehabilitation of many of the war casualties. Day-school programs came into being, which provided for the education of handicapped children who continued to live at home. With the inception of intelligence tests and the classification of retarded children into various levels, schools and programs were established for education of the trainable retarded children.

As techniques for the teaching and training of handicapped children developed, and as evidence of success with these children became known, the attitudes of both the education profession and the public gradually underwent subtle but important changes. Feelings toward handicapped children had generally been those of distaste, suspicion, even revulsion. This was true not only among the general public but even among the families of such children, often to such a degree that parents would refuse to acknowledge the existence of the child in the family. While there remains today even among enlightened people some opprobrium attached to having a retarded or handicapped child, there is far less than there was half a century ago. As social enlightenment grew, parent groups began to organize for the support of special care and education of their handicapped children. The first of these organizations to reach a large scale was the cerebral palsy movement, which began in 1940 when the parent of a cerebral-palsied child inserted a personal advertisement in *The New York Times* inquiring whether other parents with such children wished to contact the advertiser. Out of this developed the New York State Cerebral Palsy Association. Soon after, parents of mentally retarded children began to organize, and formed the National Association for Retarded Children.

As interest in, and facilities for, the handicapped increased, demand developed for special teachers. The state of Michigan played a leading role in the special-education movement. Michigan had for some years been at the forefront in having a variety of special schools and institutions for the various types of handicapped children. The first teacher-training program for special-education teachers was established in 1914 by Charles S. Berry at the Lapeer State Home and Training School in Michigan. This was a summer course for the teachers at this residential school for the mentally retarded. Soon after, the first college program in special education was organized at Michigan State Normal College in Ypsilanti, now Eastern Michigan University, under the leadership of Charles M. Elliot. To professor Elliot must go major credit for the development of special education. His pioneering efforts resulted in the establishment at Eastern Michigan of the Rackham School of Special Education, which was for many years the chief source of special-education teachers in this country.

While prior to World War II important strides were being made toward developing methods and techniques for teaching of the mentally and physically handicapped, the actual number of special programs and teachers was smaller than might have been expected. Cruickshank has pointed out that this delay was primarily due to mixed acceptance of the concept of special education, with resistance to the idea in many circles. This reflected to a great degree the then current concepts of so-called "progressive education" to which the name of John Dewey is attached. Cruickshank observes:

The professional progressive educators, oftentimes lay people in the community, carried the thoughtful concepts and theories of progressive education to an unrealistic extreme. Their thoughtless advocation of unplanned and heterogeneous grouping stimulated the abolition of many special classes with the subsequent reassignment of exceptional children, particularly the mentally handicapped, into the regular grades.

Following World War II, with the subsidence of the extreme use of progressive education, together with general progress in the status of the education profession, special education has come of age. In 1949, 77 institutions of higher learning gave sequences of courses in the teaching of exceptional children. By 1953, this number had risen to 122. The programs of teacher training for the various types of exceptional children in 1953 were distributed as follows (Cruickshank):

Blind and partially blind—9
Crippled—13
Special health problems—5
Deaf and partially deaf—90
Speech problems—115
Socially maladjusted—10
Mentally retarded—40
Exceptionally gifted—2

The above figures represent only those programs in which a sequence of courses, presumably leading to rather complete training in the specialty, are given. Additionally, there are hundreds of other institutions offering some courses or partial programs in special education.

Cruickshank expresses concern at the current rapid growth of special education, noting the dangers of inadequate preparation, the lack of sufficient numbers of trained and experienced persons of professorial rank, the lack of standardization of requirements, and, most important, the great discrepancy between supply and demand caused by overenthusiastic development of special-education programs at all levels. A course or two in special education does not prepare a person for working with handicapped children. The criteria for selection of these personnel must be high: the first requisite is emotional maturity; the second is experience gained by working under competent supervision.

Special education, if it develops properly and along sound lines, promises to become a major force in preventive psychiatry. The child psychiatrist has an increasing responsibility to communicate with the teaching profession, and this can perhaps most effectively be accomplished through the special-education teacher.

DYNAMIC PSYCHIATRY AND PSYCHOANALYSIS

Until the late nineteenth century, treatment of the mentally ill consisted largely in segregating them from society. Their care had become much more humane, a development highlighted by Pinel's courageous and celebrated undertaking of removing the chains from the patients at the Salpetriere in Paris. Nevertheless, treatment continued to be largely custodial, as there was little concept of mental illness as a dynamic process. Indeed, "the insane" were regarded for the most part as a homogeneous group, and investigations were made into such matters as the body build, blood pressure, and heart rate associated with "insanity."

A significant development was Kraepelin's descriptive classification of mental illnesses. While the Kraepelinean approach has been criticized as undynamic, nevertheless, it was in its time a significant development; it had the effect of creating some order out of chaos. It emphasized the heterogeneity of the mental disorders, and led the way to a systematic study of the causes of the various types of mental and emotional illnesses at an individual level.

At about the turn of the century two men emerged who have come to be regarded as the cofounders of modern psychiatry: Sigmund Freud and Adolf Meyer. Both of these psychiatrists epitomized the individual approach to mental illness. Both were great teachers, and both attracted an enormous following. Meyer, originally trained in psychoanalysis under Freud, is better known for his eclectic approach. He was less an investigator, more of a doer. He emphasized the total approach to the patient, and the utilization of all available facilities and therapies. Meyer urged the importance of preventive psychiatry, and the use of social work, special education, and guidance clinics. He was an early exponent of treatment rather than custodial care in the mental hospital. Meyer was much interested in the idea of child psychiatry, and was one of the first to study and treat emotionally disturbed children. He enlisted the co-operation of the pediatrics department at The Johns Hopkins University in studying the psychiatric aspects of illnesses in children. Under his aegis a chair in child psychiatry was established, and under his guiding influence the first textbook completely devoted to child psychiatry was written, Kanner's *Child Psychiatry*.

Freud's work was more in the direction of research into the determining influences of mental illnesses and of normal personality. The fundamental importance of his contributions to man's understanding of human psychology is, of course, widely recognized. Freud did not himself analyze children, with the exception of one case in which he served as supervisor, meeting the child personally on but one occasion (*Collected Papers*). Nevertheless, he long urged the psychoanalytic investigation of children, and his daughter, Anna Freud, is one of the pioneers in the field of child analysis.

While the contributions of psychoanalysis to psychology and psychiatry have been enormous, there has unfortunately been some tendency toward uncritical acceptance of analytic theory. Much has been accepted through the sheer weight and influence of those espousing it. The criticism often directed toward psychiatry, that it lacks scientific validation, has been applied even more vociferously to psychoanalysis. Analysts reply, with some justification, that much of the theory cannot be tested experimentally. It is not possible, for example, to *measure* transference, or to *prove* that a patient's anxiety is a displaced homosexual feeling toward his father. Nevertheless, it remains important to differentiate carefully between fact and opinion.

Child psychiatry has been built upon a firm foundation of psychoanalytic theory, and it is not possible to consider the two separately. At the same time, the study of children has contributed, and will contribute further, to modifications and clarifications of much of psychoanalytic theory. For example, child psychiatry has amply demonstrated that there are many conflicts other than the Oedipal conflict operant in the genesis of neurosis. Child psychiatry is able to provide data which cannot be obtained from adults, and which Freud himself long urged his colleagues to seek. Unfortunately, some adherents to analytic doctrine raise the accusation "antianalytic" against any individual or discipline not wholly and uncritically accepting of every formulation of Freud and his followers. To such polemics Freud's own continued investigations and reformulations provide the best answer. No discipline which presumes to attain to the status of a science can allow itself to fear or avoid constant scrutiny, reinvestigation, and reformulation. Nor must it expect ever to be taken on faith.

A second serious criticism of psychoanalysis has been directed against its propensity to organize into a closed group. Martin Mayer has said, "An idea dies when an organization is formed to promote it." The implication is that, if an idea is valid, it needs no promotion. In its organization, psychoanalysis has often been compared with other groups characterized by their adherence to a certain belief, such as religious orders and secret societies or cults. The parallel with religious orders has been carried further in the predilection for the analytic movement to develop "splinter groups," such as the Jungians and the Adlerians.

Enhancing the comparison of psychoanalysis with secret societies is the method for admission of new members. Applicants for training in analysis who are refused acceptance are usually not told of the reasons for refusal. Szasz has criticized the system of admission for analytic trainees in that the applicant's own analyst is usually a member of the training committee, or at least is consulted regarding the applicant. Szasz points out that this violates the first principle of the analyst-analysand relationship, namely, that the material obtained in the analysis is confidential. As a result, the analysand who is contemplating applying for analytic training cannot really be analyzed, for he is acutely aware that "whatever he says may be used against him."

Many feel that psychoanalysis has now contributed most of what it is going to contribute to psychiatry. As a therapeutic measure, it has never been a major force: It is expensive, prolonged, and there are not enough analysts to treat more than a minute portion of the population. Indeed, Freud never conceived of analysis as primarily a therapeutic technique. In child psychiatry, the analytic movement appears to be a diminishing force.

Psychiatry will continue to pay homage to the genius of Freud, for his work must forever stand as the foundation of dynamic psychiatry. But it must not be forgotten that no single discipline has a corner on the investigation and understanding of human behavior. It is quite likely that physical chemistry, ethology, or cybernetics will contribute as much to psychiatry in the second half of this century as psychoanalysis did in the first, and perhaps the psychiatrist of the next generation will adorn his office with a portrait of Linus Pauling, Konrad Lorenz, or Norbert Wiener.

PSYCHIATRIC TREATMENT OF CHILDREN

Kanner considers that the first four decades of the present century marked four rather distinct episodes in the history of child psychiatry. Kanner has characterized these as follows:

1st decade: thinking *about* children—culture
2nd decade: doing things *to* children—community
3rd decade: doing things *for* children—family and school
4th decade: working *with* children—child

Thus, while the facilities for the care and treatment of mentally ill children were being developed early in the century, it was not until the fourth decade that the child himself became actively involved in the psychotherapeutic endeavor. Prior to that time, as Kanner has aptly put it: "The principal characters in the play were still seen but not heard."

To the psychoanalysts must go a large share of the credit for first allowing the children to be heard. The names Melanie Klein and Anna

Freud, often mentioned previously in this volume, are of course most prominently associated with the true beginnings of child psychiatry. Their development of play-therapy techniques, and their application of psychoanalytic formulations to children's behavior and verbalizations, provided the foundation on which most of modern child psychiatry is based. These concepts, introduced in Europe, spread quickly to the United States. A major step was the formulation by Allen in Philadelphia, described in Chapter 16, emphasizing the relationship between therapist and child.

The concept of working *with* the child in psychotherapy is now firmly entrenched. Indeed, during the fifth decade of the century it has received overenthusiastic emphasis by some therapists, who work only with the child, excluding involvement with his environment.

The inclusion of the child in his own therapy has reached its ultimate refinement in the residential treatment center, where the therapeutic milieu is combined with individual psychotherapy. This has characterized the trend of the sixth decade of this century.

WHERE DO WE STAND TODAY, AND WHERE DO WE GO FROM HERE?

To evaluate critically the present status of child psychiatry, and to predict its future trends, while a worthy endeavor, is also a formidable task. What follows is not a prophecy; it is admittedly speculation. It gains some authority by drawing upon the declarations of the Joint Commission on Mental Health and Illness.

Perhaps the major thesis of this presentation, if a single one can be stated, is that child psychiatry has little cause for optimism or complacency. Its scope and aims are as yet poorly defined. The care of mentally ill children in this country, while an advance over the dark ages, remains for the most part a disgrace. Most of the effects of our past endeavors have not been adequately evaluated. The majority of our investigations which pass as research evidence no awareness of the basic principles of the scientific method. Internally, we are beset by petty bickerings, power struggles, the formation of groups within groups dedicated to the preservation of the status quo. Externally, our relationships with other disciplines and other medical specialties often are marked by mutual suspicion, ignorance, and resentment.

Yet the picture is not all black. There are a number of competent child psychiatrists who are daily helping to restore disturbed children to useful and happy lives. Facilities specifically designed for the treatment of children have grown from almost none to a considerable number in the past decade, and plans for many more are underway. Child psychiatry, in

1959, gained official recognition as a subspecialty under the American Board of Psychiatry and Neurology. The mental health movement continues to gain impetus, and the concept of mental illness as a public health problem finds ever increasing acceptance. Financial support for research, both public and private, has mushroomed since World War II, and a vast program of research is underway encompassing many areas of the social, behavioral, and biological sciences.

Here is the picture in greater detail:

THE AIMS

Psychiatry, like most of medicine, has traditionally held to a short-sighted point of view. Briefly stated, the aim has been to help the sick, which means waiting until a person becomes ill before doing anything for him. A noble aim, and not to be despised. But for some illnesses there is no satisfactory treatment, and many more can be prevented than can be cured. Perhaps one of the most incontrovertible of social predictions is that a major trend of medicine will be toward prevention. This is as true of psychiatry as of the rest of medicine. It means that psychiatry has a major responsibility to learn the causes of emotional maladjustment. The social structures for the application of a true preventive psychiatry cannot develop in the absence of a firm foundation of knowledge as to what produces the disorders and what must be eliminated and what must be supplied to avoid these disorders.

Because child psychiatry is charged with the responsibility of taking care of mentally disturbed children, it is in the vital position of being the only discipline able to answer many of the fundamental questions about mental disorders. This is a heavy burden, and requires among other things that we keep abreast of social developments throughout the world. For example, problems resulting from the so-called population explosion suggest that a system of population control will become a major social force in the not-distant future. Psychiatry will undoubtedly be called upon to participate, but at its present rate of growth it will be ill-equipped to do so. The problem involves a consideration of human genetics: Are we, by treating the "misfits," furthering the dissemination of "bad" genes? This question can presently be discussed with profundity, but it cannot be answered. The geneticist, H. J. Muller, has answered it in the affirmative, but his reply has aroused a storm of protest among his colleagues.

Perhaps the goal of elimination or reduction of mental illness is not only unattainable but also undesirable. Gordon Allen in 1957 made the interesting suggestion that a necessary by-product of the wide variability of brain function in the human population is the occurrence of those extremes of variability which provide the biological basis for mental disorders. Therefore behavioral variability among the human race is a desirable trait, necessary to the population's high level of adaptability and survival. It follows that significant attempts to reduce the occurrence of mental illness might of necessity reduce the race's capacity to adapt.

These are philosophical questions, and have little direct significance for the practicing psychiatrist who sees unhappy children in his office. But they are questions which the profession must surely take cognizance of. The forces of natural selection and evolution are profound and eternal in their operation. To manipulate and interfere with them from the short-sighted view of one or two generations may be to invite disaster for the children of this generation and those to come.

CHILD PSYCHIATRY AND THE ALLIED DISCIPLINES

Despite the continued growth of the orthopsychiatric movement and the homage paid to the concept of the multidisciplinary approach, child psychiatry remains, in many ways, singularly insular. Pediatrics and child psychiatry should have a great deal in common, yet there is actually little communication between the two. At a recent meeting of the Society for Pediatric Research, not a single paper was concerned with the emotional aspects of illness in children. Pediatricians generally acknowledge the importance of attending to the emotional problems of their patients, but their concern is mainly with medical disease, and it is difficult enough to keep abreast of developments in their own field. Moreover, their modus operandi is not geared to spending a leisurely hour with each child to learn what thoughts are troubling him—there are impatient mothers and fretting children in the waiting room, needing attention to their sore throats, rashes, and leukemias.

Pediatricians, for the most part, approach their patients with warmth, kindness, and consideration, and this is usually enough. If the child is chronically depressed, or eternally anxious, or savagely aggressive, the wise pediatrician calls for help. Sometimes the psychiatrist supplies the help, but often he does not. Many pediatricians express discouragement at the lack of real communication, saying that they are unable to understand what the psychiatrist is talking about. They further point out that the tenets of psychiatry are often vague, unscientific, and ephemeral. Relationships are not furthered if the psychiatrist's attitude is one of defensiveness or contempt, with denial that the criticisms of his specialty have any foundation. That this situation need not be inevitable is amply demonstrated in a number of individual instances, where relations between psychiatrist and pediatrician are marked by mutual respect, interest, and understanding.

Perhaps the most important professional group with which the child psychiatrist must deal are the educators. Here, the picture is generally brighter, and appears to be steadily improving. An important factor is the increasing number of school personnel specifically assigned to helping problem children, mainly the school psychologists, visiting teachers, and special-education teachers. The presence of these persons on the school staff, together with the increasing enlightenment of all school personnel regarding the needs of disturbed children and the functions of child psychiatry, ensure that progress will continue. The schools in many areas now seek the help and advice of child psychiatrists to a greater degree than can be supplied. This discrepancy is in part due to insufficient psychiatric personnel, but it is due also to a failure of child psychiatry to identify itself sufficiently with the preventive psychiatry movement.

THE DIRECTIONS OF RESEARCH

There has been throughout this volume the endeavor to delineate in the areas of child psychiatry and human behavior those things which are known, those which are conjectured, those about which little or nothing is known, and those about which more ought to be learned. The latter will be recapitulated briefly here.

The most pressing need is to determine the causes of emotional disorders of children. This calls for extensive and long-range programs of research. It requires longitudinal studies of a number of individuals from birth to adulthood, perhaps including more than a single generation. It requires the joint endeavors of a variety of disciplines from the social, the clinical, and the biological sciences. Such a program obviously requires careful long-range planning, and the assurance of continued support. Promising beginnings have been made by several groups of investigators. It is certain that there will be an incorporation of these beginnings into major and inclusive programs, which will proceed on a scale far beyond any presently imagined.

A second important area for wide-scale investigation is the results of psychiatric therapies. Thus far, with a few notable exceptions, psychiatry has avoided directly and systematically investigating its own worth. The introduction into psychiatry of mass techniques for evaluation of results, first with psychosurgery, then with the psychoactive drugs, has brought gradual appreciation of both the importance of, and the difficulties involved in, accurately determining results. Application of research to certain types of therapies, such as various techniques of psychotherapy and long-term institutional treatment, is much more difficult, as the problem of control becomes more complicated. Nevertheless, the urgency of research into methods of therapy is great, and it must certainly be undertaken.

The cause and the cure—these are the two great areas requiring much research in mental illness. What is the prospect that these programs of research will be adequately carried out? Frankly, it is not good. This conclusion, shared by many, has been carefully explored in the report of the Joint Commission on Mental Illness and Health, entitled *Action for Mental Health* (1961). In its chapter on research resources in mental health, the report states:

The mental health sciences address themselves to the alleviation of complex biological, psychological, and social problems that have plagued man throughout his history; mental health scientists face this task with an incredibly small fund of knowledge about causes and cures. It is a field where many qualified guesses abound and the few hard facts achieve prominence by their very scarcity.

The Commission further notes that, because of the nonresearch orientation of most members of the psychiatric profession, the lead in mental health research has clearly passed from the hands of psychiatry to other groups: physiologists, psychologists, anatomists, biochemists, and social scientists, who easily constitute 90 per cent or more of the investigators working in mental health research today. This is not necessarily an unfortunate trend. The inclusion of these fields into a program of mental health research is essential. However, it is also necessary that that group which is directly charged with the care of the mentally ill, the psychiatrists, should continue to be actively represented in such a program.

Whatever directions research in psychiatry may take, without any doubt it will be sped on its way by automatic computers. The mushroomlike growth of computerization and automatic control, already creating a revolution in industry, science, and government, will undoubtedly be incorporated on an increasing scale into the study of human behavior and mental illness. How much will be learned, and how quickly, it is useless to speculate. The possibilities are exciting. Through the handling of masses of data, totally unsuspected relations and meanings will be uncovered. The limiting factor will be accuracy of measurement. The problem will not be *what* to measure, but *how* to measure. The computer will tell us which measurements are significant. How much can be predicted of a personality from chemical and neurophysiological measurements made in infancy? Should a baby with a high serum cholinesterase be stimulated and attended to more than other babies? Does an intense withdrawal response from an electrical shock predict proneness to depression in adulthood? There are a million questions, and most of them will probably be asked—and some will be answered.

Along with the expansion of applied research as discussed above, a continued increase in basic research will certainly be seen as an integral part of the total mental health research program. The past decade has witnessed a resurgence of investigation into brain functioning; neurochemistry, neurophysiology, and neuropharmacology are increasing man's knowledge of the brain at an exciting pace. What can their discoveries be expected to provide to the field of mental health? No one knows. The problem of justifying basic research has always been a vexatious one. One can point to examples from the past, but to predict the fruits of a present endeavor is never possible. We must nevertheless continue to defend the principle that basic research is the solid foundation of all science. It provides the chief source of trained and enthusiastic workers, new techniques, and new ideas. The Joint Commission report concludes:

Unglamorous as it may sound, the only realistic approach seems to lie in a long-term program of basic and clinical research equally well supported in the broad spectrum of medical, biological, and social science disciplines and conducted in universities, in hospitals, in clinics, and in a variety of other settings.

PSYCHIATRY AND THE CHILD

The goals and the responsibilities are formidable. Hopefully, they will continue to be better defined, and better carried out. We can predict with some confidence the directions which psychiatric research will take, and the place which psychiatry will hold in a world increasingly more complex and troubled.

We can predict with even greater accuracy that the problems which beset a troubled child will always be about as they are today. He will continue to be frightened, or anxious, or angry. He will continue to need love, comfort, and control. And the child psychiatrist will remain a person who is interested in that child, who understands him, and will sit patiently in a quiet place and talk with him about his troubles.

REFERENCES

Action for Mental Health—Final Report of the Joint Commission on Mental Health and Illness. New York, Basic Books, Inc., 1961.
Allen, G. Genetic Aspects of Mental Disorder, in The Nature and Transmission

of the Genetic and Cultural Characteristics of Human Populations, New York, Milbank Memorial Fund, 1957.

Cruickshank, W. M. The Development of Education for Exceptional Children, in Education of Exceptional Children and Youth, eds. Cruickshank and Johnson, Englewood Cliffs, N.J., Prentice-Hall, Inc., 1958.

Crutcher, R. Child Psychiatry, A History of its Development, Psychiatry, 6: 191, 1943.

Freud, S. An Analysis of a Case of Phobia in a Five-Year-Old Boy, Collected Papers, London, Hogarth Press, 1953, Vol. 3.

Healy, W. The Individual Delinquent, Boston, Little, Brown & Co., 1915.

———— and Bronner, A. The Child Guidance Clinic—Birth and Growth of an Idea, in Orthopsychiatry 1923–1948, eds. Lowrey and Sloane, New York, American Orthopsychiatric Association, 1948.

Kanner, L. Child Psychiatry 3rd ed., Springfield, Ill., Charles C Thomas, 1957.

Krugman, M. Orthopsychiatry and Education, in Orthopsychiatry 1923–1948, eds. Lowrey and Sloane, New York, American Orthopsychiatric Association, 1948.

Mayer, M. The Schools, New York, Harper Bros., 1961.

Muller, H. J. Human Evolution by Voluntary Choice of Germ Plasm, Science, 134: 643, 1961.

Stevenson, G. S. Child Guidance and the National Committee for Mental Hygiene, in Orthopsychiatry 1923–1948, eds. Lowrey and Sloane, New York, American Orthopsychiatric Association, 1948.

Szasz, T. Three Problems in Contemporary Psychoanalytic Training, Arch. Gen. Psychiatry, 3: 82, 1960.

Watson, R. I. Psychology of the Child, New York, John Wiley & Sons, 1959.

AUTHOR INDEX

Ackerman, N. W., 87, 88, 90, 285, 375
Aichhorn, A., 271, 274, 338
Alderton, H. R., 399, 400
Alexander, F., 42, 55, 143, 153, 281, 285, 287, 288, 293
Alexander, T., 399, 401
Allen, F., 325, 326, 342
Allen, G., 418, 419, 423
Allen, L., 70, 299
Alpert, A., 371, 385
Alt, H., 345, 367
Altschule, M. D., 283, 285
Andersen, Hans C., 327
Arieti, S., 56, 286
Ascher, E., 311
Ausubel, D. P., 265, 270, 274

Bakst, H., 282, 286
Bakwin, H. and R., 211, 212, 234, 244, 294, 298, 299
Beach, F. A., 55
Beaumont, W., 279, 285
Beck, M. B., 386
Beers, C., 410
Bellak, L., 41, 55, 118
Bender, L., 66, 70, 97, 99, 100, 101, 105, 109, 110, 114, 117, 118, 164, 166, 167, 171, 172, 183, 202, 241, 242, 243, 244, 267, 275, 299, 300, 301, 302, 330, 333, 342, 388, 393, 395, 397, 398, 400, 401
Benedict, R. M., 47, 55
Berger, F. M., 390, 401
Berger, M., 109, 119
Berkowitz, P., 371, 386
Berry, C. S., 413
Betz, B. J., 90
Bierman, J., 146, 153
Binet, 407
Birch, H., 26, 27, 153
Blackwell, A., 293
Blanchard, P., 199, 212

Bleuler, 96
Blitzer, J. R., 288, 291, 293
Borstelmann, L. J., 400
Bowlby, J., 22, 26, 70, 235, 239, 244
Bradley, C., 176, 181, 183, 397, 401
Brauer, W., 311, 395, 401
Braustein, P., 119
Brill, A. A., 302, 343
Broca, P., 197, 212
Brodbeck, A. J., 56
Bronner, A., 267, 275, 409, 424
Brown, J., 117, 118
Brown, N., 311, 401
Brown, R., 191, 212
Bryant, K., 118
Burlingham, D., 13, 26, 236
Butler, S., 330

Cabot, R., 272
Cain, B., 305, 306, 308
Cameron, J. L., 119
Caplan, G., 118, 119
Casler, L., 236, 237, 244
Cattell, P., 257, 262
Cavanaugh, E. B., 285
Challas, G., 311, 395, 401
Chambers, W., 283, 285
Chapel, J. L., 311, 395, 401
Charcot, 52
Chess, S., 12, 26, 27, 39, 55, 88, 90, 129, 141, 153, 218, 230, 254, 262
Ching, A. Y. T., 285
Clemmens, R. S., 161, 183
Colby, K., 318, 342
Cole, M., 289, 293
Connell, G. E., 7, 27
Coolidge, J., 302, 305, 307
Corsini, R., 386
Costello, C. G., 33, 57
Cottington, F., 400
Cramer, J. B., 119
Cronbach, L. J., 257, 262

425

SUBJECT INDEX

Abstraction, language, 190–191
Academic difficulty
  in psychoneurosis, 144
  reading disability and, 203
Acalculia, 210
Acathexis, psychogenic, 239
Acculturation, diagnosis and, 83
Acting out
  in personality disorder, 223
  in reading disability, 207
Adaptability, 5
Adjustment mechanisms, 135–141. *See also*
    individual mechanisms.
Admission for residential treatment, 361–
    363
Adolescence
  delinquency in, 270–271
  personality development in, 37
  psychotherapy in, 335–338
Adoption, psychopathy and, 244
Adulthood
  brain damage in, 164–165
  personality development in, 37–38
  schizophrenia in, 97–98
Affect hunger, primary, 239
Affectionless, 239
Affects, diagnosis and, 82
Age of emotionally disturbed children, 64,
    65
  in psychotherapy, 319–320
Aggression
  in personality disorder, 220
  in psychoneurosis, 131, 137
Aggressive drive, 23–24
Agraphia, 210
Alexia, 196
American Board of Psychiatry and Neurol-
    ogy, 419
American Orthopsychiatric Association,
    172, 238, 410, 411
American Psychiatric Association, 88
Amitriptyline, 398
Amphetamines, 397–398
Anal stage, 39

Animals
  epileptiform seizures in, 6
  experimental neurosis in, 29–30
  fear in, 23
  instinct in, 18–21
  language in, 187–188
  selective breeding in, 7–10
  strain differences in, 10
Anorexia nervosa, 40, 73, 280, 287–293
  diagnosis of, 290
  differential diagnosis of, 290–291
  etiology of, 288–290
  incidence of, 288
  prognosis of, 291
  symptoms of, 289
  treatment of, 291–293
  types of, 287–288
Anticonvulsants, 400
Antidepressives, 396–399
  amphetamines, 397–398
  iminodibenzyl derivatives, 398–399
  of miscellaneous structure, 399
  monoamine oxidase inhibitors, 298
Antisocial behavior. *See also* Delinquency.
  in brain damage, 169
Anxiety
  in brain damage, 164, 166
  in psychoneurosis, 142–144
  tolerance, 141
Apathy in psychoneurosis, 147
Aphasia, 201, 210
  in brain damage, 168
  schizophrenia vs., 111
Appetite in anorexia nervosa, 289
Arithmetic achievement, reading disabil-
    ity and, 203
Art therapy, 332–333
Arthritis, rheumatoid, 280
Asthma, 73, 280, 281, 282, 283, 284
Asymbolia, 196
Atarax, 395
Ataraxic drugs, 390
Athetosis, tic vs., 309
Atypical child, 97

431